PHYSICAL ACTIVITY IN NATURAL SETTINGS

Exercise interactions with green and blue spaces offer low-cost, non-invasive solutions to public health challenges—particularly around mental health and obesity—and issues around environmental sustainability. *Physical Activity in Natural Settings* brings together multi-disciplinary, international research on physical activity, health and the natural environment, offering evidence-based guidance on implementing nature-based solutions at individual, patient and population levels.

Divided over four sections, the book assesses the current research landscape, explores the underlying psychological and physiological mechanisms of the benefits of green exercise, details applied examples of physical activity in natural settings, and suggests future directions for research and practice. It features contributions from experts from around the world and covers topics including:

- Self-determination, nature and well-being
- Visual cognition and multisensory stimuli
- Nature's role in growing resilience
- Physical education and nature
- Mindfulness and green exercise
- Positive psychology and pro-environmental behaviour

Timely and prescient, and showcasing real-life examples of green exercise prescription, *Physical Activity in Natural Settings* is fascinating and important reading for any students or researchers in the psychology or physiology of physical activity and health, physical education or outdoor studies, and policy-makers and health professionals.

Aoife A. Donnelly is a Lecturer in the School of Food Science and Environmental Health at Technological University Dublin, Ireland. Previously, she was an Environmental Protection Agency (EPA) funded post-doctoral researcher and developed an operational real time air quality forecast model using integrated parametric and non-parametric regression techniques. Her PhD studies explored background air pollution concentration variations across Ireland. She is a founding member of the GO GREEN (Going Outdoors: Gathering Research Evidence on Emotions and Nature) research initiative.

Tadhg E. MacIntyre is a Lecturer with the Health Research Institute and course director for the Masters in Sport, Exercise and Performance Psychology at the University of Limerick, Ireland. Since 2011, he has been an HCPC accredited practitioner in sport psychology in the UK and has been a member of the Irish Institute of Sport quality assurance panel since 2007. Previously, he has conducted funded research for the following agencies: World Anti-Doping Agency, the British Association of Sport and Exercise Sciences, the British Psychological Society, Erasmus + European Union funding and he is a member of the Strategic Level Expert Advisory Board of the H2020 project Re-Nature. He is a founding member of the GO GREEN (Going Outdoors: Gathering Research Evidence on Emotions and Nature) research initiative.

PHYSICAL ACTIVITY IN NATURAL SETTINGS

Green and Blue Exercise

Edited by Aoife A. Donnelly and Tadhg E. MacIntyre

LONDON AND NEW YORK

First published 2019
by Routledge
2 Park Square, Milton Park, Abingdon, Oxon OX14 4RN

and by Routledge
52 Vanderbilt Avenue, New York, NY 10017

Routledge is an imprint of the Taylor & Francis Group, an informa business

British Library Cataloguing-in-Publication Data
A catalogue record for this book is available from the British Library

Library of Congress Cataloging-in-Publication Data
Names: Donnelly, Aoife A., editor. | MacIntyre, Tadhg E, editor.
Title: Physical activity in natural settings : green and blue exercise / Edited by Aoife A. Donnelly and Tadhg E. MacIntyre.
Description: Abingdon, Oxon ; New York : Routledge, 2019. | Includes bibliographical references and index. |
Identifiers: LCCN 2019019048 | ISBN 9781138749603 (hardback) | ISBN 9781138894310 (paperback) | ISBN 9781315180144 (ebook)
Subjects: LCSH: Physical fitness. | Natural areas. | Outdoor recreation. | Public health–Environmental aspects.
Classification: LCC GV481 .P478 2019 | DDC 613.7–dc23
LC record available at https://lccn.loc.gov/2019019048

ISBN: 978-1-138-74960-3 (hbk)
ISBN: 978-1-138-89431-0 (pbk)
ISBN: 978-1-315-18014-4 (ebk)

Typeset in Bembo
by Swales & Willis, Exeter, Devon, UK
Printed and bound by CPI Group (UK) Ltd, Croydon CR0 4YY

CONTENTS

FIGURES

TABLES

BOXES

CONTRIBUTORS

Méliné Baronian
City of Versailles, France

Jo Barton
University of Essex, UK

Jürgen Beckmann
Technical University of Munich, Germany

Peter Bentsen
Steno Diabetes Center Copenhagen, Denmark

Mads Bølling
Steno Diabetes Center Copenhagen, Denmark

Noel Brick
Ulster University, UK

Giovanna Calogiuri
Inland Norway University of Applied Sciences, Norway

Massimiliano Cappuccio
United Arab Emirates University, United Arab Emirates

Marcus Collier
Trinity College Dublin, Ireland

Simone Coetzee
University of Essex, UK

Patricia M. Darcy
Staffordshire University, UK

Aoife A. Donnelly
Technical University, Dublin, Ireland

Barbara Eigenschenk
Technische Universität München, Germany

Christopher Gidlow
Staffordshire University, UK

Valerie Gladwell
University of Essex, UK

Susan Gritzka
TU Dresden, Germany

Dominic Harmon
Limerick University Hospital, Ireland

Evan Hunt
Institute of Child Education & Psychology, Europe

Eric R. Igou
University of Limerick, Ireland

Marc Jones
Staffordshire University, UK

Sinéad Kelly
University of Essex, UK

Eric Klinger
University of Minnesota, USA

Ian Lahart
University of Wolverhampton, UK

Sigbjørn Litleskare
Inland Norway School of Sport Sciences, Norway

Kat Longshore
Lafayette College, USA

Ryan Lumber
University of Derby, UK

Deirdre MacIntyre
Institute of Child Education & Psychology, Europe

Tadhg E. MacIntyre
University of Limerick, Ireland

Michelle M. McAlarnen
Minnesota State University, USA

Mike McClure
Sport Northern Ireland, UK

Christopher R. Madan
University of Nottingham, UK

Erik Mygind
University of Copenhagen, Denmark

Lærke Mygind
Deakin University, Australia

Maire-Treasa Ni Cheallaigh
Royal College of Surgeons, Ireland

Glen Nielsen
University of Copenhagen, Denmark

Mark Nieuwenhuijsen
IS Global, Spain

Moya O'Brien
Institute of Child Education & Psychology, Europe

Greig Oliver
Irish Rugby Football Union, Ireland

Jules Pretty
University of Essex, UK

Mike Rogerson
University of Essex, UK

Ryan Sappington
University of Maryland, USA

David Sheffield
University of Derby, UK

Stephen Smith
Institute of Child Education & Psychology, Europe

Matt P. Stevenson
University of Copenhagen, Denmark

Marlena Tomkalska
Collen Construction, Ireland

Wijnand A. P. van Tilburg
King's College London, UK

Andree Walkin
University of Limerick, Ireland

Giles Warrington
University of Limerick, Ireland

FOREWORD

I was raised in Killaloe overlooking the banks of the river Shannon and I am back living on her shores again. There is a pull to a place like this: the underlying sound of the longest river on these isles surrounded by the natural landscape of rolling hills. It is an area with an inherent sense of nature and with it a sense of a place to be explored and experienced. Away from the cities, it also has a sense of healthy nature-based activity. How do we make that activity more accessible?

My role as the first chairperson of Healthy Ireland, a cross-sectoral government-led initiative aimed at improving the health and well-being of the country, enabled me to cultivate partnerships with those promoting our understanding of how human and environmental health are inextricably linked. The passion for nature-based initiatives was overwhelming but the evidence was sparse. Scientists had not taken a holistic approach and instead they often operated in silos. It has taken time to recognize that mental health problems, physical inactivity, social inequity, environmental issues and climate change are not discrete issues but part of the complicated tapestry of modern life.

So we decided to have an impact where we could, at Clarisford Park in Killaloe. Some of this seems retrospective and some of it is retrospective but there were fundamental health and well-being elements central to our early discussions. And we kept getting drawn back to a more simple time.

As a child I roamed the orchards, fields and lake-side for fun, play, adventure and exploration. When we scaled the walls of the Bishops Palace at Clarisford Park demesne to climb trees or pick conkers, physical activity and well-being were never the goals. Roll on the years and over numerous coffees and conversations amongst friends, a shared vision of how our natural playground could be transformed into a bespoke multi-generational physical activity and sport facility began to take shape. One of our goals: to achieve explicitly what we implicitly did as children. Ten years later the work was completed and Clarisford Park has become the go-to spot for all types of activity, involving up to five thousand participants every week. The 10 hectare site comprising a running trail, playing pitches, an indoor pavilion and parkland, is now a designated Sports Hub and it is mapped onto the Healthy Cities and Counties Network, which is based on the European Health Policy Framework.

The Healthy Killaloe Ballina Initiative at Clarisford Park involved consideration of Special Areas of Conservation (SAC), protected habitats and unique species within Lough Derg and its environs, partnership with the communities across the twin towns, Clare and Tipperary County Council, Local Sport Partnerships, Waterways Ireland, Coillte, the Irish EPA, and local sporting, community groups and action groups. The whole project was a lesson in collaboration. At one level, I was enthused, everyone appeared to have an oar in the water, but at another they seemed to be pulling in different directions. We all had slightly different agendas. And maybe there was a bigger outcome to be had?

We decided to collaborate on a prototype that could be scaled up and replicated nationwide. We needed an evidence-based initiative, one that could speak to the multi-stakeholders, intersectoral actors and in sum, people. The evidence had to be translational and transformative. We partnered with a University of Limerick research group, GO GREEN, comprising a longstanding colleague Dr Giles Warrington and led by Tadhg MacIntyre and Aoife Donnelly (editors of this collection) with psychologist Nollaig O'Sullivan and a truly international scientific research team in support. This book is the outcome of that collaboration.

GO GREEN, *Going Outdoors: Gathering Research Evidence on Emotions and Nature* addressed this issue with evidence-based initiatives on blue and green exercise. Evidence will enable optimization of future initiatives both nationally and overseas. Killaloe is a small town but if we imagine an urban vista the bespoke multi-functional and cross-generational concept we developed has utility in developing ecosystem services from green natural spaces.

During the research for this book, I participated as an interviewee in the case-studies on green exercise. Science has many means to promote change and advancement but it was clear from this and the parallel case studies, that the individual's voice should not be lost in the service of science. One question I was asked was whether I was more attracted to green space or blue space. I find it hard to differentiate personally, I am connected to nature, be it tending to the veg in our garden, or kayaking with my boys at Moys lock on the Killaloe canal, or striding uphill on the forested slopes of Ballycuggaran.

When I stand on the top of Moylusa (532m) and absorb the panorama of the Lough Derg Blueway, nature seems all about connectivity. Connecting with nature through physical activity in green and blue settings gives me a sense of perspective on my life, my family, community and the planet. In a modern world perspective would seem to be essential.

We need leadership for change and the voices of change will resonate clearly when we have evidence for human health and well-being to support calls for action on climate change, environmental degradation and sustainability. Leadership requires evaluation research on human-nature interactions to enhance our lives and our environs. If we can achieve this at a local level, there may be the chance to extol its virtues at a county, country or even on a global level.

Keith Wood, Former International Rugby Player

PREFACE

Physical Activity in Natural Settings: Green Exercise and Blue Mind

Physical activity has been a key feature of human lives throughout evolutionary history. Early in our existence, hunter gatherers roamed endlessly over wide areas, covering an estimated 15 to 20 km per day. Later, agrarian societies engaged in physically demanding planting, harvesting and tending of their crops, and the shepherding of livestock, periodically meeting up with others to trade their products. Such active lifestyles persisted over tens of thousands of years during which our biochemistry and physiology became attuned to supporting walking, running, climbing, swimming and other physical activities, mainly in outdoor natural settings

Today, lifestyles are very different. Profound changes in the way we spend our days have taken place, especially over the last 200 years. With the industrial revolution came mass migrations into towns and cities. This has been most evident in Europe, the USA and Japan, but is now happening across the world. Urbanization and the adoption of western lifestyles has, for many, led to a tremendous reduction in active movement and in the amount of time spent in outdoor pursuits. For example, in the UK, where 85% of the population now live in urban environments, the Department of Health estimates that on average adults spend only 21% of their time outdoors while for children the value falls to just 9%. It is no coincidence that as levels of outdoor physical exercise have fallen, the number of individuals becoming obese, developing type 2 diabetes and suffering a range of mental health problems has risen to epidemic proportions. This is placing an intolerable burden on healthcare systems worldwide.

In attempting to address these challenges, public health experts have been urging people to engage in more physical exercise. Great efforts are being made to encourage visits to the gym or participation in sports. Many highly motivated individuals do so as a way of relaxing and getting fit; it is a lifestyle choice. But these activities may be too expensive or impractical for others, or may simply not appeal.

A less costly and more widely available option is to spend time being physically active in outdoor natural settings; for example, in gardens, parks, woods, forests and different types of countryside ("green space"), or by ponds, canals, rivers and lakes, or if available, seashores and coastal paths ("blue space"). Thirty minutes of exercise every day can be sufficient to maintain health and well-being. Evidence suggests that outdoor exercise actually confers greater health benefits than undertaking the same amount of exercise indoors.

The contention then is that natural settings motivate people to be physically active and thereby help to alleviate stress and foster better physical and mental health.

In this book, the editors have assembled a team of experts to rigorously explore the links between physical exercise in outdoor settings and related health benefits. The backgrounds of the chapter authors are diverse in that they hail from an array of academic departments, ranging from Life Sciences, and Exercise and Sports Medicine to Psychology and Education. This facilitates a transdisciplinary approach which delves deep into the emotions we experience in nature and how this affects our behaviours. It has also revealed new insights into generic responses and those which occur in specific circumstances, and clarifies whether responses are transient or long term.

The volume's content provides an overview of the research landscape, past and present; describes potential mechanisms through which natural settings might affect physical and mental health; offers several case studies which illuminate general principles and specific local considerations; and finally, identifies future pathways that we might follow to gain greater value from nature in relation to our health and well-being.

Each chapter is crammed with a wealth of knowledge and insightful analysis in a readable style that will help us to use nature more effectively to deliver health-related ecosystem services. They present a truly transdisciplinary perspective, so prized by the editors, to emerge strongly. The volume is an important addition to the growing library of literature concerning the intimate relationship between the natural environment, human health and well-being.

Professor Michael H. Depledge CBE, DSc, FRSB, FRCP.
Chair of Environment and Human Health,
University of Exeter Medical School,
Exeter, Devon, UK.
Honorary Professor of Public Policy,
University College,
London, UK.

PART I
The research landscape

1

FRIEND OR FOE

Salutogenic possibilities of the environment

David Sheffield and Ryan Lumber

In her seminal 1940s work about her relationship with the Cairngorms, *The Living Mountain*, Nan Shepherd (1977, p.4) describes two different experiences of nature: a place to contact and experience the elementals; and a place of fun and competition. There is good evidence to support the benefits of the latter; indeed, a systematic review by Coon et al. (2011) found evidence that psychological wellbeing benefits of exercise reported by adults was higher following practice in natural versus indoor locations. In this book and elsewhere there are further reports that the wellbeing benefits following exercise in nature on wellbeing outweigh those observed following the same exercise load indoors (e.g., Barton & Pretty, 2010; Loureiro & Veloso, 2014). There is now evidence implicating the role of contact and connecting with nature.

In this chapter, we describe how two theoretical developments have spurred a wave of research examining the benefits of connecting with nature: the biophilia hypothesis (Wilson, 2002) and salutogenesis (Antonovsky, 1979, 1987). We conclude by discussing some of the questions that remain to be answered in the light of these developments.

Antonovsky's fundamental contribution was to raise the philosophical 'salutogenic' question of what creates total health (*ease*) and to search for 'the origin of health' rather than to look for the causes of *dis-ease* in the pathogenic direction (Antonovsky, 1979, 1987). Antonovsky got the salutogenic idea from an epidemiological study of the problems in the menopause of women in Israel. In this study he used a target group of women who had survived the concentration camps of the Second World War. To his surprise he found that, among these women, there was a group that had the capability of maintaining good health and led a good life in spite of all they had gone through. Antonovsky questioned 'How the Hell can this be explained?', which led him (Antonovsky, 1996) to recognise that it is more important to focus on people's resources and capacity to create health than the pathogenic orientation on risks, ill health and disease. The ability to comprehend the whole situation and the capacity to use the resources available was called sense of coherence. This capacity was a combination of peoples' ability to assess and understand the situation they were in, to find a meaning to move in a health-promoting direction, also having the capacity to do so – that is, comprehensibility, meaningfulness and manageability, to use Antonovsky's own terms. Antonovsky also distinctly stated the salutogenesis was not limited by the disciplinary borders of one profession but was rather an interdisciplinary approach and a question of bringing coherence between disciplines and realising what connects them. Furthermore, it is not only a question of the person but an interaction between people and the structures of society – that is, the human resources and the conditions of the living context. It is not explicitly mentioned by Antonovsky himself, but it is reasonable to presume that he was also describing the natural environment. Salutogenesis, the origin of health, is a stress resource orientated concept, which focuses on resources, and maintains and improves the movement towards health. It gives the answer to why people, despite stressful situations and hardships, stay well. Thus, the key elements in the salutogenic development are the orientation towards problem solving and the capacity to use the resources available. Nature affords a range of resources to directly promote wellbeing and facilitate problem solving as Wilson (1984) recognised.

Biophilia

E. O. Wilson (1984, p.1) defined *biophilia* as

> the innate tendency [in human beings] to focus on life and lifelike process … To an extent still undervalued in philosophy and religion, our existence depends on this propensity, our spirit is woven from it, hopes rise on its currents.

Having an affiliation for life is theorised to stem from an evolutionary history of searching for survival-enhancing environments (Frumkin, 2001; Kellert & Wilson, 1993; Windhager, Atzwanger, Bookstein, & Schaefer, 2011) with the awe and wonder such settings provide responsible for the affiliation towards those survival-enhancing environments (Perkins, 2010). As urban living has occurred relatively recently in humanity's evolutionary history, the learning tendencies derived from nature are unlikely to have been erased from our biology (Nisbet, Zelenski, & Murphy, 2011). Tentative evidence exists for innate biophilia as savannah-like landscapes are more likely to be preferred by children between eight and eleven years of age, with older children preferring savannah landscapes and their home environment equally (see Wilson, 2002). However, an innate transmission of biophilia has been challenged more recently, as the evidence of the transmission of biophilic tendencies through genetic heritability is questionable; rather it is more likely a result of experiential learning instead (Simaika & Samways, 2010).

The adaptive behaviour biophilia produces will manifest in emotional connections to specific stimuli, the language used, and preferences for particular aspects of nature (Kellert & Wilson, 1993). Until recently empirical support for the hypothesis has been mixed (Kahn, 1997), yet evidence supporting the hypothesis does exist. Natural scenes and plant life contain the aesthetic qualities required for mental restoration (Kaplan, 1995) and recovery from stress (Wilson, 2002). After surgery, recovery was quicker for patients who were given natural views compared to urban brick walls (Ulrich, 1984). Physical and mental health aside, humans have an intrinsic interest in both known and unknown nature; dinosaurs continue to fascinate and inspire, acting as an icon of lost biodiversity (Wilson, 2002) while zoos have larger annual attendances compared to all the major sports combined in the United States of America (Kellert & Wilson, 1993). Such factors, along with the time invested in pet keeping (Kahn, 2011) and the popularity of wilderness activities, point to an advantage and desire to affiliate with nature through biophilia (Nisbet et al., 2011). The majority of research supporting the hypothesis does not test the rubrics of biophilia directly; the hypothesis is difficult to test scientifically as the theory's ambiguous nature makes it hard to refute (Kahn, 1999). Despite this, biophilia has been a useful catalyst for research into the human-nature relationship.

Connecting to nature

The prevailing view held by modern, westernised societies that humanity is set apart from (Vining, Merrick, & Price, 2008) and even above nature (Maller et al., 2009) was outlined as being one of principal causes of environmentally harmful behaviour (Haila, 1999). The value placed on self, animals and wider nature is therefore crucial to the attitudes held on environmental issues (Schultz, 2001) as well as behaviour (Verplanken, Walker, Davis, & Jurasek, 2008). In order for this to be achieved, an expansion of an individual's concept of self to include nature is necessary in becoming connected to nature (Mayer & Frantz, 2004; Schultz, 2001). It is thought that extending the self-concept to include nature creates a feeling of kinship (Olivos, Aragones, & Amerigo, 2011) and commonality with all life (Fox, 1990) as nature and the self are perceived as one and the same (Light, 2000). A connectedness to nature therefore creates a sense of belonging to the wider natural world as part of a larger community of nature (Mayer, Frantz, Bruehlman-Senecal, & Dolliver, 2009). The need for a connection to nature is a western notion and for indigenous cultures such as the Inuit, the natural landscape forms a crucial part of their cultural identity (Russell et al., 2013). Therefore, extending the self to include nature is not a new concept, as traditional indigenous belief systems often see the Earth and self as one and the same, with an individual's identity entwined with the fate of the wider environment (Macy, 2007). Since medieval times, the concept of 'Friluftsliv', a lifestyle of joy, freedom and experience leading to a spiritual connectedness with nature has existed in Sweden and continues to influence lifestyle and education to this day (Beery, 2013). Experience is therefore important as it informs an eco-identity which is intertwined with an active engagement with nature (Russell et al., 2013).

Anthropomorphising nature may also be important for including nature within the self-concept as it is the 'cognitive mechanism' for developing a biocentric ethos (Kahn, 1999; Vining, 2003) as natural elements are humanised, leading to feelings of similarity and empathy (Tam, Lee, & Chao, 2013). Possessing a nature self-concept leads to humanity and nature being perceived to be bound by the same natural laws, with all life having value (Schultz, Shriver, Tabanico, & Khazian, 2004). This view point is in essence biocentric (Munoz, Bogner, Clement, & Carvalho, 2009; Schroeder, 2007; Schultz, 2001; Vining et al., 2008), where nature and humanity co-exist and are not separated. Here, the selfish benefit to humanity is foresworn in order to preserve biodiversity, regardless of whether nature possesses utilitarian properties or not (Barbier et al., 2011). Therefore, everything in nature has a cultural, biological and individualistic value (Bourdeau, 2004; Drengson & Devall, 2010). Possession of this view point (and therefore a connectedness to nature) should lead to an appreciation of the richness of life and the flourishing of humanity (Naess, 2007) as harming nature when it is part of the self-concept is akin to harming oneself (Mayer & Frantz, 2004). While a sense of self and nature as one and the same may fluctuate depending on circumstance as it is thought to be comprised of an experience of nature at the individual, community and social group level (Russell et al., 2013), the nature-self ethos is vital to humanity living in balance with wider nature (Wilson, 2002).

Understanding the causes and consequences of our relationship with nature is therefore crucial. Individuals commonly report feeling emotionally close to, and an integral part of, nature, and this is reflected in the construct of nature connectedness (Mayer & Frantz, 2004). The importance of this sense of relatedness is evidenced by numerous studies linking nature connectedness with a range of wellbeing measures including hedonic ('feeling good') and eudaimonic ('functioning well') indicators (e.g. Capaldi, Dopko, & Zelenski, 2014; Nisbet & Zelenski, 2011). Indeed, in our recent review (Pritchard, Richardson, Sheffield, & McEwan, in press) we examined the relationship between nature connectedness and eudaimonic wellbeing by means of a meta-analysis and compared this with the relationship between nature connectedness and hedonic wellbeing. Eudaimonic wellbeing concerns functioning well (Ryff, 1989), akin to Antonovsky's notion of total health, and contrasts with hedonic wellbeing which focuses on feeling good. Data from 20 samples (n = 4,758) revealed a small positive correlation between nature connectedness and eudaimonic wellbeing (r = .24), indicating that individuals who are connected to nature are more likely to be flourishing and functioning well psychologically. However, the hypothesis that nature connectedness would be more strongly associated with eudaimonic wellbeing than it is with hedonic wellbeing was not supported (k=30, n=11,638, r=.20). However, one aspect of eudaimonic wellbeing was more strongly related to nature connectedness than hedonic wellbeing: personal growth, which accords well with Antonovsky's emphasis on people's resources and capacity to create health. A number of authors have suggested that nature connectedness may benefit eudaimonic wellbeing because it provides a route through which basic psychological needs can be met (e.g. Cleary, Fielding, Bell, Murray, & Roiko, 2017; Nisbet, Zelenski, & Murphy, 2009). Ryan and Deci's self-determination theory suggests three basic psychological needs – autonomy, competence and relatedness – are considered essential for psychological growth, integrity and wellbeing (Ryan & Deci, 2000). It is plausible that nature connectedness provides a route through which these basic needs are met and so leads to increased eudaimonic wellbeing. For example, the basic psychological need for relatedness could be met by being exposed to nature, which in turn is known to increase feelings of connectedness to nature (e.g. Weinstein, Przybylski, & Ryan, 2009). Howell and Passmore (2013) suggested that the relationship between nature affiliation and wellbeing could be mediated by a greater sense of social connectedness, and nature connection has been found to promote pro-social behaviour such as altruism and generosity (Weinstein et al., 2009). It also seems likely that nature connection promotes a form of relatedness distinct from social (human) connectedness and important in its own right (Cleary et al., 2017). This is supported by research from Zelenski and Nisbet (2014), who found that the concept of nature relatedness was distinct from other forms of relatedness – including connectedness with family and friends – and was a significant and distinct predictor of happiness.

Nature connectedness has been linked to a range of activities including gardening (Shaw, Miller, & Wescott, 2012), feeding birds or nurturing plants (Freeman, Dickinson, Porter, & van Heezik, 2012), walking (Mayer et al., 2009) and general wilderness experiences (Martin, 2004). Nature-based interventions for wellbeing have been found to aid recovery from stress-related mental disorders due to their facilitation of self as part of a wider existence (Pálsdóttir, Grahn, & Persson, 2014), with self-reported reductions in healthcare service attendance (Währborg, Petersson, & Grahn, 2014). Forest-based interventions lead to improvements in psychological factors for participants with depression and anxiety disorders (Sonntag-Öström et al., 2015). Of note is the Three Good Things Positive Psychology Intervention which has been used to facilitate a greater focus on gratitude that in turn reduces negative emotions while prolonging feelings of pleasure (Bryant, 2003). Three Good Things lets an individual to think and write down three good things that have happened to them, resulting in increased wellbeing even up to a six month follow up (Seligman, Steen, Park, & Peterson, 2005). The intervention has adapted to focus on the good things found in nature (Richardson, Hallam, & Lumber, 2015), finding increased nature connectedness when tested experimentally in comparison to a control group both at one week and two month follow-up (Richardson & Sheffield, 2017). Moreover, in this study, we found that changes in nature connectedness predicted increases in psychological wellbeing in the experimental group but not the control group. The benefits of 'being' in nature are not limited to the time of the intervention solely, as they extend beyond the encounter (Windhorst & Williams, 2016), which may have implications for prevention care in terms of relapse and wellbeing maintenance for individuals with depression and/or anxiety disorder. Indeed, we have replicated our notice good things in nature findings in children and in adults with diagnoses of anxiety and/or depression.

Pathways to nature connectedness

Biophilia has been framed as comprising of nine succinct values that cover a range of ways in which individuals relate to or interact with nature (Kellert, 1993) and are often unconsciously manifested in cognitions, emotive responses, artistry and ethics (Kahn, 1997, 2011). We have argued that a selection of biophilic values provide pathways to nature connectedness.

Each of the nine values may cross over into one another but they are considered to be separate values with each focused on its own particular area (Kellert & Wilson, 1993). It is suggested that affiliating with nature through the nine values leads to an appreciation for diversity and subsequent flourishing of the individual (Nisbet et al., 2009) and that interacting with nature in one or more of the biophilic values allows for an innate learning of nature through active participation (Gullone, 2000). Thus, biophilia is not a hardwired biological process, rather a predisposition for certain natural settings that may be a core human instinct (Wilson, 2002). Biophilia is therefore seen as a biocultural model that occurs through inherited prepared learning that has been maintained through reliance on and affiliation towards nature, leading to greater survival and evolutionary fitness (Wilson, 2002); biophilia may consequently be crucial to optimum human functioning both affectively and psychologically (Kellert, 1993; Nisbet et al., 2011).

In order to understand the mechanisms involved in nature connectedness we (Lumber, Richardson, & Sheffield, 2018) used the biophilia hypothesis as a framework to explore how connectedness to nature can be achieved from the perspective of individuals who engage with nature through the biophilic values. Seven themes emerged from the thematic analysis of three focus groups of 11 individuals who regularly undertook activity that involved an engagement with nature (see Table 1.1). These were investigating nature through scientific enquiry, engaging the senses, creating idyllic nature, noting nature through artistry, nature conservation, growing food and engaging with wild nature. Subsequent development of a scale examined these seven pathways in 314 adults (Lumber, Richardson, & Sheffield, 2017). Activities structured around the naturalistic, humanistic, aesthetic, moralistic and symbolic biophilic values positively predicted nature connectedness, whereas the values that involved use (utilitarian), control (dominionistic), avoidance (negativistic) and knowledge (ecologistic-scientific) did not. In order to make the activity values more accessible, while differentiating the pathways from the biophilic values to reflect humanity's current relationship with nature (in contrast to our evolutionary propensity (biophilia) due to perceived separation), new labels were created.

TABLE 1.1 Biophilic pathways (based on Kellert & Wilson, 2003)

Biophilia mapping	*Pathway*	*How nature connectedness is facilitated*
Ecologistic-scientific	Scientific enquiry of nature	Through an appreciation of the interconnectedness of all life (including humanity) by investigating nature using scientific methodology
Naturalistic	Engaging the senses	Engaging the senses including touch, sound and smell to feel deeply connected with nature
Dominionistic	Creating idyllic nature	Shaping natural spaces to become more in line with a personal ideal that facilitates restoration
Aesthetic	Noting nature through artistry	Actively taking notice of nature to experience nature connectedness and preserving the experience through artistic expression
Moralistic	Conservation of nature	Protecting local natural environments from human caused harm leading to an emotional attachment for the conserved habitat
Utilitarian	Growing food	Appreciating nature by nurturing and growing produce that is eaten to increase the value held for nature
Humanistic	Engaging with wild nature	Forming an emotional attachment to non- domesticated, wild animals through a sense of similarity through positive interactions

These were contact (naturalistic), emotion (humanistic), meaning (symbolic), compassion (moralistic), and beauty (aesthetic). Finally, in a subsequent test (n = 72), a walking intervention with activities operationalising the identified five predictors, was found to significantly increase nature connectedness when compared to walking in nature alone or walking in and engaging with the built environment (Lumber et al., 2017). These findings indicate that contact, emotion, meaning, compassion and beauty are pathways for improving nature connectedness. Thus, there is a need to go beyond activities that simply engage people with nature through knowledge and identification, to pathways that develop a more meaningful and emotional relationship with nature.

The New Economics Foundation's *Five Ways to Wellbeing* (2008) provides straightforward and popular guidance on five ways we can improve human wellbeing from a salutogenic perspective: Connect, Take Notice, Give, Be Active, Learn. These can be applied to nature-based activities based on the biophilic pathways we have found that relate to nature connectedness (Richardson, 2019).

Connect – Social relationships are important for wellbeing: be with and talk to people – about anything including nature. Humans are social animals and part of the natural world – nature offers socially isolated people a way of feeling connected.

Take notice – Noticing nature, its beauty, our emotions in nature and what nature means are key to developing a closer relationship with nature.

Give – Take part in community life, do something for a friend – do something for nature.

Be active – Walk or cycle when you can, to green spaces to connect with others, to notice, to give and learn – connect actively with nature.

Learn – Try something new, rediscover your wonder for nature, learn that people are part of the natural world and nature matters for human health.

The current trend of conservation as development that emphasises humanity as a part of nature (ergo any conservation efforts benefit both wider nature and humanity), represents a cultural shift (Flikke, 2014) that may facilitate greater behavioural change. However, any further societal-wide change in behaviour may only occur when a concern for the environment becomes part of the self in order to elicit environmentally consistent behaviours (Verplanken et al., 2008). This would emerge from a shared, human worldview (Wilson, 2002) and cultural perspective (Ernst & Theimer, 2011). Such an ideological change will involve appreciating life quality instead of quantity (Naess, 1986; Antonovsky, 1996) to allow human beings to live sustainably with nature where diversity is valued (Light, 2000) thus allowing all life to flourish (Drengson & Devall, 2010). Humanity has the capacity and responsibility to think about and protect the planet but a relationship with nature is needed as the main requirement of a much-needed and emerging environmental ethic (Wilson, 2002). Research attention has begun to turn towards the human-nature relationship (Perkins, 2010) as a route to limiting environmental damage (Tam et al., 2013). This is due to the acknowledgment that information and awareness is not enough to produce environmentally responsible behaviours (Arbuthnott, Glenn, Sutter, & Heidt, 2014). Ultimately the pressing need for change is not about saving the world, rather it is about saving humanity from a harm of its own making and to avoid the ultimate loss of other species, which form an important part of humanity's culture and identity, along with ourselves.

Future challenges

There is increasing evidence that connecting to nature through biophilic pathways has the potential to increase total health, and that this should include individuals, societies and our planet. But there remain a number of research questions to be addressed. These include: What makes natural settings so compelling? How do natural settings restore bodily health? Are some natural patterns more effective than others? Are there ways to design, manage and interpret natural environments so as to enhance their beneficial influences? How do individuals' differences and preferences impact on the effectiveness of biophilic pathways to improve wellbeing? How do childhood experiences impact on those preferences and might environmental education be tailored to encourage nature connectedness in adulthood? Finally, given the changes in climate that we are observing, how might we prevent biophilia turning to biophobia?

There is still much to learn about the ways in which humans interact with nature and how we can improve the wellbeing of both. But learning does not decrease the awe and wonder with which we can encounter nature. As Nan Shepherd (1977, p.45) describes:

> The more one learns of this intricate interplay of soil, altitude, weather, and the living tissues of plant and insect (an intricacy that has its astonishing moments, as when sundew and butterwort eat the insects), the more the mystery deepens. Knowledge does not dispel mystery.

References

Antonovsky, A. (1979). *Health, stress and coping*. San Francisco, CA: Jossey-Bass.

Antonovsky, A. (1987). *Unraveling the mystery of health. How people manage stress and stay well*. San Francisco, CA: Jossey-Bass.

Antonovsky, A. (1996). The salutogenic model as a theory to guide health promotion. *Health Promotion International*, *11*(1), 11–18.

Arbuthnott, K. D., Glenn, C., Sutter, G. C., & Heidt, C. T. (2014). Natural history museums, parks, and connection with nature. *Museum Management and Curatorship*, *29*(2), 1–20. doi:10.1080/09647775.2014.888818

Barbier, E. B., Hacker, S. D., Kennedy, C., Koch, E. W., Stier, A. C., & Silliman, B. R. (2011). The value of estuarine and coastal ecosystem services. *Ecological Monographs*, *81*(2), 169–193.

Barton, J., & Pretty, J. (2010). What is the best dose of nature and green exercise for improving mental health? A multi-study analysis. *Environmental Science and Technology*, *44*(10), 3947–3955. doi:10.1021/es903183r

Beery, T. H. (2013). Nordic in nature: Friluftsliv and environmental connectedness. *Environmental Education Research*, *19*(1), 94–117. doi:10.1080/13504622.2012.688799

Bourdeau, P. (2004). The man-nature relationship and environmental ethics. *Journal of Environmental Radioactivity*, *72*, 9–15.

Bryant, F. (2003). Savoring beliefs inventory (SBI): A scale for measuring beliefs about savouring. *Journal of Mental Health*, *12*(2), 175–196. doi:10.1080/0963823031000103489

Capaldi, C. A., Dopko, R. L., & Zelenski, J. M. (2014). The relationship between nature connectedness and happiness: A meta-analysis. *Frontiers in Psychology*, *5*, 976.

Cleary, A., Fielding, K. S., Bell, S. L., Murray, Z., & Roiko, A. (2017). Exploring potential mechanisms involved in the relationship between eudaimonic wellbeing and nature connection. *Landscape and Urban Planning*, *158*, 119–128.

Coon, T., Boddy, K., Stein, K., Whear, R., Barton, J., & Depledge, M. (2011). Does participating in physical activity in outdoor natural environments have a greater effect on physical and mental wellbeing than physical activity indoors? A systematic review. *Environmental Science & Technology*, *45*(5), 1761–1772. doi:10.1021/es102947t

Drengson, A., & Devall, B. (2010). The deep ecology movement: Origins, development & future prospects. *The Trumpeter*, *26*(2), 48–69.

Ernst, J., & Theimer, S. (2011). Evaluating the effects of environmental education programming on connectedness to nature, *Environmental Education Research*, *17*(5), 577–598. doi: 10.1080/13504622.2011.565119

Flikke, R. (2014). On the fractured, fragmented and disrupted landscapes of conservation. Forum for Development Studies, 41(2), 173-182. doi:10.1080/08039410.2014.918759

Fox, W. (1990). Transpersonal ecology: "psychologising" ecophilosophy. *The Journal of Transpersonal Psychology*, *22*(1), 59–96.

Freeman, C., Dickinson, K. J. M., Porter, S., & van Heezik, Y. (2012). "My garden is an expression of me": Exploring householders' relationships with their gardens. *Journal of Environmental Psychology*, *32*(2), 135–143. doi:10.1016/j.jenvp.2012.01.005

Frumkin, H. (2001). Beyond toxicity. Human health and the natural environment. *American Journal of Preventative Medicine*, *20*(3), 234–240.

Gullone, E. (2000). The Biophilia Hypothesis and life in the 21st century: Increasing mental health or increasing pathology? *Journal of Happiness Studies*, *1*, 293–322. doi:10.1023/A:1010043827986

Haila, Y. (1999). Biodiversity and the divide between culture and nature. *Biodiversity and Conservation*, *8*, 165–181.

Howell, A. J., & Passmore, H. (2013). The nature of happiness: Nature affiliation and mental well-being. In C. L. M. Keyes (Ed.), *Mental well-being: International contributions to the study of positive mental health* (pp. 231–257). New York: Springer.

Kahn, P. H. (1997). Developmental psychology and the Biophilia Hypothesis: Children's affiliation with nature. *Developmental Review*, *17*(1), 1–61. doi:10.1006/drev.1996.043

Kahn, P. H. (1999). *The human relationship with nature: Development and culture*. Cambridge, MA: MIT Press.

Kahn, P. H. (2011). *Technological nature: Adaptation and the future of human life*. Cambridge, MA: MIT Press

Kaplan, S. (1995). The restorative benefits of nature: Towards an integrative framework. *Journal of Environmental Psychology*, *15*(3), 169–182.

Kellert, S. H. (1993). The biological basis for human values of nature. In S. H. Kellert & E. O. Wilson (Eds.), *The Biophilia hypothesis*. (pp. 42–69). Washington, DC: Island.

Kellert, S. H., & Wilson, E. O. (1993). *The Biophilia hypothesis*. Washington, DC: Island.

Light, A. (2000). What is an ecological identity? *Environmental Politics*, *9*(4), 37–41. doi:10.1080/09644010008414551

Loureiro, A., & Veloso, S. (2014). Outdoor exercise, well-being and connectedness to nature. *Psico*, *45*(3), 299–304.

Lumber, R., Richardson, M., & Sheffield, D. (2017). Beyond knowing nature: Contact, emotion, compassion, meaning, and beauty are pathways to nature connection. *PLoS One*, *12*(5), e0177186. doi:10.1371/journal.pone.0177186

Lumber, R., Richardson, M., & Sheffield, D. (2018) The seven pathways to nature connectedness: A focus group exploration. *European Journal of Ecopsychology*, *6*, 47–68.

Macy, J. (2007). *World as lover, world as self: Courage for global justice and ecological renewal*. Berkeley, CA: Parallax Press

Maller, C., Townsend, M., Leger, L. S., Henderson-Wilson, C., Pryor, A., Prosser, L., & Moore, M. (2009). Healthy parks, healthy people: The health benefits of contact with nature in a park context. *The George Wright Forum*, *26*, 51–83.

Martin, P. (2004). Outdoor adventure in promoting relationships with nature. *Australian Journal of Outdoor Education*, *8*(1), 20–28.

Mayer, F. S., & Frantz, C. M. (2004). The connectedness to nature scale: A measure of individuals' feeling in community with nature. *Journal of Environmental Psychology*, *24*(4), 503–515. doi:10.1016/j.jenvp.2004.10.001

Mayer, F. S., Frantz, C. M., Bruehlman-Senecal, E., & Dolliver, K. (2009). Why is nature beneficial? The role of connectedness to nature. *Environment and Behaviour, 41*, 607–643. doi:10.1177/0013916508319745

Munoz, F., Bogner, F., Clement, P., & Carvalho, G. S. (2009). Teachers' conceptions of nature and environment in 16 countries. *Journal of Environmental Psychology*, 407–413. doi:10.1016/j.jenvp.2009.05.007

Naess, A. (2007). *The Selected Works of Arne Naess Volumes 1–10*. Dordrecht: Springer.

New Economics Foundation. (2008). *Five ways to wellbeing*. London: Author.

Nisbet, E. K., & Zelenski, J. M. (2011). Underestimating nearby nature: Affective forecasting errors obscure the happy path to sustainability. *Psychological Science, 22*(9), 1101–1106. doi:10.1177/0956797611418527

Nisbet, E. K., Zelenski, J. M., & Murphy, S. A. (2009). The nature relatedness scale: Linking individuals' connection with nature to environmental concern and behavior. *Environment and Behavior, 41*, 715–740.

Nisbet, E. K., Zelenski, J. M., & Murphy, S. A. (2011). Happiness is in our nature: Exploring nature relatedness as a contributor to subjective well-being. *Journal of Happiness Studies, 12*, 303–322, doi:10.1007/s10902-010-9197-7

Olivos, P., Aragones, J. I., & Amerigo, M. (2011). The connectedness to nature scale and its relationship with environmental beliefs and identity. *International Journal of Hispanic Psychology, 4*(1), 5–19.

Pálsdóttir, A. M., Grahn, P., & Persson, D. (2014). Changes in experienced value of everyday occupations after nature-based vocational rehabilitation. *Scandinavian Journal of Occupational Therapy, 21*(1), 58–68. doi:10.3109/11038128.2013.832794

Perkins, H. E. (2010). Measuring love and care for nature. *Journal of Environmental Psychology, 30*(4), 455–463. doi:10.1016/j.jenvp.2010.05.004

Pritchard, A., Richardson, M., Sheffield, D., & McEwan, K. (in press). The relationship between nature connectedness and eudaimonic well-being: A meta-analysis. *Journal of Happiness Studies*.doi:10.1007/s10902-019-00118-6

Richardson, M. (2019). 5 ways to wellbeing with nature. Finding Nature Blogpost. https://findingnature.org.uk/2019/01/28/5-ways-to-wellbeing-with-nature/

Richardson, M., Hallam, J., & Lumber, R. (2015). One thousand good things in nature: Aspects of nearby nature associated with improved connection to nature. *Environmental Values, 24*(5), 603–619. doi:10.3197/096327115X14384223590131

Richardson, M., & Sheffield, D. (2017). Three good things in nature: Noticing nearby nature brings sustained increases in connection with nature/tres cosas buenas de la naturaleza: Prestar atención a la naturaleza cercana produce incrementos prolongados en conexión con la naturaleza. *Psyecology, 8*(1), 1. doi:10.1080/21711976.2016.1267136

Russell, R., Guerry, A. D., Balvanera, P., Gould, R. K., Basurto, X., Chan, K. M.-A., Klain, S., Levine, J., & Tam, J. (2013). Humans and nature: How knowing and experiencing nature affect well-being. *Annual Review of Environment and Resources, 38*(6), 6.1–6.30. doi:10.1146/annurev-environ-012312-110838

Ryan, R. M., & Deci, E. L. (2000). Self-determination theory and the facilitation of intrinsic motivation, social development, and well-being. *American Psychologist, 55*, 66–78.

Ryff, C. D. (1989). Happiness is everything, or is it? Explorations on the meaning of psychological well-being. *Journal of Personality and Social Psychology, 57*, 1069–1081.

Schroeder, H. W. (2007). Place, experience, gestalt and the human-nature relationship. *Journal of Environmental Psychology, 37*, 293–309. doi: 10.1016/j.jenvp.2007.07.001

Schultz, P. W. (2001). The structure of environmental concern: Concern for self, other people, and the biosphere. *Journal of Environmental Psychology, 21*, 327–339. doi:10.1006/jevp.2001.0227

Schultz, P. W., Shriver, C., Tabanico, J. J., & Khazian, A. M. (2004). Implicit connections with nature. *Journal of Environmental Psychology, 24*(1), 31–42. doi:10.1016/S0272-4944(03)00022-7

Seligman, M. E. P., Steen, T. A., Park, N., & Peterson, C. (2005). Positive psychology progress. Empirical validation of interventions. *American Psychologist, 60*, 410–421. doi:10.1037/0003-066X.60.5.410

Shaw, A., Miller, K., & Wescott, G. (2012). Wildlife gardening and connectedness to nature: Engaging the unengaged. *Environmental Values, 22*(4), 483–502.

Shepherd, N. (1977). *The living mountain*. London: Canongate.

Simaika, J. P., & Samways, M. J. (2010). Biophilia as a universal ethic for conserving biodiversity. *Conservation Biology: The Journal of the Society for Conservation Biology, 24*(3), 903–906. doi:10.1111/j.1523-1739.2010.01485.x

Sonntag-Öström, S., Nordin, M., Dolling, A., Lundell, Y., Nilsson, L., & Järvholm, L.S. (2015): Can rehabilitation in boreal forests help recovery from exhaustion disorder? The randomised clinical trial ForRest. *Scandinavian Journal of Forest Research, 30*(8), 1–41.

Tam, K.-P., Lee, S.-L., & Chao, M. M. (2013). Saving Mr. Nature: Anthropomorphism enhances connectedness to and protectiveness toward nature. *Journal of Experimental Social Psychology, 49*(3), 514–521. doi:10.1016/j.jesp.2013.02.001

Ulrich, R. S. (1984). View through a window may influence recovery from surgery. *Science, 224*, 420–421.

Verplanken, B., Walker, I., Davis, A., & Jurasek, M. (2008). Context change and travel mode choice: Combining the habit discontinuity and self-activation hypotheses. *Journal of Environmental Psychology, 28*, 121–127.

Vining, J. (2003). The connection to other animals and caring for nature. *Research in Human Ecology, 10*(2), 87–99.

Vining, J., Merrick, M. S., & Price, E. A. (2008). The distinction between humans and nature: Human perceptions of connectedness to nature and elements of the natural and unnatural. *Research in Human Ecology, 15*(1), 1–11.

Währborg, P., Petersson, I. F., & Grahn, P. (2014). Nature-assisted rehabilitation for reactions to severe stress and/or depression in a rehabilitation garden: Long-term follow-up including comparisons with a matched population-based reference cohort. *Journal of Rehabilitation Medicine, 46*(3), 271–276. doi:10.2340/16501977-1259.

Weinstein, N., Przybylski, A., & Ryan, R. (2009). Can nature make us more caring? Effects of immersion in nature on intrinsic aspirations and generosity. *Personality and Social Psychology Bulletin, 35*, 1315–1329.

Wilson, E. O. (1984). *Biophilia*. London: Harvard University Press.

Wilson, E. O. (2002). *The future of life*. New York: Alfred A. Knopf

Windhager, S., Atzwanger, K., Bookstein, F. L., & Schaefer, K. (2011). Fish in a mall aquarium—An ethological investigation of Biophilia. *Landscape and Urban Planning, 99*(1), 23–30. doi:10.1016/j.landurbplan.2010.08.008

Windhorst, E., & Williams, A. (2016). Bleeding at the roots: Post-secondary student mental health and nature affiliation: Bleeding at the roots. *The Canadian Geographer/Le Géographe Canadien, 60*(2), 232–238. doi:10.1111/cag.12273

Zelenski, J. M., & Nisbet, E. K. (2014). Happiness and feeling connected: The distinct role of nature relatedness. *Environment and Behaviour, 46*, 3–23.

2

SOCIETAL CHALLENGES, METHODOLOGICAL ISSUES AND TRANSDISCIPLINARY APPROACHES

Tadhg E. MacIntyre, Giovanna Calogiuri, Aoife A. Donnelly, Giles Warrington, Jürgen Beckmann, Ian Lahart and Noel Brick

Climate change has long been referred to as a wicked problem (Head, 2008; Incropera FP, 2016; Rittel & Webber, 1973; Sun & Yang, 2016). Wicked problems have innumerable causes, morph constantly, and have no correct solution. Transdisciplinary approaches have been proposed as pathways to understanding wicked problems (Pohl et al., 2017). The focus of this chapter is to recognize the key societal challenges, climate change, increased urbanization, air pollution, mental health, and physical inactivity, and to seek approaches that may ultimately lead to solutions. The task is to at least ask the right questions about green exercise as a potential solution for the wicked problems we face.

What is transdisciplinary?

Since the biophilia hypothesis (see Chapter 1) was first proposed research could be described as progressing through three waves. Initial research and theorization focusing on the predominant explanations for human-nature interactions, the stress reduction theory (Ulrich et al., 1991) and the attention restoration theory (Kaplan & Kaplan, 1989), respectively, was largely interdisciplinary. The next wave of studies applied a largely multidisciplinary approach and large-scale projects included the FP7 funded PHENOTYPE project which investigated the benefits of nature contact for human health and well-being (Nieuwenhuijsen et al., 2014). Contemporary research is asserting a more transdisciplinary perspective and this again resonates through large-scale projects. The EU funded Blue Health project offers this approach in the study of blue natural spaces on health and well-being (Grellier et al., 2017).

In effect, researchers have progressed from using one lens (interdisciplinary) to converging lens (multidisciplinary) to stacking multiple lens together and developing a new methodology (transdisciplinary). In comparison to multidisciplinary perspectives which have typified much of the prior research, transdisciplinary approaches involve theories, concepts and knowledge, data and techniques from two or more disciplines and non-academic or non-formalized fields. Transdisciplinary approaches aim to optimize synergies across the scientific disciplines and promote multi-stakeholder engagement typical of nature-based solutions activities (see Chapter 18). The above description would not be without debate as others contest that interdisciplinary approaches offer a more cohesive approach (Seymour, 2016).

Successive studies have noted that conceptual and methodological issues have plagued the interpretation of findings on human nature interactions (Frumkin et al., 2017; Gascon, Zijlema, Vert, White, & Nieuwenhuijsen, 2017; White et al., 2013), and the complexity of physical activity as an additional variable only exacerbates the problems. Thus, the purpose of this chapter is to:

- Review the societal challenges that influence the potential of green exercise as an intervention,
- Provide a critical overview of the state of the art of the field,
- Evaluate and discuss methodological challenges and limitations of the current scientific literature, and
- Present a series of recommendations for future research and for those who intend to implement green exercise initiatives.

Societal challenges

i. Global health challenge 1 – mental health

In 2013, the World Health Organization (WHO) predicted that depression, then ranked the fourth leading disease burden, would be the top ranked problem by 2030. This estimate was surpassed 13 years earlier than predicted and moreover, the scale of the problem may continue to be widely underestimated due to the prevailing stigmas which surround mental health issues (WHO, 2018b). Mental health is reported as the greatest burden of disease globally (WHO, 2018b) and the total costs of mental ill-health are over EUR 600 billion – or more than 4% of GDP – across the 28 EU countries. These findings are not unrelated to urbanisation where urban living compounds risk factors. Mental health and well-being are complex constructs closely linked to economic indices, cultural differences and indeed variations in access to natural green space (WHO, 2016). Individuals may show prejudice against those with a mental health condition and thus be service averse with regard to coping with their own mental health challenges. Stigma impacts care seeking when individuals attempt to avoid being labelled with the culturally-determined stereotypes associated with mental health illness. Interventions that target mental health directly (e.g. mental health first aid) may also be stigmatized and have reduced acceptability among users. Nature-based interventions, including green exercise, have the potential to be a non-invasive low-stigma preventative intervention for positive mental health and well-being.

ii. Global health challenge 2 – physical inactivity

Regular physical activity is a well-known protective factor for the prevention and treatment of several non-communicable diseases, such as heart disease, stroke, diabetes and different types of cancer. Physical activity is also known to promote good mental health, delay the onset of dementia, and improve people's quality of life and well-being (WHO, 2018a). In spite of this, it is estimated that 23% of adults and 81% of adolescents worldwide do not meet WHO's recommendations of at least 150 minutes of aerobic moderate-intensity (or equivalent amounts of vigorous-intensity) physical activity per week (WHO, 2010). Noticeably, according to WHO, the minimum recommended levels of physical activity can be attained across multiple domains, including purposeful exercise but also occupational activities (e.g. paid work and domestic work), transportation activities (e.g. walking and cycling), and recreational activities (e.g. playing and gardening) (WHO, 2014). Therefore, there is an urgent need to tackle the problem of physical inactivity at a population level. There has been a growth in the interest of the role that natural environments can play in increasing physical activity levels and potentially providing additional improvements in health and well-being compared to built-up or indoor environments (Thompson Coon et al., 2011). Natural environments may promote physical activity by facilitating safe, accessible and attractive venues and a motivation to engage in physical activity (Mytton, Townsend, Rutter, & Foster, 2012). Furthermore, physical activity in a natural environment has been proposed to provide additional benefits, such as restoration from stress and mental fatigue and improvements in mood, social networking, physical activity adherence, appreciation of nature, and self-esteem, above that experienced following physical activity in a built or indoor environment (Barton and Pretty, 2010; Thompson Coon et al., 2011,). These positive effects have the potential to enhance people's attitudes toward physical activity and thus foster more active lifestyles (Calogiuri & Chroni, 2014). In this chapter, we will further assess the evidence regarding the suggested role natural environments play in promoting physical activity.

iii. Global health challenge 3 – climate change

Global climate change is one of society's grand challenges (American Psychological Association, 2008). A substantial global disease burden is a likely consequence of climate change (van den Bosch & Depledge, 2015). Nevertheless, the Lancet commission has recognized that tackling climate change could be the greatest global health opportunity of the 21st century (Wang & Horton, 2015). Doherty and Clayton (2011) propose that the psychological impact of climate change is predicted to occur by three pathways: direct (e.g., acute or traumatic effects of extreme weather events and a changed environment); indirect (e.g. threats to emotional well-being based on observation of impacts and concern or uncertainty about future risks); and psychosocial (e.g. chronic social and community effects of heat, drought, migrations, and climate-related conflicts, and post-disaster adjustment). Nature-based interventions allied to nature-based solutions (NBS) may have a role in the promotion of resilience, a prerequisite for coping with adverse future events.

iv. Global health challenge 4 – increasing urbanization

Coupled with climate change is the problem of global urbanization – with more than 50% of the world's population now residing in urban areas with limited access to greenspace for physical activity. This figure is set to rise further, with 70% of people projected to be living in towns and cities by 2050 (Intergovernmental Panel on Climate Change, 2014) and almost 10% predicted to be inhabitants of mega-cities (pop. > 10m) by 2030 (United Nations, 2016). The World Economic Forum (2019) identified social, environmental and health challenges arising from poorly planned urbanization and associated infrastructure as a societal risk in their assessment of global risks and the emerging climate risks are concentrated in urban areas. Increased urbanization and densification within cities can lead to degradation of ecosystems and resource depletion creating differential risks for communities (van den Bosch & Depledge, 2015). One consequence of the degradation of ecosystems and denaturing of landscapes is that people are increasingly disconnected from nature.

v. Global health challenge 5 – air pollution

Air pollution is the "biggest environmental risk" to public health in Europe, causing an estimated 400,000 premature deaths a year, with many EU countries failing to meet air quality standards (CAFE directive 2008/50/EC). Future risk from climate change exacerbates what are termed the often-unseen mental health effects (Watts et al., 2018). It is now well known that exposure to poor ambient air quality contributes to a significant global burden of respiratory and allergic diseases and increased mortality rates (EEA, 2012; Guerreiro, Foltescu, & de Leeuw, 2014; Hettelingh et al., 2013; Kunzli et al., 2000). Ambient pollutants such as nitrogen dioxide (NO_2), ozone (O_3) and fine particulate matter (PM) have been associated with poorer health outcomes in many epidemiological studies (Beelen et al., 2014; Laumbach & Kipen, 2012; Pascal et al., 2013; Raaschou-Nielsen et al., 2013). Indeed concern extends beyond that of direct human health impacts and acidifying pollutant emissions (e.g. nitrogen oxides (NO_x), sulfur dioxide (SO_2) and ammonia (NH_3)) can also impact on sensitive ecosystems by contributing to acidification and eutrophication

(Guerreiro et al., 2014) and have indirect secondary impacts on human health by affecting ecological status and agricultural productivity (Galloway et al., 2004; Staelens et al., 2012). Degradation of the natural environment thus has the potential to cause a degree of distress among the population and subsequently, as we try to ascertain the positive effects to be gained from interacting with it, the quality of that environment is certainly influential.

The knowledge gap

The use of green natural spaces for health promotion, or nature-based interventions (i.e. nature is the *setting* of an intervention) includes the promotion of green exercise, which refers to the completion of physical activity in natural settings (Barton & Pretty, 2010). Simply accessing natural environments with limited physical activity has the potential to enhance individual well-being. When compared with indoor exercise or exercise in built environments, green exercise has been exhibited to have efficacy in conferring additional psychological benefits (e.g., enhanced mood, reduced stress) (Thompson Coon et al., 2011). This review, the authors acknowledged, was limited by the quality of the available research and only included 11 trials (n = 833). Given the perils of ever increasing urbanization, it is vital to evaluate if it can be both a more sustainable form of exercise than indoor activity (see Chapter 16) and secondly, if it confers additional benefits in terms of adherence, well-being, reduced exertion, etc.

Comprehensive study approaches are lacking that would enable mediators and moderators relating to the potential psychological benefits of nature contact to be identified. A systematic review by Gascon et al. (2017) investigating the potential health benefits of outdoor blue spaces (lakes, rivers, sea, etc.) reported that, among the small number of available studies, there was “a large degree of heterogeneity in terms of study design, exposure metrics and outcome measures, making synthesis difficult” (p. 1207). A further issue arises from the lack of evidence regarding which metrics of nature (e.g. biodiversity, air quality, soundscape) best predict various mental health benefits. A variety of in-situ measures have been used to quantify the quality of natural settings (e.g. natural environment scoring tool (NEST); Gidlow et al., 2018) but, without consensus on the optimum tools, comparisons across studies are restricted.

Recent decades have seen huge developments in the field of environmental monitoring. From advanced analytical techniques to large scale deployment of minuscule sensors it would appear that we can now measure anything and everything whenever we want. However, the simple fact remains that we cannot yet determine what the quality of the environment is; all that we can do is estimate it at a given point in space and a given point in time. And once you move away from that given spatial dimension or as time passes, that value that you once had is no longer representative. So the questions must then be asked:

- Does this really matter?
- Why do we care if it does?

Assuming that it does matter and we do care, this variability poses many challenges for environmental scientists as they must try to account for both naturally influencing factors and anthropogenic factors when estimating environmental quality. While measurements form an important aspect of air quality assessment, on their own they are unlikely to be sufficient to provide an accurate spatial and temporal description of the pollutant concentrations and as a result, models are often needed (Moussiopoulos, 1997). Improvements in computational speed, efficiency and overall ability have allowed for the application of statistical, deterministic and probabilistic models on scales ranging from street level to global and everything in between. Where we have suitably detailed and accurate input data models can provide us with information that monitoring alone simply cannot. While the use of models continues to increase, one should always remember the words of renowned British statistician George E.P. Box: "Essentially, all models are wrong, but some are useful" (Box & Draper, 1987). Data collection itself, be it by means of directly monitoring or by modelling, is only the first step in estimating environmental quality. These data then need analysis, and the very nature of environmental data as auto correlated, non-normally distributed time series subject to a range of short and long-term external effects tends to complicate the process. The perceived quality of that environment should also then be considered and there is currently a lack of understanding of how perception of environmental quality and actual environmental quality are related in a range of situations. Chapter 16 discusses further the importance of the ambient environment in which we exercise, paying particular attention to gyms, and suggests ways in which we can improve exercise-related sustainability

Finally, concerns have been raised regarding the extent to which experimental studies have succeeded in re-creating equivalent exercise stimuli in green exercise treatments as compared with comparisons or control conditions (e.g., exercise indoors, Rogerson, Gladwell, Gallagher, & Barton, 2016).

A lack of conceptual clarity abounds with nature exposure, nature connectedness, environmental quality perception and sensory engagement all providing competing explanations on related but distinct concepts. Given the zeitgeist and the pressures emerging from the future growth of cities, it is imperative that such methodological and conceptual challenges be overcome rapidly.

State of the art and beyond

In 1984, E. O. Wilson developed the biophilia hypothesis to explain our innate need to connect with living organisms and nature. This theory spawned over three decades of research largely within the framework of environmental psychology, and two classic theoretical accounts of nature contact on cognition and stress (van den Berg & Staats, 2018). Attention restoration theory (Kaplan & Kaplan, 1989) and stress reduction theory (Ulrich et al., 1991) have illuminated the field, linking exposure to natural stimuli with positive psychological outcomes. However, different dimensions of nature have been studied by different scientific disciplines with a lack of integration, and the theorizing could now be enhanced, extended, and deepened (van den Berg & Staats, 2018).

Nature connectedness is unfortunately a blurred construct with a range of competing concepts developed in order to describe the human-nature relationship, including connectedness to nature (Mayer & Frantz, 2004), and environmental identity (Clayton, 2003). Mayer & Frantz (2004) described connectedness to nature as a "measure of an individual's trait levels of feeling emotionally connected to the natural world" (p. 503) and is explicitly conceptualized as assessing the affective component of the human-nature connection. Attention should be paid to what is understood by nature as individual differences in nature connectedness could be influenced by how people conceive it (Duffy & Verges, 2009). Lack of consensus on the measurement of this most fundamental concept – *How we connect to nature* – undermines our ability to understand the determinants of human-nature interaction. For example, the Connectedness to Nature Scale (CNS; Mayer and Frantz, 2004) is a widely used measure of the subjective cognitive connection between individuals and nature. Recent studies using item response theory suggested that using a reduced version of the scale after eliminating the items that display inappropriate behavior may be more reliable (Pasca, Aragonés, & Coello, 2017). Accurate evaluation of the impact of nature connectedness necessitates a clear consensus on its definition.

The cues and clues present in natural scenes that promote well-being have rarely been the focus of research despite the range of natural environmental settings that have been employed across naturalistic, experimental, and epidemiological studies (Depledge, Stone, & Bird, 2011). While "greenness" may be a relevant cue, such preferences may be culturally bound. Surveys in Dresden and Leipzig indicated that urban brownfields are perceived ambivalently. Although negative attitudes dominate, in particular with respect to urban brownfields with spontaneous vegetation, there are, however, residents who view brownfields in a clearly positive manner (Mathey, Arndt, Banse, & Rink, 2018). These settings can contribute to biodiversity and yet may be undervalued by the predominant measures for assessing green natural spaces, e.g. normalized difference vegetation index (NDVI). The rise of quasi-public spaces in cites, in London, for example, is another confound for such methods, which are valuable for planning but may overlook person-based viewpoint experiences such as walkability or noise pollution.

Contact with nature has often been simplified to the level of "nature exposure" in an attempt to operationalize the specific form of nature contact they are studying (Frumkin, Frank, & Jackson, 2004). Frumkin et al. (2017) refer to nature as "areas containing elements of living systems that include plants and nonhuman animals across a range of scales and degrees of human management, from a small urban park through to relatively 'pristine wilderness'" (Bratman, Hamilton, & Daily, 2012), together with abiotic elements such as sunset or mountain views. The application of exposure science can account for duration but may overlook the psychological state (e.g. mindfulness) and the level of awareness of the environment. Environmental enrichment and technological nature are other means of promoting nature contact. Technological nature can include virtual environments, digital nature windows, and viewing phone images of natural stimuli (Calogiuri et al., 2018). For instance, Brick, Macintyre, and Campbell (2014) identified that during high intensity exercise attention is focused upon internal sensory monitoring, outward monitoring, and active self-regulation with natural scenery providing involuntary or voluntary distraction. Meta-cognitive processes during exercise or mindfulness need to be considered to accurately appreciate human-nature interactions (MacIntyre, Igou, Campbell, Moran, & Matthews, 2014).

Despite the complexity of our interactions with nature, a narrow set of outcomes have been investigated based on the aforementioned classic models from environmental psychology. Among the more commonly measured outcome variables is well-being. Across an array of studies concerned with the impact of nature, green exercise, or residential proximity to green space, evidence suggests that different types of nature exposure are associated with different aspects of well-being (Wyles et al., 2017). Consequently, not only is the choice of measurement tool vital but findings may be skewed unless the full gamut of dimensions of subjective well-being are included.

Interdisciplinary approaches have consequently been undermined by the aforementioned issues. A value-laden approach may have also hampered research efforts to explore the negative impact of nature-based interventions. Transdisciplinary perspectives that account for air quality, environmental stressors, physical activity, cognition and affect, and biodiversity offer potential for the fertile research landscape to yield the benefits, opportunities, and innovations necessary to tackle societal challenges.

Progressing beyond the state of the art

In order to elucidate the assessment of human-nature interactions and natural environmental quality the following innovative approaches beyond the state of the art are evaluated:

1. New theoretical frameworks and concepts with different outcome measures,
2. Technological nature and health,
3. Neuroscientific and psychobiological perspectives (e.g., fMRI; EEG; eye-tracking, biomarkers),
4. Integration of technologies for the assessment of natural environmental quality (e.g., Google Earth Streetview; Twitter Sentiment Analysis) with tToolkits (e.g. BlueHealth Environmental Assessment Tool (BEAT), NEST), and
5. The integration of perceived and ambient pollutants and soundscape measurement.

New theoretical frameworks and concepts with different outcome measures

Environmental psychology has arguably paved the way for contemporary research through an extant scientific literature dominated by North American studies and anchored by biophilia theory. Alternative theoretical accounts have been somewhat overlooked in the literature. For example, the conservation of resources theory can account for stress, resilience, and psychological recovery (Hobfoll, 2001). Recovery processes can occur during various temporal and environmental settings ranging from, for example, visits to nature (e.g. nature walk or green exercise), to more informal breaks, so-called micro-breaks (Sonnentag, Venz, & Casper, 2017). Awareness of the different types of experience can provide useful metacognitive knowledge for the autonomous regulation of well-being (Macintyre et al., 2017), and this theoretical account moves beyond that posited by environmental psychologists (attention restoration theory (Kaplan, 1995); stress reduction theory (Ulrich et al., 1991)).

The term "resilience" is integral to ecological systems and is defined as the capacity of a complex system to remain within a regime in the face of external perturbations and/or internal change (Holling, 1973). Within the psychological tradition it has typically been viewed as the ability to recover from setbacks, conceived as an outcome not a process. Contemporary research in psychology now views resilience as "encompassing the capacity to maintain regular functioning through diverse challenges or to rebound through the use of facilitative resources" (Bryan, O'shea, & Macintyre, 2017, p. 8). This conceptualization is aligned with the aforementioned conservation of resources theory and resilience is conceived of as a state rather than a trait. Resilience of ecosystems and psychological resilience resonates with the necessity to adapt with climate change and the possible adverse consequences (American Psychological Association, 2008). It is surprising therefore that there is a paucity of research on the topic of psychological resilience from human-nature interactions (Ingulli & Lindbloom, 2013). This stream of research has the potential to help understand how nature contact and specifically green exercise can influence human resilience.

Technological nature and health

Researchers have been keen to couple technology with nature interactions, and determine whether technology can be utilized to enhance the positive psychological and health outcomes associated with nature contact. This topic is discussed in detail in Chapter 15, so suffice to say that the prevalence of smartphone use among digital natives offers the potential for interventions on the macros-scale. For example, Bakolis et al. (2018) availed of a smartphone-based tool in order to examine how exposure to natural features within the built environment affects mental well-being in real time (Urban Mind). An ecological momentary assessment methodology was employed for one week with over 100 participants. The interactive tool captured images of the environment in addition to their perceptions of the setting. The findings, as predicted, suggested that being outdoors, seeing trees, hearing birds singing, seeing the sky, and feeling in contact with nature were associated with higher levels of momentary mental well-being. The novel approach enabled the time course cessation of the positive effects to be assessed. These beneficial effects could still be observed even if the participant was no longer outdoors and no longer had access to nature. This lagged effect indicates a time-lasting impact of nature on mental well-being that can still be observed after several hours, demonstrating the opportunity of employing technologies that enable real-time assessment.

Neuroscientific and psychobiological perspectives

Examining brain activity and structure can provide additional insight into the neurobiological mechanisms underlying the observed behavioral effects of human-nature contact (see Chapter 6). Studies that have investigated natural stimuli have typically focused only on comparisons of activation in response to viewing natural and built environment. Interestingly, Gidlow, Randall, Gillman, Smith, and Jones (2016) reported that a biomarker, hair cortisol concentration, had potential as a chronic stress biomarker in larger studies of natural environment and health. Mean cortisol concentrations were higher in areas with less natural environment. Combining biomarkers with self-report, behavioral (e.g. eye-tracking), and neuroscientific metrics would provide a major addition to the depth of the research base for human-nature interactions.

Integration of technologies for the assessment of natural environmental quality

Emerging technologies such as smartphone apps that allow people to describe their surroundings, may play an important role here (Schootman et al., 2016). Such crowd-sourced data need to be evaluated in terms of validity and generalizability. There is increasing interest in identifying specific characteristics of the social and built environments that are adversely affecting health outcomes (Schootman et al., 2016). Emerging technologies have conceivable benefits in the assessment of green space quality and accessibility (e.g., Google Earth Streetview; Twitter Sentiment Analysis). Coupled with new tools from EU funded studies on green and blue natural spaces, the above technologies can augment the most frequently used measure, the NDVI, which assesses the density of photosynthetically active biomass based on satellite imagery (Gascon et al., 2016). Preliminary support for the validity of the NEST has been reported (Gidlow et al., 2018). It aims to provide in-situ assessment of diverse natural environments that might support a variety of uses, and to explore associations between natural environment quality, and objectively measured amounts of natural environment and neighborhood-level socio-economic status.

Similarly, the BEAT measures objective environmental conditions (terrestrial and aquatic) and blue infrastructure, including an evaluation of water quality, accessibility, litter and vandalism, signage, etc. (Grellier et al., 2017).

Integration of perceived and ambient pollutants and soundscape analyzes

The prevalence of noise and air pollution within urban settings is a well-established stressor. Integration of both ambient measures and the people's perception of the environment is important to understanding individual behavior preferences. Some previous studies have compared perceived and measured outdoor air quality and found associations between the perception of air quality and specific air pollutants (Atari, Luginaah, & Fung, 2009). In contrast, Egondi et al. (2013) found that despite high levels of exposure to air pollutants, knowledge of pollution sources among respondents was low and the need for increased awareness of air pollution levels was emphasized.

Similarly, research in psychoacoustics focuses on the concept of soundscape, which is used to describe the sound environment from a listener's perspective (Garmestani & Benson, 2013). ISO defines soundscape as an "acoustic environment as perceived or experienced and/or understood by people, in context". A key issue is to understand how the soundscape perceived affects an individual's physiological/psychological health, and contemporary research suggests that the design of urban furniture can enhance the soundscape and influences people's perception of their built environment (Fusaro, D'Alessandro, Baldinelli, & Kang, 2018). In addition, urban natural environments with natural sounds have a positive effect on the restoration of an individual's attention (Zhang & Kang, 2004). It is important to consider ambient pollution levels and their perception as emerging technologies (e.g. Google Street View) do not provide data about specific environmental contaminants.

Recommendations for future research and practice

Recommendation 1 – purposeful sampling and mixed methods

Firstly, we advocate a strength-based approach which would focus on purposive sampling of those that are sport-engaged (see Figure 2.1). This would overcome the challenge of recruiting sedentary participants for whom the challenge of adherence to any sustained physical activity may be overwhelming. Sport participants in natural settings (e.g. adventure sports) may have knowledge both meta-cognitive and declarative which mediates their persistent participation in such activities in natural settings. Mixed-methods approaches could be a key route to unlocking the expertise of such sport participants with regard to their often life-long pursuit of adventure sport.

RECOMMENDATIONS FOR RESEARCH

Use purposeful sampling

Target cohorts that have specific characteristics of interest and already have formed habits of green exercise for example. Measure individual variation in nature connection, childhood experience with nature and relevant factors using mixedmethods approaches.

Apply a transdisciplinary approach

Assess the quality of the environments (e.g. co-hazards of air and noise pollution), typology, biodiversity and soundscape and perceptions of the natural setting.

Measure the exercise component

Ratings of Perceived Exertion, physiological parameters, preexercise intentions and beliefs and future implementation intentions should be assessed.

Measure psychological variables

Typical outcome measures should be augmented by other variables including resilience, psychological recovery, emotional regulation, empathy and attitudes towards the environment and sustainability.

FIGURE 2.1 Recommendations for the study of green exercise

Recommendation 2 – make use of boosted green exercise

Secondly, a positive psychology approach based on the concepts of meaningful life, flow, and savoring can augment both prior and emerging research in this area. For example, savoring is a form of emotion regulation used to prolong and enhance positive emotional experiences. This can be trained using a psychological literacy framework – one that goes beyond previous conceptualizations which focused on educational attainment of psychology graduates. More specifically, to maximize the health outcomes of green exercise initiatives, we propose a *5-component approach for green exercise* interventions:

Component 1: Active engagement Transcendent experience has been found to positively affect flow and happiness (Tsaur, Yen, & Hsiao, 2013). Green exercise interventions should strive to direct the participants' attention to the experience of exercising outdoors in nature, rather than focus their attention on the sensation of effort or pacing or time outcomes. In natural environments people tend to shift their focus of attention toward the external environment rather than toward internal thoughts and feelings. However, the level of engagement with the natural environment might still be superficial if they are for example exercising at high intensity when their attentional focus may be on maintaining effort (Brick et al., 2014). Moreover, their motive may be unrelated to the natural environment and they may not explicitly engage with nature. A recent study showed that green exercisers are not only motivated by their enjoyment of nature, but also by "convenience motives", such as having the opportunity to exercise free of charge and at the time that suits them better (Calogiuri & Elliott, 2017). An active engagement with nature, on the other hand, can lead to greater and more meaningful impacts of potentially restorative experiences, which question a basic dose-response interaction (Shanahan et al., 2016) (see Figure 2.2).

Component 2: Post-exercise savoring A concept from positive psychology, savoring is defined as regulating the emotional impact of positive events by one's cognitive or behavioral responses, and leads to increased positive emotions (Bryant & Veroff, 2007). The positive impact of nature on well-being and the possible reciprocal effects on mental well-being from engagement with nature are integral to future intervention studies. This approach could include, for example, use of an off-the-shelf smartphone application, which would enable the user to choose from a list of pre-determined emotions and tag their digital image with this information. Technology-based applications for enhancing happiness and managing stress have been demonstrated to be effective ways to increase mental well-being and help people to better understand and develop appropriate responses for their moods (Morris et al., 2010). Therefore, eliciting savoring after green exercise experiences, for example by giving "savoring tasks" to participants, might strengthen the positive psychological responses and lead to greater mental health outcomes. Technological nature offers a useful avenue for the exploration of savouring in everyday settings (Kahn, 2011).

Component 3: Positive constructive mental imagery Mental imagery, a symbolic sensory experience that may occur in many sensory models is a cognitive tool which is widely applied on sport contexts. Mental imagery interventions have been demonstrated to enhance motor skills in sport and other contexts (e.g., mental practice) (Weinberg, 2008). Recent research has reported that imagery ability is associated with optimism and the capacity

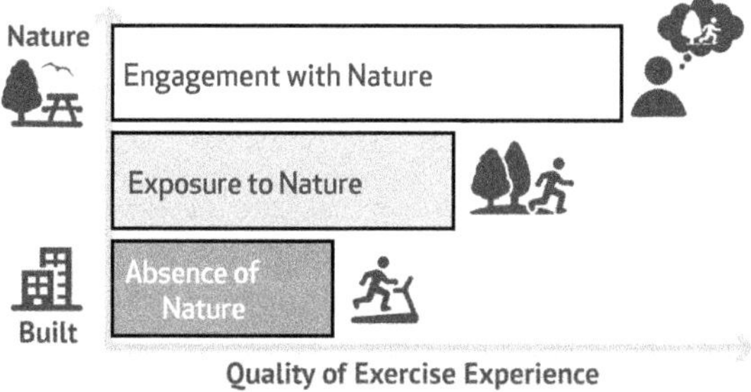

FIGURE 2.2 Differential engagement with nature across settings

to regulate implementation intentions (Blackwell et al., 2013). Education on the application of mental imagery for coping, savoring and planning future bouts of green exercise can build upon pre-existing competencies of participants in green exercise interventions (see Chapter 6). Imagery can be elicited, for example, through online instruction that can augment prior knowledge of motor imagery with ways to apply imagery for coping and mental well-being.

Component 4: Habit formation training Habits are formed when a goal-directed behavior is performed frequently and consistently in a similar context for the same purpose. Knowledge of how habits work can facilitate habit formation, which occurs when the mental representation of the plan to initiate a given activity is accessed implicitly without significant conscious effort (Danner, Aarts, & de Vries, 2008). Habit formation is a vital element of behavioral change interventions to promote adherence in physical activity-based interventions. Here the "behavior" is the additional natural environment engagement whilst undertaking a familiar activity (rather than trying to increase physical activity). The elements of habit formation consist of repetition of the behavior (i.e., boosted green exercise cues and triggers; positive reinforcement; and implementation intentions), which can all be supported using technology (Lally & Gardner, 2013).

Component 5: Environmental education Motivation for pro-environmental behavior may come from variety of internal and external sources but there are several that are frequently posited. These are biocentric motives, altruistic motives, and egoistic motives (Clark, Kotchen, & Moore, 2003). It has been shown that recovery from stress is faster and more complete when people are exposed to natural rather than urban environments (Ulrich et al., 1991). It is not surprising then that promoting connectedness with nature is possible through environmental education, even if the evidence to support the efficacy of such programmes in changing pro-environmental behavior is not as robust. Experiences in nature are known to elicit enhanced feelings of connectedness with nature, which not only can lead to enhanced environmental awareness and engagement in pro-environmental behaviors, but can also magnify the participants' mental health outcomes and exercise adherence. Enhanced nature connectedness could be further boosted by providing culturally and geographically and climatically bespoke knowledge on aspects of the environment to enhance environmental literacy to participants.

Recommendation 3 – take a transdisciplinary approach to understand environmental quality, its impacts and perception versus reality

Nature connectedness may be enhanced under certain environmental conditions and the benefits of understanding our environments and the effects we have on them should not be underestimated in such studies. The quality of the ambient environment may also impact on behaviors that result from any intervention.

Taking air quality as an example, there is much evidence to suggest that air pollution can cause exacerbations of pre-existing asthma in adults (Guarnieri & Balmes, 2014). Thus any intervention should consider vulnerable members of society and take account of the actual and perceived (for its influence on behaviors) environmental quality. Accurate quantification of environmental quality is thus key, as is communication of this information to stakeholders.

In the age of big data an increasingly important but also increasingly rare first step in data analytics is the graphical analysis stage. Consider for a moment the simple plots in Figure 2.3 which show nitrogen dioxide (NO_2) levels measured at a rural site in Ireland. These normalized plots are based on hourly monitoring data that has been simply split into four different groups prior to plotting. Based on this graph alone we can make some fairly well grounded guesses on what is influencing NO_2 concentrations at this location:

- Weekend values are significantly lower than weekday values in both seasons
    - Conclusion → Anthropogenic factors are affecting concentration levels
- There is a relatively greater diurnal variation during the week than at weekends
    - Conclusion → Some of the diurnal variation is caused by anthropogenic factors

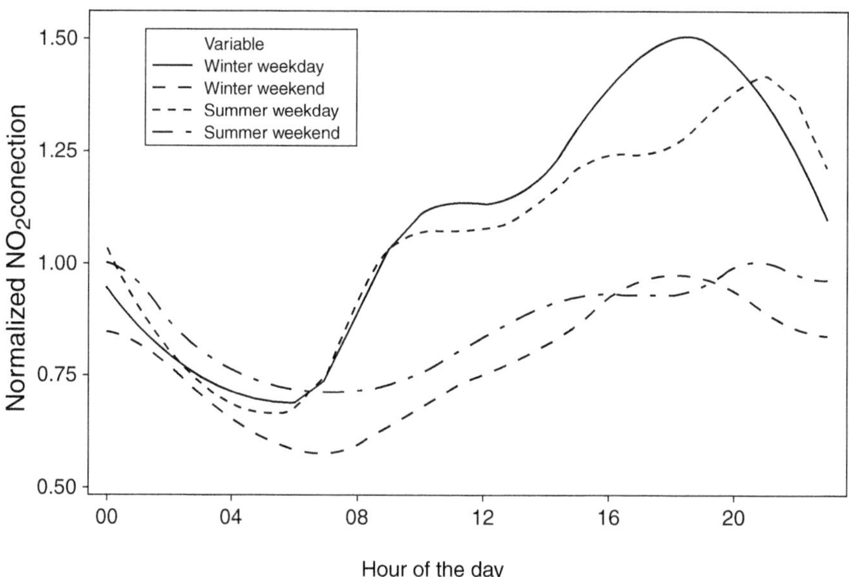

FIGURE 2.3 Diurnal variation in NO_2 concentrations at a background location in Ireland

- The normalized diurnal variation between the hours of midnight and 5am is similar on weekdays and weekends
  - Conclusion → Night time variations in concentrations are influenced by natural factors

- The peak concentration is reached later in the evening in summer months than in winter months both at weekends and during the week
  - Conclusion → Difference in daylight hours affects concentrations.

While we cannot of course be 100% sure that the above conclusions are true, they represent good guesses based on a very simple graphical analysis. Using this information alone, it would be possible to design interventions in ways to minimize exposure to increased NO_2 concentrations. We can easily see, using this graph, when the best time to go for a run might be (on average) during the winter months.

Furthermore, nature connectedness, the current perspective on human-nature relationships, could be expanded to include a dimension of attachment. This could be enhanced by including an emphasis on the degree of engagement with nature during exposure, which, in the case of green exercise, would include methodological advances from the endurance sport domain (e.g. thought-sampling). Neuroscientific methods and a transdisciplinary approach would further elucidate the interaction between nature, metacognitive beliefs, and our concern for the environment, all of which can address key questions about the major societal challenges.

Conclusions

While this chapter provides only a very brief introduction to the potential for transdisciplinary approaches to study the synergistic benefits for mental well-being, cognitive function, and health resulting from the combination of exercise and natural settings together with an engagement mindset, it presents an idea of the wealth of information that is available or can be collected for future analysis. The well-established relationship between lack of physical activity and premature mortality coupled with the significant portion of the global population who are insufficiently active presents an urgent need to tackle the problem of physical inactivity at a population level. We have proposed three recommendations for research in green exercise to reach a gold standard required for an evidence-based approach. In particular future research should *use purposeful sampling and mixed methods*, make *use of boosted green exercise* (through active engagement, post-exercise savoring, positive constructive mental imagery, habit formation training, and environmental education), and take a *transdisciplinary approach* to understand environmental quality, its impacts and perception versus reality.

References

American Psychological Association. 2008. *Society's grand challenges: Insights from psychological science: Climate change*. Washington, DC: APA.

Atari, D., Luginaah, I. & Fung, K. 2009. The relationship between odour annoyance scores and modelled ambient air pollution in Sarnia, "Chemical Valley", Ontario. *International Journal of Environmental Research and Public Health*, 6, 2655–2675.

Bakolis, I., Hammoud, R., Smythe, M., Gibbons, J., Davidson, N., Tognin, S. & Mechelli, A. 2018. Urban mind: Using smartphone technologies to investigate the impact of nature on mental well-being in real time. *BioScience*, 68, 134–145.

Barton, J. & Pretty, J. 2010. What is the best dose of nature and green exercise for improving mental health? A multi-study analysis. *Environmental Science & Technology*, 44, 3947–3955.

Beelen, R., Raaschou-Nielsen, O., Stafoggia, M., Andersen, Z. J., Weinmayr, G., Hoffmann et al et et . 2014. Effects of long-term exposure to air pollution on natural-cause mortality: An analysis of 22 European cohorts within the multicentre ESCAPE project. *The Lancet*, 383, 785–795.

Blackwell, S. E., Rius-Ottenheim, N., Schulte-Van Maaren, Y. W., Carlier, I. V., Middelkoop, V. D., Zitman, F. G., Spinhoven, P., Holmes, E. A. & Giltay, E. J. 2013. Optimism and mental imagery: A possible cognitive marker to promote well-being? *Psychiatry Research*, 206, pp.56–61.

Box, G. E. & Draper, N. R. 1987. *Empirical model-uilding and Response Surfaces*. New York: Wiley.

Bratman, G. N., Hamilton, J. P. & Daily, G. C. 2012. The impacts of nature experience on human cognitive function and mental health. *Annals of the New York Academy of Sciences*, 1249, 118–136, PMID: 22320203, doi:10.1111/j.1749-6632.2011.06400.x.

Brick, N., Macintyre, T. & Campbell, M. 2014. Attentional focus in endurance activity: New paradigms and future directions. *International Review of Sport and Exercise Psychology*, 7, 106–134.

Bryan, C., O'shea, D. & Macintyre, T. 2017. Stressing the relevance of resilience: A systematic review of resilience across the domains of sport and work. *International Review of Sport and Exercise Psychology*, 12(1), 70–111.

Bryant, F. B. & Veroff, J. 2007. *Savoring: A new model of positive experience*. Mahway, NJ: Psychology Press.

Calogiuri, G., & Chroni, S. 2014. The impact of the natural environment on the promotion of active living: an integrative systematic review. *BMC Public Health*, 14, 873. doi:10.1186/1471-2458-14-873

Calogiuri, G. & Elliott, L. 2017. Why do people exercise in natural environments? Norwegian adults' motives for nature-, gym-, and sports-based exercise. *International Journal of Environmental Research and Public Health*, 14, 377.

Calogiuri, G., Litleskare, S., Fagerheim, K. A., Rydgren, T. L., Brambilla, E. & Thurston, M. 2018. Experiencing nature through immersive virtual environments: Environmental perceptions, physical engagement, and affective responses during a simulated nature walk. *Frontiers in Psychology*, 8, 2321.

Clark, C. F., Kotchen, M. J. & Moore, M. R. 2003. Internal and external influences on pro-environmental behavior: Participation in a green electricity program. *Journal of Environmental Psychology*, 23, 237–246.

Clayton, S. 2003. Environmental identity: A conceptual and an operational definition. In S. Clayton & S. Opotow (Eds.), *Identity and the natural environment: The psychological significance of nature* (pp. 45–65). MIT Press.

Danner, U. N., Aarts, H. & de Vries, N. K. 2008. Habit vs. intention in the prediction of future behaviour: The role of frequency, context stability and mental accessibility of past behaviour. *British Journal of Social Psychology*, 47, 245–265.

Depledge, M., Stone, R. & Bird, W. J. 2011. Can natural and virtual environments be used to promote improved human health and wellbeing? *Environmental Science & Technology*, 45, 4660–4665.

Doherty, T. J. & Clayton, S. 2011. The psychological impacts of global climate change. *American Psychologist*, 66, 265.

Duffy, E., & Verges, M. 2009. It matters a hole lot: Perceptual affordances of waste containers influence recycling compliance. *Environment and Behavior*, 41(5), 741–745.

EEA. 2012. *Evaluation of progress under the EU national emissions ceilings directive. Progress towards EU air quality objectives*. Copenhagen: European Environment Agency. EEA Technical Report No 14/2012.

Egondi, T., Kyobutungi, C., Ng, N., Muindi, K., Oti, S., Vijver, S., Ettarh, R. & Rocklöv, J. 2013. Community perceptions of air pollution and related health risks in Nairobi slums. *International Journal of Environmental Research and Public Health*, 10, 4851–4868.

Frumkin, H., Bratman, G. N., Breslow, S. J., Cochran, B., Kahn, P. H., Jr, Lawler, J. J., ... Wood, S. A. (2017). Nature Contact and Human Health: A Research Agenda. *Environmental Health Perspectives*, 125(7), 075001. doi:10.1289/EHP1663

Frumkin, H., Frank, L. & Jackson, R. J. 2004. *Urban Sprawl and Public Health: Designing, Planning, and Building for Healthy Communities*. Washington, DC: Island Press.

Fusaro, G., D'alessandro, F., Baldinelli, G. & Kang, J. 2018. Design of urban furniture to enhance the soundscape: A case study. *Building Acoustics*, 25, 61–75.

Galloway, J. N., Dentener, F. J., Capone, D. G., Boyer, E. W., Howarth, R. W., Seitzinger, S. P., Asner, G. P., Cleveland, C. C., Green, P. A., Holland, E. A., Karl, D. M., Michaels, A. F., Porter, J. H., Townsend, A. R. & Vörösmarty, C. J. 2004. Nitrogen cycles: Past, present, and future. *Biogeochemistry*, 70, 153–226.

Garmestani, A. & Benson, M. 2013. A framework for resilience-based governance of social-ecological systems.

Gascon, M., Cirach, M., Martínez, D., Dadvand, P., Valentín, A., Plasència, A. & Nieuwenhuijsen, M. J. 2016. Normalized difference vegetation index (NDVI) as a marker of surrounding greenness in epidemiological studies: The case of Barcelona city. *Urban Forestry & Urban Greening*, 19, 88–94.

Gascon, M., Zijlema, W., Vert, C., White, M. P. & Nieuwenhuijsen, M. J. 2017. Outdoor blue spaces, human health and well-being: A systematic review of quantitative studies. *International Journal of Hygiene and Environmental Health*, 220, 1207–1221.

Gidlow, C., van Kempen, E., Smith, G., Triguero, M., Kruize, H., Gražulevičienė, R., Ellis, N., Hurst, G., Masterson, D. & Cirach, M. 2018. Development of the Natural Environment Scoring Tool (NEST). *Urban Forestry & Urban Greening*, 29, 332–333.

Gidlow, C. J., Randall, J., Gillman, J., Smith, G. R. & Jones, M. V. 2016. Natural environments and chronic stress measured by hair cortisol. *Landscape and Urban Planning*, 148, 61–67.

Grellier, J., White, M. P., Albin, M., Bell, S., Elliott, L. R., Gascón, M., Gualdi, S., Mancini, L., Nieuwenhuijsen, M. J., Sarigiannis, D. A. & van Den Bosch, M. 2017. BlueHealth: A study programme protocol for mapping and quantifying the potential benefits to public health and well-being from Europe's blue spaces. *BMJ Open*, 2, 7.

Guarnieri, M. & Balmes, J. R. 2014. Outdoor air pollution and asthma. *The Lancet*, 383, 1581–1592.

Guerreiro, C. B. B., Foltescu, V. & de Leeuw, F. 2014. Air quality status and trends in Europe. *Atmospheric Environment*, 98, 376–384.

Hettelingh, J.-P., Posch, M., Velders, G. J. M., Ruyssenaars, P., Adams, M., de Leeuw, F., Lükewille, A., Maas, R., Sliggers, J. & Slootweg, J. 2013. Assessing interim objectives for acidification, eutrophication and ground-level ozone of the EU National Emission Ceilings Directive with 2001 and 2012 knowledge. *Atmospheric Environment*, 75, 129–140.

Hobfoll, S. E. 2001. The influence of culture, community, and the nested-self in the stress process: Advancing conservation of resources theory. *Applied Psychology*, 50, 337–421.

Holling, C. S. 1973. Resilience and stability of ecological systems. *Annual Review of Ecology and Systematics*, 4, 1–23.

Incropera FP. 2016. *Climate Change: A Wicked Problem*. New York: Cambridge University Press.

Ingulli, K. & Lindbloom, G. 2013. Connection to nature and psychological resilience. *Ecopsychology*, 5 (1), 52–55.

Intergovernmental Panel on Climate Change. 2014. Climate change 2014 impacts, adaptation, and vulnerability.

Kahn, P. H. 2011. *Technological nature: Adaptation and the future of human life*. Cambridge, MA: MIT Press.

Kaplan, R., & Kaplan, S. (1989). *The experience of nature: A psychological perspective*. New York: Cambridge University Press.

Kaplan, S. 1995. The restorative benefits of nature – Toward an integrative framework. *Journal of Environmental Psychology*, 15, 169–182.

Lally, P. & Gardner, B. 2013. Promoting habit formation. *Health Psychology Review*, 7, S137–S158.

Laumbach, R. J. & Kipen, H. M. 2012. Respiratory health effects of air pollution: Update on biomass smoke and traffic pollution. *Journal of Allergy and Clinical Immunology*, 129, 3–13.

MacIntyre, T. E., Igou, E. R., Campbell, M. J., Moran, A. P., & Matthews, J. 2014. Metacognition and action: A new pathway to understanding social and cognitive aspects of expertise in sport. *Frontiers in Psychology*, 5, 1155. doi: 10.3389/fpsyg.2014.01155

Macintyre, T. E., Jones, M., Brewer, B. W., van Raalte, J., O'shea, D. & Mccarthy, P. J. 2017. Mental health challenges in elite sport: Balancing risk with reward. *Frontiers in Psychology*, 8, 1892.

Mathey, J., Arndt, T., Banse, J. & Rink, D. 2018. Public perception of spontaneous vegetation on brownfields in urban areas—Results from surveys in Dresden and Leipzig (Germany). *Urban Forestry & Urban Greening*, 29, 384–392.

Mayer, F. S. & Frantz, C. M. 2004. The connectedness to nature scale: A measure of individuals' feeling in community with nature. *Journal of Environmental Psychology*, 24, 503–515.

Morris, M. E., Kathawala, Q., Leen, T. K., Gorenstein, E. E., Guilak, F., Deleeuw, W. & Labhard, M. 2010. Mobile therapy: Case study evaluations of a cell phone application for emotional self-awareness. *Journal of Medical Internet Research*, 12, e10.

Moussiopoulos, N. 1997. *Ambient air quality, pollutant dispersion and transport models*. Office for Official Publications of the European Communities. Brussels: European Commission.

Mytton, O. T., Townsend, N., Rutter, H. & Foster, C. 2012. Green space and physical activity: An observational study using Health Survey for England data. *Health & Place*, 18, 1034–1041.

Nieuwenhuijsen, M. J., Kruize H., Gidlow, C., Andrusaityte, S., Antó, J. M., Basagaña, X., … Grazuleviciene, R. 2014. Positive health effects of the natural outdoor environment in typical populations in different regions in Europe (PHENOTYPE): A study programme protocol. *BMJ Open*, 4(4), e004951. doi: 10.1136/bmjopen-2014-004951

Pasca, L., Aragonés, J. I. & Coello, M. T. 2017. An analysis of the connectedness to nature scale based on item response theory. *Frontiers in Psychology*, 8, 1330.

Pascal, M., Corso, M., Chanel, O., Declercq, C., Badaloni, C., Cesaroni, G., Henschel, S., Meister, K., Haluza, D., Martin-Olmedo, P. & Medina, S. 2013. Assessing the public health impacts of urban air pollution in 25 European cities: Results of the Aphekom project. *Science of the Total Environment*, 449, 390–400.

Raaschou-Nielsen, O., Andersen, Z. J., Beelen, R., Samoli, E., Stafoggia, M., Weinmayr, G., et al. 2013. Air pollution and lung cancer incidence in 17 European cohorts: Prospective analyses from the European Study of Cohorts for Air Pollution Effects (ESCAPE). *The Lancet Oncology*, 14, 813–822.

Pohl, C., Truffer, B., & Hirsch Hadorn, G. (2017). Addressing wicked problems through transdisciplinary research. In R. Frodeman, J. Thompson Klein, & R. C. S. Pacheco (Eds.), *The Oxford handbook of interdisciplinarity* (pp. 319-331). doi:10.1093/oxfordhb/9780198733522.013.26

Rittel, H. W. J., & Webber, M. M. (1973). Dilemmas in the general theory of planning. *Policy Sciences*, 4, 155–169. doi:10.1007/BF01405730

Rogerson, M., Gladwell, V., Gallagher, D. & Barton, J. 2016. Influences of green outdoors versus indoors environmental settings on psychological and social outcomes of controlled exercise. *International Journal of Environmental Research and Public Health*, 13, 363.

Schootman, M., Nelson, E. J., Werner, K., Shacham, E., Elliott, M., Ratnapradipa, K., Lian, M. & Mcvay, A. 2016. Emerging technologies to measure neighborhood conditions in public health: Implications for interventions and next steps. *International Journal of Health Geographics*, 15, 20.

Seymour, V. 2016. The human-nature relationship and its impact on health: A critical review. *Frontiers in Public Health*, 4, 260. doi:10.3389/fpubh.2016.00260

Shanahan, D. F., Bush, R., Gaston, K. J., Lin, B. B., Dean, J., Barber, E. & Fuller, R. A. 2016. Health benefits from nature experiences depend on dose. *Scientific Reports*, 6, 28551.

Sonnentag, S., Venz, L. & Casper, A. 2017. Advances in recovery research: What have we learned? What should be done next? *Journal of Occupational Health Psychology*, 22, 365.

Staelens, J., Wuyts, K., Adriaenssens, S., van Avermaet, P., Buysse, H., van Den Bril, B., Roekens, E., Ottoy, J.-P., Verheyen, K., Thas, O. & Deschepper, E. 2012. Trends in atmospheric nitrogen and sulphur deposition in northern Belgium. *Atmospheric Environment*, 49, 186–196.

Sun, J., & Yang, K. (2016). The Wicked Problem of Climate Change: A New Approach Based on Social Mess and Fragmentation. *Sustainability*, 8(12), 1312. doi:10.3390/su8121312

The World Economc Forum. 2019. The global risks report 2019.

Thompson Coon, J., Boddy, K., Stein, K., Whear, R., Barton, J. & Depledge, M. H. 2011. Does participating in physical activity in outdoor natural environments have a greater effect on physical and mental wellbeing than physical activity indoors? A systematic review. *Environmental Science & Technology*, 45, 1761–1772.

Tsaur, S. H., Yen, C. H. & Hsiao, S. L. 2013. Transcendent experience, flow and happiness for mountain climbers. *International Journal of Tourism Research*, 15, 360–374.

Ulrich, R. S., Simons, R. F., Losito, B. D., Fiorito, E., Miles, M. A. & Zelson, M. 1991. Stress recovery during exposure to natural and urban environments *Journal of Environmental Psychology*, 11(3), September 1991, 201–230, 201–203.

United Nations. 2016. The world's cities in 2016, data booklet (ST/ESA/SER. A/392). United Nations, Department of Economic and Social Affairs, Population ….

van den Berg, A. E., & Staats, H. 2018. Environmental psychology. In M. van den Bosch & W. Bird (Eds.), *Oxford textbook of nature and public health: The role of nature in improving the health of a population* (pp. 51–56). Oxford, UK: Oxford University Press. doi: 10.1093/med/9780198725916.003.0035

van den Bosch, M. & Depledge, M. 2015. Healthy people with nature in mind. *BMC Public Health*, 15, 1232. https://doi.org/10.1186/s12889-015-2574-8

Wang, H. & Horton, R. 2015. Tackling climate change: The greatest opportunity for global health. *The Lancet*, 386, 1798–1799.

Watts, N., Amann, M., Ayeb-Karlsson, S., Belesova, K., Bouley, T., Boykoff, M., et al. 2018. The 2017 report of the lancet countdown on health and climate change: From 25 years of inaction to a global transformation for public health. *The Lancet*, 391(10120): 581-630. doi:10.1016/S0140-6736(17)32464-9

Weinberg, R. 2008. Does imagery work? Effects on performance and mental skills. *Journal of Imagery Research in Sport and Physical Activity*, 3(1), Article ID 1. doi:10.2202/1932-0191.1025

WHO. 2010. *Global Recommendations on Physical Activity for Health.* In: PRESS, W. H. O. (ed.). Geneva: World Health Organization.

WHO. 2018a. *Governance: Development of a draft global action plan to promote physical activity.* Geneva: World Health Organization.

World Health Organization. 2014. *Global status report on noncommunicable diseases.* Geneva: World Health Organization.

World Health Organization. 2016. *Urban Green Spaces and Health.* Copenhagen: WHO Regional Office for Europe.

World Health Organization. 2018b. *The Health and Well-Being of Men in the WHO European Region: Better Health through a Gender Approach.* Available online at www.euro.who.int/en/publications/abstracts/the-health-and-well-being-of-men-in-the-who-european-region-better-health-through-a-gender-approach-2018

Wyles, K. J., White, M. P., Hattam, C., Pahl, S., King, H. & Austen, M. 2017. Are some natural environments more psychologically beneficial than others? The importance of type and quality on connectedness to nature and psychological restoration. *Environment and Behavior*, 51(2), 111–143. 0013916517738312.

Zhang, M. & Kang, J. 2004. Evaluation of urban soundscape by future architects. *The Journal of the Acoustical Society of America*, 115, 2497.

3

KNOWN KNOWNS

A systematic review of the effects of green exercise compared with exercising indoors

Ian Lahart, Patricia M. Darcy, Christopher Gidlow and Giovanna Calogiuri

The idea that exercising in a natural environment (green exercise) offers health benefits is not new. The Ancient Greek physician, Hippocrates (c. 450 to c. 380 BCE), for example, championed both walking as "man's best medicine" and nature as "the best physician". Contemporary researchers have extensively examined the first of Hippocrates' aphorisms, and have found favourable effects of exercise on a range of disease and health-related outcomes (Durstine, Gordon, Wang, & Luo, 2013; World Health Organization, 2010). The health effects of exposure to nature (Bowler, Buyung-Ali, Knight, & Pullin, 2010) and exercising in natural environments, however, have received considerably less attention (Calogiuri & Chroni, 2014; Thompson Coon et al., 2011).

The green exercise concept proposed in this book (see Chapter 1 for a detailed explanation) posits that natural environments not only provide a venue for exercise, but can also increase exercise intentions, enjoyment, and adherence, promote social interactions, and generate favourable health outcomes. However, to date evidence is equivocal that simply having better access to natural environments (e.g., parks, playing fields or woodlands) fosters physical activity. Reviews of epidemiologic studies exploring exercise and objectively measured access to green space, and park proximity report positive associations in less than half of studies, and mixed or null findings in the remaining studies (Kaczynski & Henderson, 2007; Lachowycz & Jones, 2011).

As noted by Hartig, Mitchell, de Vries, & Frumkin (2014), despite some evidence of positive associations between green space and exercise, there is marked variation in associations between population subgroups and types of exercise (e.g., walking for recreation vs. walking for transport). This variation is compounded by the profound effect of study design and measurement choices. This field of research is dominated by studies with cross-sectional design, which prevents the identification of causal relationships between the availabilit ural environments and exercise (Lee & Maheswaran, 2011).

Natural environments have also been proposed to influence health by facilitating greater duration and intensity of exercise. When in green space, people might be more likely to engage in exercise (Joseph & Maddock, 2016), be active for longer (Peacock, Hine, & Pretty, 2007), or at higher intensities (Pennebaker & Lightner, 1980).

Finally, some review-level evidence supports the theory that exercise in natural environments confers additional psychological and health benefits compared with those that would result from the equivalent activity in an urban/built or indoor environment (Bowler et al., 2010; Thompson Coon et al., 2011). A 2010 review of 25 studies comparing responses to exposure to natural versus outdoor built or indoor environments, found that the former were associated with more favourable psychological outcomes, such as higher energy and lower anxiety, anger, fatigue, and sadness (Bowler et al., 2010). Similarly, Thompson Coon et al. (2011) conducted a systematic review of the effects of exercise in natural environments compared with exercise indoors on mental and physical wellbeing, health-related quality of life, and long-term exercise adherence. The authors reported statistically beneficial effects of green exercise on a range of psychological outcomes, such as revitalisation, positive engagement, tension, confusion, anger, depression, and energy. There was also evidence of greater enjoyment and satisfaction with outdoor activity, with indications of greater intent to repeat the activity. The review, however, was limited by a small number of included papers (n = 11), as well as the "poor methodological quality of the available evidence and the heterogeneity of outcome measures employed", which prevented a meta-analysis.

In summary, despite inconsistent evidence that access to natural environments can increase exercise levels, previous reviews do offer some support for the benefits of green exercise, particularly for psychological outcomes. Given the recent proliferation of work in this area, this chapter provides an update and expansion of the review by Thompson Coon et al. (2011). Therefore, our aim in this chapter was to review the evidence for three comparisons: 1) the longitudinal effects of exercising in an outdoor natural environment ("real green" exercise) versus exercising indoors without exposure to nature (indoor exercise); 2) the acute effects of real green exercise versus exercising indoors without exposure to nature (indoor exercise); and 3) the acute effects of virtual green exercise versus exercising indoors without exposure to nature (indoor exercise).

Method

Search strategy

The present review represents an update of Thompson Coon et al. (2011), whose searches were conducted April 2010. We applied the same search strategy as Thompson Coon et al. to search for eligible trials within the following databases:

PubMed, CENTRAL, Embase (via OVID), and PsycINFO, GreenFile, and Sports DISCUS (via EBSCO) (see Table 3.1 for the PubMed search strategy, and https://osf.io/mgfsd/ for all search strategies). We retained the eligible trials from Thompson Coon et al. (2011), but screened them for eligibility. All searches were run from 1 January 2010 to 28 March 2018. In addition, to database searches, we also checked the references of included articles for any additional references.

Eligibility screening and data extraction

We applied similar eligibility criteria as Thompson Coon et al. (2011), but we were more explicit regarding the classification of "green exercise" (see full eligibility criteria in Table 3.2).

Two authors (IML, PD) screened the titles and abstracts of articles, and subsequently the full texts of articles to find eligible trials. We (IML, PD) extracted data, such as trial, sample, and intervention characteristics, from all trials that met our eligibility criteria (see Table 3.3 for study characteristics). Any disagreements during screening or data extraction were resolved by the two other authors (CG, GC). Authors were contacted to supply missing data where necessary.

Assessment of risk of bias

Risk of bias was assessed using the Cochrane "risk of bias" tool (Higgins & Green, 2011) in the included randomised controlled trials (RCTs). For crossover trials, we applied a modified "risk of bias" tool (Ding et al., 2015). Briefly, this

TABLE 3.1 Search strategy for PubMed (adapted for the other databases)

1. green exercis*.tiab
2. green gym*.tiab
3. ecotherapy.tiab
4. (outdoor* or outside*).tiab
5. (exercis* or physical activit* or walk* or physical fit*).tiab
6. 4 and 5
7. park*.tiab
8. 5 and 7
9. (greenspace* or green space*).tiab
10. 5 and 9
11. natural environment*.tiab
12. 5 and 11
13. nature.tiab
14. 5 and 13
15. (indoor or inside or laboratory or gym*).tiab
16. 1 or 2 or 3 or 6 or 8 or 10 or 12 or 14
17. 15 and 16

Key: tiab: title and abstract.

TABLE 3.2 Green exercise review eligibility criteria

Population	• Adults or children
Interventions	• Studies must include experimental conditions in which participants were *explicitly/purposefully* exposed to views of nature (sceneries containing elements of nature such as trees, plants, grass, mountains, water, etc.) while engaging in exercise. • The nature exposure could be achieved by having the participants exercising in *outdoor environments containing nature elements* or by exposing them to virtual sceneries of nature (e.g., images or videos of nature projected on a screen or viewed using virtual reality goggles).
Comparison	• Exercise initiatives conducted indoors with no exposure to nature (real or virtual). • The exercise must be of the same volume, duration, intensity, and mode as in the green exercise condition.
Outcomes	• Any outcome related to physical and mental wellbeing.
Study design	• Randomised crossover (RXTs) or controlled/comparative trials (RCTs), quasi-RXTs and quasi-RCTS, or non-RXTs and non-RCTs (both acute and longitudinal trials were considered)

tool includes additional bias domains, such as appropriateness of crossover design, potential carry-over effects, and presentation of unbiased data, to the six domains (randomisation, allocation concealment, blinding, incomplete outcome data, selective reporting, and "other issues") of the RCT "risk of bias" tool.

Data synthesis

We performed a meta-analysis on an outcome only if ≥2 studies assessed that same outcome, but not if outcomes were too diverse. We used the inverse variance random-effects method (DerSimonian & Laird, 1986) via RevMan software. When trials measured an outcome using the same measurement method or scale we expressed the effects as mean difference (MD), whereas we used SMD when trials used different instruments to measure the same outcome. We presented pooled intervention effect estimates and their 95% confidence intervals (CIs) for each outcome.

For trials that included more than one applicable green exercise or comparison group (e.g., Irandoust & Taheri, 2017), we created (where possible) a single pair-wise comparison by combining outcome data (Higgins & Green, 2011). If variability was presented by measures other than standard deviation (SD), such as standard errors, we obtained an estimate of the SD via the inbuilt RevMan calculator (Higgins & Green, 2011).

We conducted a meta-analysis of crossover data only when trials provided results of paired analyses (Elbourne et al., 2002). For comparisons where meta-analysis was not possible and for outcomes where at least two trials were available we produced harvest plots to summarise effects (Crowther, Avenell, Maclennan, & Mowatt, 2011; Ogilvie et al., 2008). For all other outcomes we provided a narrative summary.

In our meta-analysis, we assessed study heterogeneity using the I^2 statistic. In accordance with Higgins and Green (2011), we interpreted I^2 values as follows: 0% to 40% as "might not be important"; 30% to 60% as "may represent moderate heterogeneity"; 50% to 90% as "may represent substantial heterogeneity"; 75% to 100% as showing "considerable heterogeneity".

Results

Search results

We retained 10 of the 11 eligible trials in Thompson Coon et al. (2011)—one trial (Hug, Hansmann, Monn, Krütli, & Seeland, 2008) was excluded because the study design did not meet with our eligibility criteria. The updated search revealed 14 new trials (Figure 3.1). Therefore, we included a total of 24 eligible

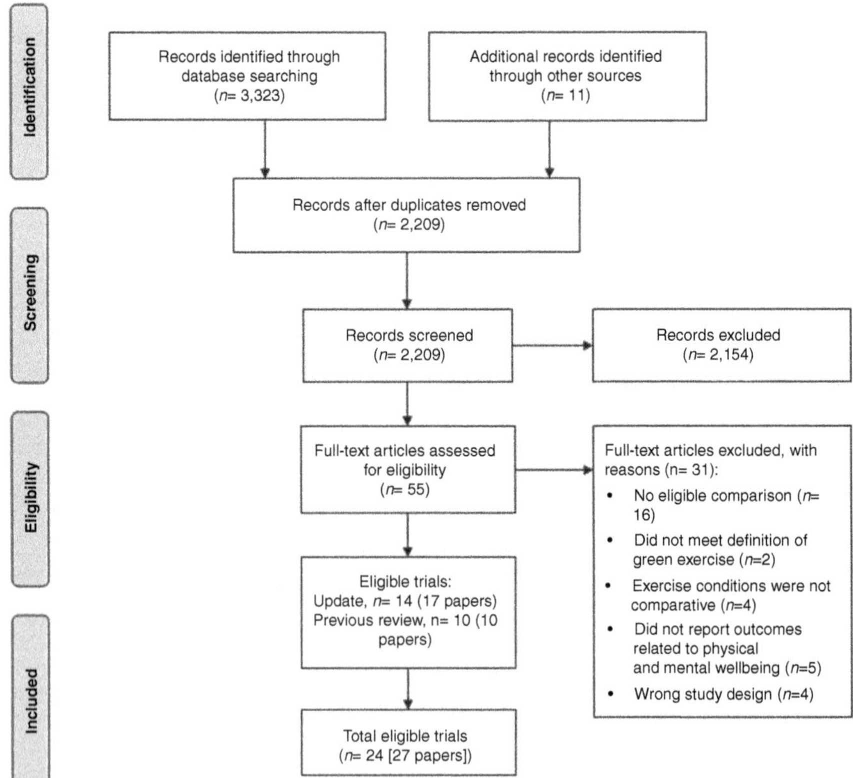

FIGURE 3.1 Flow of studies diagram

trials (27 articles). Three trials had two publications each (Calogiuri et al., 2016; Calogiuri, Nordtug, & Weydahl, 2015; Lacharité-Lemieux, Brunelle, & Dionne, 2015; Lacharité-Lemieux & Dionne, 2016; Niedermeier, Einwanger, & Hartl, 2016; Niedermeier, Einwanger, Hartl, & Kopp, 2017). The characteristics of eligible trials can be found in Table 3.3; however, we include a brief summary of the key characteristics below.

Trial design characteristics

Most trials investigated the acute effects of exercise (*n* = 21), whereas only three (all RCTs) examined longitudinal effects (Calogiuri et al., 2016; Irandoust & Taheri, 2017; Lacharité-Lemieux et al., 2015). One longitudinal trial consisted of a brief intervention involving just two bouts of each exercise condition over a fortnight (with a 10 week follow-up assessment). The remaining two studies were both 12 weeks duration (Calogiuri et al., 2016). Of the acute studies, eight were randomised crossover trial (RXT) design, seven were non-RXTs, and the remaining six adopted a RCT parallel group design.

Participant characteristics

A total of 1,039 (median: 33, min–max: 8–154) participants were recruited to the 24 eligible trials. The total sample of the three longitudinal RCTs was 112 (median: 31, min–max: 14–75), and comprised postmenopausal women who were sedentary (Lacharité-Lemieux et al., 2015), Iranian women with severe depression, obesity (Body Mass Index, BMI, range: 30–35 kg/m^2) and vitamin D deficiency (Irandoust & Taheri, 2017), and office workers (50% women) (Calogiuri et al., 2016). In the 21 acute trials, a total of 927 (median: 35, min–max: 8–154) participants were recruited. The samples comprised university students (*n* = 7 studies), university students and staff (*n* = 1), recreational or competitive athletes (*n* = 5), healthy adults (*n* = 4), postmenopausal women (*n* = 2), patients post-stroke (*n* = 1), and primary school kids (*n* = 1).

Intervention characteristics

Longitudinal trials

All three eligible longitudinal RCTs compared outdoor green exercise with indoor exercise (Calogiuri et al., 2016; Irandoust & Taheri, 2017; Lacharité-Lemieux et al., 2015). One trial used running as their mode of exercise (Irandoust & Taheri, 2017) whereas, another trial utilised a combined cycling and strength training intervention (Calogiuri et al., 2016), and similarly, Lacharité-Lemieux et al. (2015) combined resistance training with aerobic circuit training. The intensity of exercise prescribed was moderate in two trials (Calogiuri et al.,

TABLE 3.3 Characteristics of eligible studies

Study (country)	*Design and Sample*	*Green Exercise Conditions*	*Eligible Comparison Conditions*	*Outcomes (measure)*
Calogiuri 2015 (also 2016) (Norway)	**Design:** RCT Brief longitudinal, 2 sessions with 2 week and 10 week follow-up **Sample:** 14 healthy employees, sedentary or moderately active (50% female and 50% male) Age (mean ± SD): 49 ± 8 y BMI (mean ± SD): 25.2 ± 2.5 kg/m^2 VO_2max (mean ± SD): 3.6 ± 0.8 L/min HRrest (mean ± SD): 61 ± 5 bpm PA (mean ± SD): 6.5 ± 4.5 h/wk CNS (mean ± SD): 3.4 ± 0.6	Two sessions of 25-min outdoor cycling, and 20-min outdoor strength session using elastic rubber bands with handles (intensity: 55% HRR, overall) **Description:** "track in a forest area nearby both workplaces. Strength session took place in a grass yard" (image provided) **Month:** Sept **Temperature:** 8–10°C	Two sessions of 25-min indoor spinning cycling, and 20-min strength session using elastic rubber bands with handles (intensity: 55% HRR, overall) **Description:** "'typical' exercise setting (gym-hall), and, the subjects did not have visual contact with nature" (image provided) **Temperature:** 20°C	Affect (PAAS); BP; Effort (6–20 Borg RPE scale); Enjoyment (1-item scale); Exercise behaviour (modified LTEQ); Future exercise intention (3-item scale TBP-based); HR (% of HRR); Perceived potential for restoration (PRS); Stress (salivary CAR and serum cortisol concentration).
Carvalho 2010 (Sweden)	**Design:** RXT Acute, 3 trials separated by at least 5-min rest **Sample:** 36 post-stroke patients (31% female and 69% male) Two groups based on self-selected walking speed:	Outdoor 6MWT at self-selected on a 30 m course and 30 m walk test at max speeds. **Description:** "an outdoor walkway in a calm garden and quiet neighborhood"	Indoor 6MWT at self-selected and max speeds on a 30 m course in basement or clinical setting **Description:** A) basement: "empty corridor" B) clinical: "corridor in a clinic rehabilitation unit".	CRF (6MWT distance); Walking performance (self-selected and max speed over 30 m).

	A: <0.8 m/s (n = 10), and B: ≥0.8 m/s (n = 26). Age (mean ± SD): A, 60 ± 3 y; B, 60 ± 3 yMonths post-stroke (mean ± SD): A, 69 ± 43; and B, 59 ± 27 Assistive device (n): A, 10; B, 1.	**Temperature:** NR ("the walkway was free of snow and ice and was treated with sand")	"The two indoor corridors had the same regular wall-to-wall plastic carpet with an even surface, well kept, and well lit" **Temperature:** NR	
Duncan 2014 (UK)	**Design:** Non-RXT, counterbalanced Acute, 2 visits separated by 24 h **Sample:** 14 year 5 (ages 9–10) primary school children (50% female and 50% male) Age (mean ± SD): 10 ± 1 y BMI (mean ± SD): 19.2 ± 2.9 kg/m^2	15-min of cycle ergometer exercise at a moderate intensity (50% HRR and cadence of 70–80 rpm) while watching a nature video **Description: "**film of cycling in a forest environment (Through the Forest; World Nature Video, Lunteren, The Netherlands)" **Temperature:** NR	15-min cycle ergometer exercise at a moderate intensity (50% HRR and cadence of 70–80 rpm) while viewing a blank screen **Description:** "blank screen … Walls were blank and there were no visible windows" **Temperature:** NR	BP; HR average and rest (Polar HR monitor); Mood (BRUMS).
Focht, 2009 (USA)	**Design:** RXT, counterbalanced Acute 2 single visits 48 h apart **Sample:** 35 physically active college-age women Ethnicity: 30 Caucasians, 4 African Americans, 1 Native American Age (mean ± SD): 22.1 ± 1.7 y	10-min outdoor walk at a self-selected intensity (59 ± 8% HRmax) **Description:** "standardized route on sidewalks and walking paths". Clear views of nature such as grass, trees, and plants.* **Temperature:** 21°C (range: 14–28°C)	10-min walk at a self-selected intensity (57 ± 8% HRmax) on an indoor treadmill **Description:** "laboratory setting" **Temperature:** NR	Affect (FS, FAS, and EFI); Effort (Borg 6–20 RPE scale); Intention to exercise (single-item percentage scale); PA enjoyment (PACES).

(*Continued*)

TABLE 3.3 (Cont.)

Study (country)	*Design and Sample*	*Green Exercise Conditions*	*Eligible Comparison Conditions*	*Outcomes (measure)*
	BMI (mean ± SD): 22.6 ± 2.6 kg/m^2 LTEQ PA (mean ± SD): mild, 3.3 ± 2.6 h/wk; moderate, 3.9 ± 1.6 h/wk; strenuous, 3.5 ± 1.4 h/wk			
Harte 1995 (Australia)	**Design:** Non-RXT, counterbalanced Acute, 4 single visits on separate days **Sample:** 10 male amateur triathletes or marathon runners Mean (range) age: 27 (18–37) y	12 km run completed course in less than 45-min **Description:** "12 km run outdoors on a designated route around James Cook University campus" **Temperature:** NR (all tests took place between 5–8am)	Two 45-min indoor runs on treadmill: 1) run in indoor setting with outdoor noises; 2) run in indoor setting with sound of heartbeat and breathing. **Description:** "6 x 6m sports physiology laboratory with brick walls and high-set windows" **Temperature:** NR	Attention (attention checklist); Effort (9-point Borg scale); evaluation of activity; Mood (POMS); Recent life events (RLEQ); Systolic BP; Urinary adrenaline, noradrenaline, cortisol (expressed as a % of creatinine).
Irandoust 2017 (Iran)	**Design:** RCT, parallel group Longitudinal, 12 weeks **Sample:** 75 "severely depressed women" with Vitamin D deficiency (15 outdoor PA with vitamin D, and 15 without vitamin D; 15 indoor PA with vitamin D, and 15, without vitamin D; 15 control)	Four 1-hour outdoor exercise sessions/week for 12 weeks. Exercise sessions: 5-min stretching, 50-min running at target HR 55–75% (Intensity progression: weeks 1–2, 55%; weeks 3–4, 65%, weeks 5–12, 75%) and RPE 11–12, and 5-min stretching	Four 1-hour indoor exercise sessions per week for 12 weeks (same structure and intensity of outdoor condition) **Description:** "treadmill walking under supervision at a health club" **Temperature:** NR	25-Hydroxyvitamin D; BDI; Bodyweight, BF %, BMI, and WHR.

	Age (mean ± SD): 43.2 ± 12.4 y BMI (range): 30.0–35.0 kg/m^2	**Description:** "outdoor conditions"* **Temperature:** NR (sessions took place at 11–12am in the Fall of 2015 in Qazvin, Iran)		
Kerr 2006 (Japan)	**Design:** Non-RXT, counterbalanced Acute, 2 single visits 1 week apart **Sample:** 44 male students, recreational (50%) and competitive (50%) runners Age (mean ± SD): recreational runners, 22.7 ± 1.7 y, and competitive middle and long distance runners, 20.6 ± 1.3 y	5 km run at 60% HRR in natural environment **Description:** "participants ran 5 km on a tree-lined footpath … outdoor running pathway ran alongside two small lakes, through woods and playing fields and the road had only occasional traffic" **Temperature:** NR ("weather and ground conditions were similar (sunny, no wind, dry ground)")	5 km indoor run at 60% HRR on a treadmill **Description:** "treadmill located in the university sports medicine laboratory" **Temperature:** NR ("Temperature and humidity conditions in the laboratory were similar to conditions outside")	Emotional response (TESI).
Lacharité-Lemieux 2015 (also 2016) (Canada)	**Design:** RCT, parallel groups Longitudinal, 12 weeks **Sample:** 23 healthy, sedentary postmenopausal women divided into two groups (11, indoor, and 12, outdoor) Age (mean ± SD): indoor, 59.4 ± 3.8 y; and outdoor, 62.0 ± 5.5 y BMI (mean ± SD): indoor, 25.7 ± 1.8 kg/m^2; and outdoor, 25.4	Three weekly 1-hour mixed aerobic (10-min: "performing movements" and 20-min: circuit training; intensity 65%–95% HRmax) and resistance training (15-min) sessions conducted in outdoor natural park **Description:** "mainly natural park beside a body of water, where paths were lined with large	Three weekly 1-hour mixed aerobic (10-min: "performing movements" and 20-min: circuit training; intensity 65%–95% HRmax) and resistance training (15-min) conducted in indoor room **Description:** "Research Center on Aging … The floor was carpeted and the room had many	Affect (EFI; FS; FAS); BMI, fat mass, LBM, and muscle mass index (DXA); BP (automatic BP monitor); CRF (via modified Balke test); Depressive symptoms (BDI); Effort (via Borg 6–20 RPE); Exercise adherence (% of sessions attended); Fasting glucose, insulin, and plasma lipids; HR

(Continued)

TABLE 3.3 (Cont.)

Study (country)	*Design and Sample*	*Green Exercise Conditions*	*Eligible Comparison Conditions*	*Outcomes (measure)*
	± 1.9 kg/m^2 PASE PA (mean ± SD): indoor, 148.0 ± 75.2 kcal/wk; and outdoor, 148.3 ± 54.5 kcal/wk Environmental preference (indoor/outdoor): indoor, 5/6; and outdoor, 5/7	trees and rich biodiversity … river and some old pine trees" **Months**: Apr–Jul **Temperature:** NR ("On days with heavy rain, the group exercised under the large tent located in the center of the park near the water")	windows, with a view of the parking lot on both sides" **Temperature:** NR ("participants in both groups experienced the same temperature conditions on hot days … indoor participants avoided the cold days of early April")	(Polar HR monitor); Muscular endurance (max number of repetitions at 70% 1RM); Muscular strength (1RM test); PA (PASE).
Langhammer 2009 (Norway)	**Design:** RCT Longitudinal, 2.5 weeks average duration **Sample:** 39 patients with stroke (59% female and 41% male) attending a private rehabilitation centre Age (mean ± SD): outdoors, 75 ± 10.4 y; treadmill, 74 ± 13.3 y Weight (mean ± SD): outdoors, 67 ± 17.3 y; and treadmill, 75 ± 15.0 y Days post-stroke (mean ± SD): outdoors, 349 ± 820 d; and treadmill, 419 ± 1034 d	30-min of outdoor walking at a comfortable speed on 5 days/week for 2.5 weeks on average. Additional: balance, strength, and coordination; strength, flexibility, balance, and endurance; group therapy; group exercises; relaxation, physiotherapy, and education; self-directed exercise (~21 h/week) **Description:** "Norwegian scenery with nature, trees, a beautiful view of the Oslo fjord and mountains"	30-min of walking at a comfortable speed on treadmills on 5 days/week for 2.5 weeks on average. Same additional exercise as outdoor group **Description:** "exercises were carried out with the treadmill in a flat position" **Temperature:** NR	CRF (6MWT); Motor function (MAS); Quality of walking (10-m walk test)

		Temperature: NR ("walks were performed regardless of weather conditions")		
McMurray 1988 (USA)	**Design:** Non-RXT Acute, 2 single visits on separate days **Sample:** 8 male runners Age (range): 21–41 years Weight (mean ± SEM): 70.2 ± 1.3 kg VO_2max (mean ± SEM): 59 ± 3 ml/kg/min	10 mile outdoor run (same intensity as indoor run) **Description:** "outdoors on a predetermined, fairly level, 10 mile course" (First and final laps were performed on a - 400 m athletics track) **Temperature** (mean ± SD): 25 ± 2°C (slight breeze) **Humidity** (mean ± SD): 65 ± 6%	10 mile run on indoor treadmill at speed and grade setting equal to 70% VO_2 max **Description:** Indoor "laboratory" setting **Temperature** (mean ± SD): 22 ± 1°C (cooling fans were used for all runs) **Humidity** (mean ± SD): 40 ± 12%	Affect (GAS); VO_2 (via open circuit spirometry and Douglas Bags); HR (via ECG and palpitation); Plasma beta-endorphin and lactate concentrations (via blood samples).
Mieras 2014 (USA)	**Design:** RXT, counterbalanced Acute, 2 sessions (no fewer than 2 days and no longer than 2 weeks apart) **Sample:** 12 recreationally trained male cyclists Ethnicity: 11 Caucasian, 1 African-American	40 km outdoor cycling on set course at self-selected intensity (consistent effort) **Description:** "outdoor trials were completed along a relatively flat, out and back course on a paved recreation trail (Keystone Trail, Omaha, NE, USA)"	Laboratory cycling on 40 km at self-selected training intensity (consistent effort) **Description:** "Exercise physiology laboratory, where environmental conditions remain relatively constant"	Attentional focus (via TAF scale); Bodyweight; Core temperature (CBTC); Effort (Borg 6–20 RPE scale); HR; Performance power output (power meter); Skin temperature (Thermostor patch); USG (via digital refractometer).

(*Continued*)

TABLE 3.3 (Cont.)

Study (country)	*Design and Sample*	*Green Exercise Conditions*	*Eligible Comparison Conditions*	*Outcomes (measure)*
	Age (mean ± SD): 37 ± 2 y Weight (mean ± SD): 82.1 ± 4.8 kg BF % (mean ± SD): 15.1 ± 1.8% VO_2max (mean ± SD): 53 ± 2 ml/kg/min	**Month**: Aug–Oct **Temperature** (Mean ± SD): 22.1 ± 0.2°C **Humidity** (Mean ± SD): 32.0 ± 1.4% **Wind speed** (Mean ± SD): 2.5 ± 0.6 m/s^{-1} Heat Index, Dew point, wet bulb, and pressure similar between-conditions	**Temperature** (Mean ± SD): 22.0 ± 0.1°C **Humidity** (Mean ± SD): 38.3 ± 3.4% **Wind speed** (Mean ± SD): 0.0 ± 0.0 m/s^{-1}	
Niedermeier 2017a (also 2017b) (Austria)	**Design:** RXT Acute 3 single sessions with mean time between sessions of 1 week (1–14 day range) **Sample:** 42 healthy adults (48% female and 52% male) Age (mean ± SD): 32 ± 12 y BMI (mean ± SD): 23.0 ± 2.0 kg/m^2 PA (mean ± SD): 8 ± 5 h/week Mountain tours (mean ± SD): 27.2 ± 26.2 tours/year	3-h of outdoor mountain hiking in groups of five (6 km of uphill walking in ~1.5 h to 1500m at average speed 4 km/h; 10-min rest; walking downhill for 70-min at average speed 5.2 km/h **Description**: "famous hiking area and started at the northern edge of Innsbruck with direct access to natural environment" **Month:** May, Aug, Sept/Oct **Temperature:** NR	3-h of indoor treadmill walking in groups of five (6 km of walking uphill on inclination of 10% for 1.5 h at 4 km/h; 10-min rest; 70-min of level walking at average speed 5.2 km/h **Description:** "situated in a fitness centre" **Temperature:** NR	Affect (FS, FAS); Affective states (MSS & STAI); BP; Effort (Borg 6–20 RPE scale); HR (Polar HR monitor); HRV; Salivary cortisol.
Nisbet 2011 (Canada)	**Design:** RCT x 2	1) 17-min walk in nature in groups of 1–11 students.		Affect (PANAS); Nature Relatedness (INS scale);

	Acute, single session in both study 1 and 2. **Sample:** Study 1) 150 University students (57% female, 37% male, and 6% unspecified) Age (mean ± SD): 20.8 ± 5.0 y Study 2) 80 participants (no participant characteristics were reported)	**Description:** "walking and biking path along the Rideau Canal … a green corridor … 8 km through the heart of Ottawa.. relatively picturesque … urban nature" 2) Participants received description of walk and rated their anticipated effect before walking in a different outdoor environment to above **Description:** "on-campus and followed a walking path between a road and a river that borders the campus, ending near a campus building" **Temperature:** 2.5–14.6°C ("Walks conducted in Fall on days with no rain")	1) 17-min walk in indoor environment in groups of 1–11 students **Description:** "proceeded to their destination, the athletics building, via tunnels" 2) Participants received description of walk & rated their anticipated effect before they walked in an indoor environment **Description:** "different building than the indoor route in Study 1, but also used parts of the university tunnel system" **Temperature:** NR	Relaxation, Fascination, curiosity, and interest (modified PANAS scale).
Peacock 2007 (UK)	**Design:** Non-RXT Acute 2 single visits 1 week apart **Sample:** 20 participants (65% female and 35% male) Age range: 31–70 y (aged 31–50 y: 47%; aged 51–70 y: 53%)	30-min outdoor walk. No intensity provided but "continuous walking was preferred … participants were allowed to stop briefly to admire the scenery … social interaction was also encouraged" **Description:** "Belhus Woods Country Park, which has a	30-min indoor walk. No intensity provided but "continuous walking was preferred … participants were allowed to stop briefly to admire … hop windows, and a certain level of social interaction was also encouraged"	Enjoyment (via 1–5 Likert scale); Mood (POMS); Self-esteem (RSE scale).

(Continued)

TABLE 3.3 (Cont.)

Study (country)	*Design and Sample*	*Green Exercise Conditions*	*Eligible Comparison Conditions*	*Outcomes (measure)*
		diverse landscape of woodlands, grasslands and lakes" **Temperature:** NR	**Description:** "walking around Lakeside shopping centre" **Temperature:** NR	
Plante 2003 (USA)	**Design:** RCT, parallel groups Acute, 4 single visits on separate days **Sample:** 154 undergraduate psychology students (66% female and 34% male) Age: NR BMI (mean ± SD): outside, women 21.1 ± 2.7 kg/m^2 and men 24.6 ± 3.7 kg/m^2; laboratory, women 23.5 ± 3.3 kg/m^2 and men 24.1 ± 2.3 kg/m^2	1) 20-min brisk (~3 mph) outdoor walk. **Description:** "Garden at the campus of Santa Clara University"* 2) 20-min VR with walking (speed: 2.7–3.5 mph) in laboratory. **Description:** "same route around campus that walkers used in condition 1 (see above)" (sunny conditions) **Temperature:** NR ("no participant was made to walk in rainy weather or at night")	20-min of walking on a treadmill (speed: 2.7–3.5 mph) without any VR technology **Description:** "No visual stimulus was presented before the walk to the participants" **Temperature:** NR	Mood (AD-ACL); Social Desirability or defensiveness (MC-SDS)
Plante 2006 (USA)	**Design:** RCT, parallel groups Acute, 2 single visits on separate days	1) 20-min brisk outdoor walk (speed ~4.8 km/h)	No non-green exercise intervention included.	Mood (AD-ACL); PA enjoyment (PACES); Social Desirability or defensiveness (MC-SDS).

	Sample: 112 undergraduate psychology students (58% female and 42% male) (no participant characteristics were reported)	**Description:** "Garden at the campus of Santa Clara University"* 2) 20-min walking (speed: 4.3–5.6 km/h) on a laboratory treadmill while watching a video projected on a screen of the same route around campus that walkers in condition 1 (see above) completed (sunny day) **Temperature:** NR ("northern California during the fall … no participant was made to walk in rainy weather or at night")		
Plante 2007 (USA)	**Design:** RCT, parallel groups Acute, single visit **Sample:** 88 female undergraduate students Age (mean ± SD): 19 ± 1 y	1) 20-min moderate intensity walk (60–70% HRmax) along a prescribed route on the university campus 2) Same walk as above but accompanied by a friend All conditions performed "same exercise task in terms of type and intensity of exercise" **Description:** "Garden at the campus of Santa Clara University"*	1) 20-min moderate intensity walk (60–70% HRmax) alone on a treadmill 2) Completed the same treadmill walk as above but did so alongside a friend who walked on an adjacent treadmill **Description:** "University fitness facility on campus" **Temperature:** NR	Mood (AD-ACL); PA enjoyment (PACES).

(Continued)

TABLE 3.3 (Cont.)

Study (country)	*Design and Sample*	*Green Exercise Conditions*	*Eligible Comparison Conditions*	*Outcomes (measure)*
		Temperature: NR		
Rider 2016 (Canada)	**Design:** RXT, counterbalanced Acute, 2 10-minute walks Study 1) participants studied a word list, then walked; Study 2) participants walked, then studied a word list. **Sample:** Study 1) 24 undergraduate students (83% female and 17% male) Mean age: 22 y Study 2) 24 undergraduate students (79% female and 21% male) Mean age: 22 y	10-minute (~0.5 km) nature walk (intensity not reported) **Description:** "walk through a number of stands of trees, bushes, and grassy areas along a relatively quiet asphalt path on University campus" (image provided) **Month:** Sept–Oct 2014 **Temperature:** -5°C to 21°C (weekday mornings or afternoons)	10-minute (~0.5 km) indoor walk (intensity not reported) **Description: "**hallways on three floors of the University building and did not provide much exposure to natural or urban outdoor elements" **Temperature:** -5°C to 21°C	Memory (Free recall test, Forced-choice recognition test); Mood (11-point scale, -5 = very negative, 0 = neutral, +5 = very positive); Rating of experience (asked to indicate which walk was most enjoyable, most beautiful, least distracting).
Rogerson 2016 (UK)	**Design:** RXT, counterbalanced Acute, 3 visits—baseline, indoors, outdoors (baseline to first condition separated by 6 ± 3 d; condition 1 and 2 separated by 9 ± 8 d). Participants took part	15-min on cycle ergometer at 50% HRR. Participants advised that they were free to talk as much or as little as they liked **Description: "**Exercise was performed outside, on the	15-min on cycle ergometer at 50% HRR. Participants advised that they were free to talk as much or as little as they liked. **Description:** Exercise was performed in a laboratory (8.3	Directed attention (backwards digit span task); Effort (Borg RPE); Mood (30-item POMS); Intention for future (VAS [0–100] to rate enjoyment of session, intention to attend a session

	in pairs (who already knew each other) **Sample:** 24 participants (79% female and 21% male) (1 staff member, 10 students, 13 public) Age (mean ± SD): 35.1 ± 20.1 y Weight (mean ± SD): 70 ± 15 kg	University sports fields, a large area of largely level gradient, maintained grassland, lined and partly interspersed with trees" (image provided) **Temperature:** NR	x 4.9 m) with a view of a white painted brick wall (image provided) **Temperature:** NR	in the future—if offered free); Social interaction time (accumulated interaction time [visual and verbal] was measured by the experimenter).
Rogerson 2015 (UK)	**Design:** RXT, counterbalanced Acute, 4 visits separated by 7–25 days (average: 13 days) **Sample:** 12 healthy adult participants (50% female and 50% male) Age (mean ± SD): 27.8 ± 5.5 y Weight (mean ± SD): 65.4 ± 10.5 kg	1) 15-min bout of exercise on the treadmill, at 60% VO_2 peak (via gas analysis) while watching nature video 2) run at 85% VO_2 peak to voluntary exhaustion while watching nature video **Description:** video consisted of scenes extracted from "Evening Run through Endless Forest" (all videos played at the same speed without auditory sound) **Temperature:** NR (time of day was consistent between occasions within 2 hours)	1) 15-min bout of exercise on the treadmill, at 60% VO_2 peak (via gas analysis) while watching 1) blank screen and 2) watching built environment video 2) run at 85% VO_2 peak to voluntary exhaustion while watching 1) "blank white screen" and 2) watching built environment video **Temperature:** NR	Directed Attention (subtraction of serial sevens test, spelling words backwards, and backwards digit span test); Effort (Borg 6–20 RPE scale); Energy expenditure (gas analysis method not reported); HR average; Respiratory exchange ratio (gas analysis method not reported); TTE at 85% VO_2 peak.
Ryan 2010 (USA)	**Design:** RCT, parallel groups (study 2)	15-min walk in outdoor setting (no intensity reported)	15-min walk in indoor setting (no intensity reported)	State vitality (SVS)

(*Continued*)

TABLE 3.3 (Cont.)

Study (country)	*Design and Sample*	*Green Exercise Conditions*	*Eligible Comparison Conditions*	*Outcomes (measure)*
	Acute, single visit **Sample:** 80 undergraduate university students (82% female and 18% male) Mean (range) age: 20 (18–22) y	**Description:** "Participants in the outdoor condition walked on a largely tree-lined footpath along a river that runs parallel to the university campus" **Month:** Sept–Oct **Temperature:** NR (walks completed 11am–4pm)	**Description:** "series of underground hallways and tunnels that were devoid of living things" **Temperature:** NR (walks completed 11am–4pm)	
Teas 2007 (USA)	**Design:** Non-RXT Acute 2 single visits 1 week apart **Sample:** 19 healthy, non-smoking, postmenopausal women Ethnicity (n): European American, 13; African-American, 6 Age (mean ± SD): 58 ± 4 y BMI (mean ± SD): 27 ± 6 kg/m^2	1-hour walk at a "comfortable" self-chosen speed (mean: 5.1 km/h) outdoors **Description:** "campus horseshoe (grassy area lined with brick paths, old trees, and flowerbeds)" **Month:** May **Temperature:** 22°C (women walked together on same day at 6:20–7:20 pm) **Humidity:** 45% (Light: 220 lux; Noise: 65 decibels)	1-hour walk at a "comfortable" self-chosen speed (mean: 4.3 km/h) on a treadmill **Description:** "gym lab was located in the university gym, and provided an environment similar to that found in a commercial gym" **Temperature:** 23°C (walk completed 5–6:45pm) **Humidity:** 46% (Light: 180 lux; Noise: 74 decibels)	Negative affect (NAS); Positive affect (PAS); Salivary cortisol and alpha amylase
Turner 2017 (UK)	**Design:** RXT, counterbalanced	6 km run—first 3 km at steady-state pace, second 3 km at	6 km run—first 3 km at steady-state pace, second 3 km at	

	Acute, 2 visits at least 24 hours apart **Sample:** 22 adult competitive and recreational runners (36% female and 64% male) Age (n): 18–34 y, 14; 35–51 y, 8 BMI (n): ≤ 24.9 kg/m^2, 16; ≥ 25.0 kg/m^2, 6 Relatedness to nature (n): high, 19; low: 3	maximum intensity (fast as possible) with the second half completed at maximum effort, followed by 10-min recovery **Description:** "Large woodland area, with walking/running trails lined with trees and bushes … Dog walkers and other runners were present" **Temperature:** 17.5°C (typically cloudy with sunny intervals)	maximum intensity (fast as possible) with the second half completed at maximum effort, followed by 10-min recovery **Description:** Treadmill in a large fitness suite. "Digital screens on the treadmill displaying feedback data remained visible, to allow for self-pacing. Other users of the fitness suite were present" **Temperature:** 19°C	Affect (FS, FAS); Effort (Borg 6–20 RPE scale); State vitality (7-item SVS).
White 2015 (UK)	**Design:** RXT Acute, 4 visits ~1 week apart **Sample:** 37 postmenopausal women Age (mean ± SD): 50.1 ± 3.7 y BMI (mean ± SD): 25.3 ± 4.7 kg/m^2 Self-reported instances of at least 30-min of light-moderate exercise per week (mean ± SD): 4.5 ± 2.9 instances.	Cycle ergometer for 15-min while watching a 1) green video and 2) blue video. **Description:** Green video: 3 x 5-min scenes of fields with sheep, hedgerows and a small wood. Blue video: 3 x 5-min clips from a headland overlooking a beach and of views from beach height across rocks and the sea **Temperature:** NR	Cycle ergometer for 15-min while facing 1) a blank wall (control) or 2) watching an "urban video". **Temperature:** NR	Affect (FS, FAS); BP; Effort (Borg RPE scale); Experience (Enjoyment of session); HR; Time perception (asked participants for how long they felt they had been cycling).
Yeh 2017 (UK)	**Design:** Non-RXT, counterbalanced	1) 20 minute treadmill run at self-selected pace looking at static image of nature (visual only)	20 min treadmill at self-selected pace focusing on self-selected entertainment (music = 23;	Affect: happiness, anxiety, dejection, anger, and excitement (SEQ); Distance (via treadmill);

(*Continued*)

TABLE 3.3 (Cont.)

Study (country)	*Design and Sample*	*Green Exercise Conditions*	*Eligible Comparison Conditions*	*Outcomes (measure)*
	Acute, 3 20-min treadmill runs with minimum 7 day gap between-conditions **Sample:** 30 adults (40% female and 60% male) Age (mean ± SD): 28 ± 9 y BMI (mean ± SD): 22.2 ± 2.1 kg/m^2	2) 20 minute treadmill run at self-selected pace looking at dynamic image of nature (visual only) **Description:** Dynamicimage condition: video of the "Sheffield Botanical Gardens … series of paths within the gardens, capturing the trail through lawns, trees and flower beds … sunny spring afternoon" **Temperature:** NR	movies with sound = 6; viewing a picture = 1) **Description:** "self-selected, preferred entertainment where participants were able to choose preferences that included visual and/or auditory information" **Temperature:** NR	HR (Polar HR watch).

Key: RXT: Randomised crossover trial; BMI: Body Mass Index; RCT: Randomised comparative trial; VR: virtual reality; VO_2max/peak: maximal/peak oxygen uptake; CVD: cardiovascular disease; HR: heart rate; HRV: Heart Rate Variability; PA: physical activity; CRF: Cardiorespiratory Fitness; SF: short form; BP: blood pressure; LTEQ: Godin's Leisure Time Exercise Questionnaire; CNS: Connectedness to Nature Scale (1–5 scale, higher the score, greater the connectedness to nature); PAAS: Physical Activity Affective Scale; PRS: Perceived Restorativeness Scale; CAR: Cortisol Awakening Response; 6MWT: 6-min walk test; BRUMS: Brunel Mood State Inventory; FS: Feeling Scale; FAS: Felt Arousal Scale; EFI: Exercise-Induced Feeling Inventory; GAS: General affect scale; MSS: Mood Scale Score; STAI: State-Trait Anxiety Inventory; PACES: Physical Activity Enjoyment Scale; ZIPERS: Zuckerman's Inventory of Personal Reactions; NCPCT: Necker Cube Pattern Control task; RPE: Rate of Perceived Exertion; DXA: dual energy X-ray absorptiometry; SVS: Subjective Vitality Scale; PAS: Positive Affect Scale; NAS: Negative Affect Scale; WHR: Waist-Hip Ratio; BF: body fat; TESI: Tension and Effort Stress Inventory; RSE: Rosenberg Self-esteem; POMS: Profile Of Mood States; RLEQ: Recent Life Events Questionnaire; AD-ACL: Activation–Deactivation Adjective Check List; TTE: time to exhaustion; PANAS: Positive and Negative Affect Schedule; MC-SDS: Marlowe-Crowne Social Desirability Scale; TAF: Tammen Attentional Focus; PASE: Physical Activity Scale for the Elderly; CBTC: Core Body Temperature Capsule; USG: Urine Specific Gravity; INS: Inclusion of Nature in Self; SEQ: Sport Emotion Questionnaire; 1-RM (one repetition-maximum); *: Additional information received from author.

2016; Irandoust & Taheri, 2017), and moderate-to-high in the other (Lacharité-Lemieux et al., 2015). Exercise duration ranged from 45 (Calogiuri et al., 2016) to 60 minutes (Lacharité-Lemieux et al., 2015).

Acute trials

Of the 16 studies that compared outdoor green exercise with indoor exercise, seven were RXTs (Carvalho, Sunnerhagen, & Willén, 2010; Focht, 2009; Mieras, Heesch, & Slivka, 2014; Niedermeier et al., 2016; Rider & Bodner, 2016; Rogerson, Gladwell, Gallagher, & Barton, 2016; Turner & Stevinson, 2017), five were non-RXTs (Harte & Eifert, 1995; Kerr et al., 2006; McMurray, Berry, Vann, Hardy, & Sheps, 1988; Peacock et al., 2007; Teas, Hurley, & Ghumare, 2007), and four were RCTs (Nisbet & Zelenski, 2011; Plante et al., 2003, 2007; Ryan et al., 2010). In most, the chosen mode of exercise was walking (n = 10) or running (n = 4), whereas, the remaining two used cycling (Mieras et al., 2014; Rogerson et al., 2016). Another study, however, compared mountain hiking in an Austrian Alpine region with treadmill walking flat and on an incline (Niedermeier et al., 2016).

Exercise intensity was moderate in all but one of the 16 studies; Turner and Stevinson (2017) instructed participants to run as fast as possible in the last 3 km of a 6 km run. Short duration exercise bouts ≤20 min were used in most of the 16 studies (n = 8), whereas, only two trials included exercise bouts of 60 min (Teas et al., 2007) or longer (Niedermeier et al., 2016, 3-h). Four studies used a set distance rather than prescribed exercise duration (Kerr et al., 2006, 5 km; McMurray et al., 1988, 10 miles; Mieras et al., 2014, 40 km; Turner & Stevinson, 2017, 6 km).

Of the five trials that compared virtual green exercise with indoor exercise, four were either RXTs (Rogerson et al., 2016; White, Pahl, Ashbullby, Burton, & Depledge, 2015) or non-RXTs (Duncan et al., 2014; Yeh, Stone, Churchill, Brymer, & Davids, 2017), and one was a RCT (Plante et al., 2003). Five of the trials included moderate intensity conditions (Duncan et al., 2014; Plante et al., 2003; Rogerson et al., 2016; White et al., 2015; Yeh et al., 2017). Rogerson et al. (2016) also included a high-intensity (85% VO_2max) exercise condition. Exercise duration was either 15-min (Duncan et al., 2014; Rogerson et al., 2016; White et al., 2015) or 20-min (Plante et al., 2003; Yeh et al., 2017).

Study outcomes and measures

Full details of the outcomes and measurement tools assessed in the eligible studies can be found in Table 3.3. Of the three longitudinal RCTS that compared green exercise with indoor exercise, all included measurements for both subjective and objective outcomes (Calogiuri et al., 2016; Irandoust & Taheri, 2017; Lacharité-Lemieux et al., 2015). Subjective outcomes reported included affect, depression, restoration, perceived effort, enjoyment, physical activity levels and physical activity intention, of which most were measured using reliable and validated scales. Objective outcomes included biomarkers, cardiovascular responses, anthropometric measurements, cardiorespiratory fitness, exercise adherence, and muscular strength and endurance.

In the eligible acute trials subjective outcomes included affect/mood, emotions (e.g., energy, tension, calmness depression, etc.) enjoyment, self-esteem, perceived effort, physical activity intention, time perception, perceived restoration, and cyber sickness. Objective outcomes across eligible acute trials included attention and cognitive function, cardiovascular and physiological responses (e.g., heart rate and blood pressure), biological markers, power output, walking/running, speed, distance covered, and time to completion and exhaustion.

Risk of bias

Authors' judgements and rationales for risk of bias can be found here: https://osf.io/mgfsd/. Below we briefly summarise the risk of bias for RCTs and crossover trials.

Randomised comparative trials

Two RCTs were at a high risk of selection bias because the allocation was not concealed. In the remaining six RCTs, the risk of selection bias was unclear as insufficient information was provided about randomisation procedures. We judged all eight trials at high risk of performance bias due to the inability to blind participants to the nature of the intervention (exercise) and the environment (outdoor vs. indoor). Only one trial stated that they blinded outcome assessors to the intervention—all other trials were judged at high risk of detection bias. All trials were deemed at low risk of attrition bias due to minimal or no loss to follow-up. One trial was deemed at a high risk of selective reporting bias; the remaining seven were judged to have an unclear risk of selective reporting due to a lack of pre-registration. One trial each was considered to have a high and unclear risk of other bias.

Crossover trials

In three out of the 16 crossover trials we judged that the crossover design employed may not have been appropriate due to a short wash-out period between-conditions. Nine (53%) trials had an appropriate design, whereas, in four trials it was unclear. We judged seven trials at a high or unclear risk of a carry-over effect influencing study results due mainly to insufficient wash-out periods or insufficient information available. All trials were deemed to have included unbiased data because data from all treatment periods were provided.

The seven eligible non-RXTs were judged to be at a high risk of selection bias. Of the nine RXTs, seven were deemed to have an unclear risk of selection bias because the randomisation method was not reported. Only two trials provided their randomisation method. No trials adequately concealed condition order allocation from study personnel. All trials were again judged at high risk of performance bias. No trial stated that they blinded outcome assessors to the intervention, and were therefore, deemed to be at high risk of detection bias.

Most trials (n = 13) reported minimal loss to follow-up. Three trials were judged at high risk of attrition bias, because some participants (10–20%) did not complete all conditions. All trials had an unclear risk of selective reporting due to a lack of pre-registration. Six trials were deemed at risk of other biases.

1. **Summary of effects: Longitudinal effects of outdoor green exercise versus indoor exercise**

Results of possible meta-analysis are presented in Table 3.4. All trials reported post-intervention values (none provided mean changes). Each analysis involves data from just two trials, so caution is advised when interpreting the results of our meta-analysis. Of the analyses performed, slightly higher post-intervention diastolic blood pressure and lower RPE values with green exercise were the only statistically significant findings observed (Table 3.4).

Outcomes not in the meta-analysis

Psychological-related outcomes

One longitudinal RCT (Calogiuri et al., 2016) found that compared with exercising indoors, outdoor exercise results in statistically higher perceived restorativeness of the environment (fascination and being away, both $p<.001$), enjoyment after outdoor biking ($p = .02$; overall enjoyment, $p<.05$), and intention to exercise in the future after correcting for previous exercise behaviour ($p<.01$). Lacharite-Lemieux and colleagues (2015), however, reported no statistical changes in revitalisation and fatigue scores as a function of time or environment.

Exercise adherence, exercise intensity, and physical fitness

Only one trial included adherence, exercise intensity, and physical fitness outcomes (Lacharité-Lemieux et al., 2015). This trial reported statistically higher adherence to exercise in the outdoor versus indoor exercise groups (97% vs. 91% of prescribed sessions completed), but no statistical between-condition differences in average or maximal heart rates during exercise (bpm and %, p's≥.05), and cardiorespiratory fitness (via estimated VO_2max). A statistical pre- to post-intervention increase in VO_2max, however, was observed in the indoor exercise group ($p = .01$), but not the outdoor exercise group ($p = .082$). Lacharité-Lemieux and colleagues (2015) also reported no statistical time by environment interaction for upper or lower body muscular strength or muscular endurance (p's≥.05).

TABLE 3.4 The longitudinal effects of outdoor green exercise versus indoor exercise on emotions and enjoyment: meta-analysis of parallel RCTs

Outcome	*Trials*	*Sample*	*Statistical Method*	*Effect Estimate*	I^2
Positive affect/ engagement	2	51	SMD (IV, Random, 95% CI)	0.94 [-0.59, 2.46]	84%
Tranquillity	2	37	SMD (IV, Random, 95% CI)	0.25 [-0.40, 0.90]	0%
Depressive symptoms	2	83	SMD (IV, Random, 95% CI)	-0.58 [-1.81, 0.64]	84%
RPE	2	37	MD (IV, Random, 95% CI)	-1.02 [-1.88, -0.16]	0%
Average HR [% HRmax]	2	37	MD (IV, Random, 95% CI)	-0.76 [-4.66, 3.14]	0%
Systolic blood pressure [mmHg]	2	37	MD (IV, Random, 95% CI)	3.39 [-2.80, 9.58]	0%
Diastolic blood pressure [mmHg]	2	37	MD (IV, Random, 95% CI)	4.45 [0.54, 8.37]	0%
Physical activity	2	37	SMD (IV, Random, 95% CI)	1.36 [-0.50, 3.22]	79%
Mass [Kg]	2	83	MD (IV, Random, 95% CI)	-0.15 [-2.10, 1.80]	0%
BMI [Kg/m^2]	2	83	MD (IV, Random, 95% CI)	-0.10 [-1.01, 0.80]	0%
Body fat [%]	2	83	MD (IV, Random, 95% CI)	-1.43 [-5.12, 2.27]	63%

Key: SMD, standardised mean difference; MD, mean difference; RPE, rate of perceived exertion; HR, heart rate; BMI, body mass index.

Anthropometric variables

One trial reported statistical pre to post-intervention reductions in waist-to-hip ratio in all exercise groups (*p*'s>.05), but not in a non-exercise control (Irandoust & Taheri, 2017). Whereas another trial, correcting for muscle mass index and physical activity levels, found no statistical time by environment interaction effect for any anthropometric variable (Lacharité-Lemieux et al., 2015).

Biomarkers

All three longitudinal trials included biological marker outcomes. Calogiuri et al. (2016) observed statistical improvements in salivary cortisol awakening response (CAR) area under the curve with respect to increase (AUCI) in the green exercise group versus the indoor exercise group (p = .04), but no between-group differences in CAR area under the curve with respect to the ground and serum cortisol concentration. Another trial found statistically higher serum 25-hydroxyvitamin D (25-OH vitamin D) concentrations with a 12-week green exercise intervention with and without vitamin D supplementation versus indoor exercise with and without vitamin D (*p*'s<.05) (Irandoust &

Taheri, 2017). In the third trial, Lacharité-Lemieux et al. (2015) found no statistical changes in fasting glucose and insulin, Homeostasis Model Assessment-insulin resistance, triglycerides, and total, low-density lipoprotein, and high-density lipoprotein cholesterol with either outdoor green or indoor exercise.

2. Summary of effects: acute effects of real green exercise versus indoor exercise without exposure to nature

Twelve crossover trials and four parallel RCTs compared the effects of acute outdoor green exercise conditions with indoor exercise conditions. Only four of these trials were sufficiently powered to detect at least moderate effects on affective states (Focht, 2009; Niedermeier et al., 2016), affective valence (Turner & Stevinson, 2017), and power output (Mieras et al., 2014). Two of these trials, however, based their sample size calculation upon an anticipated moderate (d = 0.5) or large effect size (d = 0.8), which may have been optimistic and underestimated required sample size.

General affect

Eight trials assessed a range of general affect constructs with a variety of tools (Figure 3.2). All but two of the trials examined the acute effects of exercise bouts of 30 min or less, and only one did not use walking or running as the exercise mode (Rogerson et al., 2016, stationary cycling). Half of the trials (2 RXTs and 2 non-RXTs) showed no statistical differences in general affect between real green and indoor exercise, whereas, the other four trials (2 RXTs, 1 RCT, and 1 non-RXT) showed statistical improvements in favour of green exercise (Figure 3.2). Nisbet and colleagues (2011) also reported statistically lower negative affect in the green exercise condition compared with indoor exercise in both the original trial (p<.05, d = 0.51) and its replication (p<.05, d = 0.47).

Only three trials (all RXTs) included affective valence (assessed via FS) and perceived activation (via FAS) as outcomes (Figure 3.2). Two trials (10 min nature walk and 3-h of mountain hiking) observed statistically higher affective valence scores in green exercise conditions compared with indoor exercise. Only one out of three trials reported a moderate statistical improvement in perceived activation with a 10-min nature walk versus an indoor treadmill walk (d = 0.41). Two trials employed Bonferroni corrections lowering their threshold for statistical significance to p>0.025 and p>0.0125 (Niedermeier et al., 2016; Turner & Stevinson, 2017).

Emotions

Seven (3 RXTs, 2 RCTs, and 2 non-RXTs) of the 10 trials that included a measure of "energy" found no difference between real green exercise and indoor exercise (Figure 3.3). Most trials (n = 4/6, 67%) observed no statistical

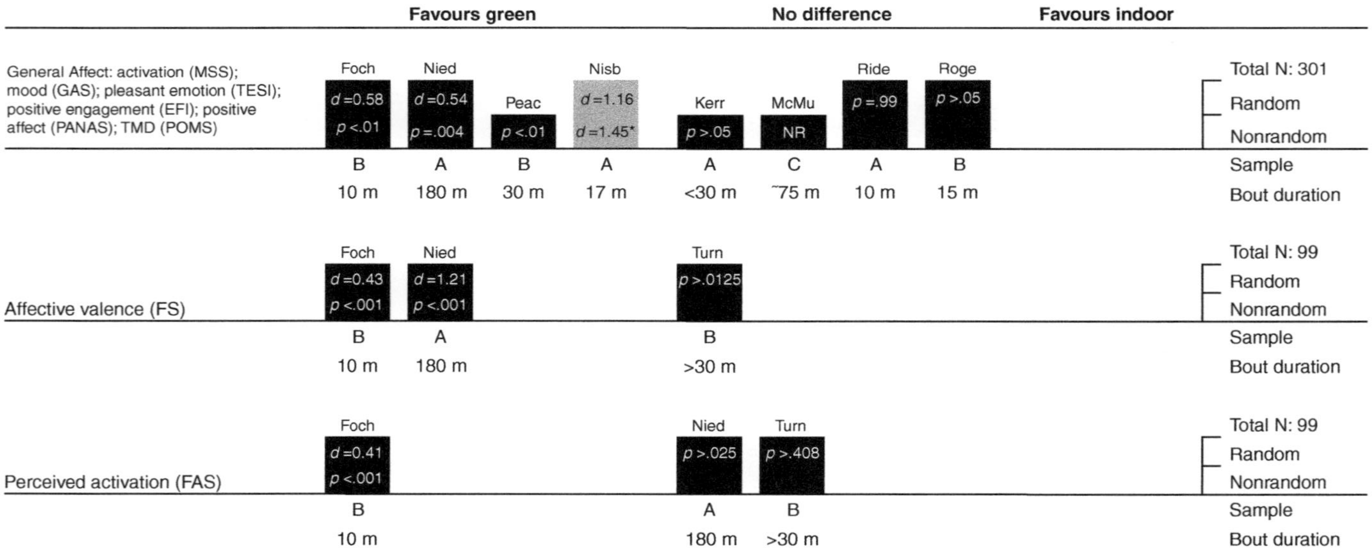

	Favours green				No difference				Favours indoor	
General Affect: activation (MSS); mood (GAS); pleasant emotion (TESI); positive engagement (EFI); positive affect (PANAS); TMD (POMS)	Foch d =0.58 p <.01	Nied d =0.54 p =.004	Peac p <.01	Nisb d =1.16 d =1.45*	Kerr p >.05	McMu NR	Ride p =.99	Roge p >.05		Total N: 301 Random Nonrandom
	B	A	B	A	A	C	A	B		Sample
	10 m	180 m	30 m	17 m	<30 m	˜75 m	10 m	15 m		Bout duration
Affective valence (FS)	Foch d =0.43 p <.001	Nied d =1.21 p <.001			Turn p >.0125					Total N: 99 Random Nonrandom
	B	A			B					Sample
	10 m	180 m			>30 m					Bout duration
Perceived activation (FAS)	Foch d =0.41 p <.001				Nied p >.025	Turn p >.408				Total N: 99 Random Nonrandom
	B				A	B				Sample
	10 m				180 m	>30 m				Bout duration

FIGURE 3.2 Harvest plots of trials investigating general affect in outdoor green exercise versus indoor exercise without exposure to nature. A: studies with ≥40 participants; B: studies with 20–39 patients; C: studies with <19 patients. We also provide the total sample across trials for each comparison. The large bars represent randomised trials in this comparison, and small bars represent non-randomised trials. Grey bars indicate parallel group design trials, whereas black bars represent crossover design trials. P-values and effect sizes (i.e. Cohen's d) are provided inside each bar where this information is available. Exercise bout duration is provided in minutes (Kerr et al., 2006 consisted of 5km runs, which we characterised as less than 30 min; whereas Turner et al., 2017 included 6km runs, which we characterised as >30 min). The name on top of each bar represents the study: Foch=Focht, 2009; Kerr=Kerr, 2006; McMu=McMurray, 1998; Nied=Niedermeier, 2017; Nisb=Nisbet, 2011; Peac=Peacock, 2008; Ride=Rider & Bodner, 2016; Roge=Rogerson, 2016; Turn=Turner & Stevinson, 2017. Key: EFI: Exercise-Induced Feeling Inventory; FS: Feeling Scale; FAS: Felt Arousal Scale; GAS: General Affect Scale; PANAS: Postive and Negative Affect Schedule; POMS: Profle of Mood States; TESI: Tension and Effort Stress Inventory; TMD: Total Mood Disturbance. *Replication study results.

effect of real green exercise versus indoor exercise on measures related to calmness. The two trials finding a statistical effect of green exercise reported small to large effects (d = 0.27 and 1.09). Half (4/8) of the trials that included a measure of anxiety/tension/worry found a favourable statistical effect of real green exercise versus indoor exercise. These four crossover trials used walking as a mode of exercise, three trials employed a non-randomised design and the other was randomised, and two trials had sample sizes below 20 participants. Out of the six trials (2 RXTs and 4 non-RXTs), only two non-RXTs found a beneficial statistical effect of green exercise versus indoor exercise on anger. These same two trials also found a statistical improvement in depression. Statistically lower fatigue scores were observed with green versus indoor exercise in three (1 RCT, 1 RXT, and 1 non-RXT) of the seven trials that included this outcome. Plante et al. (2003), however, observed a statistical effect only in female participants. Only one non-RXT reported statistical improvements in confusion with green versus indoor exercise. Compared with equivalent duration indoor treadmill walking, a statistical improvement in happiness (including elation) was observed after 3 h of mountain hiking (Niedermeier et al., 2016), but not after a 60 min nature walk (Teas et al., 2007).

Three out of four trials found statistically higher enjoyment or satisfaction scores after real green exercise (10 and 20 min walks, and 12 km run) versus indoor exercise (see Figure 3.3). One trial reported slightly higher average enjoyment (0–5 scale) scores after green exercise compared with indoor exercise condition, but did not perform a statistical analysis (Peacock et al., 2007). In Rider and Bodner (2016), 11 of the 21 participants chose a nature walk as more enjoyable compared with an indoor walk.

Some emotion outcomes were reported only in one trial; therefore, we provide a narrative summary of these outcomes. Compared with 60 min of treadmill walking, one non-RXT trial (Teas et al., 2007) found a statistical improvement in pleased (p = .03) and frustrated (p = .03), but not in delighted (p = .05), and joy (p = .07) scores following a 60 min walk in nature. Compared with indoor exercise, green exercise resulted in statistically higher fascination and nature relatedness (p<.01, d = 1.13 and p<.01, d = 0.86, respectively) in one trial (Nisbet & Zelenski, 2011), and self-esteem in another (Peacock et al., 2007, p<.05). Kerr et al. (2006) reported statistically greater feelings of pride (p<.05) in recreational runners and higher tension stress and effort stress scores in competitive athletes (λ = 0.82, p<.05) after green versus indoor exercise (5 km run). No statistical between-group differences were found in total pleasant somatic, total unpleasant, total unpleasant somatic emotions, and other emotions (boredom, placidity, anger, provocativeness, humiliation, modesty, shame, gratitude, resentment, virtue, and guilt). Lastly Niedermeier et al. (2016) reported no statistical effect of three hours of mountain hiking versus treadmill walking on contemplation (p = .272).

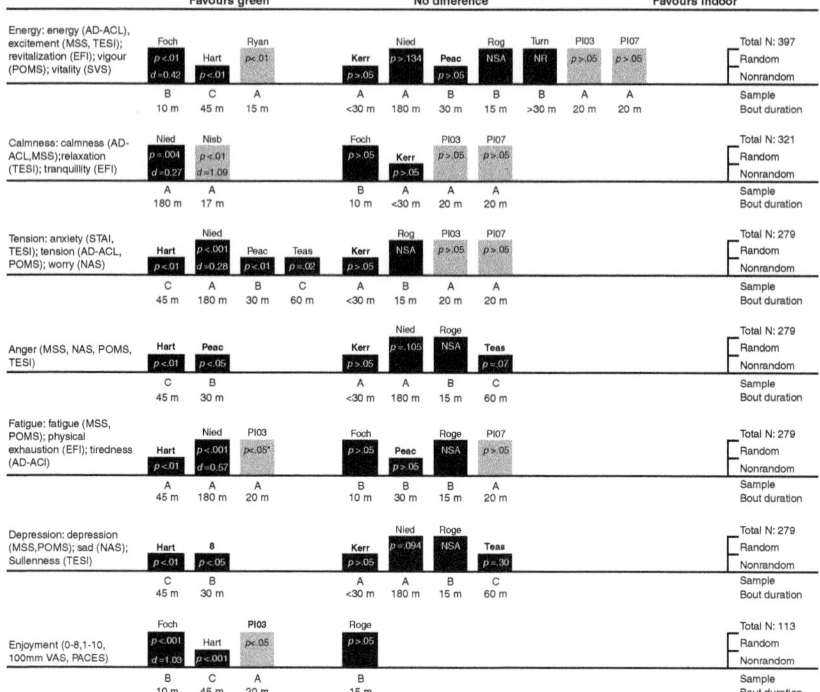

FIGURE 3.3 Harvest plots of trials investigating emotion in outdoor green exercise versus indoor exercise without exposure to nature. A: studies with ≥40 participants; B: studies with 20–39 patients; C: studies with <19 patients. We also provide the total sample across trials for each comparison. The large bars represent randomised trials in this comparison, and small bars represent non-randomised trials. Grey bars indicate parallel group design trials, whereas black bars represent crossover design trials. P-values and effect sizes (i.e. Cohen's d) are provided inside each bar where this information is available. Exercise bout duration is provided in minutes (Kerr et al., 2006 consisted of 5km runs, which we characterised as less than 30 min; whereas Turner et al., 2017 included 6km runs, which we characterised as >30 min). The name on top of each bar represents the study: Foch=Focht, 2009; Hart=Harte & Eifert, 1995; Kerr=Kerr, 2006; Nied=Niedermeier, 2017; Nisb=Nisbet, 2011; Peac=Peacock, 2008; Pl03=Plante, 2003; Pl07=Plante, 2007; Ride=Rider & Bodner, 2016; Roge=Rogerson, 2016; Ryan=Ryan, 2010; Teas=Teas, 2017; Turn=Turner & Stevinson, 2017. **Key:** AD-ACL: Activation-Deactivation Adjective Check List; EFI: Exercise-Induced Feeling Inventory; GAS: General Affect Scale; MSS: Mood Scale Score; NAS: Negative Affect Scale; PACES: Physical Activity Enjoyment Scale; PANAS: Postive and Negative Affect Schedule; PAS: Positive Affect Scale; POMS: Profle of Mood States; STAI: State-Trait Anxiety Inventory; SVS: Subjective Vitality Scale; TESI: Tension and Effort Stress Inventory; VAS: Visual Analogue Scale.

Intention for future exercise behaviour and social interaction time

One trial (Focht, 2009) found statistically greater intention for future participation ($p<.001$; $d = 0.92$) following outdoor versus indoor walking, whereas another trial found no between-group differences (Rogerson et al., 2016). The latter trial did report a statistical greater social interaction time (via direct observation) for green versus indoor exercise ($p<.001$, $\eta p^2 = 0.67$).

Attention and memory

Two crossover trials reported statistically improved attention [via a 28-item checklist of words, $p<.001$ (Harte & Eifert, 1995); and digit span backwards task, $p = .02$, (Rogerson et al., 2016)]. Mieras et al. (2014), however, reported no between-condition differences in Tammen attentional focus scale scores ($p = .261$). Similarly, Rider and Bodner (2016) found no statistical effect of 10-min walks in nature, urban, and indoor environments on recall and recognition for word lists.

Perceived exertion, cardiovascular responses, and exercise performance

Six trials (5 RXTs and 1 non-RXT) that measured perceived exertion via Borg's RPE scale (6–20) reported no statistical difference between conditions (Figure 3.4). Two RXTs reported statistically higher heart rates during an outdoor exercise condition versus indoor [$p<.05$ (Mieras et al., 2014); $p = .001$, $d = 0.59$ (Niedermeier et al., 2016)]. Another two trials found similar between-condition heart rate responses (Focht, 2009; McMurray et al., 1988). McMurray et al. (1988) also found similar oxygen uptake and beta-endorphin responses, but statistically higher average blood lactate values after green exercise compared with indoor exercise (mean: 4.1 vs. 1.8 mmol/L). No statistical differences were found in blood pressure responses (Harte & Eifert, 1995; Niedermeier et al., 2016) or heart rate variability (Niedermeier et al., 2016) with real green versus indoor exercise.

Mieras et al. (2014), powered to detect power output differences, found statistically higher power output ($p<.001$), lower time to completion ($p<.001$), larger thermal gradient for heat dissipation ($p<.001$), lower skin temperature ($p<.001$), but not core temperature, urine specific gravity, bodyweight, or sweat rate, with outdoor versus indoor cycling. Conversely, one trial each found similar between-conditions time to completion (Turner & Stevinson, 2017, $p = .64$) and self-chosen walking speeds (Teas et al., 2007, $p>.05$). Carvalho and colleagues (2010) observed that patients recovering from stroke with a self-selected walking speed of ≥0.8m/s covered statistically greater distances in six-minute walk test outdoors compared with indoors ($p = .01$), but no differences in those with slower walking speeds and 30-m walk performance.

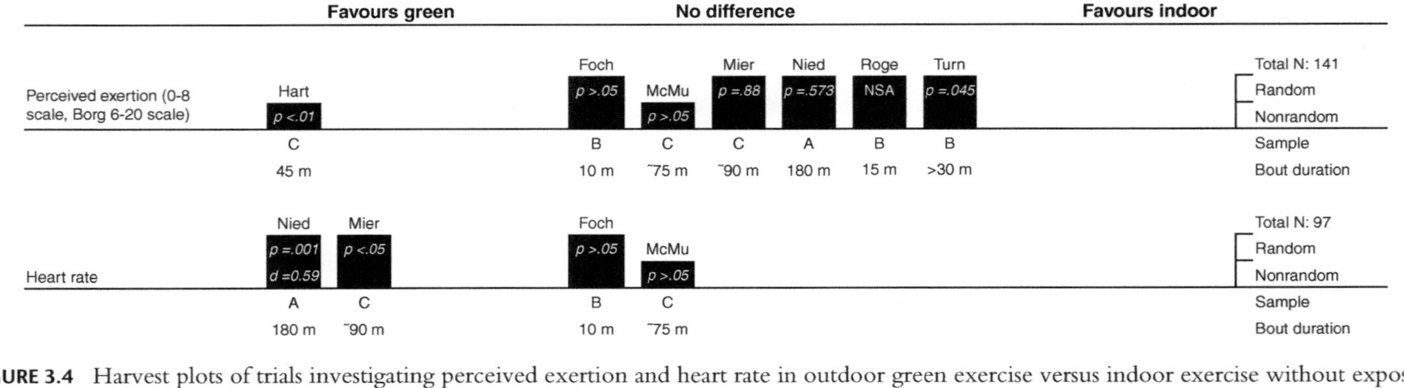

FIGURE 3.4 Harvest plots of trials investigating perceived exertion and heart rate in outdoor green exercise versus indoor exercise without exposure to nature. A: studies with ≥40 participants; B: studies with 20–39 patients; C: studies with <19 patients. We also provide the total sample across trials for each comparison. The large bars represent randomised trials in this comparison, and small bars represent non-randomised trials. Grey bars indicate parallel group design trials, whereas black bars represent crossover design trials. P-values and effect sizes (i.e. Cohen's d) are provided inside each bar where this information is available. Exercise bout duration is provided in minutes (Turner et al., 2017 included 6km runs, which we characterised as >30 min). The name on top of each bar represents the study: Foch=Focht, 2009; Hart=Harte & Eifert, 1995; McMu=McMurray, 1998; Mier=Mieras 2014; Nied=Niedermeier, 2017; Roge=Rogerson, 2016; Turn=Turner & Stevinson, 2017.

Biomarkers

Of the three crossover trials that included a measure of salivary cortisol, one reported differences between-conditions only for statistically higher cortisol after the indoor run with internal attention focus (Harte & Eifert, 1995), another found no statistical difference between groups (Niedermeier et al., 2016), whereas the other trial only examined associations between moods and post-exercise salivary cortisol and log alpha amylase (no environmental effects were examined) (Teas et al., 2007). Harte and Eifert (1995) also observed statistically higher noradrenaline concentrations but not adrenalin, with green versus indoor exercise.

3. Acute effects of virtual green exercise versus indoor exercise without exposure to nature

Four crossover trials and one RCT compared the effects of acute virtual green exercise conditions with other indoor exercise conditions [blank/neutral screen (Duncan et al., 2014; Plante et al., 2003; Rogerson & Barton, 2015; White et al., 2015); self-selected entertainment conditions (Yeh et al., 2017)].

General affect

One RXT (White et al., 2015) revealed statistically higher affective valence (via FS) scores pre to 5-min during cycling exercise for virtual green versus indoor exercise ($p<.001$). However, no statistically significant time by condition interaction was observed for perceived activation scores (via FAS).

Emotions

For emotion outcomes, one RCT (Plante et al., 2003) and two non-RXT (Duncan et al., 2014; Yeh et al., 2017) reported no statistical differences between virtual green exercise and indoor exercise (for energy, fatigue/tiredness, calmness, and anger; Figure 3.5). Only one trial found statistically lower tension after indoor exercise compared with after virtual green exercise, but this finding was only observed in women (Plante et al., 2003). Of the other emotions, Yeh and colleagues (2017) found participants were happier in groups exercising while exposed to either a dynamic or static nature image compared with self-selected entertainment ($p<.05$). All three trials included exercise bouts with durations of 15 or 20 min, and two of the trials had relatively small sample sizes (≤30). None of the trials included a power calculation or primary outcomes.

White and colleagues (2015) observed that participants in a virtual green exercise condition reported a more positive evaluation (0–6 scale), and a greater preference and willingness to repeat the exercise ($p<.001$), compared those who exercised while viewing a blank wall (p's$<.001$).

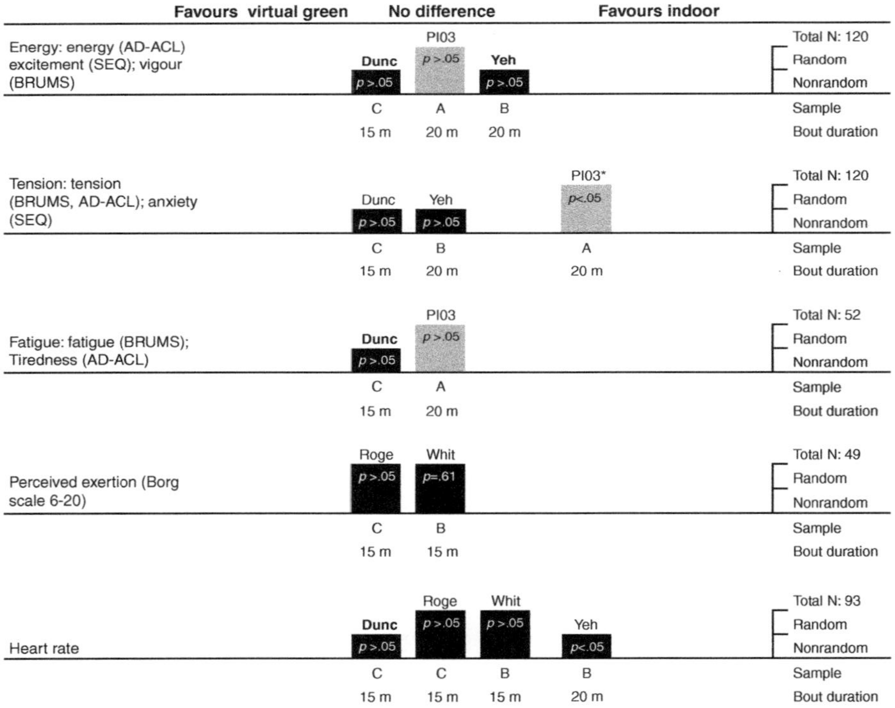

Favours virtual green | No difference | Favours indoor

Energy: energy (AD-ACL) excitement (SEQ); vigour (BRUMS)
Dunc p >.05 | PI03 p >.05 | Yeh p >.05
Sample: C | A | B
Bout duration: 15 m | 20 m | 20 m
Total N: 120 — Random / Nonrandom

Tension: tension (BRUMS, AD-ACL); anxiety (SEQ)
Dunc p >.05 | Yeh p >.05 | PI03* p<.05
Sample: C | B | A
Bout duration: 15 m | 20 m | 20 m
Total N: 120 — Random / Nonrandom

Fatigue: fatigue (BRUMS); Tiredness (AD-ACL)
Dunc p >.05 | PI03 p >.05
Sample: C | A
Bout duration: 15 m | 20 m
Total N: 52 — Random / Nonrandom

Perceived exertion (Borg scale 6-20)
Roge p >.05 | Whit p=.61
Sample: C | B
Bout duration: 15 m | 15 m
Total N: 49 — Random / Nonrandom

Heart rate
Dunc p >.05 | Roge p >.05 | Whit p >.05 | Yeh p<.05
Sample: C | C | B | B
Bout duration: 15 m | 15 m | 15 m | 20 m
Total N: 93 — Random / Nonrandom

FIGURE 3.5 Harvest plots of trials investigating effects of virtual green exercise versus indoor exercise. A: studies with ≥40 participants; B: studies with 20–39 patients; C: studies with <19 patients. We also provide the total sample across trials for each comparison. The large bars represent randomised trials in this comparison, and small bars represent non-randomised trials. Grey bars indicate parallel group design trials, whereas black bars represent crossover design trials. P-values and effect sizes (i.e. Cohen's d) are provided inside each bar where this information is available. Exercise bout duration is provided in minutes (Turner et al., 2017 included 6km runs, which we characterised as >30 min). The name on top of each bar represents the study: Foch=Focht, 2009; Hart=Harte & Eifert, 1995; McMu=McMurray, 1998; Mier=Mieras 2014; Nied=Niedermeier, 2017; Roge=Rogerson, 2016; Turn=Turner & Stevinson, 2017.

Attention and time perception

In the one trial (Rogerson & Barton, 2015) that assessed directed attention (via backwards digit span), improvements were found for virtual green exercise ($p<.001$), but not for indoor exercise. Another trial observed no statistical differences on time perception between the simulated green and indoor blank screen exercise conditions (White et al., 2015).

Perceived exertion, exercise intensity, cardiovascular responses, and exercise performance

Two RXTs (Rogerson & Barton, 2015; White et al., 2015) found no statistical differences in perceived exertion scores (via Borg's RPE 6–20 scale) between 15 min of virtual green exercise and indoor exercise conditions. One non-RXT (Yeh et al., 2017) found statistically higher heart rates when participants exercised with self-selected entertainment versus with exposure to a dynamic nature image and a static nature image ($p<.05$). Conversely, three trials (2 RXTs and 1 non-RXT) observed no statistical between-group differences in heart rate. In one RXT, no statistical differences in energy expenditure and respiratory exchange ratio were found between exercise conditions (Rogerson & Barton, 2015).

Duncan and co-workers (Duncan et al., 2014) reported that systolic blood pressure 15-min post-exercise was statistically lower after virtual green cycling exercise compared with cycling while viewing a blank screen ($p = .01$). No statistical differences were observed between the conditions for diastolic blood pressure. Similarly, White et al. (2015) reported no statistical time by environment interaction for mean arterial pressure. Yeh et al. (2017) reported statistically greater distance run in the self-selected entertainment compared with the static nature image condition (p<.05), but not the dynamic nature image. Whereas, the RXT reported no statistical between-conditions differences in time to exhaustion ($p = .203$) (Rogerson & Barton, 2015).

Discussion

This current review updates and expands upon the work of Thompson Coon et al. (2011), who systematically reviewed studies comparing green exercise with indoor exercise to examine evidence for potential added health benefits of green exercise. We identified 27 eligible trials (17 trials from the updated search and 10 from Thompson Coon et al., 2011) that made various comparisons between green exercise and indoor exercise (i.e. real green exercise vs. indoor exercise; virtual green exercise vs. indoor exercise; or real green exercise vs. virtual green exercise).

Across the 27 eligible studies, we found largely inconclusive evidence that green exercise is more beneficial than indoor exercise. In our meta-analysis of three RCTs investigating the longitudinal effects of repeated episodes of green versus indoor exercise, the only statistical findings were slightly higher post-intervention diastolic blood pressure and lower perceived exertion values with green exercise. It was not possible to make conclusions regarding many of the outcomes assessed in the longitudinal trials because most of the outcomes were assessed by only one study.

Of the affect and emotion outcomes examined in the 16 acute trials that compared outdoor (real) green exercise with indoor exercise without exposure to nature, only affective valence appeared to be more favourably affected by green exercise compared with indoor exercise—although the number of trials that assessed this outcome was small. More studies (3 out of 4) reported greater enjoyment or satisfaction after green versus indoor exercise. There were, however, consistent null findings (6 out of 7 trials) for the effect of green versus indoor exercise on perceived exertion, and equivocal findings for the effects on exercise intensity (walking/running speed, and heart rate). Compared with indoor exercise, we found no consistent statistical effects on energy, tension, fatigue, perceived exertion, or heart rate with virtual green exercise.

The lack of consistent findings in the current review is in slight contrast with a previous meta-analysis (Bowler et al., 2010), which found statistically more favourable feelings of energy, anxiety, anger, fatigue, and sadness after direct exposure to a natural versus synthetic environment. In addition to the inclusion of a greater number of more recent trials, there are three important differences between the current review and Bowler and colleagues (2010), which make comparisons between the two reviews difficult. Firstly, in addition to green exercise conditions, Bowler et al. (2010) included non-exercise conditions that involved exposure to a natural environment while remaining passive or sedentary. Secondly, Bowler and colleagues (2010) "synthetic environment" conditions included built outdoor environments as well as indoor environments. Finally, Bowler et al. (2010) performed a meta-analysis of outcomes, whereas, in the current review, in agreement with Thompson Coon et al. (2011), we decided this approach would not be appropriate (due to a paucity of reported paired analysis). In their meta-analysis, Bowler et al. (2010) did not take trial design into consideration, treating crossover trials as comparative trials (i.e. assumes treatment arms are independent), and combined both trial designs in the meta-analysis. This is the least desirable approach to combining crossover trials, and can overestimate the variability of the within-study treatment effect (Nolan et al., 2016).

In the 2011 systematic review, Thompson Coon et al. found favourable effects on feelings of anger, confusion, depression, energy, enjoyment and satisfaction, positive engagement, revitalisation, and tension, but negative effects on feelings of calmness, with green exercise compared with exercising indoors. Similar to the current review, Thompson Coon and colleagues (2011) identified a number of issues with the available evidence, such as poor methodological quality and the diversity of outcome measures assessed, that impedes the interpretation and generalisation of findings. These common methodological issues include: i) small sample sizes and inadequate statistical power (only 4 trials performed a power calculation); ii) dearth of longitudinal studies; iii) insufficient or unclear wash-out periods in trials with crossover design, meaning that effects of one environmental exposure might have influenced responses to the subsequent environment; iv) risk of bias through lack of randomisation, non-blinding of outcome assessors, and potential contamination in controls (e.g., possible exposure to green environments on way to indoor facilities); v) limited generalisability of evidence due to overrepresentation of young, university student participants; vi) heterogeneity of "green" setting, exercise (duration and type), and outcome variables (very few trials measured the same outcomes); vii) lack of control of the exercise intensity; viii) use of only single episodes of exercise (repeated bout effects are unknown); and viii) lack of control for multiple comparisons (only three trials corrected for this).

The absence of multiple comparison control combined with low statistical power has likely led to an increased risk of type I (false positives: a statistically significant *p*-value when null hypothesis is true) and type II (false negatives: a non-statistically significant *p*-value when null hypothesis is false) errors across the included trials. Furthermore, because the analyses performed may have lacked statistical power to detect a true effect, trials cannot claim there is no effect when $p<.05$ (Lakens, 2017). There is, therefore, great uncertainty regarding the effects of real or virtual green exercise versus indoor exercise.

Within this field, there will be an inevitable tension between the need for internal and ecological validity; that is, trying to control for the effects of extraneous factors, while allowing responses to environmental exposures that are "typical" or "real". However, based on the studies reviewed here, there is a clear need for researchers to conduct trials with large enough samples to achieve sufficient statistical power and to improve methodological rigour through, for example, using appropriate randomisation, allocation concealment, and blinding procedures, and sufficient wash-out periods. Better reporting of crossover trials is required so future trials can be combined in meta-analysis—crossover trial authors should follow guidance provided in a recent CONSORT extension to within-person randomised trials (Pandis, Chung, Scherer, Elbourne, & Altman, 2017). More studies assessing the long-term effects of green exercise are needed, as well studies assessing the adherence to and cost-effectiveness of green exercise compared with exercising indoors. More studies assessing the long-term effects of green exercise are needed, as well studies assessing the adherence to and cost-effectiveness of green exercise compared with exercising indoors.

We unfortunately failed to achieve the primary objective of our review—to establish the known of the effects of green exercise—instead, we appear to have uncovered only further known unknowns.

References

Bowler, D., Buyung-Ali, L., Knight, T., & Pullin, A. (2010). A systematic review of evidence for the added benefits to health of exposure to natural environments. *BMC Public Health*, *10*(1), 456.

Calogiuri, G., & Chroni, S. (2014). The impact of the natural environment on the promotion of active living: an integrative systematic review. *BMC Public Health*, *14*, 873. doi:10.1186/1471-2458-14-873

Calogiuri, G., Evensen, K., Weydahl, A., Andersson, K., Patil, G., Ihlebæk, C., & Raanaas, R. K. (2016). Green exercise as a workplace intervention to reduce job stress. Results from a pilot study. *Work*. https://doi.org/10.3233/WOR-152219

Calogiuri, G., Nordtug, H., & Weydahl, A. (2015). The potential of using exercise in nature as an intervention to enhance exercise behavior: Results from a pilot study. *Perceptual and Motor Skills*, *121*(2), 350–370. https://doi.org/10.2466/06.PMS.121c17x0

Carvalho, C., Sunnerhagen, K. S., & Willén, C. (2010). Walking speed and distance in different environments of subjects in the later stage post-stroke. *Physiotherapy Theory and Practice*. https://doi.org/10.3109/09593980903585042

Crowther, M., Avenell, A., Maclennan, G., & Mowatt, G. (2011). A further use for the Harvest plot: A novel method for the presentation of data synthesis. *Research Synthesis Methods*. https://doi.org/10.1002/jrsm.37

DerSimonian, R., & Laird, N. (1986). Meta-analysis in clinical trials. *Controlled Clinical Trials*, 7, 177–188. https://doi.org/10.1016/0197-2456(86)90046-2

Ding, H., Hu, G. L., Zheng, X. Y., Chen, Q., Threapleton, D. E., & Zhou, Z. H. (2015). The method quality of cross-over studies involved in Cochrane Systematic Reviews. *PLoS One*, *10*(4), e0120519. https://doi.org/10.1371/journal.pone.0120519

Duncan, M., Clarke, N., Birch, S., Tallis, J., Hankey, J., Bryant, E., & Eyre, E. (2014). The effect of green exercise on blood pressure, heart rate and mood state in primary school children. *International Journal of Environmental Research and Public Health*, *11*(4), 3678–3688.

Durstine, J. L., Gordon, B., Wang, Z., & Luo, X. (2013). Chronic disease and the link to physical activity. *Journal of Sport and Health Science*, *2*(1), 3–11. https://doi.org/10.1016/j.jshs.2012.07.009

Elbourne, D. R., Altman, D. G., Higgins, J. P. T., Curtin, F., Worthington, H. V., & Vail, A. (2002). Meta-analyses involving cross-over trials: Methodological issues. *International Journal of Epidemiology*, *31*, 140–149. https://doi.org/10.1093/ije/31.1.140

Focht, B. C. (2009). Brief walks in outdoor and laboratory environments: Effects on affective responses, enjoyment, and intentions to walk for exercise. *Research Quarterly for Exercise and Sport*. https://doi.org/10.1080/02701367.2009.10599600

Harte, J. L., & Eifert, G. H. (1995). The effects of running, environment, and attentional focus on athletes' catecholamine and cortisol levels and mood. *Psychophysiology*, *32*, 49–54.

Hartig, T., Mitchell, R., de Vries, S., & Frumkin, H. (2014). Nature and health. *Annual Review of Public Health*, *35*, 207–228.

Higgins, J. P. T., & Green, S. (2011). *Cochrane handbook for systematic reviews of interventions*. Version 5.1.0 [updated March 2011]. London, UK: The Cochrane Collaboration.

Hug, S. M., Hansmann, R., Monn, C., Krütli, P., & Seeland, K. (2008). Restorative effects of physical activity in forests and indoor settings. *International Journal of Fitness*, *4*(2), 25–37.

Irandoust, K., & Taheri, M. (2017). The effect of vitamin D supplement and indoor vs outdoor physical activity on depression of obese depressed women. *Asian Journal of Sports Medicine*. https://doi.org/10.5812/asjsm.13311

Joseph, R. P., & Maddock, J. E. (2016). Observational Park-based physical activity studies: A systematic review of the literature. *Preventive Medicine*, *89*, 257–277. https://doi.org/10.1016/j.ypmed.2016.06.016

Kaczynski, A. T., & Henderson, K. A. (2007). Environmental correlates of physical activity: A review of evidence about parks and recreation. *Leisure Sciences*, *29*, 315–354.

Kerr, J. H., Fujiyama, H., Sugano, A., Okamura, T., Chang, M., & Onouha, F. (2006). Psychological responses to exercising in laboratory and natural environments. *Psychology of Sport and Exercise*, 7, 345–359.

Lacharité-Lemieux, M., Brunelle, J. P., & Dionne, I. J. (2015). Adherence to exercise and affective responses: Comparison between outdoor and indoor training. *Menopause*. https://doi.org/10.1097/GME.0000000000000366

Lacharité-Lemieux, M., & Dionne, I. J. (2016). Physiological responses to indoor versus outdoor training in postmenopausal women. *Journal of Aging and Physical Activity*, *24*(2), 275–283. https://doi.org/10.1123/japa.2015-0019

Lachowycz, K., & Jones, A. P. (2011). Greenspace and obesity: A systematic review of the evidence. *Obesity Reviews*, *12*(5), e183–e189. https://doi.org/10.1111/j.1467-789X.2010.00827.x

Lakens, D. (2017). Equivalence tests: A practical primer for t tests, correlations, and meta-analyses. *Social Psychological and Personality Science*, *8*(4), 355–362. https://doi.org/10.1177/1948550617697177

Lee, A., & Maheswaran, R. (2011). The health benefits of urban green spaces: A review of the evidence. *Journal of Public Health*, *33*. https://doi.org/10.1093/pubmed/fdq068

McMurray, R. G., Berry, M. J., Vann, R. T., Hardy, C. J., & Sheps, D. S. (1988). The effect of running in an outdoor environment on plasma beta endorphins. *Annals of Sports Medicine*, *3*(4), 230–233.

Mieras, M. E., Heesch, M. W. S., & Slivka, D. R. (2014). Physiological and psychological responses to outdoor vs. laboratory cycling. *Journal of Strength and Conditioning Research*. https://doi.org/10.1519/JSC.0000000000000384

Niedermeier, M., Einwanger, J., & Hartl, A. (2016). Acute affective responses in uphill mountain hiking-a randomised controlled trial. *European Health Psychologist*, *18*(S), 1044.

Niedermeier, M., Einwanger, J., Hartl, A., & Kopp, M. (2017). Affective responses in mountain hiking—A randomized crossover trial focusing on differences between indoor and outdoor activity. *PLoS One*. https://doi.org/10.1371/journal.pone.0177719

Nisbet, E. K., & Zelenski, J. M. (2011). Underestimating nearby nature: Affective forecasting errors obscure the happy path to sustainability. *Psychological Science*. https://doi.org/10.1177/0956797611418527

Nolan, S. J., Hambleton, I., & Dwan, K. (2016) The Use and Reporting of the Cross-Over Study Design in Clinical Trials and Systematic Reviews: A Systematic Assessment. *PLoS ONE*, 11, e0159014.

Ogilvie, D., Fayter, D., Petticrew, M., Sowden, A., Thomas, S., Whitehead, M., & Worthy, G. (2008). The harvest plot: A method for synthesising evidence about the differential effects of interventions. *BMC Medical Research Methodology*. https://doi.org/10.1186/1471-2288-8-8

Pandis, N., Chung, B., Scherer, R. W., Elbourne, D., & Altman, D. G. (2017). CONSORT 2010 statement: Extension checklist for reporting within person randomised trials. *BMJ (Online)*. https://doi.org/10.1136/bmj.j2835

Peacock, J., Hine, R., & Pretty, J. (2007). *Got the blues, then find some greenspace: The mental health benefits of green exercise activities and green care*. Mind Week Report. Available online: http://psykinfo.regionsyddanmark.dk/dwn109161.pdf (accessed on 1 March 2019).

Pennebaker, J. W., & Lightner, J. M. (1980). Competition of internal and external information in an exercise setting. *Journal of Personality and Social Psychology, 39*(1), 165–174. https://doi.org/10.1037/0022-3514.39.1.165

Plante, T. G., Aldridge, A., Su, D., Bogdan, R., Belo, M., & Kahn, K. (2003). Does virtual reality enhance the management of stress when paired with exercise? An exploratory study. *International Journal of Stress Management*. https://doi.org/10.1037/1072-5245.10.3.203

Plante, T. G., Gores, C., Brecht, C., Carrow, J., Imbs, A., & Willemsen, E. (2007). Does exercise environment enhance the psychological benefits of exercise for women? *International Journal of Stress Management, 14*, 88–98.

Rider, N., & Bodner, G. (2016). Does taking a walk in nature enhance long-term memory? *Ecopsychology*. https://doi.org/10.1089/eco.2015.0042

Rogerson, M., & Barton, J. (2015). Effects of the visual exercise environments on cognitive directed attention, energy expenditure and perceived exertion. *International Journal of Environmental Research and Public Health*. https://doi.org/10.3390/ijerph120707321

Rogerson, M., Gladwell, V. F., Gallagher, D. J., & Barton, J. L. (2016). Influences of green outdoors versus indoors environmental settings on psychological and social outcomes of controlled exercise. *International Journal of Environmental Research and Public Health*. https://doi.org/10.3390/ijerph13040363

Ryan, R. M., Weinstein, N., Bernstein, J., Brown, K. W., Mistretta, L., & Gagné, M. (2010). Vitalizing effects of being outdoors and in nature. *Journal of Environmental Psychology*. https://doi.org/10.1016/j.jenvp.2009.10.009

Teas, J., Hurley, T., & Ghumare, S. (2007). Walking outside improves mood for healthy post-menopausal women. *Clinical Medicine Insights: Oncology, 2007*, 35. (CMO-1-Teas-et-al)

Thompson Coon, J., Boddy, K., Stein, K., Whear, R., Barton, J., & Depledge, M. H. (2011). Does participating in physical activity in outdoor natural environments have a greater effect on physical and mental wellbeing than physical activity indoors? A systematic review. *Environmental Science & Technology, 45*(5), 1761–1772. https://doi.org/10.1021/es102947t

Turner, T. L., & Stevinson, C. (2017). Affective outcomes during and after high-intensity exercise in outdoor green and indoor gym settings. *International Journal of Environmental Health Research*. https://doi.org/10.1080/09603123.2017.1282605

White, M. P., Pahl, S., Ashbullby, K. J., Burton, F., & Depledge, M. H. (2015). The effects of exercising in different natural environments on psycho-physiological outcomes in post-menopausal women: A simulation study. *International Journal of Environmental Research and Public Health*. https://doi.org/10.3390/ijerph120911929

World Health Organization. (2010). *Global recommendations on physical activity for health*. Geneva: WHO.

Yeh, H. P., Stone, J. A., Churchill, S. M., Brymer, E., & Davids, K. (2017). Physical and emotional benefits of different exercise environments designed for treadmill running. *International Journal of Environmental Research and Public Health*. https://doi.org/10.3390/ijerph14070752

4

THE GREEN EXERCISE CONCEPT

Two intertwining pathways to health and well-being

Mike Rogerson, Jo Barton, Jules Pretty and Valerie Gladwell

The green exercise concept and the two potential pathways

Over the last 15 years, researchers have examined how and why environmental exercise settings might influence health and well-being. 'Green exercise' – a term coined by researchers at the University of Essex in 2003, refers to engaging in physical activity whilst simultaneously experiencing nature (Pretty, 2004; Pretty, Griffin, Sellens, & Pretty, 2003; Pretty, Peacock, Sellens, & Griffin, 2005), and has sometimes been referred to as 'exercise squared' (Selhub & Logan, 2012). The concept blends the psychological, physiological, social and other benefits of exercise, with those promoted by nature-based environments such as parks, woodlands and countryside. A systematic review of research in this area showed that compared with either indoor, or more 'built' urban outdoor environments, green spaces such as parks can boost the mood- and self-esteem-enhancing properties of exercise (Thompson Coon et al., 2011). Green exercise can benefit all social groups (Gladwell, Brown, Wood, Sandercock, & Barton, 2013). For example, although a meta-analysis found that the extent of green exercise-associated mood and self-esteem improvements are influenced by age and sex (Barton & Pretty, 2010), the majority of such well-being benefits from participation are universally obtainable across those and a range of other factors (Rogerson, Brown, Sandercock, Wooller, & Barton, 2015).

To date, research has demonstrated that there are two pathways by which environments influence exercise outcomes. **Firstly**, simple exposure to nature is both acutely and chronically salutogenic (Berman, Jonides, & Kaplan, 2008; Keniger, Gaston, Irvine, & Fuller, 2013; Seymour, 2016), and exercise facilitates access to nature and green space. In this context, it has been important for research to establish whether the outlined benefits of nature environments are attainable during exercise to the same extent as they are via simple exposure at rest. **Second**, environments shape behaviours, including exercise behaviours, which themselves influence health and well-being (Figure 4.1). Just as having chairs in a room encourages people to sit rather than stand, outdoor, natural settings and green spaces facilitate certain exercise behaviours that indoor, or more urbanised environments do not. Further to facilitating exercise in the first place, environments also shape how that behaviour progresses, and how it is experienced. Blue space (spaces including water) is as important as green: it is not the colour that matters but the opportunity to behave in a particular way that improves well-being (White et al., 2016b).

Brymer et al. outline that at the level of individual-environment interaction, affordances (behavioural invitations or possibilities) exist, which are products of characteristics relating to both the individual and environment (Brymer & Davids, 2012, 2014). In this way, ecological dynamics can be considered to underpin both proposed pathways (Figure 4.1).

Health encompasses physical, mental, and social well-being (Grad, 2002). In this chapter, we draw on green exercise research findings to demonstrate how our proposed two intertwining pathways influence each of these facets of health and well-being.

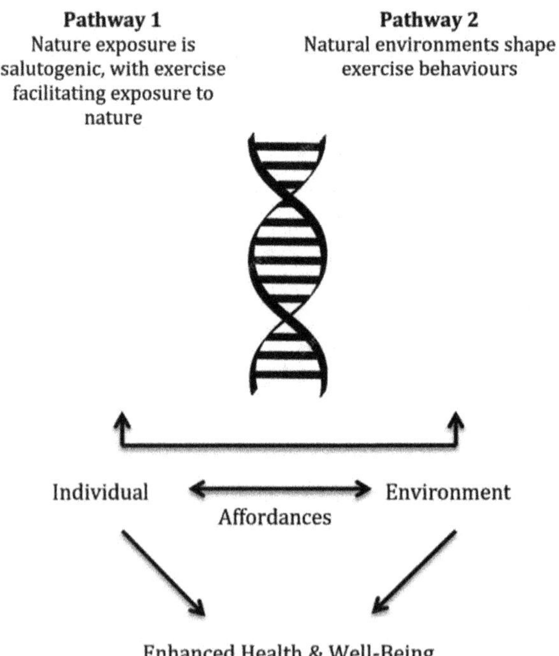

FIGURE 4.1 Two intertwining pathways showing how environments influence exercise and health-related outcomes

Psychological benefits of both pathways

Nature exposure promotes psychological health

Positive acute influences of exposure to nature on affect and well-being have been reported. Often compared with urban or 'built' environment types, simple exposure to nature environments is psychologically restorative (Chang, Chen, Hammitt, & Machnik, 2007), has beneficial influences on individuals' emotions (Mayer, Frantz, Bruehlman-Senecal, & Dolliver, 2008; Ulrich, 1979; Ulrich et al., 1991) and enhances the ability to reflect on life problems (Mayer et al., 2008). Theoretical explanations for some of these reported influences of nature environments on human psychological well-being have been suggested. From a psycho-evolutionary perspective, humans have, until very recently, always lived, survived and thrived in natural environments, so it makes sense that when there is an absence of perceived threat, we respond in an emotionally positive way to these places (Pretty, 2014).

Further, the Stress Reduction Theory hypothesises that natural environments provide positive distractions from daily stresses and invoke feelings of interest, pleasantness and calm, thereby reducing stress symptoms and promoting positive affect (Ewert, Overholt, Voight, & Wang, 2011; Herzog & Strevey, 2008; Ulrich, 1984, 1981). Simple exposure to nature is associated with reductions in stress measures such as blood pressure (although physiological markers of stress are often measured, original perception of the stressor in these cases is psychological), heart rate and stress hormones. After viewing a psychologically stressful video, viewing scenes of nature improves recovery of parasympathetic activity, compared to viewing urban scenes (Ulrich et al., 1991). Similarly, viewing nature scenes prior to a stressor also improves autonomic recovery from a state of stress (Brown, Barton, & Gladwell, 2013). Viewing still images of natural scenes elicits lower heart rate compared to a baseline measure, than do urban scenes (Laumann, Gärling, & Stormark, 2003).

Furthermore, Attention Restoration Theory (Kaplan & Kaplan, 1989; Kaplan, 1995) suggests that one's affective state is linked to attentional resources, and defines two types of attention: directed attention and involuntary attention. Directed attention, which we regularly use in our everyday lives, involves mental effort and concentration, and if overused leads to directed attention fatigue, accompanied by worsened affective state. Natural environments have been shown to promote the use of involuntary attention, providing an opportunity for recovery from mental fatigue, which is associated with positive change in affect (Berman et al., 2008; Taylor & Kuo, 2009). For example, Ottoson and Grahn (2005) reported that resting for one hour in an outdoor garden resulted in greater improvements in directed attention than equivalent rest indoors; whilst nature views or the presence of plants within the workplace have demonstrated reductions in mental fatigue (Berto, 2005; Kaplan, 1993; Raanaas, Evensen, Rich, Sjøstrøm, & Patil, 2011).

Exercise offers participants an opportunity to access these psychological benefits of natural environments. Here, green exercise research has shown that beyond the influences of exercise, nature-based exercise environments promote greater improvements in psychological states than exercise in other environment types. In a systematic review of studies comparing indoor and outdoor physical activity, Thompson Coon et al. (2011) found that, compared with walking indoors, outdoor walking was associated with more positive mood, increased self-esteem, vitality, energy and pleasure, alongside reductions in frustration, worry, confusion, depression and tiredness. Running and other exercise outside has also been associated with lower somatic anxiety, greater satisfaction and greater mood improvements than exercise indoors (Harte & Eifert, 1995; LaCaille, Masters, & Heath, 2004; Lowton, Brymer, Clough, & Denovan, 2017). Walking in oak-sycamore woodland nature settings increases positive affect and reduces anger, whereas urban walks in a city retail and office development promote opposite affective outcomes (Hartig, Evans, Jamner, Davis, & Gärling, 2003). Measures of brain activity have supported the role of environmental settings for psychological restoration. Electroencephalogram data showed that, in line with attention restoration theory, movement from an urban shopping street to a green space was associated with change in brain activity patterns indicative of reductions in arousal, frustration and engagement, and increased meditation (Aspinall, Mavros, Coyne, & Roe, 2015). An investigation of competitive runners failed to identify influence of exercise environments on affective outcomes (Kerr et al., 2006), possibly due to competitive exercisers focusing on internal cues to a greater extent, therefore reducing mindful engagement/immersion with environmental settings. Green exercise also promotes greater pre- to post-exercise restoration of fatigued directed attention than does exercise in other environment types. Berman et al. (2008) found that although walking in a downtown environment and a botanical garden both facilitated improvements in directed attention, the improvement was significantly greater after botanical garden walking. Compared with walks in urban environments, walks in green and blue environments are associated with greater restoration and cognitive function improvements that persist for at least 30-minutes post-exercise (Gidlow et al., 2016). By controlling the exercise component across indoor and outdoor exercise trials (thus ensuring the physiological alterations were similar), Rogerson et al. (2016) concluded that outdoor nature environments facilitate exercise-associated directed attention improvements to a greater extent than indoors (Rogerson & Barton, 2015; Rogerson, Gladwell, Gallagher, & Barton, 2016).

Psychological aspects of environments shaping exercise experiences and behaviour

Environments play an important role in shaping the psychological experience of exercise, which impacts on behavioural aspects of the exercise, which can in turn enhance health and well-being outcomes.

Perceptions of exertion and exercise intensity

Exercise environments can influence perceived exertion, that is, how hard an individual feels they are physically working during activity, and linked to this, the actual physiological intensity of physical activity. In research, perceptions of exertion are usually measured by Borg's Rated Perceived Exertion scale (Borg, 1970; 1982; 1998); and exercise intensity can also be instructively prescribed using the same scale. When exercising at an instructed perceived exertion, individuals work harder (measured by walking speed, heart rate and blood lactate concentration) during outdoor exercise than during indoor treadmill exercise (Ceci & Hassmén, 1991; Dasilva et al., 2011). Concurrently, and perhaps more interestingly in terms of environments shaping behaviour, during self-paced exercise (i.e. no instruction given about exertion levels), individuals walk faster and work harder (measured by heart rate), yet report lower perceived exertion during outdoor walking compared to indoor treadmill walking (Focht, 2009). These findings may be partly explained by the notion that synthetic environments demand greater directed attention processing (Kaplan & Kaplan, 1989; Kaplan, 1995, 2001; Ulrich et al., 1991), as cognitive fatigue makes exercise feel harder and impairs exercise performance (Marcora, Staiano, & Manning, 2009). Additionally, greater extent of optic flow is afforded by exercise in nature environments than when using equipment in a traditional gym setting. Optic flow is defined as the expanding flow on the retina caused by moving through an environment that forms the representational basis of egomotion (estimating motion relative to a rigid or static scene) (Gibson, 1950, 1954; Parry, Chinnasamy, & Micklewright, 2012; Warren & Rushton, 2009). Slower optic flow has been associated with lower perceived exertion during cycling exercise (Parry et al., 2012), however no optic flow occurs when using traditional stationary ergometers in gym settings, and this may be confusing for brain and body. It is proposed that, alongside other factors such as prior experience, optic flow functions as an important cue for an individual's internal 'performance template' (Tucker & Noakes, 2009), which is used to assess fatigue and exertion in relation to performance expectations. Restrictions of this cue, as associated with ergometer-based exercise, may therefore heighten perceived level of exertion.

Future exercise behaviour

Beyond the impact of environments shaping exercise experiences and behaviour in this acute sense, they may also influence exercise behaviour in the longer term. Although there are many confounding factors that can interrupt such a pathway, exercise intensity and perceived exertion can influence future exercise behaviours via affective responses and intention (Dasilva et al., 2011; Ekkekakis, Parfitt, & Petruzzello, 2011; Williams et al., 2008). A repeated finding of research studies is that green exercise is associated with more positive affective valence (such as boosts in mood and self-esteem) compared to equivalent exercise in either indoor, or 'built' or urban settings (Thompson Coon et al., 2011). Environmental settings may thereby provide a mode of manipulation by which adherence to exercise behaviours might be influenced. In a comparison of outcomes of outdoor walks versus laboratory-based treadmill walks, individuals reported significantly greater positive affect and intention to engage in future exercise behaviours following outdoors walking (Focht, 2009). Another study, which focused on postmenopausal women, found that, following a 12-week exercise programme, outdoor exercise led to both significantly greater affective responses and significantly greater adherence compared to indoor exercise (97% versus 91% respectively) (Lacharité-Lemieux, Brunelle, & Dionne, 2015). Green exercise participation also offers opportunity both for individuals to either form or amend their perceptions of specific green spaces (e.g. local parks), and for enhancement of individuals' feelings of nature connection, both of which play an important role in the relationship between green space and physical activity (Flowers, Freeman, & Gladwell, 2016).

Physiological benefits of both pathways

Nature exposure promotes physiological benefits

Numerous direct benefits of acute doses of nature have been reported outside of the exercise context. In China, compared to visiting an urban environment, two-day visits to a forest environment were found to result in reduced oxidative stress and both pro-inflammatory biomarker and serum cortisol levels (Mao et al., 2012). Research in Germany found that spending one day per school week learning in a forest environment benefits children's diurnal cortisol rhythm across the year (Dettweiler, Becker, Auestad, Simon, & Kirsch, 2017). Sitting in forest environments can enhance vagal activity and reduce diastolic blood pressure (Park, Tsunetsugu, Kasetani, Kagawa, & Miyazaki, 2010). Japanese research has highlighted the potentially important role of phytoncides in relation to these physiological impacts. Phytoncides are essential wood oils that are airborne in abundance in forest environments. When inhaled, phytoncides function to regulate sympathetic nervous activity (Tsunetsugu et al., 2007), decrease levels of adrenaline and contribute to an increase in NK cell activity (Li & Kawada, 2013; Li et al., 2009). Indeed, forest bathing (a short, leisurely visit to a forest environment), as a specific example of a nature-based intervention, has been associated with a range of physiological outcomes relating to the immune and endocrine systems (Li, 2016). Under controlled conditions, simply viewing images or videos of nature scenes can enhance vagal activity and decrease heart rate compared to viewing equivalent 'built' urban environments (Gladwell et al., 2012; Laumann et al., 2003; Ulrich et al., 1991). Just as simply viewing nature scenes at rest can elicit acute physiological responses, viewing nature scenes during exercise impacts on post-exercise physiology. In a seminal study, greater reductions in both systolic and diastolic BP were observed after viewing pleasant rural scenes compared to a control (blank wall) and urban unpleasant scenes during gentle jogging (Pretty et al., 2005). Likewise, in a study focusing on a child sample, systolic blood pressure 15 minutes after exercise was significantly lower following green exercise compared to a control condition (Duncan et al., 2014).

Indeed, many such physiological health outcomes seem to be accessible via physical activity. Compared with either exercising in or viewing built or urban scenes during exercise, exercising whilst being exposed to nature environments has significantly greater beneficial effects on blood pressure (Li et al., 2011; Pretty et al., 2005), other measures of cardiovascular and autonomic function (Brown et al., 2013; Brown, Barton, Pretty, & Gladwell, 2014; Gladwell et al., 2013; Gladwell, Kuoppa, Tarvainen, & Rogerson, 2016), and endocrine and immune function (Lee et al., 2012; Li et al., 2007, 2011). For example, compared with walks through a built setting, lunchtime walks through nature settings resulted in significantly greater overall heart rate variability and parasympathetic cardiac contribution during sleep later that night (Gladwell et al., 2016). Further, twenty minutes' walk in a Japanese forest was reported to result in significantly lower prefrontal cerebral activity and significantly lower concentration of salivary cortisol than did an equivalent walk in a downtown city area (Park et al., 2007). Walks through a forest environment during a 3-day visit resulted in significantly enhanced immune functioning and proliferation of anti-cancer proteins that lasted for more than seven days (Li et al., 2008, 2007). Physical activity can be seen as a vehicle for obtaining beneficial doses of phytoncides, both in serving as the visit purpose and as it promotes increased respiration. Air quality is one of the pathways outlined in Hartig et al.'s model of links between nature environments and health and well-being (Hartig, Mitchell, De Vries, & Frumkin, 2014). As discussed by Donnelly et al. (2016), both short and long-term exposure to pollutant atmospheric particulate matter, such as $PM_{2.5}$ result in adverse health impacts, even where exposure is below the current World Health Organization's recommended annual limit of 10 $\mu g/m^3$, and there is significant evidence from toxicological and clinical studies that short duration exposure to combustion-derived particles leads to immediate detrimental physiological change (World Health Organization, 2013). Reviews of the research evidence report that urban green spaces can decrease levels of air pollution and reduce atmospheric carbon dioxide through carbon storage and sequestration (Bowler, Buyung-Ali, Knight, & Pullin, 2010; Calfapietra et al., 2016; World Health Organization, 2016). Accessing nature environments via exercise can serve as respite from polluted urban air, and given the increased respiration associated with exercise, reduced pollution becomes of even greater importance. Of particular relevance to urban residents or workers, this indicates the importance of accessing urban green spaces as areas of at least marginally reduced air pollution.

Environments shaping physiological exercise experiences and behaviour

Environments shape physical activity behaviours both at the acute level within single exercise bouts, and at a more general level. At the general, epidemiological level, nature environments seem to be spaces that afford, or invite physical activity per se, as the two are frequently reported to be positively associated (World Health Organization, 2016). Although the importance of physical activity to the link between green space level and health is still debated (Maas, Verheij, Spreeuwenberg, & Groenewegen, 2008; Mytton, Townsend, Rutter, & Foster, 2012; Richardson, Pearce, Mitchell, & Kingham, 2013), natural environments provide the context for a large proportion of recreational physical activity, for example, over 8 million adults per week engage in green exercise in England alone (White et al., 2016a). Physical activity is one of the pathways outlined in Hartig et al.'s model of links between nature environments and health and well-being (Hartig et al., 2014); nature environments often facilitate physical activity behaviour, as a product of their characteristics, or behavioural affordances (Brymer, Davids, & Mallabon, 2014; Calogiuri & Chroni, 2014; Sharma-Brymer & Bland, 2016). The provision of good access to green spaces in urban areas can help promote population physical activity (Coombes, Jones, & Hillsdon, 2010; Picavet et al., 2016), and association has been reported between having more green space closer to home and doing more moderate-vigorous physical activity. (Coutts, Chapin, Horner, & Taylor, 2013). The presence of and proximity to neighbourhood green spaces helps to maintain recreational walking over a period of four years (Sugiyama et al., 2013). One study found that odds of achieving the recommended amount of physical activity was over four times greater for people who visited local green space once per week compared to never going (Flowers et al., 2016). After controlling for age, sex and socio-economic deprivation, research in New Zealand reported that levels of physical activity were higher in greener neighbourhoods than less green neighbourhoods (Richardson et al., 2013). In Beijing, accessibility of parks within 500 metres from residents' homes significantly correlates with their physical activity level (Liu, Li, Li, & Zhang, 2017). Indeed, green space in the home neighbourhood may be protective against decline in physical activity among older people as they age, with activities such as dog walking serving as potential mechanisms in this relationship (Dalton, Wareham, Griffin, & Jones, 2016). Children frequently use nature environments for moderate to vigorous physical activity (Lachowycz, Jones, Page, Wheeler, & Cooper, 2012); and the behavioural affordances typical of those environments may increase interest in physically active behaviours (Sharma-Brymer & Bland, 2016). In urban areas, half of children's outdoor moderate to vigorous physical activity throughout the year takes place in green space at the weekend (Lachowycz et al., 2012). Compared to break- and lunch-times spent on a school playground, school fields promote greater moderate to vigorous physical activity (Wood, Gladwell, & Barton, 2014).

Environments also shape physiological aspects of acute physical activity bouts, including biomechanical properties and the pacing of continuous aerobic exercise such as walking and running. Although there are general similarities between overground and treadmill running gaits (Fellin, Manal, & Davis, 2010; Riley et al., 2008), there are significant biomechanical and neuromuscular differences. For example, compared to overground running, treadmill running is associated with flatter foot landing, 12 degrees reduction in hip flexion at foot-strike, 6 degrees reduction in ankle excursion to peak angle, 6 degrees greater peak ankle eversion, and both lower magnitude of maximal plantar pressure and a lower maximum plantar force at the plantar areas (Hong, Wang, Li, & Zhou, 2012; Nigg, De Boer, & Fisher, 1995; Sinclair et al., 2013). There are also significant differences in knee kinematics, peak ground reaction forces, joint movements and joint power trajectories (Riley et al., 2008). Treadmill running elicits weaker amplitudes of soleus neuromuscular activity during the push-off phase of running than does overground running (Baur, Hirschmüller, Müller, Gollhofer, & Mayer, 2007). That is, the environmental context of exercise shapes its likely biomechanical properties; in this case, the mechanics of treadmill running cannot be simply generalised to the overground running typical of green exercise (Sinclair et al., 2013). Indeed, exercise behaviour is also shaped in relation to homeostasis and pacing fluctuations. Without effortful control of pacing, non-conscious mechanisms regulate and promote exercise-pacing fluctuations in line with maintaining homeostasis (Billat, Wesfreid, Kapfer, Koralsztein, & Meyer, 2006; Gibson & Noakes, 2004; Lambert, Gibson, & Noakes, 2005; Noakes, 2008; Tucker et al., 2006). Consistent with this, compared with self-paced 10,000 metre running, completing this distance at the same overall average speed via enforced pacing elicits greater physiological strain as measured by mean oxygen consumption, heart rate and blood lactate concentration (Billat et al., 2006). Where the treadmill removes the option to vary pace, green exercise environments are amenable to self-regulated pacing changes.

Psychophysiological influences of environmental settings on the linked aspects of perceived exertion and exercise intensity have been discussed earlier in this chapter. Green exercise settings promote lower rated perception of exertion, and with this, tendency to exercise at a greater intensity can in turn boost physiological outcomes of the exercise; that is, physiological adaptations that occur in response to greater physiological load or strain. Of course, as well as enabling coaches to 'dupe' athletes into training harder (Rogerson, 2017), this affect may also pose a risk that requires consideration for individuals with physiological vulnerabilities, such as cardiac rehabilitation patients.

Social benefits of both pathways

Nature exposure promotes social benefits

The value attached to relationships constitutes a form of capital, which has come to be known as social capital. This includes an individual's contacts and networks;

the common rules, norms and sanctions that regulate behaviour together with the reciprocity and exchanges that build friendships, respect and ultimately trust (Pretty, 2003; Putnam, 1995). People engage with the outdoors not just for the connection to nature, but to provide the setting for the building of social capital (Kawachi, Kennedy, Lochner, & Prothrow-Stith, 1997; Krenichyn, 2004). Social contact plays a considerable role in the building of social cohesion. For example, green spaces in Zurich have been found to encourage children and adolescents to make contacts and develop friendships across cultures (Seeland, Dübendorfer, & Hansmann, 2009). The process of strengthening social networks and spending time socialising, and the trusting relationships that come from these benefit health and well-being (Dolan, Peasgood, & White, 2008; Kawachi et al., 1997; Pretty, 2003). In these ways, green spaces are important for increasing social capital (World Health Organization, 2016); and social contact and cohesion can mediate the relationship between green space and health (de Vries, van Dillen, Groenewegen, & Spreeuwenberg, 2013; Maas, Van Dillen, Verheij, & Groenewegen, 2009; Ward Thompson, Aspinall, Roe, Robertson, & Miller, 2016). A meta-analysis of 148 studies found a 50% increased likelihood of survival over seven years for those people with strong relationships (Holt-Lunstad, Smith, & Layton, 2010).

Exercise can provide individuals with the occasion for social contact. Accessing green spaces via exercise also offers opportunity for place making – exercisers become attached to the environments that they exercise in (Hitchings & Latham, 2016). Place making promotes a positive trajectory towards healing and good well-being; a sense of place encapsulates each of its social (communal) physical, functional and spiritual elements (Atkinson et al., 2012). Place making is not only a social construction; the human brain develops complex, specific patterns of interaction with places (Lengen & Kistemann, 2012), and exercise can be a vehicle for creating a place that can function throughout the life-course as a pro-health and well-being resource, as well as a medium for social identity and meaning. For example, places and place making play an important role in restoring well-being and promoting 'becoming at home' for resettled youth with refugee backgrounds (Sampson & Gifford, 2010).

Social aspects of environments shaping exercise experiences and behaviour

On comparing the mood outcomes of outdoor and indoor (treadmill) walks, Teas, Hurley, Ghumare, and Ogoussan (2007, p. 40) noted:

> The women, almost all of whom were strangers to each other, began walking along the campus path at about the same time, and ended about the same time. The pace was self-regulated, and many women fell into conversation with other participants during the walk. In theory, this could have contributed to greater social contact and satisfaction, particularly at the second exercise period. However, although the treadmill exercise

> period followed the campus walk, none of the same women conversed with their neighbors while on the side by side treadmills in the exercise lab. This could have been related to the music or the unfamiliar setting of the gym .... Although it is possible to bring personal audio equipment into the gym, most gyms play loud music with a heavy beat so it was a reasonable part of our simulated gym setting.

Beyond the research design issues regarding the non-randomisation of condition order within this study (all participants completed the outdoor walk first, before completing the treadmill walk a week later), what Teas et al. effectively reported on here, was the influence of the environmental setting in shaping social aspects of the participants' exercise behaviour. Similarly, when Rogerson et al. asked participants to cycle in pairs, they spent 20% more of the exercise time being socially interactive outdoors compared to indoors (Rogerson et al., 2016). A further finding of this study was that social interaction time significantly predicted intention for future exercise in the outdoors condition, but did not in the indoor condition, alluding that environments can influence longer-term behavioural choices via a pathway involving social experience (Rogerson et al., 2016). Availability of exercise partners can also play an important role in exercise motivation for and adherence to exercise behaviours (Phillips, Schneider, & Mercer, 2004), and whereas health club or gym memberships limit options, in that not all potential exercise partners might afford membership, green spaces allow for physical activity with all partners. Social support can indirectly influence exercise through self-efficacy and outcome expectations (Resnick, Orwig, Magaziner, & Wynne, 2002). Even in instances that social expectations or motivations may be slightly greater for indoor than outdoor exercise (Calogiuri & Elliott, 2017; Hug, Hartig, Hansmann, Seeland, & Hornung, 2009), the previously outlined findings suggest that actual experience can be quite the opposite.

Intertwining of the pathways

Green exercise research, and adjacent research on exercise, environments, health and well-being, tends to consider its findings largely in isolation. Similarly within the current chapter, findings have been discussed in isolation so to outline the two pathways via which green exercise offers health and well-being benefits. However, it is most likely that in many instances, exercise-associated beneficial outcomes of nature exposure, and the role of environments in shaping exercise experiences and behaviours, complexly interact – especially in real world practice. At a snapshot, the two intertwined pathways of affects appear not as they are – something of a very loose double-helix structure, but as a blurred wall of outcomes. Findings are simply listed, for example, individuals may report greater enjoyment of green exercise compared to exercise in other settings (Focht, 2009; Teas et al., 2007), and lunchtime walks through nature settings promote greater parasympathetic cardiac contribution during sleep later that night compared to walks through a built environment (Gladwell et al., 2016). The points at which the pathways link within themselves and across to one other, and what those links are, are understandably difficult to decipher, and many outcomes and shaped behaviours will not link to others. Links between accessing qualities of nature-based environments, and future behaviours, have been discussed by some studies (Focht, 2009; Rogerson et al., 2016), drawing on previously theorised relationships, such as that linking exercise intensity – affect – and intention (Ekkekakis et al., 2011). Many other impactful instances of intertwining are also likely to occur. As discussed by Rogerson et al. (Rogerson et al., 2016, p. 11):

> dual-mode theory proposes that the interplay between and shifting relative importance of collections of cognitive (e.g., self-efficacy, self-presentational concerns) and physiological elements (e.g., acidosis, core temperature) of exercise experiences influence the exercise-affect relationship … aside from a possible pathway involving attention restoration, as the social setting of the exercise in the current study was different from that of previous research, affect associated with social interactions during the exercise might have functioned to distract from or over-ride other pathways via which both exercise and environments influence affect.

This 'interplay' that the authors describe might be beneficial to health and well-being in some respects, and not so in others. Figure 4.2 draws together some of the research discussed in this chapter, in order to give just one example of how the two described pathways of green exercise may intertwine.

Conclusions

This chapter has reviewed both green exercise and adjacent research findings in such a way as to outline the two pathways by which green exercise serves to improve health and well-being. The first pathway outlines that exercise functions as a vehicle for accessing the acute and chronic salutogenic impacts of green spaces and other nature-based environments. The second pathway is that of environmental shaping of exercise behaviour, which itself is health and well-being-linked. Both pathways are important in their own right, delivering a wide range of psychological, physiological and social benefits. Additionally, in some instances, the two pathways can intertwine, whereby aspects of one pathway impact on aspects of the other, which may in turn impact back on the first.

If green space or green exercise were considered as a drug for health and well-being, more detailed understanding of its mechanisms can lead to optimal dosage, and knowledge of when and for whom it might work best (Barton & Rogerson, 2017). As well as reporting health and well-being impacts per se, better understanding might be aided by consideration of research findings in

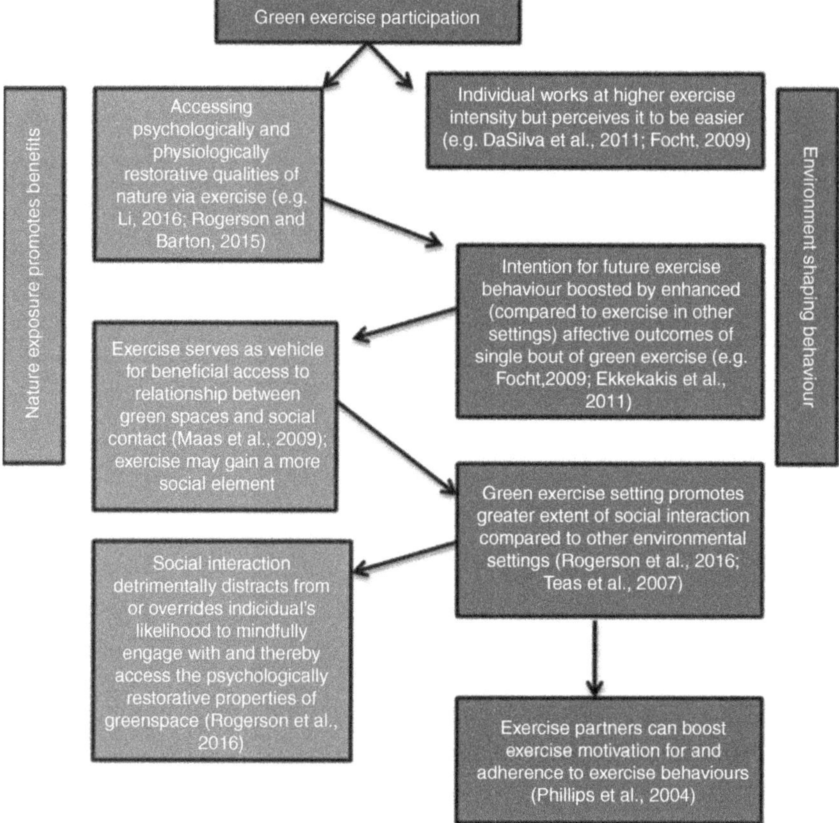

FIGURE 4.2 Example of the pathways intertwining

relation to each of the two pathways, and possibilities of where and how the pathways might intertwine.

References

Aspinall, P., Mavros, P., Coyne, R., & Roe, J. (2015). The urban brain: Analysing outdoor physical activity with mobile EEG. *British Journal of Sports Medicine*, *49*(4), 272–276.

Atkinson, S., Fuller, S., Painter, J., Atkinson, S., Fuller, S., & Painter, J. (2012). Wellbeing and place. In *Wellbeing and Place*, pp. 1–14. Oxon: Routledge.

Barton, J., & Pretty, J. (2010). What is the best dose of nature and green exercise for improving mental health? A multi-study analysis. *Environmental Science & Technology*, *44* (10), 3947–3955.

Barton, J., & Rogerson, M. (2017). Themed editorial: The importance of green space for mental health. *BJPsych International*, *14*(4), 79–81.

Baur, H., Hirschmüller, A., Müller, S., Gollhofer, A., & Mayer, F. (2007). Muscular activity in treadmill and overground running. *Isokinetics and Exercise Science*, *15*(3), 165–171.

Berman, M. G., Jonides, J., & Kaplan, S. (2008). The cognitive benefits of interacting with nature. *Psychological Science, 19*(12), 1207–1212.

Berto, R. (2005). Exposure to restorative environments helps restore attentional capacity. *Journal of Environmental Psychology, 25*(3), 249–259.

Billat, V. L., Wesfreid, E., Kapfer, C., Koralsztein, J. P., & Meyer, Y. (2006). Nonlinear dynamics of heart rate and oxygen uptake in exhaustive 10,000 m runs: Influence of constant vs. freely paced. *The Journal of Physiological Sciences, 56*(1), 103–111.

Borg, G. (1970). Perceived exertion as an indicator of somatic stress. *Scandinavian Journal of Rehabilitation Medicine, 2*, 92–98.

Borg, G. (1998). *Borg's perceived exertion and pain scales*. Champaign, IL: Human Kinetics.

Borg, G. A. (1982). Psychophysical bases of perceived exertion. *Medicine & Science in Sports & Exercise, 14*(5), 377–381.

Bowler, D. E., Buyung-Ali, L., Knight, T. M., & Pullin, A. S. (2010). Urban greening to cool towns and cities: A systematic review of the empirical evidence. *Landscape and Urban Planning, 97*(3), 147–155.

Brown, D. K., Barton, J. L., & Gladwell, V. F. (2013). Viewing nature scenes positively affects recovery of autonomic function following acute-mental stress. *Environmental Science & Technology, 47*(11), 5562–5569.

Brown, D. K., Barton, J. L., Pretty, J., & Gladwell, V. (2014). Walks4Work: Assessing the role of the natural environment in a workplace physical activity intervention. *Scandinavian Journal of Work, Environment & Health, 40*(4), 390–399.

Brymer, E., & Davids, K. (2012). Ecological dynamics as a theoretical framework for development of sustainable behaviours towards the environment. *Environmental Education Research, 19*(1), 45–63.

Brymer, E., & Davids, K. (2014). Experiential learning as a constraint-led process: An ecological dynamics perspective. *Journal of Adventure Education & Outdoor Learning, 14*(2), 103–117.

Brymer, E., Davids, K., & Mallabon, L. (2014). Understanding the psychological health and well-being benefits of physical activity in nature: An ecological dynamics analysis. *Ecopsychology, 6*(3), 189–197.

Calfapietra, C., Morani, A., Sgrigna, G., Di Giovanni, S., Muzzini, V., Pallozzi, E., … Fares, S. (2016). Removal of ozone by urban and peri-urban forests: Evidence from laboratory, field, and modeling approaches. *Journal of Environmental Quality, 45*(1), 224–233.

Calogiuri, G., & Chroni, S. (2014). The impact of the natural environment on the promotion of active living: An integrative systematic review. *BMC Public Health, 14*(1), 873.

Calogiuri, G., & Elliott, L. R. (2017). Why do people exercise in natural environments? Norwegian adults' motives for nature-, gym-, and sports-based exercise. *International Journal of Environmental Research and Public Health, 14*(4), 377.

Ceci, R., & Hassmén, P. (1991). Self-monitored exercise at three different RPE intensities in treadmill vs field running. *Medicine & Science in Sports & Exercise, 23*(6), 732–738.

Chang, C.-Y., Chen, P.-K., Hammitt, W. E., & Machnik, L. (2007). Psychophysiological responses and restorative values of wilderness environments.

Coombes, E., Jones, A. P., & Hillsdon, M. (2010). The relationship of physical activity and overweight to objectively measured green space accessibility and use. *Social Science & Medicine, 70*(6), 816–822.

Coutts, C., Chapin, T., Horner, M., & Taylor, C. (2013). County-level effects of green space access on physical activity. *Journal of Physical Activity and Health, 10*(2), 232–240.

Dalton, A. M., Wareham, N., Griffin, S., & Jones, A. P. (2016). Neighbourhood greenspace is associated with a slower decline in physical activity in older adults: A prospective cohort study. *SSM-Population Health*, *2*, 683–691.

Dasilva, S. G., Guidetti, L., Buzzachera, C. F., Elsangedy, H. M., Krinski, K., De Campos, W., … Baldari, C. (2011). Psychophysiological responses to self-paced treadmill and overground exercise. *Medicine & Science in Sports & Exercise*, *43*(6), 1114–1124.

de Vries, S., van Dillen, S. M., Groenewegen, P. P., & Spreeuwenberg, P. (2013). Streetscape greenery and health: Stress, social cohesion and physical activity as mediators. *Social Science & Medicine*, *94*, 26–33.

Dettweiler, U., Becker, C., Auestad, B. H., Simon, P., & Kirsch, P. (2017). Stress in school. Some empirical hints on the circadian cortisol rhythm of children in outdoor and indoor classes. *International Journal of Environmental Research and Public Health*, *14*(5), 475.

Dolan, P., Peasgood, T., & White, M. (2008). Do we really know what makes us happy? A review of the economic literature on the factors associated with subjective well-being. *Journal of Economic Psychology*, *29*(1), 94–122.

Donnelly, A. A., MacIntyre, T. E., O'Sullivan, N., Warrington, G., Harrison, A. J., Igou, E. R., … Lane, A. M. (2016). Environmental influences on elite sport athletes well being: from gold, silver, and bronze to blue green and gold. *Frontiers in Psychology*, 7, 1167. doi: 10.3389/fpsyg.2016.01167.

Duncan, M. J., Clarke, N. D., Birch, S. L., Tallis, J., Hankey, J., Bryant, E., & Eyre, E. L. (2014). The effect of green exercise on blood pressure, heart rate and mood state in primary school children. *International Journal of Environmental Research and Public Health*, *11* (4), 3678–3688.

Ekkekakis, P., Parfitt, G., & Petruzzello, S. J. (2011). The pleasure and displeasure people feel when they exercise at different intensities. *Sports Medicine*, *41*(8), 641–671.

Ewert, A., Overholt, J., Voight, A., & Wang, C. C. (2011). Understanding the transformative aspects of the wilderness and protected lands experience upon human health.

Fellin, R. E., Manal, K., & Davis, I. S. (2010). Comparison of lower extremity kinematic curves during overground and treadmill running. *Journal of Applied Biomechanics*, *26*(4), 407.

Flowers, E. P., Freeman, P., & Gladwell, V. F. (2016). A cross-sectional study examining predictors of visit frequency to local green space and the impact this has on physical activity levels. *BMC Public Health*, *16*(1), 420.

Focht, B. C. (2009). Brief walks in outdoor and laboratory environments: Effects on affective responses, enjoyment, and intentions to walk for exercise. *Research Quarterly for Exercise and Sport*, *80*(3), 611–620.

Gibson, A. S. C., & Noakes, T. (2004). Evidence for complex system integration and dynamic neural regulation of skeletal muscle recruitment during exercise in humans. *British Journal of Sports Medicine*, *38*(6), 797–806.

Gibson, J. J. (1950). The perception of the visual world.

Gibson, J. J. (1954). The visual perception of objective motion and subjective movement. *Psychological Review*, *61*(5), 304.

Gidlow, C. J., Jones, M. V., Hurst, G., Masterson, D., Clark-Carter, D., Tarvainen, M. P., … Nieuwenhuijsen, M. (2016). Where to put your best foot forward: Psycho-physiological responses to walking in natural and urban environments. *Journal of Environmental Psychology*, *45*, 22–29.

Gladwell, V., Brown, D., Barton, J. L., Tarvainen, M., Kuoppa, P., Pretty, J., … Sandercock, G. (2012). The effects of views of nature on autonomic control. *European Journal of Applied Physiology*, *112*(9), 3379–3386.

Gladwell, V. F., Brown, D. K., Wood, C., Sandercock, G. R., & Barton, J. L. (2013). The great outdoors: How a green exercise environment can benefit all. *Extreme Physiology & Medicine*, *2*(1), 1–7.

Gladwell, V. F., Kuoppa, P., Tarvainen, M. P., & Rogerson, M. (2016). A lunchtime walk in nature enhances restoration of autonomic control during night-time sleep: Results from a preliminary study. *International Journal of Environmental Research and Public Health*, *13*(3), 280.

Grad, F. P. (2002). The preamble of the constitution of the World Health Organization. *Bulletin of the World Health Organization*, *80*(12), 981–984.

Harte, J. L., & Eifert, G. H. (1995). The effects of running, environment, and attentional focus on athletes' catecholamine and cortisol levels and mood. *Psychophysiology*, *32*(1), 49–54.

Hartig, T., Evans, G. W., Jamner, L. D., Davis, D. S., & Gärling, T. (2003). Tracking restoration in natural and urban field settings. *Journal of Environmental Psychology*, *23*(2), 109–123.

Hartig, T., Mitchell, R., De Vries, S., & Frumkin, H. (2014). Nature and health. *Annual Review of Public Health*, *35*, 207–228.

Herzog, T. R., & Strevey, S. J. (2008). Contact with nature, sense of humor, and psychological well-being. *Environment and Behavior*, *40*(6), 747–776.

Hitchings, R., & Latham, A. (2016). Indoor versus outdoor running: Understanding how recreational exercise comes to inhabit environments through practitioner talk. *Transactions of the Institute of British Geographers*, *41*(4), 503–514.

Holt-Lunstad, J., Smith, T. B., & Layton, J. B. (2010). Social relationships and mortality risk: A meta-analytic review. *PLOS Medicine*, 7(7), e1000316.

Hong, Y., Wang, L., Li, J. X., & Zhou, J. H. (2012). Comparison of plantar loads during treadmill and overground running. *Journal of Science and Medicine in Sport*, *15*(6), 554–560.

Hug, S.-M., Hartig, T., Hansmann, R., Seeland, K., & Hornung, R. (2009). Restorative qualities of indoor and outdoor exercise settings as predictors of exercise frequency. *Health & Place*, *15*(4), 971–980.

Kaplan, R. (1993). The role of nature in the context of the workplace. *Landscape and Urban Planning*, *26*(1), 193–201.

Kaplan, R., & Kaplan, S. (1989). *The experience of nature: A psychological perspective*. New York, NY: Cambridge University Press.

Kaplan, S. (1995). The restorative benefits of nature: Toward an integrative framework. *Journal of Environmental Psychology*, *15*(3), 169–182.

Kaplan, S. (2001). Meditation, restoration, and the management of mental fatigue. *Environment and Behavior*, *33*(4), 480–506.

Kawachi, I., Kennedy, B. P., Lochner, K., & Prothrow-Stith, D. (1997). Social capital, income inequality, and mortality. *American Journal of Public Health*, *87*(9), 1491–1498.

Keniger, L. E., Gaston, K. J., Irvine, K. N., & Fuller, R. A. (2013). What are the benefits of interacting with nature? *International Journal of Environmental Research and Public Health*, *10*(3), 913–935.

Kerr, J. H., Fujiyama, H., Sugano, A., Okamura, T., Chang, M., & Onouha, F. (2006). Psychological responses to exercising in laboratory and natural environments. *Psychology of Sport and Exercise*, 7(4), 345–359.

Krenichyn, K. (2004). Women and physical activity in an urban park: Enrichment and support through an ethic of care. *Journal of Environmental Psychology*, *24*(1), 117–130.

LaCaille, R. A., Masters, K. S., & Heath, E. M. (2004). Effects of cognitive strategy and exercise setting on running performance, perceived exertion, affect, and satisfaction. *Psychology of Sport and Exercise*, *5*(4), 461–476.

Lacharité-Lemieux, M., Brunelle, J.-P., & Dionne, I. J. (2015). Adherence to exercise and affective responses: Comparison between outdoor and indoor training. *Menopause*, *22* (7), 731–740.

Lachowycz, K., Jones, A. P., Page, A. S., Wheeler, B. W., & Cooper, A. R. (2012). What can global positioning systems tell us about the contribution of different types of urban greenspace to children's physical activity? *Health & Place*, *18*(3), 586–594.

Lambert, E., Gibson, A. S. C., & Noakes, T. (2005). Complex systems model of fatigue: Integrative homoeostatic control of peripheral physiological systems during exercise in humans. *British Journal of Sports Medicine*, *39*(1), 52–62.

Laumann, K., Gärling, T., & Stormark, K. M. (2003). Selective attention and heart rate responses to natural and urban environments. *Journal of Environmental Psychology*, *23*(2), 125–134.

Lee, J., Li, Q., Tyrväinen, L., Tsunetsugu, Y., Park, B.-J., Kagawa, T., & Miyazaki, Y. (2012). Nature therapy and preventive medicine. *Public Health-Social and Behavioral Health*, *16*, 325–350.

Lengen, C., & Kistemann, T. (2012). Sense of place and place identity: Review of neuroscientific evidence. *Health & Place*, *18*(5), 1162–1171.

Li, Q. (2016). Forest bathing in Japan. In J. Barton, R.Bragg, C. Wood, & J. Pretty (Eds.), *Green exercise: Linking nature, health and well-being*, pp. 79–88. Oxon: Routledge.

Li, Q., & Kawada, T. (2013). Possibility of clinical applications of forest medicine. *Nihon Eiseigaku Zasshi. Japanese Journal of Hygiene*, *69*(2), 117–121.

Li, Q., Kobayashi, M., Wakayama, Y., Inagaki, H., Katsumata, M., Hirata, Y., … Park, B. (2009). Effect of phytoncide from trees on human natural killer cell function. *International Journal of Immunopathology and Pharmacology*, *22*(4), 951–959.

Li, Q., Morimoto, K., Kobayashi, M., Inagaki, H., Katsumata, M., Hirata, Y., … Wakayama, Y. (2008). Visiting a forest, but not a city, increases human natural killer activity and expression of anti-cancer proteins. *International Journal of Immunopathology and Pharmacology*, *21*(1), 117–127.

Li, Q., Morimoto, K., Nakadai, A., Inagaki, H., Katsumata, M., Shimizu, T., … Miyazaki, Y. (2007). Forest bathing enhances human natural killer activity and expression of anti-cancer proteins. *International Journal of Immunopathology and Pharmacology*, *20* (2 Suppl), 3–8.

Li, Q., Otsuka, T., Kobayashi, M., Wakayama, Y., Inagaki, H., Katsumata, M., … Shimizu, T. (2011). Acute effects of walking in forest environments on cardiovascular and metabolic parameters. *European Journal of Applied Physiology*, *111*(11), 2845–2853.

Liu, H., Li, F., Li, J., & Zhang, Y. (2017). The relationships between urban parks, residents' physical activity, and mental health benefits: A case study from Beijing, China. *Journal of Environmental Management*, *190*, 223–230.

Lowton, E., Brymer, E., Clough, P., & Denovan, A. (2017). The relationship between the physical activity environment, nature relatedness, anxiety and the psychological well-being benefits of regular exercisers. *Frontiers in Psychology*. doi:10.3389/fpsyg.2017.01058

Maas, J., Van Dillen, S. M., Verheij, R. A., & Groenewegen, P. P. (2009). Social contacts as a possible mechanism behind the relation between green space and health. *Health & Place*, *15*(2), 586–595.

Maas, J., Verheij, R. A., Spreeuwenberg, P., & Groenewegen, P. P. (2008). Physical activity as a possible mechanism behind the relationship between green space and health: A multilevel analysis. *BMC Public Health, 8*(1), 206.

Mao, G. X., Lan, X. G., Cao, Y. B., Chen, Z. M., He, Z. H., Lv, Y. D., … Jing, Y. (2012). Effects of short-term forest bathing on human health in a broad-leaved evergreen forest in Zhejiang Province, China. *Biomedical and Environmental Sciences, 25*(3), 317–324.

Marcora, S. M., Staiano, W., & Manning, V. (2009). Mental fatigue impairs physical performance in humans. *Journal of Applied Physiology, 106*(3), 857–864.

Mayer, F. S., Frantz, C. M., Bruehlman-Senecal, E., & Dolliver, K. (2008). Why is nature beneficial? The role of connectedness to nature. *Environment and Behavior, 41*(5), 607–643.

Mytton, O. T., Townsend, N., Rutter, H., & Foster, C. (2012). Green space and physical activity: An observational study using health survey for England data. *Health & Place, 18* (5), 1034–1041.

Nigg, B. M., De Boer, R. W., & Fisher, V. (1995). A kinematic comparison of overground and treadmill running. *Medicine & Science in Sports & Exercise, 27*(1), 98–105.

Noakes, T. D. (2008). Testing for maximum oxygen consumption has produced a brainless model of human exercise performance. *British Journal of Sports Medicine, 42*(7), 551–555.

World Health Organization. (2016). *Urban green spaces and health: A review of the evidence.* Copenhagen: WHO Regional Office for Europe.

Ottosson, J., & Grahn, P. (2005). A comparison of leisure time spent in a garden with leisure time spent indoors: On measures of restoration in residents in geriatric care. *Landscape Research, 30*(1), 23–55.

Park, B.-J., Tsunetsugu, Y., Kasetani, T., Hirano, H., Kagawa, T., Sato, M., & Miyazaki, Y. (2007). Physiological effects of Shinrin-yoku (taking in the atmosphere of the forest)-using salivary cortisol and cerebral activity as indicators. *Journal of Physiological Anthropology, 26*(2), 123–128.

Park, B. J., Tsunetsugu, Y., Kasetani, T., Kagawa, T., & Miyazaki, Y. (2010). The physiological effects of Shinrin-yoku (taking in the forest atmosphere or forest bathing): Evidence from field experiments in 24 forests across Japan. *Environmental Health and Preventive Medicine, 15*(1), 18–26.

Parry, D., Chinnasamy, C., & Micklewright, D. P. (2012). Optic flow influences perceived exertion during cycling. *Journal of Sport & Exercise Psychology, 34*(4), 444–456.

Phillips, E. M., Schneider, J. C., & Mercer, G. R. (2004). Motivating elders to initiate and maintain exercise. *Archives of Physical Medicine and Rehabilitation, 85*, 52–57.

Picavet, H. S. J., Milder, I., Kruize, H., de Vries, S., Hermans, T., & Wendel-Vos, W. (2016). Greener living environment healthier people?: Exploring green space, physical activity and health in the Doetinchem Cohort Study. *Preventive Medicine, 89*, 7–14.

Pretty, J. (2003). Social capital and the collective management of resources. *Science, 302* (5652), 1912–1914.

Pretty, J. (2004). How nature contributes to mental and physical health. *Spirituality and Health International, 5*(2), 68–78.

Pretty, J. (2014). *The edge of extinction: Travels with enduring people in vanishing lands.* Ithaca: Cornell University Press.

Pretty, J., Griffin, M., Sellens, M., & Pretty, C. (2003). Green exercise: Complimentary roles of nature, exercise and diet in physical and emotional well-being and implications for public health policy. *CES Occasional Paper, University of Essex., 2003-1.*

Pretty, J., Peacock, J., Sellens, M., & Griffin, M. (2005). The mental and physical health outcomes of green exercise. *International Journal of Environmental Health Research, 15*(5), 319–337.

Putnam, R. D. (1995). Bowling alone: America's declining social capital. *Journal of Democracy, 6*(1), 65–78.

Raanaas, R. K., Evensen, K. H., Rich, D., Sjøstrøm, G., & Patil, G. (2011). Benefits of indoor plants on attention capacity in an office setting. *Journal of Environmental Psychology, 31*(1), 99–105.

Resnick, B., Orwig, D., Magaziner, J., & Wynne, C. (2002). The effect of social support on exercise behavior in older adults. *Clinical Nursing Research, 11*(1), 52–70.

Richardson, E. A., Pearce, J., Mitchell, R., & Kingham, S. (2013). Role of physical activity in the relationship between urban green space and health. *Public Health, 127*(4), 318–324.

Riley, P. O., Dicharry, J., Franz, J., Croce, U. D., Wilder, R. P., & Kerrigan, D. C. (2008). A kinematics and kinetic comparison of overground and treadmill running. *Medicine and Science in Sports and Exercise, 40*(6), 1093.

Rogerson, M. (2017). Commentary: environmental influences on elite sport athletes well being: from gold, silver, and bronze to blue, green and gold. *Frontiers in Psychology, 8* (78). doi:10.3389/fpsyg.2017.00078

Rogerson, M., & Barton, J. (2015). Effects of the visual exercise environments on cognitive directed attention, energy expenditure and perceived exertion. *International Journal of Environmental Research and Public Health, 12*(7), 7321–7336.

Rogerson, M., Brown, D. K., Sandercock, G., Wooller, J.-J., & Barton, J. (2015). A comparison of four typical green exercise environments and prediction of psychological health outcomes. *Perspectives in Public Health.* doi:10.1177/1757913915589845

Rogerson, M., Gladwell, V. F., Gallagher, D. J., & Barton, J. L. (2016). Influences of Green Outdoors versus indoors environmental settings on psychological and social outcomes of controlled exercise. *International Journal of Environmental Research and Public Health, 13*(4), 363.

Sampson, R., & Gifford, S. M. (2010). Place-making, settlement and well-being: The therapeutic landscapes of recently arrived youth with refugee backgrounds. *Health & Place, 16*(1), 116–131.

Seeland, K., Dübendorfer, S., & Hansmann, R. (2009). Making friends in Zurich's urban forests and parks: The role of public green space for social inclusion of youths from different cultures. *Forest Policy and Economics, 11*(1), 10–17.

Selhub, E. M., & Logan, A. C. (2012). *Your brain on nature: The science of nature's influence on your health, happiness and vitality.* Ontario, Canada: John Wiley & Sons.

Seymour, V. (2016). The human–nature relationship and its impact on health: A critical review. *Frontiers in Public Health, 4*, 260. doi: 10.3389/fpubh.2016.00260.

Sharma-Brymer, V., & Bland, D. (2016). Bringing nature to schools to promote children's physical activity. *Sports Medicine, 46*(7), 955–962.

Sinclair, J., Richards, J., Taylor, P. J., Edmundson, C. J., Brooks, D., & Hobbs, S. J. (2013). Three-dimensional kinematic comparison of treadmill and overground running. *Sports Biomechanics, 12*(3), 272–282.

Sugiyama, T., Giles-Corti, B., Summers, J., Du Toit, L., Leslie, E., & Owen, N. (2013). Initiating and maintaining recreational walking: A longitudinal study on the influence of neighborhood green space. *Preventive Medicine, 57*(3), 178–182.

Taylor, A. F., & Kuo, F. E. (2009). Children with attention deficits concentrate better after walk in the park. *Journal of Attention Disorders, 12*(5), 402–409.

Teas, J., Hurley, T., Ghumare, S., & Ogoussan, K. (2007). Walking outside improves mood for healthy postmenopausal women. *Clinical Medicine: Oncology*, *1*, 35–43.

Thompson Coon, J., Boddy, K., Stein, K., Whear, R., Barton, J., & Depledge, M. H. (2011). Does participating in physical activity in outdoor natural environments have a greater effect on physical and mental wellbeing than physical activity indoors? A systematic review. *Environmental Science & Technology*, *45*(5), 1761–1772.

Tsunetsugu, Y., Park, B.-J., Ishii, H., Hirano, H., Kagawa, T., & Miyazaki, Y. (2007). Physiological effects of Shinrin-yoku (taking in the atmosphere of the forest) in an old-growth broadleaf forest in Yamagata Prefecture, Japan. *Journal of Physiological Anthropology*, *26*(2), 135–142.

Tucker, R., Bester, A., Lambert, E., Noakes, T. D., Vaughan, C. L., & Gibson, A. S. C. (2006). Non-random fluctuations in power output during self-paced exercise. *British Journal of Sports Medicine*, *40*(11), 912–917.

Tucker, R., & Noakes, T. D. (2009). The physiological regulation of pacing strategy during exercise: A critical review. *British Journal of Sports Medicine*, *43*(6), e1-e1.

Ulrich, R. (1984). View through a window may influence recovery. *Science*, *224*(4647), 224–225.

Ulrich, R. S. (1979). Visual landscapes and psychological well-being. *Landscape Research*, *4* (1), 17–23.

Ulrich, R. S. (1981). Natural versus urban scenes some psychophysiological effects. *Environment and Behavior*, *13*(5), 523–556.

Ulrich, R. S., Simons, R. F., Losito, B. D., Fiorito, E., Miles, M. A., & Zelson, M. (1991). Stress recovery during exposure to natural and urban environments. *Journal of Environmental Psychology*, *11*(3), 201–230.

Ward Thompson, C., Aspinall, P., Roe, J., Robertson, L., & Miller, D. (2016). Mitigating stress and supporting health in deprived urban communities: The importance of green space and the social environment. *International Journal of Environmental Research and Public Health*, *13*(4), 440.

Warren, P. A., & Rushton, S. K. (2009). Optic flow processing for the assessment of object movement during ego movement. *Current Biology*, *19*(18), 1555–1560.

White, M., Elliott, L., Taylor, T., Wheeler, B., Spencer, A., Bone, A., … Fleming, L. (2016a). Recreational physical activity in natural environments and implications for health: A population based cross-sectional study in England. *Preventive Medicine*, *91*, 383–388.

White, M. P., Bell, S., Elliott, L. R., Jenkin, R., Wheeler, B. W., & Depledge, M. H. (2016b). The health benefits of blue exercise in the UK. In J. Barton, R. Bragg, C. Wood, & J. Pretty (Eds.), *Green exercise: Linking nature, health and well-being*, pp. 69–78. Oxon: Routledge.

Williams, D. M., Dunsiger, S., Ciccolo, J. T., Lewis, B. A., Albrecht, A. E., & Marcus, B. H. (2008). Acute affective response to a moderate-intensity exercise stimulus predicts physical activity participation 6 and 12 months later. *Psychology of Sport and Exercise*, *9*(3), 231–245.

Wood, C., Gladwell, V., & Barton, J. (2014). A repeated measures experiment of school playing environment to increase physical activity and enhance self-esteem in UK school children. *PLoS One*, *9*(9), e108701.

World Health Organization. (2013). *Review of evidence on health aspects of air pollution–REVIHAAP project*. Copenhagen, Denmark: Author.

5

MEANING, NATURE AND WELL-BEING

Jürgen Beckmann, Eric R. Igou and Eric Klinger

Introduction

Meaning can be considered a comprehensive theme in human life. According to Frankl (1985) the will to meaning is a motive central to human existence. It involves having aims and being absorbed by something that stimulates awe, curiosity, pleasure and other positively evaluated experiences (Klinger, 1977). For Frankl (1985) meaning in life is a core element for human beings and is crucial for survival. Finding meaning in life is essential for health and well-being according to Frankl. Different paths to achieving meaning in life have been proposed (see Wong, 2012). In this chapter we will present recent research which has shown that nature can be a source of awe and positive affect (see also Chapter 1), and potentially mediate a reduction in ruminations. Consequently, we propose that nature can mediate the experience of meaning and thereby increase individuals' health and well-being. Throughout this chapter, we will elaborate further on the effects of both exposure to and engagement with nature (see also Chapter 2). We will argue that engagement with nature increases perceived meaningfulness, resulting in higher resilience to non-communicable diseases and promoting well-being.

Approaching an understanding of meaning in life

Within the context of this chapter, Joske's (1981) earlier characterisation of meaning is noteworthy. Joske (1981) states:

> people who ask about the meaning in life ... wish to know whether the world is the sort of place which justifies and gives significance to what might otherwise seem to be a drudgery of a typical human existence. In

> other words, they are asking whether or not the world confers derivative meaning upon life.
>
> *(p. 250)*

For Baumeister (1991) meaning "connects things", which makes a complex world more explainable and predictable. Similarly, Heine, Proulx, and Vohs (2006) define meaning "as relation".

These notions of meaning are related to Klinger's (2012, p. 26) conviction that "the disposition to live purposively is built into the most fundamental architecture of zoological organisms, and the disposition to seek meaning stems straightforwardly from the evolution of purposiveness together with human intellect". Survival depends to a large degree on actively seeking out life's necessities and effectively mastering them. Empirical findings by Van Tilburg and Igou (2013) provide support for the idea that lay people understand meaningful behaviour as behaviour that is highly instrumental in serving an important goal in life.

However, this may not fully capture the significance of meaning in humans' lives. Several authors point out that meaning involves something that goes beyond a single individual's concerns, transcending the individual's life. For people in many cultures spirituality in different forms can become an ultimate concern. Religion, or cultural value systems in a broader sense may serve the purpose of reducing complexity, increasing personal coherence and providing meaning in life (Emmons, Cheung, & Tehrani, 1998). This may then reduce the amount of what appears to be incomprehensible, which most of all may be addressing the ultimate concern of managing fear of death (Greenberg, Pyszczynski, & Solomon, 1986).

Martela and Steger (2016) suggest that there are three different meaning concepts: coherence, purpose, significance. *Coherence* is a key term in Antonovsky's (1979) salutogenic model and it is viewed as crucial for health and well-being. For Antonovsky (1979) the "Sense of Coherence" is a global orientation that is characterised by a pervasive, enduring though dynamic feeling of confidence that one's environment is predictable and that things will work out well. At the core of the concept are meaningfulness, comprehensibility and manageability. In Antonovsky's model meaningfulness refers to how much one feels that life makes sense, and that challenges are worthy of commitment. This is the base for a perception of comprehensibility (i.e. my world is understandable) and furthermore, a perception of manageability (i.e. my world is manageable).

Fundamental to Antonovsky's (1979) model is to view human beings in interaction with their environment. Thus, the focus is on the individual in a more or less complex context. In this context, the sense of coherence describes a person's basic attitude towards the world and his/her own life. It reflects a person's view of life and his/her capacity to respond to stressful situations. With a high sense of coherence life is seen as structured, manageable and meaningful. Thus, a high sense of coherence reduces complexity by providing inner trust in the world and oneself (Eriksson & Lindström, 2006). The more pronounced a person's sense of coherence the more resilient a person is to health problems and the more speedily he/she is going to get well. This has interesting health implications and the evidence to support this proposition is emerging.

A series of studies by King et al. (2006) has shown that measures of life's perceived meaningfulness are substantially correlated with measures of positive affect. They also found that increasing participants' mood by having them read happy scenarios positively affected their perception of life being meaningful. Similarly, Van Tilburg and Igou (2019) found that striving for happiness served the goal to live a meaningful life, at least for participants who searched for meaning in life. However, this finding does not imply that meaningfulness can be reduced to positive affect. Further qualification of the findings show that positive affect only predicted meaning scores for people who had few sources of meaning or who were low in religious commitment or lacked strong supportive personal relationships. High scorers on these variables reported high levels of meaning in their lives independent of the mood induction.

Another indication that positive affect is not the whole story in predicting a person's sense of meaningfulness (as measured by purpose in life) scores arises from unpublished data collected by Stuchlikova and Klinger (Klinger, 2012, p. 39):

> Regression analyses that included both positive affect and negative affect confirmed that neither motivational structure nor affect substantially accounts for the ability of the other to predict purpose in life. Together, however, their multiple correlation with purpose in life scores was 0.63, thus accounting for a very large proportion of the variance of purpose in life meaning scores. One may infer that both positive affect and goal-striving patterns are associated independently with the sense of one's life feeling meaningful.

Thus, there may be different mediators of the perception of meaning in life. Nature is assumed to be one of them, and in this chapter we will review evidence supporting this contention. Wong (2012, p. 6) postulates a "meaning mindset", which he assumes "to facilitate the dual process of striving for authentic happiness" and "overcoming adversities". In humanistic psychology, humans are considered "meaning-seeking and meaning-making creatures" (Wong, 2006, p. 203). For Wong (2007), the meaning mindset also involves understanding the structure, functions and processes of meaning. It determines how one looks at life and makes significant choices. It involves a commitment to a higher purpose, such as an ultimate concern. "People's lives will be meaningful to the extent their human spirit is able to tune in on the ultimate meaning" (Frankl, 1985, p. 141). This ultimate meaning cannot be grasped simply in rational terms. It involves transcendence and spirituality.

Interference with meaning

Already Franco-Swiss philosopher Jean-Jacques Rousseau (1712–1778) saw a shift in values in the developing modern societies in the 18th century; that is, to sacrifice meaning for achieving success in comparison to others. The meaning mindset can be associated with a growth orientation found in different humanistic approaches (Maslow, 1962). But modern societies frequently instigate an opposing mindset parallel with Rousseau's observations, a "fixed mindset" which focuses on competition and stable abilities or talents (Dweck, 2006). The challenge of the fixed mindset is the problem of alienation from one's own true needs. Because a person is highly focused on functioning in the world in roles given to him/her, meeting the demands of society may involve blocking access to one's true needs or the implicit self. However, according to Lukas (1986) experiencing meaning requires achieving congruence, which involves awareness of one's true needs (implicit needs) as well as capacities and limitations. Personality research has in fact supported the view that personality congruence or coherence is an important factor in promoting individuals' perceptions that their lives are meaningful (e.g. Cervone & Shoda, 1999).

Rousseau saw the development of 18th century society not in response to human needs but as the result of pride and vanity. He proposed that societal development had crushed individual liberty. In his *Discourse on the Origin and Basis of Inequality Among Men* (Rousseau, 1755) he explains how the desire to have value in the eyes of others comes to undermine personal integrity and authenticity in a society marked by interdependence, hierarchy and inequality. In other words, societal demands may block access to the individual's real but implicit needs, thereby creating conflict and reducing the experience of meaning. Twentieth century sociology and psychology have addressed this issue. For instance, Kuhl and Beckmann (1994) describe a loss-of-autonomy cycle that leads to blocked access to the implicit self. Interactions occur sequentially between 1. Control (socialisation) with a suppression of self, leading to 2. Conflict (accumulation) increasing uncontrollable intrusions into a 3. State Orientation (blocking of consciousness and negative affect) with a subsequent impairment of auxiliary volitional functions, whereby 4. Volition (globally impaired) is linked to a compensatory increase of control (Kuhl & Beckmann, 1994).

To explain, complying with role expectations or duties in the work place or in the family may require suppressing individual needs. To a large degree socialisation prepares individuals to function in society and not to live their dreams. Through self-control the pursuit of personal concerns that are not in line with current demands is blocked. Over time, however, conflict between the implicit personal needs and demands by others will accumulate. Frequently ruminations result from this conflict accumulation. The perception of not acting in line with personal needs or concerns will eventually cause a kind of void, a perception of meaninglessness which is accompanied by an increase in negative affect. The negative affect according to Kuhl's Personal Systems Interactions theory (Kuhl, 2001) will further block access to the implicit self and ways to regulate one's life in a meaningful way. In a kind of downward spiral more and more self-control, i.e., coercing oneself to fulfil one's duty, is required.

Interestingly, this reduction in autonomy aligns with more recent accounts from the self-determination perspective. For example, Ryan et al. (2006) would partly attribute the conflict to failures of internalisation of societal values and demands. At the same time these authors concede that many social mores, behaviours and values are imposed or forced on individuals which may become introjects. People may then enact externally valued behaviours or express socially prescribed meanings simply to avoid guilt, and/or receive social awards without privately accepting these values and behaviours as their own (Deci et al., 1994).

Research by Beckmann (1997) has shown that monotonous tasks like working on an assembly line are associated with the perception of powerlessness and meaninglessness which is related to an increased perception of stress. These perceptions can result in an alienation from one's preferences on subsequent activities (Kuhl & Beckmann, 1994) and increased levels of conformity (Beckmann, 1997). In these experiments, not all individuals are affected in such a way. Individuals with chronic high negative affect accompanied by a tendency to ruminate (state orientation) were found to be unable to cope with the experience of a monotonous task. Only individuals with such a disposition to state orientation were unable to make a choice in line with their preferences after working on the monotonous task and showed high levels of conformity using the Asch paradigm (Asch, 1951). If they were informed that they had control over the assembly line and the responsibility to stop it in case of malfunctioning to prevent costly damage, their subjective experience of the situation changed: This was the case even though objectively the situation was just the same – no need for action ever occurred. With such a framing of the situation perception of powerlessness was largely reduced and perceived meaning increased. Stress was reduced. As a consequence, participants were now able to make choices in line with their actual preferences (Kuhl & Beckmann, 1994). In the conformity experiments, their level of conformity decreased significantly (Beckmann, 1997).

There appears to be a categorical difference between perceiving a presence of meaning and seeking meaning. If individuals indicate that they are seeking meaning, they tend to lack meaning. Steger et al. (2006) found that a perception of presence of meaning was correlated with positive affect. If individuals stated that they were seeking meaning, correlations with depression were found.

Effects of nature engagement on meaning of life

Interestingly, according to Wong (1998), self-transcendence is part of the sources of meaning that make life worth living. This conception might fit into Angyal's (1965) holistic theory in which homonomy is an integration into a larger world that transcends the self. It is the tendency to fit oneself to the environment by willingly subordinating oneself to something that one perceives as larger than the individual self. This could be related to a spirituality that is found in Eastern philosophy. Interestingly, such a concept is found in Csikszentmihalyi's (1992) flow concept which he characterises as the inner experiences that make life worthwhile as well as ideas on a spiritual connectedness to nature (e.g. Fabjanski & Brymer, 2017; Kamitsis & Francis, 2013).

Frankl (1985) suggested three ways of finding meaning: 1) giving or contributing something to the world through our work, 2) experiencing something or encountering someone, and 3) choosing a courageous attitude toward unavoidable suffering. Frankl's second way of finding meaning very neatly fits the assumption of finding meaning in nature. His "experiencing something" involves savouring every moment of every experience, and appreciating the gifts from nature. It relates to being mindful of what is around us, being open to what, for example, nature has to offer, and being sensitive and grateful.

In a study by Klinger (1977), enjoying nature was rated as being important in giving their life meaning by 83% of participants. Burkhardt (1989) stated that interacting with nature was an experience that adds meaning to life and put things into a larger perspective. And in fact, a number of studies have reported increased perceived meaning through nature contact and engagement (Howell, Passmore, & Buro, 2013; O'Connor & Chamberlain, 1996).

Nature mindset

Primate brains display forms of tuning which range from the recognition of faces, to the recognition of emotions, to other social and cultural phenomena. In fact, according to Hubel and Wiesel (1962) the brain could be viewed as a collection of tuned filters. Schwarz (2002) addresses cognitive tuning as individuals' spontaneously adopted reasoning style triggered among other things by environmental cues. Thus, we all possess what could be called cognitive tuning sets that involve expectations of what is relevant, of what may occur in the situation, and what kind of action may be required. Panksepp (1998) proposed in an account of affective neuroscience that there are fixed reaction patterns in our brains which are referred to as "Read Only Memories". Such a reaction pattern based on cognitive tuning is sometimes referred to as a mindset. According to Wong (2012, p. 5) "we all have assumptions, beliefs, values, and worldviews that help us make sense of our lives" and every such philosophy of life leads to the development of a certain mindset. For Wong (2012, p. 5) a mindset is "a frame of reference or prism through which we make value judgments". A meaning mindset, according to Wong (2012) focuses on the person as a meaning-seeking and meaning-making creature, a mindset that facilitates the dual process of striving for authentic happiness and overcoming adversities. Nature, in all its forms is no ordinary stimulus, and its ubiquitous presence offers us the opportunity to reflect on ourselves within a global context.

More than thirty years ago Wilson (1984) proposed the biophilia hypothesis to explain the innate need to connect with living organisms and nature (see also Chapter 1). This appears to be something universal for not only humans but also other primates. In an anecdote reported by Stamp Dawkins (1993), when a couple in Africa went up to a mountain ridge to watch the sun go down they found that the romantic spot was already occupied by a chimp couple watching the sun set.

Given the significance of an interaction with nature for human beings it would be surprising if there were no innate response tendencies that are triggered by features of natural settings. Certainly, because humans originally evolved in natural settings, sky, sun, plants, wild animals, natural water sources, etc., must have been things humans evolved around, along with storms, cold, heat, hungry wild animals, etc. This would account for innate behavioural tendencies in reacting to them. They could be construed as collectively constituting a latent, innate "mindset". This may perhaps be related to what Jung (1981) referred to as an archetype, or a symbol for something significant to humans such as the "mother figure", the "father", etc. The "mother figure", for example, has caring qualities; she is dependable and compassionate. In Jung's view, these archetypes are universal, an "inherited mode of psychic functions". Among those archetypes can be found the idea of "mother nature". Interestingly, in Jung's view, modern humans have by and large become unable to activate archetypes because there are very few demands in modern society to resort to archetypes. Alternatively, perhaps the probability of their activation is reduced because of all the competing associations we have acquired to the corresponding stimuli. Therefore, humans may have to learn how to activate a nature-related archetype or nature mindset.

A nature mindset could be considered as something like a basic pattern that all human beings share. Interestingly Schwarz (2002) and others speak of the "wisdom of feeling". An interaction with nature could have the potential of triggering a set of cognitive and emotional reactions of which one would not necessarily be fully consciously aware. However, as suggested above, socialisation in modern societies may block access to the full potential of a nature mindset.

This conceptualisation implies that a nature mindset does not have to be learned. What it needs are resources that can evoke it. What needs to be learned is how to access these. Mindfulness training may be helpful in this context (see also Chapter 18).

What is a positive natural environment?

Which features of nature have positive effects still needs further investigation. Kaplan (1995) characterises "restorative environments" as settings that allow escape from pressures, restful occupation of the mind, moderate or "quiet fascination". This author points out that they should be compatible with an individual's inclination. In Chapter 8, Igou and Van Tilburg argue that the positive effects of nature are based on the typical high levels of brightness, saturation and contrast in natural visual stimuli. In a recent narrative review, van den Bosch, Thompson, and Grahn (2018) postulate that identifying one's restorative natural space can provide a pathway to well-being for individuals.

For many researchers, including Antonovsky (1979), the complexity of the environment is a crucial variable. Too much complexity may induce confusion, anxiety and conflict. This was addressed by Berlyne (1960) in his arousal theory. Berlyne saw an arousal potential in various properties of the environment. Those properties include ambiguity, novelty and change, surprise, complexity, uncertainty and conflict. The arousal potential determines a resulting arousal level which can have positive or negative hedonic values resulting in approach or avoidance tendencies. Once an "absolute threshold" has been crossed, positive hedonic value builds to a peak as arousal potential increases. Any subsequent increases in arousal potential lead to a decline in hedonic value and eventually to increasingly negative values. Very broadly speaking, Berlyne (1960) saw low levels of complexity of the environment generating a low arousal level which is perceived as unpleasant. A typical description would be boredom (see also Chapter 8). High levels of complexity result in high levels of arousal which are also experienced as unpleasant. A medium level of complexity or arousal potential leads to an arousal level that is perceived as pleasant. Therefore, environments are preferred that can produce a pleasurable rise in arousal but at the same time possess properties that are potentially arousal decreasing such as familiarity and patterning. Similarly, Wohlwill (1983) postulated that natural environments with an intermediate level of complexity, characterised by irregular and curvilinear lines and edges, continuous gradations of shape and colour, and irregular, rough textures would be desirable. Recent research on fractal analyses of silhouettes revealed that "people prefer the most natural looking fractals – those with a visual complexity that is neither too low nor too high" a D-value of 1.3, where 1 represents no complexity and 2 high complexity (Hägerhall et al., 2018, p. 80).

Certain mechanisms can reduce the negative effects of complexity. Luhmann (1968) for example saw trust as the basic mechanism for reducing the perception of threat in a complex environment. This relates to Antonovsky's sense of coherence. Mindsets as unconscious reaction patterns could convey ways of positive feeling or positive affect that the person can trust that a situation is not threatening.

Positive experience in natural environments and nature as a resource

Overwhelming evidence has demonstrated the psychological benefits of residential proximity to nature comprising green and blue natural spaces (see also Chapter 2). For example, it was reported that chronic stress, measured by salivary cortisol, is higher in residential areas with less access to green space (Roe et al.,

2013). As discussed later in detail in Chapter 7, nature contact is associated with an increase in positive affect (McMahan & Estes, 2015) and a reduction of rumination (Bratman et al., 2015). In fact, nature might help to disengage from personal losses (Klinger, 1977). People often report that they feel *awe* when exposed to a "breathtaking" view of nature, which makes them and also the magnitude of their problems reduce upon reflection (see also Chapter 1).

People often face negative experiences; some are mundane (e.g. boredom; Van Tilburg & Igou, 2012, 2017) while others are rather serious (e.g. disillusionment; Maher, Igou, & Van Tilburg, 2018). Literature in psychology has documented thoroughly that particular stimuli and experiences have buffering or restorative functions such as self-affirmations, certainty, experienced helping (e.g., Heine et al., 2006 for an overview in coping with various meaning threats). We certainly would not want to state unequivocally that exposure to nature or engagement with nature enables people to master serious problems in life, although it is certainly plausible that it may help in this regard. More importantly, it seems that nature has a positive effect on people's psychological state when negative experiences are rather mundane and mild. This is, of course, important given that frequent mundane negative experiences may still have a profound effect on people's lives across the lifespan. One such experience is boredom (see Chapter 8). It is defined by Eastwood et al. (2012) as "the aversive experience of wanting, but being unable, to engage in satisfying activity" (p. 482).

Studies show that boredom is a rather mild negative experience, described by people as a state of meaninglessness, lacking challenge and attention (e.g. Eastwood et al., 2012; Van Tilburg & Igou, 2017). In Chapter 8, Igou and Van Tilburg) describe how nature stimuli serve as an antidote to boredom. In this respect, nature "helps" to reduce this perception of the meaninglessness that boredom conveys.

We can thus conclude that nature's buffering and restorative effects in relation to negative experiences might be explained by the meaningfulness that people experience when facing nature. We certainly do not want to claim that these effects result from all natural stimuli. It is more plausible that they are limited to some. As stated above, in line with Berlyne's theorising and the findings of Hägerhall et al. (2018), nature has to have some arousal potential that results from medium complexity. This is also reflected in Chapter 8 where it is stated that the positive effects of nature are based on the typical high levels of brightness, saturation and contrast in natural visual stimuli (see also Chapter 6). These nature-typical features seem to be effective in reducing boredom and by doing so restore a sense of meaning in life. This also suggests that some, rather atypical, visual stimuli representing nature are less effective in battling boredom and the associated meaninglessness.

Research must in parallel explore and evaluate the *type of negative experiences* that people have. Above, we already distinguished mild from severe experiences. Further, some negative experiences are relatively strongly linked to hedonics and relatively unrelated to meaninglessness (e.g. wine with a corky taste, freezing hands). It is unclear whether natural stimuli also elevate positivity in people if the original experiences are hedonically negative. This might be the case if natural stimuli are themselves associated with hedonism (e.g. sunny beach, big mushrooms). We admit, these ideas are rather speculative and call for systematic investigation.

Future research directions

- Theory-driven approaches should be applied to understand the interaction of meaning (Klinger, 2012), arousal (Berlyne, 1960) and motivation (Kuhl & Beckmann, 1994).
- Nature might help to disengage from personal losses through a process of detachment or perspective and researchers should explore the array of pathways that nature offers for restoration, recovery and the promotion of well-being.
- The specific type of negative experiences should be considered on the individual level.
- Nature-typical features require further investigation (e.g. levels of brightness, saturation and contrast in natural visual stimuli, Hägerhäll, et al., 2018).

In sum, research suggests that nature contact has positive effects on people's psychological state. This might especially be the case if they experience mild threats to their meaning system. One example is the exposure to natural stimuli when people face boredom. Systematic research on the positive effects of nature on buffering against and elevating negative experience is still in its infancy. It is important to distinguish *types of negative experience* and the particular *features of nature* that have positive effects. Further, it is important to distinguish between the types of positivity effect, whether they affect assessments of meaning in life, as we stress here, of experiences that are rather unrelated to meaning. We believe that research into these dynamics is very promising. We will continue highlighting some important and intriguing findings to date demonstrating that engagement with nature (e.g. through green exercise) can have existential consequences: they affect health and people's sense of meaning in life.

Nature-based interventions to promote meaning and increase well-being

Nature-based interventions employ nature as the setting of an intervention (van den Bosch et al., 2018). Nature-based interventions include green exercise (see Chapter 4), which refers to physical activity in natural settings (Barton & Pretty, 2010). Already in the mid-18th century Rousseau (1755) saw an opportunity to restore healthy, meaningful living through nature. He suggested bringing children up in the countryside, where, according to his beliefs, humans are most naturally suited, rather than in a city, where we only learn bad habits, both physical and intellectual.

According to Antonovsky (1979), health is understood as a multidimensional concept including physical, social, mental and spiritual health. Health is regarded as a lifelong dynamic process with people as active participants in a context. Finally, health is seen not as an end in itself but as a means to live a good life (McCuaig, Quennerstedt, & Macdonald, 2013, p. 113).

And the evidence to support the role of nature as a preventative solution for mental health is accumulating. Empirical findings show that more time spent in green space is associated with higher scores on mental health and vitality scales, independent of cultural and climatic contexts (van Den Berg et al., 2016).

Green exercise in the right mind: mindful connection with nature

In order to increase resilience or restore health and well-being through nature, mere exposure to green or blue spaces may not be enough. As outlined in Chapter 3 and Chapter 4, exercise is beneficial for health and well-being) but exercising in nature may have broader effects than mere physical activity. Furthermore, a green exercise that does not involve high intensity training (high heart rate) but focuses on experiencing nature (i.e. involves nature connectedness) is applicable to a broader group of people (see also Chapter 2). Frequently, people with mental health problems (e.g. depressives) may also suffer from comorbid issues including obesity or critical heart conditions (cf. Hare et al., 2014; Luppino et al., 2010). High intensity training is not always feasible for these patient groups.

Accessing nature even with limited physical activity can enhance well-being (Bell et al., 2017). Beckmann et al. (2002) conducted an intervention study in which six participants with and four without somatic impairments learned scuba diving. After an extensive training period at the swimming pool of a German Olympic training centre participants began with open water diving in German lakes. Eventually, a ten-day open water diving experience in Egypt's Red Sea concluded the project. Initially, physical complaints (Complaints Schedule, Zerssen, 1976) were moderate (for participants without impairments) to high (for participants with impairments). On the *Beck Depression Inventory* (BDI; Beck, Steer, & Brown, 1996) the mean score for participants without impairments was almost zero. The Mean BDI score for participants with impairments was 18, indicating a mild depression on average. In the seminal Blumenthal et al. (1999) study on the effects of exercise training on depression, participants in the exercise conditions exercised in a group setting three times per week at 70–85% of their heart rate reserve. Following 16 weeks of treatment the exercise training was found to be as effective as anti-depressive medication. In the Beckmann et al. (2002) study, physical exercise intensity was at the low-moderate level (e.g. 45–55% of maximal heart rate). The focus was on drifting balanced through the water observing nature. After one year of participating in the project perceived physical complaints were reduced by approximately 50%. The average BDI score in the group with impairments dropped to 10 during the project (indicating minimal depression) and with an average score of 15.8 was still significantly below the initial score 6 months after the end of the project. Furthermore, qualitative interviews revealed increased optimism ("I can still learn"). At the onset of the project a paraplegic participant described her life as "going to rehab and waiting for death". At the end of the project, the same person stated "having new purposes in life". Thus the experiences made in the project can be said to have rebuilt a perception of meaning in life.

Effects of an exposure to nature on meaning of life and health and well-being

Accumulating research has examined how mental health measures, such as depression, are affected by natural environments, with green space, such as grass, forests and parks, being the most prominent settings analysed (e.g. Alcock et al., 2014; De Vries et al., 2016; Mitchell & Popham, 2007). Suicide is the most severe consequence of depression. Frankl (1985) associates a loss of meaning in life with suicide. Von Andics (1947, p. 65) in an investigation on suicides wrote that "those who had committed suicide were people who had become weary of life for such reasons as maladjustment to their environments". Heisel and Flett (2004) found that purpose in life and satisfaction with life accounted for variability in suicide ideation scores above and beyond that accounted for by the negative psychological factors alone. Purpose in life also mediated the relation between satisfaction with life and suicide ideation and moderated the relation between depression and suicide ideation. More generally, several studies provide evidence that finding or having a purpose in life may promote greater longevity (Boyle et al., 2009; Hill & Turiano, 2014; Krause, 2009; Sone et al., 2008). In the context of the present chapter, it is especially relevant that exposure to a natural environment seems to contribute to a prevention of suicide. In a recent study, Helbich et al. (2018) found that municipalities with a large proportion of green or a moderate proportion of green space showed a reduced suicide risk (using standardised suicide ratios) compared to municipalities with less green space. This result emerged with several covariates (e.g., unemployment, religion, marital status, urban vs. rural areas) being controlled for and these findings align with previous research on aspects of well-being (e.g. Gascon et al., 2015).

As the following example from the first author's applied work as a sport psychologist demonstrates, even the mere imagining of physical exercise in a natural environment with positive qualities can have beneficial effects on an individual's well-being and performance capacity. A German professional football club had asked for psychological consultation for one of their players. The 27-year-old Brazilian player had had severe knee injury and was on rehabilitation treatment for six months after surgery. Upon his return to the club, he had announced that he would quit playing football. During the psychologist's first session with the player it became clear that the decision to quit was not really thought through and that playing on a professional football team remained his ambition. He said that the reason for wanting to quit playing was that he did not fully trust his knee post-surgery. Additionally, he noted that the training system at a German club was very different from the circumstances he was used to in Brazil. Particularly, he complained about high demands for discipline and a lack of spontaneity. In other words, he perceived reduced self-determination. In the next session he was asked if he would like to engage in a hypnotic guided imagery exercise. When he agreed, the "Safe Place" exercise was selected. After induction of hypnotic trance, the player was asked to imagine a place where he felt completely well and safe. He came up with the beach in his home town in Brazil. When he was asked to describe what he was doing and experiencing he said the he was jogging along the waterline, seeing the turquoise ocean and smelling it. He said he was jogging without a shirt and feeling the warm sun on his body. When asked if he was wearing shoes he answered that he was of course barefooted. He continued to describe how he was feeling the warm sand under the soles of his feet. He said he was feeling completely well and free. Eventually, he was asked, "How about your operated knee while you are jogging?" At first, he was surprised and then responded that he had not thought about his knee at all and that it was absolutely fine. The posthypnotic order given to him was to return to his safe place and savour the experience whenever he felt that the training conditions were pulling him down. As a result, he continues to play and is back to being a top performer on the team.

Concluding remarks

Nature-based interventions for treating illness, and promoting health and well-being have a long tradition, with evidence dating back to 406 BC (Huelat, 2003). Medieval monasteries as a predominant source of care often featured therapeutic or recovery gardens. Urbanisation and societal change have led to a rapid reduction in access to natural stimuli and lower levels of pro-environmental behaviour (Townsend et al., 2018). To some degree, humans probably have to re-learn to become mindfully connected to nature (see also Chapter 18). In this chapter we have presented evidence that activating a nature mindset can result in increased perceptions of meaningfulness. Perceived meaningfulness is crucial for health and well-being. Examples were given of the reduction of depression along with an increased perception of meaning in life through a mindful nature experience in the paraplegic participant in the Beckmann et al. (2002) study. Another example of nature experience is the recovery of the Brazilian football player through guided imagery of jogging on the beach of his hometown. In a case study by Weerasuriya (2016) a patient described his nature experience as "It takes you away from that medical model, into a … sense of being part of life again" (quote in Townsend et al., 2018, p. 60).

References

Alcock, I., White, M.P., Wheeler, B.W., Fleming, L.E., & Depledge, M.H. (2014). Longitudinal effects on mental health of moving to greener and less green urban areas. *Environmental Science and Technolology, 48*, 1247–1255.

Angyal, A. (1965). *Neurosis and treatment: A holistic theory*. New York, NY: Wiley.

Antonovsky, A. (1979). *Health, stress and coping*. San Francisco: Jossey-Bass.

Asch, S.E. (1951). Effects of group pressure on the modification and distortion of judgments. In H. Guetzkow (Ed.), *Groups, leadership and men* (pp. 177–190). Pittsburgh, PA: Carnegie Press.

Barton, J. & Pretty, J. (2010). What is the best dose of nature and green exercise for improving mental health. A multi-study analysis. *Environmental Science and Technology, 44*, 3947–3955.

Baumeister, R.F. (1991). *The meanings of life*. New York: Guilford.

Beck, A.T., Steer, R.A., & Brown, G.K. (1996). *Beck depression inventory-II*. New York: Pearson.

Beckmann, J. (1997). *Alienation and conformity. Manuscript*. München: Max-Planck-Institute for Psychological Research.

Beckmann, J. Rode, J., Wefers, U., Dargel, N., Krüger, T., & Wick, D. (2002). Tauchen mit Behinderten und Nichtbehinderten [Scuba diving with physically impaired and non- impaired people]. In H. Ohlert & J. Beckmann (Eds.), *Sport Ohne Barrieren [Sport without Barriers]* (pp. 166–180). Schorndorf: Karl Hofmann.

Bell, S.L., Westley, M., Lovell, R., & Wheeler, B.W. (2017). Everyday green space and experienced well-being: The significance of wildlife encounters. *Landscape Research, 43* (1), 8–19. doi:10.1080/01426397.2016.1267721

Berlyne, D. E. (1960). *Conflict, arousal, and curiosity*. New York, NY, US: McGraw-Hill.

Blumenthal, J.A., Babyak, M.A., Moore, K.A., Craighead, W.E., Herman, S., Khatri, P., Waugh, R., Napolitano, M.A., Forman, L.M., Appelbaum, M., Doraiswamy, P.M., & Krishnan, K.R. (1999). Effects of exercise training on older patients with major depression. *Archives of Internal Medicine, 159*(19), 2349–2356.

Boyle, P.A., Barnes, L.L., Buchman, A.S., & Bennett, D.A. (2009). Purpose in life is associated with mortality among community-dwelling older persons. *Psychosomatic Medicine, 71*, 574–579.

Bratman, G.N., Daily, G.C., Levy, B.J., & Gross, J.J. (2015). The benefits of nature experience: Improved affect and cognition. *Landscape and Urban Planning, 138*, 41–50.

Burkhardt, M.A. (1989). Spirituality: An analysis of the concept. *Holistic Nursing Practice, 3*, 69–77.

Cervone, D., & Shoda, Y. (1999). Social-cognitive theories and the coherence of personality. In D. Cervone & Y. Shoda (Eds.), *The coherence of personality: Social-cognitive bases of consistency, variability, and organization* (pp. 3–33). New York: Guilford Press.

Csikszentmihalyi. (1992). *Flow: The psychology of happiness*. London: Rider.

De Vries, S., Ten Have, M., van Dorsselaer, S., van Wezep. M., Hermans, T., & de Graaf, R. (2016). Local availability of green and blue space and prevalence of common mental disorders in the Netherlands. *British Journal of Psychiatry Open, 2*, 366–372.

Deci, E.L., Eghrari, H. Patrick, B.C., & Leone, D.R. (1994). Facilitating internalization: The self-determination theory perspective. *Journal of Personality, 62*, 119–142.

Dweck, C. (2006). *Mindset. The new psychology of success.* Ney York: Ballentine Books.

Eastwood, J. D., Frischen, A., Fenske, M. J., & Smilek, D. (2012). The unengaged mind: Defining boredom in terms of attention. *Perspectives on Psychological Science*, 7, 482–495. doi:10.1177/1745691612456044

Emmons, R.A., Cheung, C., & Tehrani, K. (1998). Assessing spirituality through personal goals: Implications for research on religion and SWB. *Social Indicators Research, 45*, 391–422.

Eriksson, M., & Lindström, B. (2006). Antonovsky's sense of coherence scale and the relation with health: A systematic review. *Journal of Epidemiology and Community Health, 60* (5), 376–381. doi:10.1136/jech.2005.041616

Fabjanski, M., & Brymer, E. (2017). Enhancing health and wellbeing through immersion in nature: A conceptual perspective combining the stoic and Buddhist traditions. *Frontiers in Psychology, 8*, 1573. doi:10.3389/fpsyg.2017.01573

Frankl, V. (1985). *Man's search for meaning: An introduction to logotherapy.* (Originally published 1946). New York: Washington Square Press.

Gascon, M., Triguero-Mas, M., Martínez, D., Dadvand, P., Forns, J., Plasència, A. & Nieuwenhuijsen, M.J. (2015). Mental health benefits of long-term exposure to residential green and blue spaces: A systematic review. International. *Journal of Environmental Research in Public Health, 12*, 4354–4379.

Greenberg, J., Pyszczynski, T. & Solomon, S. (1986). The causes and consequences of a need for self-esteem: A terror management theory. In R.F. Baumeister (Ed.), *Public self and private self* (pp. 189–212). New York: Springer.

Hägerhall, C.M., Sang, A.O., Englund, J., Ahlner, F., Rybka, K., Huber, J. & Burenhult, N. (2018). Do humans really prefer semi-open natural landscapes? A cross-cultural reappraisal. *Front.Psychol.* 9, 822. doi: 10.3389/fpsyg.2018.00822

Hare, D.L., Toukhsati, S.R., Johansson, P., & Jaarsma, T. (2014). Depression and cardiovascular disease: A clinical review. *European Heart Journal, 35*(21), 1365–1372.

Heine, J. S., Proulx, T., & Vohs, K. D. (2006). The meaning maintenance model: On the coherence of social motivations. *Personality and Social Psychology Review, 10*, 88–110. doi:10.1207/s15327957pspr1002_1

Heisel, M.J., & Flett, G.L. (2004). Purpose in life, satisfaction with life, and suicide ideation in a clinical sample. *Journal of Psychopathology and Behavioral Assessment, 26*(2), 127–135.

Helbich, M., de Beurs, D., Kwan, M.-P., O'Connor, R., & Groenewegen, P.P. (2018). Natural environments and suicide mortality in the Netherlands: A cross-sectional, ecological study. *Lancet Planet Health, 2*, 134–139.

Hill, P. L., & Turiano, N. A. (2014). Purpose in life as a predictor of mortality across adulthood. *Psychological Science, 25*(7), 1482–1486. doi:10.1177/0956797614531799

Howell, A. J., Passmore, H.-A., & Buro, K. (2013). Meaning in nature: Meaning in life as a mediator of the relationship between nature connectedness and well-being. *Journal of Happiness Studies, 14*(6), 1681–1696. doi:http://dx.doi.org/10.1007/s10902-012-9403-x

Hubel, D.H., & Wiesel, T.N. (1962). Receptive fields, binocular interaction and functional architecture in the cat's visual cortex. *Journal of Physiology, 160*, 106–154.

Huelat, B.J. (2003). *Healing environments: Design for the body, mind, and spirit.* Arlington, VA: MEDEZYN in collaboration with PEECAPRESS.

Joske, W. D. (1981). Philosophy and the meaning of life. In E. D. Klemke (Ed.), *The meaning of life* (pp. 248–261). New York: Oxford University Press.

Jung, C.G. (1981). *The archetypes and the collective unconscious.* Princeton, NJ: Princeton University Press.

Kamitsis, I., & Francis, A. J.P. (2013). Spirituality mediates the relationship between engagement with nature and psychological wellbeing. *Journal of Environmental Psychology, 36*, 136–143.

Kaplan, S. (1995). The restorative benefits of nature: Towards an integrative framework. *Journal of Environmental Psychology, 15*, 169–182.

King, L.A., Hicks, J.A., Krull, J.L., & Del Gaiso, A.K. (2006). Positive affect and the experience of meaning in life. *Journal of Personality and Social Psychology, 90*(1), 179–196.

Klinger, E. (1977). *Meaning and void: Inner experience and the incentives in people's lives*. Minneapolis: University of Minnesota Press.

Klinger, E. (2012). The search for meaning in evolutionary goal-theory perspective and its clinical implications. In P.T.P. Wong (Ed.), *The human quest for meaning. Theories, research, and applications* (pp. 23–56). New York, London: Routledge.

Krause N. (2009). Meaning in life and mortality. *Journal of Gerontology: Social Sciences., 64*, 517–527.

Kuhl, J. (2001). *Motivation und Persönlichkeit*. Göttingen: Hogrefe.

Kuhl, J. & Beckmann, J. (1994). Alienation. Ignoring one's preferences. In J. Kuhl & J. Beckmann (Eds.), *Volition and personality: Action and state orientation* (pp. 375–390). Seattle: Hogrefe.

Luhmann, N. (1968). *Vertrauen. Ein Mechanismus zur Reduktion von Komplexität*. Stuttgart: Enke.

Lukas, E. (1986). *Meaning in suffering: Comfort in crisis through logotherapy*. Berkeley, CA: Institute of Logotherapy Press.

Luppino, F.S., de Wit, L.M., Bouvy, P.F., Stijnen, T., Cuijpers, P., Penninx, B.W., & Zitman, F.G. (2010). Overweight, obesity, and depression: A systematic review and meta-analysis of longitudinal studies. *Archives of General Psychiatry, 67*(3), 220–229. doi:10.1001/archgenpsychiatry.2010.2

Maher, P. J., Igou, E. R, & Van Tilburg, W. A. P. (2018). Brexit, Trump, and the polarizing effect of disillusionment. *Social Psychological and Personality Science*.

Martela, F., & Steger, M.F. (2016). The three meanings of meaning in life: Distinguishing coherence, purpose, and significance. *The Journal of Positive Psychology, 11*(5), 531–545. doi:http://dx.doi.org/10.1080/17439760.2015.1137623

Maslow, A. H. (1962). *Toward a psychology of being*. Princeton: D. Van Nostrand Company.

McCuaig, L., Quennerstedt, M., & Macdonald, D. (2013). A salutogenic, strengths-based approach as a theory to guide HPE curriculum change. *Asia-Pacific Journal of Health, Sport and Physical Education, 4*(2), 109–125.

McMahan, E. A., Estes, D. (2015). The effect of contact with natural environments on positive and negative affect: A meta-analysis. *Journal of Positive Psychology, 10*, 507–519. doi:10.1080/17439760.2014.994224

Mitchell, R., & Popham, F. (2007). Greenspace, urbanity and health: Relationships in England. *Journal of Epidemiology and Community Health, 61*, 681–683.

O'Connor, K., & Chamberlain, K. (1996). Dimensions of life meaning: A qualitative investigation at mid-life. *British Journal of Psychology, 87*, 461–477.

Panksepp, J. (1998). *Affective neuroscience: The foundations of human and animal emotions*. Oxford: Oxford University Press.

Roe, J. J., Thompson, C. W., Aspinall, P. A., Brewer, M. J., Duff, E. I., Miller, D., … Clow, A. (2013). Green space and stress: Evidence from cortisol measures in deprived urban communities. *International Journal of Environmental Research and Public Health, 10* (9), 4086–4103. doi:http://doi.org/10.3390/ijerph10094086

Rousseau, J.J. (1755). *Discours sur l'origine et les fondements de l'inégalité parmi les hommes*. Amsterdam: Marc-Michel Rey.

Ryan, R.M., Deci, E.L., Grolnick, W.S., & La Guardia, J.G. (2006). The significance of autonomy and autonomy support in psychological development and psychopathology. In D. Cicchetti & D.J. Cohen (Eds.), *Developmental psychopathology* (pp. 795–849). Hoboken, NJ: Wiley.

Schwarz, N. (2002). Situated cognition and the wisdom of feelings: Cognitive tuning. In L. Feldman Barrett & P. Salovey (Eds.), *The wisdom in feeling* (pp. 144–166). New York, NY: Guilford Press.

Sone, T., Nakaya, N., Ohmori, K., Shimazu, T., Higashiguchi, M., Kakizaki, M., & Tsuji, I. (2008). Sense of life worth living (*ikagai*) and mortality in Japan: Ohsaki study. *Psychosomatic Medicine*, *70*, 70–715.

Stamp Dawkins, M. (1993). *Through our eyes only. The search for animal consciousness*. Oxford, UK: W.H. Freeman.

Steger, M. F., Frazier, P., Oishi, S., & Kaler, M. (2006). The meaning in life questionnaire: Assessing the presence of and search for meaning in life. *Journal of Counseling Psychology*, *53*, 80–93.

Townsend, M., Henderson-Wilson, C., Ramkissoon, H., & Werasuriya, R. (2018). Therapeutic landscapes, restorative environments, place attachment, and well-being. In M. van den Bosch & W. Bird (Eds.), *Oxford textbook of nature and public health. The role of nature in improving the health of a population* (pp. 57–62). Oxford, UK: Oxford University Press.

van Den Berg, M., van Poppel, M., van Kamp, I., Andrusaityte, S., Balseviciene, B., Cirach, M., Danileviciute, A., Ellis, N., Hurst, G., Masterson, D., Smith, G., Triguero-Mas, M., Uzdanaviciute, I., de Wit, P., van Mechelen, W., Gidlow, C., Grazuleviciene, R., Nieuwenhuijsen, M.J., Kruize, H., & Maas, J. (2016). Visiting green space is associated with mental health and vitality: A cross-sectional study in four European cities. *Health Place*, *38*, 8–15. doi:10.1016/j.healthplace.2016.01.003

van den Bosch, M., Ward Thompson, & Grahn, P. (2018). Preventing stress and promoting mental health. In M. van den Bosch & W. Bird (Eds.), *Oxford textbook of nature and public health. The role of nature in improving the health of a population* (pp. 108–115). Oxford, UK: Oxford University Press.

Van Tilburg, W. A. P., & Igou, E. R. (2012). On boredom: Lack of challenge and meaning as distinct boredom experiences. *Motivation & Emotion*, *36*, 181–194. doi:10.1007/s11031-011-9234-9

Van Tilburg, W. A. P., & Igou, E. R. (2013). On the meaningfulness of behavior: An expectancy x value approach. *Motivation and Emotion*, *37*, 373–388. doi:10.1007/s11031-012-9316-3

Van Tilburg, W. A. P., & Igou, E. R. (2017). Boredom begs to differ: Differentiation from other negative emotions. *Emotion*, *17*, 309–322. doi:10.1037/emo0000233

Van Tilburg W. A. P., & Igou, E. R. (2019). Dreaming of a brighter future: Anticipating happiness instils meaning in life. *Journal of Happiness Studies*, 20, 541–559. doi:10.1007/s10902-018-9960-8

Von Andics, M. (1947). *Suicide and the meaning of life*. London: William Hodge & Co.

Weerasuriya, R. (2016). The health and wellbeing experiences accessing nature in gardens within a healthcare setting. Unpublished PhD thesis, Deakin University.

Wilson, E.O. (1984). *Biophilia. The human bond with other species*. Cambridge, MA: Harvard University Press.

Wohlwill, J.F. (1983). The concept of nature: A psychologist's view. In I. Altman, & J. F. Wohlwill (Eds.), *Behavior and the natural environment. Advances in theory and research, Vol. 6* (pp. 85–125). New York: Plenum.

Wong, P.T.P. (1998). Implicit theories of meaningful life and the development of the personal meaning profile. In P.T.P. Wong (Ed.), *The human quest for meaning: A handbook of psychological research and clinical applications* (pp. 111–140). Mahwah, NJ: Erlbaum.

Wong, P.T.P. (2006). Existential and humanistic theories. In M. Hersen, & J. C. Thomas (Eds.), *Comprehensive Handbook of Personality and Psychopathology* (pp.192-211). New York: Wiley.

Wong, P.T.P. (2007). Positive psychology and a positive revolution. In P.T.P. Wong, M. McDonald, & D. Klaassen (Eds.), *The positive psychology of meaning and spirituality* (pp. 1–8). Abbotsford, BC: INPM Press.

Wong, P.T.P. (Ed.). (2012). *The human quest for meaning: Theories, research, and applications* (2nd ed. ed.). New York, NY: Routledge.

Zerssen, D.V. (1976). *Die Beschwerden-Liste.* Weinheim: Beltz.

PART II
Possible mechanisms

Part II

Possible mechanisms

6

THE COGNITIVE NEUROSCIENCE OF NATURE

From motor cognition to grounded cognition

Christopher R. Madan, Tadhg E. MacIntyre, Jürgen Beckmann and Massimiliano Cappuccio

One of the most memorable moments during childhood is our first visit to a natural green or blue space. Our recollections of climbing a tree immersed in nature can resonate for many years. Similarly, the first time one gets hit by an ocean wave provides a robust memory that has a long legacy. Nature provides a distinctive memorable experience in three ways. The stimuli of these natural experiences are both qualitatively (emotionally) and quantitatively (i.e. visual percepts) distinct to those of non-endogenous stimuli (e.g. first visit to a city). Typically, our early experiences in nature are linked to positive emotions (i.e. at least when we recall them later), and often possess a distinctive multi-sensory dimension (e.g. tactile, kinesthetic, visual and auditory). Put simply, how we perceive, experience and recall our nature experiences has been demonstrated to have unique characteristics. Not surprisingly cognitive neuroscientists have been increasingly concerned with understanding our human-nature interactions. In this chapter we will review the commonly applied neuroscientific methods used to study our perception of nature, our activation during exercise and our subsequent responses. We propose a broader conceptualisation than has previously been advocated (Frumkin et al., 2017) with the application of a converging methods approach (Kosslyn & Koenig, 1992) augmented by a strength-based approach (MacIntyre et al., 2013) to optimize the research impact and avoid succumbing to the seductive allure of neuroscience (Uttal, 2011; Farah & Hook, 2013). Additionally, we will propose sample research questions which in our view deserve attention for future research.

Firstly, we propose a rationale for the application of neuroscientific tools to explore the neural substrates of specific human-nature interactions. Figure 6.1 illustrates the range of methods (1–3) applied in studies of human-nature interactions, and transcranial magnetic stimulation (TMS) is among the novel approaches that can be applied. Here we shall briefly review a selection of the

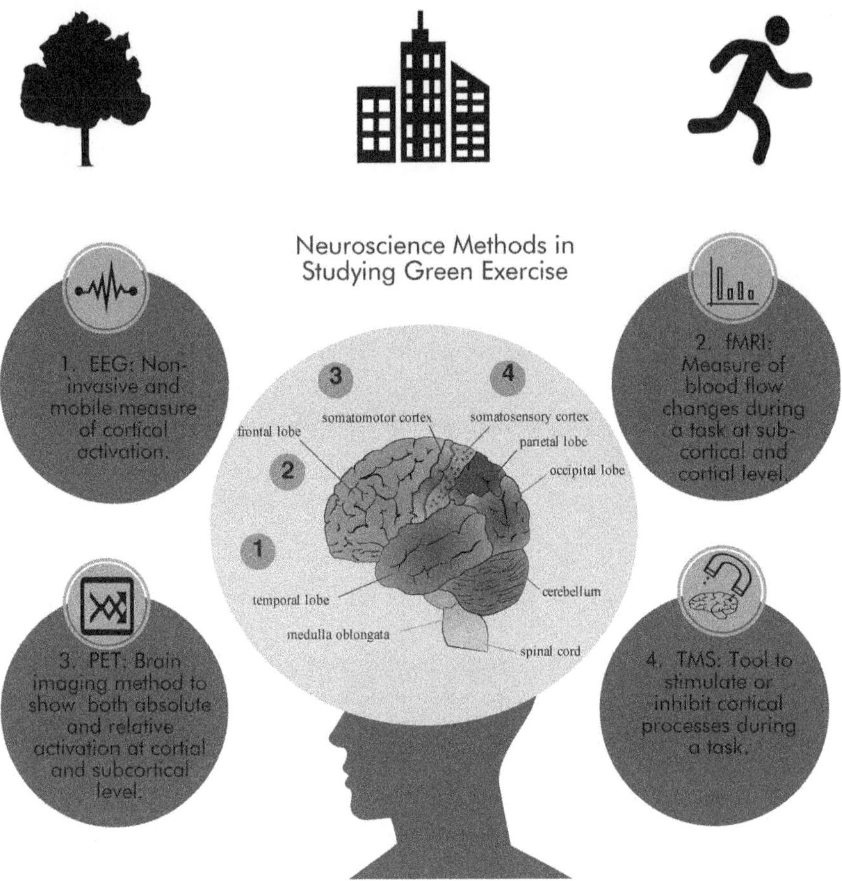

FIGURE 6.1 Neuroscientific methods for the study of green exercise

extant literature. However, it is firstly useful to explain why the memorability of human-nature interactions, and specifically, green exercise (comprising a range of action experiences and motor events), are attracting increasing scholarly concern from researchers.

The introductory chapters (Chapters 1 and 2) specifically outlined the increased concern with understanding human-nature interactions from a stress reduction, attention restoration and physical activity promotion perspective, respectively (Kaplan & Kaplan, 1989; Thompson Coon et al., 2011; Ulrich et al., 1991). Nature in its many forms provides a predominantly visual experience, which explains the proliferation of virtual reality interventions in recent years, for example (see also Chapter 15). The examples of the breaking wave and being surrounded by natural features in a forest highlight the potential multi-sensory nature of these experiences. From a cognitive psychology viewpoint, in addition to their multi-sensory basis such memories could be considered as involving several types of memory: procedural (movement-based), episodic (vivid memories of past events) and autobiographical (personal narratives) with a strong emotional component. Put simply, the neural neighborhoods activated by such experiences are blocks rather than streets, and are interconnected and link cognitive, affective and motor systems.

Consequently, one could surmise that *recalling* oneself walking or jogging on a forest trail provides a highly memorable experience (Madan & Singhal, 2012a) which is dependent upon prior knowledge and experiences, the degree of engagement with the environment, the fidelity of the natural setting and the intensity of the exercise, for example. This type of thought is often mediated by "motor imagery" which is commonly defined as a dynamic mental state during which the representation of a given motor act or movement is rehearsed in working memory without any overt motor output (Guillot & Collet, 2010). The timing of the first wave of research on human-nature interactions (Kaplan & Kaplan, 1989; Ulrich et al., 1991) paralleled the culmination of neuroscientific research and was labelled the "decade of the brain" by the US Congress. One consequence was an upsurge in visual cognition research which was grounded in a converging methods approach comprising behavioural data, computer modeling and neuroscientific data (Kosslyn & Koenig, 1992). This research led subsequently to a study of non-visual but motoric processes (Moran et al., 2011). Furthermore, affective neuroscience or social cognitive neuroscience grew from this research which ultimately linked action representation with empathy (Decety & Stevens, 2009). More recent shifts towards achieving a greater understanding of happiness, thriving, growth, meaning and resilience from the field of positive psychology (Seligman & Csikszentmihalyi, 2000) provided a zeitgeist for the cultivation of research that is concerned with the affective consequences of nature interactions.

The spawning of technologies to measure aspects of neural activation, originally concerned with establishing localisation hypotheses (e.g. what neural structures support specific functions), are now advanced and can provide a critical input into our understanding of the mechanisms underlying human-nature interactions (Kuo et al., 2018). As illustrated in Figure 6.1, EEG or electroencephalography, an early method uses multiple scalp electrodes to measure surface level electrical brain activity and is particularly useful in establishing the immediate temporal effects of a stimulus on our attentional system. Brain imaging methods including fMRI (functional magnetic resonance imaging) and PET (positron-emission tomography) techniques indicate activation based on differences in the about of oxygen consumed and both have high spatial extent (i.e. cortical and sub-cortical structures) and high resolution. The aforementioned approaches have been augmented by TMS (Walsh & Cowey, 2000) which applied a magnetic pulse to inhibit or facilitate function.

One key limitation of all but one of the above methods (EEG) is the inability to be applied in an ecologically valid way to measure movement *during* even nature contact. Participants are usually prone in a scanner and movement is limited to small finger presses or flexion. This barrier can be overcome by exploring recall of our nature experiences, for example, studying the cognitive simulation (e.g. mental imagery) of previous green exercise bouts. This approach can preserve the resolution of imaging techniques to enable appropriate measurement of neural activation in different environmental settings. A key methodological issue is the expertise of the participant in generating mental imagery of their experience, and we propose a strength-based approach as a solution here (MacIntyre et al., 2013). Thus participants should be evaluated on their imagery abilities prior to selection for fMRI testing. Researchers have advocated fMRI as a powerful tool to elucidate the urban stress based on emotional and cognitive processes (Seiyama et al., 2018). In general, for brain-based methods the main contrast has been the urban environment whereas from an exercise context, a comparison with indoor would also be of merit (see Chapter 2).

Providing early support for one of the classic explanations from environmental psychology, stress reduction theory (SRT), Ulrich (1981) presented participants with pictures of several types of landscapes and measured scalp brain activity, using EEG. This technique involves applying highly sensitive electrodes to measure electrical fields generated by activity within the brain. Using this approach, EEG can be used as a measure of physiological arousal and anxiety. Heart rate was also measured using electrocardiography (ECG), along with self-reported ratings of pleasantness. The landscape pictures consisted of either: (1) nature with water, (2) nature with primarily green vegetation, or (3) urban without water or green vegetation. Ulrich found both types of nature scenes led to less EEG-estimated arousal than for the urban scenes, and convergently, ratings of the pictures indicated that participants found the nature scenes more pleasant to look at than the urban scenes.

Similarly, Attention Restoration Theory (ART; Kaplan & Kaplan, 1989), which suggests that viewing natural, or otherwise pleasant scenes can facilitate in restoring attentional resources from fatigue, has been subjected to EEG measures. ART is based on the idea that natural scenes can attract automatically attract attentional resources, thereby decreasing demands on executive function and allowing for the recovery of attention. Over the years, ART has been increasingly supported by studies with patients (Berman et al., 2012; Cimprich & Ronis, 2003) and shown to be beneficial to measures of mental health and mood (Berman et al., 2008; Bodin & Hartig, 2003; Roe & Aspinall, 2011). However, Ohly and colleagues (2016) conducted a systematic review of ART and found results to be mixed. This variation was suggested to be largely due to the variety of experimental designs used to implement and assess the ART, which was proposed as a largely descriptive theory, so may not necessarily be indicating that the ART itself is unreliable.

The study by Roe and Aspinall (2011), a notable exception, is a fMRI study in which participants were assigned to either (a) a nature walk or (b) an urban walk both of 90 minutes duration. Post exercise testing indicated decreased rumination and reduced activation in brain areas linked to maladaptive functioning for the nature walk. Theory based hypotheses in studies integrating structural and fMRI as well as electroencephalography (EEG) techniques, have vast potential in this realm in terms of the identification of pathways as well as outcomes.

Using a portable electro-encephalogram, Aspinall et al. (2015) demonstrated not only that walking through a green space helped participants to recover from an increased stress induced by walking on a trafficked city road, but it also prevented high levels of stress emerging when they walked again on the trafficked road right after. This field study provides support to theories, such as ART and SRT, that postulate that exposure to nature elicits relief from stress as well as reducing future stress. This emerged also from the report of our participants.

Images of natural, as opposed to urban, settings have been found to lead to reduced activation in the medial prefrontal cortex, among other regions (Bratman et al., 2015). These studies have suggested this result as a preference for nature scenes, however, differences have also been found in activation of middle occipital gyrus, though these studies were unable to account for this difference in visual activity (Bratman et al., 2015). This secondary result is quite important – to accurately understand the effects of nature environments on cognition and mental health, it is necessary to consider potential confounding factors whereby natural environments differ from built environments. While it may not be possible to adequately control for the "nature" of natural settings, these differences, such as in the low-level visual features, must be at the very least considered.

Natural environments are more free-flowing than urban environments and are largely devoid of other people and man-made structures. In contrast, built environments often feature buildings, which are inherently comprised of repeating structural components (such as columns of windows) and other man-made constructs of concrete and metal. These man-made constructs are considered by many to be somewhat visually unpleasant, particularly when contrasted with images of rolling hills and mountains. Thus, here we suggest at least two dimensions that differentiate natural and built scenes that are often not controlled for experimentally, low-level visual features (such as edge density, feature congestion, and spatial frequency [subband entropy]; see Rosenholtz et al., 2007; Madan et al, 2018) and emotional valence. Indeed, low-level visual features have been successfully used to predict participants' ratings of naturalness of images (Berman et al., 2014; Kardan et al., 2015). Valtchanov and Ellard (2015) provide evidence supporting our prediction of differences in rated pleasantness for natural vs. built environment images (also see Kardan et al., 2015), while also showing that altered versions of the images that modulated the spatial frequency could attenuate differences in pleasantness ratings as well as relate to measures of eye movements.

More recent work has still continued to examine variations in brain activity in relation to viewing of nature scenes. Grassini et al. (2019) used a different approach, known as event-related potentials (ERPs), to examine fluctuations in the aforementioned EEG measured electrical fields in relation to the presentation of nature pictures and the ART. Grassini et al. found differences in early visual processing, in the period between 100 and 400 meters from the picture being presented, for pictures of nature versus urban scenes. These differences also related to self-reported ratings of how relaxing the pictures were perceived to be.

In a large-scale survey, Schebella et al. (2017) asked 447 respondents about their favorite nature spaces and why they enjoyed them, to get a better characterisation about the attributes that drew people to natural environments. The most popular nature spaces were nature parks (39.5%), followed by botanical gardens (14.5%) and private green spaces (14.5%). The least popular nature spaces were school parks (0.3%) and sports parks (2.3%). Through following questions, it was determined that one of the most relevant aspects that drew people to prefer some nature spaces over others was the species diversity, across birds, plants, and wildlife. In the same survey, it was also found that respondents most viewed the restorative aspects of nature to be associated with fascination with natural features (50.2%), rather than reasons such as being away (13.0%) or feeling a compatibility with nature (18.4%). As outlined in this survey, urban environments do not need to necessarily be divorced from nature, however. In an innovative review, Cameron et al. (2012) outline how domestic gardens can be used to provide some of the benefits of nature to urban environments, enhancing both well-being and environmental factors (e.g., air quality, biodiversity).

Shifting towards life outcomes, Cherrie et al. (2018) examined the influence of green spaces on age-related cognitive decline in a cohort study of 70-year olds (N=281 participants) and found that local availability of parks during childhood and adulthood had significant effects on maintaining cognitive abilities. Convergently, Kühn et al. (2017) found proximity to nature had beneficial effects on brain connectivity structural integrity in a sample of 341 older adults.

Almost four decades of environmental neuroscience and studies that have investigated natural stimuli have typically focused only on comparisons of activation in response to viewing natural and built environments.

Nature engagement

The interactions between green exercise, nature relatedness and mental health and mental well-being is complex and, to date, has not produced an active stream of research. Given the growing needs of citizens and, importantly, those in urban environments for solutions for mental health promotion, for the potential of nature-based interventions to be realized neurally plausible models are required.

Future pathways

Four suggestions for future research are now outlined and these augment the previous comments in this chapter (e.g. TMS methods). Research design advances including longitudinal studies now require a different level of analysis than previously warranted. Consequently, functional connectivity, structural MRI, grounded cognition approaches and indeed, neuroeconomics are all addressed.

Connectivity

Research using fMRI to study the effects of nature have been influenced by the localisation hypothesis – that is what brain regions are activated and what we can infer from the level of relative activation. In order to develop neutrally plausible models that explain the mechanisms underlying the observed behavioural effects of green exercise longitudinal research is required. One interesting approach used in exercise science involved a 16 week randomly controlled trial (RCT) of aerobic exercise (indoor), by Tozzi et al. (2016). This investigation of the impact of acute exercise on longitudinal functional connectivity used reported resting-state modifications in adults after their extended periods of aerobic exercise. Not only was connectivity from the parahippocampal gyrus to motor, sensory integration and mood regulations areas strengthened after regular exercise but self-reported mood was predicted by changes in connectivity. A variant of this study with exercise outdoors in both natural and built environments would enable differentiation of the relative impact of exercise setting on changes in mood and, additionally, time course cessation effects could be monitored post exercise using novel approaches (e.g. ecological momentary sampling).

Morphological changes

Another approach is integrating structural and functional MRI as well as EEG techniques into the proposed work. This would enable direct measurement of how how physical activity and exercise change an individual's brain structure and relate to brain activity. Novel computational methods to characterize brain structure have been found to be more sensitive to individual differences (Madan & Kensinger, 2016, 2017a; Madan, 2019). Specifically, a measure of structural complexity, mathematically calculated based on the so-called fractal dimensionality of a brain region, has been shown to be more sensitive to age-related differences than cortical measures such as cortical thickness and gyrification (Madan & Kensinger, 2016, 2018) and subcortical volume (Madan & Kensinger, 2017a; Madan, 2019a). This computational approach is also has higher test-retest reliability (Madan & Kensinger, 2017b) and resilence to head-motion (Madan, 2018) than conventional measures of brain structure. Other novel methods, such as the quantification of sulcal morphology (Madan, 2019b), will also provide advances in understanding brain structure relative to extant measures. It is vital to explore long-term changes from green exercise, and evidence (see Chapter 2) suggests that it promotes greater adherence than gym-based equivalent exercise bouts. In practice, long-term implementation intentions appear to be stronger for those using green exercise, and understanding the mechanism underlying this effect has implications for exercise initiation and maintenance.

Grounded cognition

Since Jeannerod (1994) first proposed a simulation theory of action, it has been largely accepted that motor imagery is based on the motor representation that underlies actual motor performance. As a consequence, motor imagery research enables researchers to explore embodied cognition – the idea that cognitive representations are "grounded in, and simulated through, sensorimotor activity" (Slepian et al., 2011, p.26). Converging evidence supports both the embodied cognition (Cappuccio, 2019) and grounded cognition approach and with respect to motor imagery (Madan & Singhal, 2012b; MacIntyre et al., 2019) may be coupled with action, in what are termed quasi-movements (Nikulin et al. 2008). Moreover, evidence supporting the embodiment viewpoint has emerged from studies of action words, action observation and other phenomena explained by simulation theory. Typically, these effects are displayed among expert samples where neural signatures of expertise lead to differentiation in both the intensity and magnitude of the motor resonance. This is based on the recently proposed "strength-based approach" to understanding mental imagery and motor cognition whereby researchers are recommended to focus on expert samples in specific activities to elucidate further the processes underlying motor cognition (Madan & Singhal, 2012b; MacIntyre et al., 2013; Wilson & Golonka, 2013).

Recent research has confirmed that exposure to nature as direct physical and/or sensory contact with the natural environment is as important for well-being as income and education. Positive effects have been shown for primary as well as secondary and tertiary prevention (e.g., Hennigan, 2010; Nisbet et al., 2011). These effects are related to what has been addressed as embodied cognition over the last decades in psychology (Barrett, 2011). According to this psychological approach human cognition is influenced, or even determined by experiences in the physical world. Whereas sensory inputs and motor outputs were secondary in traditional psychological approaches, they are seen as integral to cognitive processes in embodied cognition. From this perspective also cognitive and emotional processing in the brain are regarded as inseparable. In this context, especially regarding interactions with a natural environment, frequently the term "spirituality" is embraced. In general, interacting with nature is seen as an experience that adds meaning to life and puts things into a larger perspective (cf. Burkhardt, 1989). Meaning and void has been an important topic in health related psychology (Klinger, 1977). Alienation from one's implicit self is associated with negative ruminations (Kuhl & Beckmann, 1994) which in turn is connected to lack of recovery (Beckmann & Kellmann, 2004) and proneness to mental disorders (e.g., Beckmann, 1999; Bratman et al., 2015; Nolen-Hoeksema, 2000). Neurophysiological evidence for the effects of nature experience has been found (e.g., Bratman et al., 2015). These effects are related to psychological mechanisms increasing mental well-being such as promotion of positive affect (Mayer et al. 2009), cognitive functioning (e.g., Kaplan 2001), and reduced stress (Wells & Evans, 2003). Other studies have shown that these mediating mechanisms reduce alienation and thereby promote access to the self and health (Kuhl & Baumann, 2000).

Certain prerequisites seem to be warranted to produce the positive effects of exposure to nature. Most important appears to be a Nature Relatedness (Nisbet et al., 2009) which describes individuals' connectedness to the natural environment in which they find themselves, involving a general appreciation for nature and understanding of environmental issues. Another aspect relates to the actual "production functions" of the natural environment (Kareiva et al., 2011). Not all natural environments may have the same psychological effects on all people. The environments should have a "restorative" quality for an individual (Hartig & Staats, 2006). Research has in fact shown that that individuals tend to select favourite environments as means to transform negative psychological states to more positive ones (Korpela, et al., 2001). In general, pleasing positive qualities of natural environments encompass open views, and a lack of loud, distracting noises (Herzog et al., 2003). Another requirement for positive effects of nature experience is that the nature experience is explicitly incorporated into activities. Otherwise, familiarity or habituation to a natural environment in everyday life may diminish the impact of nature exposure (Kamitsis & Francis, 2013).

Neuroeconomics

A growing literature in the field of cognitive neuroscience has demonstrated evidence of a "common currency" of value in the brain (e.g. Landreth & Bickle, 2008; Montague & Berns, 2002). This hypothesis has shown that across a variety of types of "value", there are common brain structures involved in the execution of value-based decision making, including regions such as orbitofrontal cortex and posterior parietal cortex. To investigate the neural processes involved in decisions related to environmental resources, such as deciding to preserve or destroy natural park lands, Sawe and Knutson (2015) conducted an innovative fMRI study. Here participants were shown images of national parks and asked to make hypothetical donations related to supporting different uses of the land (e.g., mining). While procedure is based on a well-established task design in economics, known as willingness-to-pay, the content of the decisions is not merely economic. Indeed, Sawe and Knutson found value-related brain activations in regions associated with reward, but also regions associated with social and belief attitudes, such as the temporoparietal junction.

These additional regions found in the Sawe and Knutson study parallel those found in studies of moral and preference judgements (Theriault et al., 2017). While this may appear to challenge the common currency hypothesis, it is important to acknowledge that this hypothesis was principally borne out of research that is not only about value per se, but is more specifically developed within the field of neuroeconomics. As such, it is reasonable to consider that value-based decisions related to one's self, including decisions involving monetary gains, pleasant music, and attractive faces, may not be shared with decisions about one's morals and ethical viewpoints – which may be more relevant to that person's views on the "value" of nature.

Conclusions

Frumkin et al. (2017, p. 5) recently posed a critical question for the field: "Does nature-based physical activity confer benefits above and beyond equivalent physical activity in nature-free settings?" To answer this question, neuroscientific approaches are increasingly being recognized as a useful tool and many novel questions will be posed to enable greater specificity on the underlying mechanisms to be elucidated.

References

Aspinall, P., Mavros, P., Coyne, R., & Roe, J. (2015). The urban brain: analysing outdoor physical activity with mobile EEG. British Journal of Sports Medicine, 49(4), 272–276. doi:10.1136/bjsports-2012-091877

Barrett, L. (2011). Beyond the brain: how the body and the environment shape cognition. Princeton, NJ: Princeton University Press.

Beckmann, J. (1999). Alienation und Introjektion. Verlust des individuellen Selbst als Merkmal schizophrener Erkrankung [Alienation and introjection. loss of the individual self as characteristic of schizophrenic disorder]. In M. Lasar & H. Ribbert (Eds.), Kognitive und motivationale prozesse bei schizophrener erkrankung [Cognitive and Motivational Processes in Schizophrenic Disorders] (41–53). Regensburg: Roderer.

Beckmann, J., & Kellmann, M. (2004). Self-regulation and recovery: approaching an understanding of the process of recovery from stress. Psychological Reports, 95, 1135–1153.

Berman, M., Jonides, J., & Kaplan, S. (2008). The cognitive benefits of interacting with nature. Psychological Science, 19, 1207–1212.

Berman, M., Kross, E., Krpan, K., Askren, M., Burson, A., & Deldin, P., et al. (2012). Interacting with nature improves cognition and affect for individuals with depression. Journal of Affective Disorders, 140, 300–305.

Berman, M. G., Hout, M. C., Kardan, O., Hunter, M. R., Yourganov, G., Henderson, J. M., et al. (2014). The perception of naturalness correlates with low-level visual features of environmental scenes. PLoS ONE, 9(12), e114572. https://doi.org/10.1371/journal.pone.0114572.

Bodin, M., & Hartig, T. (2003). Does the outdoor environment matter for psychological restoration gained through running? Psychology of Sport and Exercise, 4, 141–153.

Bratman, G.N., Hamilton, J.P., Hahn, K.S., Daily, G.C., & Gross, J.J. (2015). Nature experience reduces rumination and sugenual prefrontal cortex activation. PNAS, 112, 8567–8572. www.pnas.org/cgi/doi/10.1073/pnas.1510459112.

Burkhardt, M.A. (1989). Spirituality: an analysis of the concept. Holistic Nursing Practice, 3, 69–77.

Cameron, R.W., Blanuša, T., Taylor, J.E., Salisbury, A., Halstead, A.J., Henricot, B., & Thompson, K. (2012). The domestic garden–its contribution to urban green infrastructure. Urban Forestry & Urban Greening, 11, 129–137.

Cappuccio, M.L. (2019). Handbook of embodied cognition and sport psychology. Cambridge, MA: MIT Press.

Cherrie, M.P., Shortt, N.K., Mitchell, R.J., Taylor, A.M., Redmond, P., Thompson, C. W., … Pearce, J.R. (2018). Green space and cognitive ageing: A retrospective life course analysis in the Lothian Birth Cohort 1936. Social Science & Medicine, 196, 56–65.

Cimprich, B., & Ronis, D. (2003). An environmental intervention to restore attention in women with newly diagnosed breast cancer. Cancer Nursing, 26, 284–292.

Decety, J., & Stevens, J.A. (2009). Action representation and its role in social interaction. In K.D. Markman, W.M.P. Klein, & J.A. Suhr (Eds.), Handbook of imagination and mental simulation (3–20). New York: Psychology Press.

Farah, M.J., & Hook, C.J. (2013). The seductive allure of "seductive allure". Perspectives on Psychological Science, 8(1), 88–90. doi:10.1177/1745691612469035

Frumkin, H., Bratman, G. N., Breslow, S. J., Cochran, B., Kahn, P. H., Jr, Lawler, J. J., et al. (2017). Nature contact and human health: a research agenda. *Environmental Health Perspectives*, 125(7), 075001. doi:10.1289/EHP1663.

Grassini, S., Revonsuo, A., Castellotti, S., Petrizzo, I., Benedetti, V., & Koivisto, M. (2019). Processing of natural scenery is associated with lower attentional and cognitive load compared with urban ones. Journal of Environmental Psychology, 62, 1–11.

Guillot, A. & Collet, C. (2010). The neurophysiological foundations of mental and motor imagery. Oxford: OUP.

Hartig, T., & Staats, H. (2006). The need for psychological restoration as a determinant of environmental preferences. *Journal of Environmental Psychology*, *26*, 215–226.

Hennigan, K. (2010). Therapeutic potential of time in nature: implications for body image in women. Ecopsychology, 2, 135–140.

Herzog, T.R., Maguire, C.P., & Nebel, M.B. (2003). Assessing the restorative components of environments. Journal of Environmental Psychology, 23, 159–170.

Jeannerod, M. (1994). The representing brain: neural correlates of motor intention and imagery. Behavioral and Brain Sciences, 17(2), 187–245. doi:10.1017/s0140525x00034026.

Kamitsis, I., & Francis, A.J.P. (2013). Spirituality mediates the relationship between engagement with nature and psychological wellbeing. Journal of Environmental Psychology, 36, 136–143.

Kaplan, R., & Kaplan, S. (1989). The experience of nature. Cambridge: Cambridge University Press.

Kardan, O., Gozdyra, P., Misic, B., Moola, F., Palmer, L. J., Paus, T., et al. (2015). Neighborhood greenspace and health in a large urban center. Scientific Reports, 5, 11610. doi:10.1038/srep11610.

Kareiva, P.K., Tallis, H., Ricketts, T.H., Daily, G.C., & Polasky, S. (2011) Natural capital: theory & practice of mapping ecosystem services. Oxford, UK: Oxford Univercity Press.

Klinger, E. (1977). Meaning and void. The inner experiences and the incentives in people's life. Minneapolis, MN: The University of Minnesota Press.

Korpela, K. M., Hartig, T., Kaiser, F. G. & Fuhrer, U. (2001). Restorative experience and self-regulation in favorite places. Environment and Behavior, 33, 572-589.

Kosslyn S.M., Koenig O. (1992). Wet mind. The new cognitive neuroscience. New York/Toronto: The Free Press.

Kuhl, J. & Baumann, N. (2000). Self-regulation and rumination: negative affect and impaired self-accessibility. In W.J. Perrig & A. Grob (Eds.), Control of human behavior, mental processes, and consciousness (283–305). Mahwah, NJ: Erlbaum.

Kuhl, J., & Beckmann, J. (1994). Alienation. Ignoring one's preferences. In J. Kuhl & J. Beckmann (Eds.), Volition and personality: action and state orientation (375–390). Seattle, WA:Hogrefe.

Kühn, S., Düzel, S., Eibich, P., Krekel, C., Wüstemann, H., Kolbe, J., … & Lindenberger, U. (2017). In search of features that constitute an "enriched environment" in humans: associations between geographical properties and brain structure. Scientific Reports, 7, 11920.

Kuo, M., Browning, M.H., & Penner, M.L. (2018). Do lessons in nature boost subsequent classroom engagement? Refueling students in flight. Frontiers in Psychology, 8, 2253.

Landreth, A., & Bickle, J. (2008). Neuroeconomics, neurophysiology and the common currency hypotheses. Economics and Philosophy, 24, 419–429.

MacIntyre, T., Madan, C.R., Brick, N.E., Beckmann, J., & Moran, A.P. (2019). Imagery, expertise and action: a window into embodiment, In M.L. Cappuccio (Ed.), Handbook of embodied cognition and sport psychology (625–650). Cambridge, MA: MIT Press.

MacIntyre, T.E., Moran, A.P., Collet, C., & Guillot, A. (2013). An emerging paradigm: A strength-based approach to exploring mental imagery. Frontiers in Human Neuroscience, 7, 104. doi:10.3389/fnhum.2013.00104

Madan, C. R., & Singhal, A. (2012a). Using actions to enhance memory: Effects of enactment, gestures, and exercise on human memory. *Frontiers in Psychology*, 3, 507.

Madan, C. R., & Singhal, A. (2012b). Motor imagery and higher-level cognition: Four hurdles before research can sprint forward. *Cognitive Processing*, 13, 211–229.

Madan, C. R. (2018). Age differences in head motion and estimates of cortical morphology. PeerJ, 6, e5176. doi:10.7717/peerj.5176.

Madan, C. R. (2019a). Shape-related characteristics of age-related differences in subcortical structures. Aging & Mental Health, 23, 800–810.

Madan, C. R. (2019b). Robust estimation of sulcal morphology. Brain Informatics, 6, 5.

Madan, C. R., & Kensinger, E. A. (2016). Cortical complexity as a measure of age-related brain atrophy. NeuroImage, 134, 617–629.

Madan, C. R., & Kensinger, E. A. (2017a). Age-related differences in the structural complexity of subcortical and ventricular structures. Neurobiology of Aging, 50, 87–95.

Madan, C. R., & Kensinger, E. A. (2017b). Test-retest reliability of brain morphology estimates. Brain Informatics, 4, 107–121.

Madan, C. R., & Kensinger, E. A. (2018). Predicting age from cortical structure across the lifespan. European Journal of Neuroscience, 47, 399–416.

Madan, C. R., Bayer, J., Gamer, M., Lonsdorf, T., & Sommer, T. (2018). Visual complexity and affect: ratings reflect more than meets the eye. Frontiers in Psychology, 8, 2368.

Mayer, F.S., Frantz, C.M., Bruehlman-Senecal, E., & Dolliver, K. (2009). Why is nature beneficial? The role of connectedness to nature. Environment and Behavior, 41, 607–643.

Montague, P.R., & Berns, G.S. (2002). Neural economics and the biological substrate of valuation. Neuron, 36, 265–284.

Moran, A., Guillot, A., MacIntyre, T., & Collet, C. (2011). Re-imagining motor imagery: building bridges between cognitive neuroscience and sport psychology. British Journal of Psychology. doi: 10.1111/j.2044-8295.2011.02068.x.

Nikulin, V. V., Hohlefeld, F. U., Jacobs, A. M., & Curio, G. (2008). Quasi-movements: a novel motor-cognitive phenomenon. Neuropsychologia, 46, 727–742. doi: 10.1016/j.neuropsychologia.2007.10.008.

Nisbet, E.K., Zelenski, J.M., & Murphy, S.A. (2009). The nature relatedness scale: Linking individuals' connection with nature to environmental concern and behavior. Environment and Behavior, 41, 715–740.

Nisbet, E.K., Zelenski, J.M., & Murphy, S.A. (2011). Happiness is in our nature: Exploring nature relatedness as a contributor to subjective well-being. Journal of Happiness Studies, 12, 303–322.

Ohly, H., White, M.P., Wheeler, B.W., Bethel, A., Ukoumunne, O.C., Nikolaou, V., & Garside, R. (2016). Attention restoration theory: a systematic review of the attention restoration potential of exposure to natural environments. Journal of Toxicology and Environmental Health, Part B, 19, 305–343.

Roe, J., & Aspinall, P. (2011). The restorative benefits of walking in urban and rural settings in adults with good and poor mental health. Health & Place, 17, 103–113.

Rosenholtz, R., Li, Y., & Nakano, L. (2007). Measuring visual clutter. Journal of Vision, 7, 17.

Sawe, N., & Knutson, B. (2015). Neural valuation of environmental resources. NeuroImage, 122, 87–95.

Schebella, M.F., Weber, D., Lindsey, K., & Daniels, C.B. (2017). For the love of nature: exploring the importance of species diversity and micro-variables associated with favorite outdoor places. Frontiers in Psychology, 8, 2094.

Seiyama, A., Yamada, K., Osaki, K., Nakai, R., Matsumoto, J., & Yoshimura, A. (2018). Neural bases on cognitive aspect of landscape evaluation: a study using functional magnetic resonance imaging. Journal of Neurology and Neuroscience, 9(4), 263. Doi: 10.21767/2171-6625.1000263.

Seligman, M. E. P., & Csikszentmihalyi, M. (Eds.) (2000). Positive psychology—an introduction. American Psychologist, 55, 5-14.

Slepian, M. L., Weisbuch, M., Rule, N. O., & Ambady, N. (2011). Tough and tender: embodied categorization of gender. Psychological Science, 22, 26-28.

Theriault, J., Waytz, A., Heiphetz, L., & Young, L. (2017). Examining overlap in behavioral and neural representations of morals, facts, and preferences. Journal of Experimental Psychology General, 146, 1586–1605.

Thompson-Coon, J. T., Boddy, K., Stein, K., Whear, R., Barton, J., & Depledge, M. H. (2011). Does participating in physical activity in outdoor natural environments have a greater effect on physical and mental wellbeing than physical activity indoors? a systematic review. Environmental Science & Technology, 45(5), 1761–1772.

Tozzi, L., Carballedo, A., Lavelle, G., Doolin, K., Doyle, M., Amico, F., et al. (2016). Longitudinal functional connectivity changes correlate with mood improvement after regular exercise in a dose-dependent fashion. European Journal of Neuroscience, 43, 1089–1096.

Ulrich, R.S. (1981). Natural versus urban scenes: some psychophysiological effects. Environment and Behavior, 13, 523–556.

Ulrich, R. S., Simons, R. S., Losito, B. D., Fiorito, E., Miles, M. A., & Zelson, M. (1991). Stress recovery during exposure to natural and urban environments. Journal of Environmental Psychology, 11, 201–230.

Uttal, W.R. (2011). Mind and brain: a critical appraisal of cognitive neuroscience. MIT Press.

Walsh, V., & Cowey, A. (2000). Transcranial magnetic stimulation and cognitive neuroscience. Nature Reviews Neuroscience, 1(1), 73–79. doi:10.1038/35036239

Wells, N.M., & Evans, G.W. (2003). Nearby nature: A buffer of life stress among rural children. Environment and Behavior, 35, 311–330.

Wilson, A.D., & Golonka, S. (2013). Embodied cognition is not what you think it is. Frontiers in Psychology, 4, 58. http://dx.doi.org/10.3389/fpsyg.2013.00058

7

AFFECTIVE RESPONSES TO NATURAL ENVIRONMENTS

From everyday engagement to therapeutic impact

Patricia M. Darcy, Marc Jones and Christopher Gidlow

The environment with which we engage is recognised as a determinant of health (World Health Organization, WHO, 2014). Natural environments include green spaces, blue spaces (coastal and inland waterways) and urban green space (UGS; urban space covered by vegetation of any kind) and differ from the built urban environment (grey space) in relation to restoration and mental health outcomes (Cox et al., 2017; Hartig, Mitchell, De Vries, & Frumkin, 2014; Ulrich et al., 1991). In the present chapter we explore the impact of engagement with natural environments on one aspect of health and well-being – affective states. First, we provide an overview of the relationship between engaging with natural environments and health and well-being. Second, we explain why our affective state is an important part of our health and well-being, define what we mean by affective states and how these may be influenced by engagement with natural environments. Third, the main body of the chapter considers how engagement with natural environments may help clinical populations as a therapeutic intervention. Finally, we consider the design of natural environments to promote positive affective responses.

Natural environments, health and well-being

Natural environments have the potential to act as health promoting and health supporting environments, through a combination of natural environment interactions, exposures and pathways. Three types of natural environment interaction have been identified in the literature: intentional, incidental and indirect (Keniger, Gaston, Irvine, & Fuller, 2013). Intentional interactions are defined as purposely being in or experiencing natural environments, such as hill-walking. Incidental interactions result where one is physically present in natural environments; however the interaction is unintended, such as walking to work and encountering street trees. Finally, indirect interaction does not require one to be physically present in natural environments; for example, a view of a garden through a window.

Natural environments also impact on our health and well-being through direct and indirect pathways. Direct pathways include passive nature exposure (i.e. viewing nature or being in the presence of nature but not engaging in an activity), quasi-passive nature exposure (i.e. exploring nature such as smelling and touching plants) and active nature exposure (i.e. actively engaging with the environment) which can bring about restoration from mental fatigue, reduce stress, and improve mood. Indirect pathways include the increased positive affect associated with physical activity in natural environments, and enhanced emotional well-being generated through connecting with others while present in natural environments.

In addition, the beneficial impact of natural environments on health and well-being can be understood across a continuum of interaction which includes regular engagement with nature in everyday life (e.g., gardening), the integration of natural environments in health promotion initiatives and activities aimed at the general population (e.g., green exercise "Parkruns"; WHO, 2016), and the application of prescriptive therapeutic interventions for individuals with defined needs (e.g. green care., Bragg & Leck, 2017).

The central role that natural environments play in impacting on health and well-being may be explained by psycho-evolutionary theories such as the biophilia hypothesis (Kellert & Wilson, 1995; Wilson, 1984), which stipulates that as humans adapted to live in natural environments they developed an innate connection with and preference for natural settings. An absence of a connection to natural environments reflected in our modern lifestyles may create a "mismatch", unconsciously representing a threatening environment and triggering a resulting stress response. Stress Reduction Theory (SRT; Ulrich, 1983) suggests that the aesthetic value of environments has a direct effect on psycho-physiological arousal. Environments that are appraised as attractive promote increased positive affect and reduce negative thoughts and psycho-physiological stress. Attention Restoration Theory (ART; Kaplan & Kaplan, 1989) proposes that natural environments restore depleted mental capacities through effortless or indirect attention. Recent evolutionary theories such as Green Mind Theory (GMT; Pretty, Rogerson, & Barton, 2017) focuses on the link between the brain, body and the environment through reciprocal relationships that connect the body with natural and social environments. GMT proposes that well-being can be improved by environments which influence the body, brain and mind. In turn, the mind changes behaviours which benefits health, and influences pro-social behaviour and greener economies (Pretty et al., 2017).

The role that environments have in determining our health and well-being may have greater relevance than ever due to major demographic changes, such as urbanisation and an increasing older population, in addition to some of the negative consequences of modern, urban living, such as chronic stress and sedentary lifestyles. Urbanisation, where there is a growing trend for people to live in urban settings, presents risk for physical and psychological health, particularly in certain population groups (e.g., children and older people; Tenkate, 2009). Presently 74% of the European population live in an urban environment and globally this is anticipated to be 68% of the population by 2050 (United Nations, 2018).

Urban environments can be detrimental to health. One reason is because of greater levels of pollutants, such as air and noise pollution (e.g., Dadvand et al., 2012). Further, there is greater stimulation from a busy urban environment meaning less opportunity for rest and recuperation, with implications for chronic stress. Indeed, students currently living in urban areas had a stronger amygdala activity in response to social stress compared to students currently living in rural areas (Lederbogen et al., 2011). Further data from the same study showed that students who grew up in a city also showed a stronger response in the cingulate gyrus, compared to those who grew up in a rural area. These findings link the mental health risks of living in an urban environment to stress processing in the brain. They suggest that brain regions differ in vulnerability to social stress depending on living in urban or rural areas across the lifespan, with individuals living in natural environments showing a more resilient response (at least neurobiologically) to stress. Finally, there is evidence that urban upbringing doubles a child's chances of developing schizophrenia in adulthood, with low social cohesion and high crime rates in urban areas being potential contributory factors (e.g., Newbury et al., 2016).

In addition to our changing living environment, it is predicted that by 2030 the proportion of people aged 60 years and older will increase worldwide by over 50%, with significantly greater numbers of older people living in urban settings (United Nations, 2015a; WHO, 2015). Physical inactivity and social isolation are important risk factors to health and well-being (Blair, 2009; Cacioppo, Hughes, Waite, Hawkley, & Thisted, 2006; Holt-Lunstad, Smith, Baker, Harris, & Stephenson, 2015), where physical activity levels decline with age (Chodzko-Zajko et al., 2009) and older people are at greater risk for social isolation and loneliness (Luanaigh & Lawlor, 2008). Research suggests that older people may experience less loneliness and greater social support when they live in green areas (Maas et al., 2009).

Modern living is also associated with an increase in sedentary lifestyles, alongside reduced opportunities to engage with natural environments (McMichael, 2000). In the UK, the proportion of urban population with access to a private garden is reducing (Department for Communities and Local Government, 2010), while the average European spends 90% of their time indoors and, for vulnerable groups (i.e., children and the elderly), this figure can be up to 100% (Galea et al., 2013). The Monitor of Engagement with the Natural Environment survey identified that 12% of children do not visit the natural environment each year (Natural England, 2010).

Natural environments as restorative environments

Natural environments have the potential to act as restorative environments, where a restorative environment is one that promotes restoration (Hartig, 2004). Restoration in this context is defined as "the process of renewing, recovering, or re-establishing physical, psychological, and social resources or capabilities diminished in ongoing efforts to meet adaptive demands" (Hartig, 2004, p. 273). Environmental restoration theories suggest that while not all urban environments lack components that may be restorative, similarly not all natural environments contain components that are (Berto, 2011; Berto, Baroni, Zainaghi, & Bettella, 2010; Kaplan & Kaplan, 1989; Ulrich, 1983). Certain aspects and qualities of natural environments may be more restorative than others (Grahn & Stigsdotter, 2010; Kaplan, 2001). Restoration is often related to environmental preference (Hidalgo, Berto, Galindo, & Getrevi, 2006; Peron, Berto, & Purcell, 2002; Van Den Berg, Koole, & Van der Wulp, 2003) where environments that are appraised as restorative and elicit greater positive affect are most often preferred and sought out to facilitate recovery of depleted resources (Korpela & Hartig, 1996; Staats, Kieviet, & Hartig, 2003).

Specifically, in relation to ART (Kaplan & Kaplan, 1989) attention is easily and almost effortlessly held by natural scenes; referred to as "soft fascination" (Kaplan & Kaplan, 1989). When nature captures attention, executive systems that regulate directed attention get to rest, pessimistic thoughts are blocked, and negative emotions are replaced by positive ones. To illustrate, participants reported higher levels of attention restoration having been for a 30 minute walk in a green or blue environment than an urban environment (Gidlow et al., 2016). In relation to SRT (Ulrich, 1983) natural environments have the potential to act as affective landscapes through alleviating or offsetting the effects of stress, generating positive affect and decreasing negative affect (Bowler, Buyung-Ali, Knight, & Pullin, 2010; Ulrich et al., 1991).

Affect and engagement with nature

In the present chapter we use affect as a broad term referring to the experiential component of all valenced responses, such as emotions and moods (cf. Ekkekakis & Petruzzello, 2000; Rosenberg, 1998). Affect refers to how we feel, and how we feel matters. For example, in the UK in 2016/2017 work-related stress, anxiety, depression (SAD) accounted for 40% of all work-related ill health, and 49% of working days lost due to ill health (HSE, 2016), while chronic stress is a significant contributor to the global increase in non-communicable diseases (NCDs) such as obesity and type II diabetes (Vos et al., 2016). Further, one third of the European population will experience mental health problems at some point in their life with depression and anxiety (considered to be stress-related disorders), the most prevalent mental health disorders (WHO, 2013). Depression is the leading cause of ill-health and disability worldwide (WHO, 2016), and is one of the main reasons for patients to consult with health services, adding significantly to both the economic and health burden (Choi, Lee, Matejkowski, & Baek, 2014). Chapter 10 discusses in detail the potential mechanisms of how engaging with natural environment influences psychological states. We now consider in turn the evidence for the impact on mood and chronic stress.

Natural environments and mood

There is a large body of research which suggests that exposure to nature is associated with increased emotional well-being, lower physiological arousal, higher positive affect and less negative affect in those exposed to natural environments compared to urban or built environments (Hartig, Evans, Jamner, Davis, & Gärling, 2003; Lee et al., 2011; Park et al., 2007). McMahan and Estes (2015) concluded that despite heterogeneity of study design and effect sizes, brief contact with natural environments was associated with higher positive affect (moderate effect size) and reduced negative affect (smaller, but consistent effect size) compared to other environments. Natural environments can have a salutogenic impact by the generation of positive states such as friendliness, happiness and vitality. In comparison, a nature-deficit environment can adversely impact on well-being through the production of negative affect such as anger, aggression, frustration, sadness and fear. Compared to natural environments in laboratory settings (for example virtual nature), actual natural environments elicit greater positive mood (McMahan & Estes, 2015). Similar findings have also been reported where a decrease in negative affect and clinically relevant moods (SAD) was observed after exposure to real or virtual nature (Brooks, Ottley, Arbuthnott, & Sevigny, 2017). However, a greater positive mood was only found for actual nature exposure. Interestingly, while most studies within this area have limited natural environment exposure to summer months, Brooks et al. (2017) examined nature exposure across seasons. Regardless of season, improvements in mood were observed, and this was most evident for actual nature exposure.

While the evidence suggests that even brief nature supports emotional well-being through promoting positive affect, and to a lesser extent, decreasing negative affect, Nisbet and Zelenski (2011) propose that one's level of nature connectedness, developed as a result of time spent in natural environments, may moderate this effect. Specifically, those who report higher levels of nature connectedness also report higher levels of subjective well-being. Despite this, many individuals underestimate the degree to which even brief contact with the natural environment can promote positive affect (Nisbet & Zelenski, 2011). The underusage of natural environments, stemming from a chronic disconnection with nature associated with modern lifestyles, has led to underestimating the positive affect associated with natural environment contact (Nisbet & Zelenski, 2011).

Green and blue exercise

It is widely regarded that regular physical activity is beneficial for health and well-being and a preventative risk factor in many chronic diseases (Fortier, Duda, Guerin, & Teixeira, 2012; Hopper, Billah, Skiba, & Krum, 2011; Murphy, Nevill, Murtagh, & Holder, 2007; Tate, Jeffery, Sherwood, & Wing, 2007). Physical activity in natural environments (referred to as "green exercise") seems to confer an added psychological benefit over the equivalent activity in indoor environments (Thompson Coon et al, 2011) or in synthetic environments (indoors or outdoor built environments; Bowler et al., 2010; Pretty, Peacock, Sellens, & Griffin, 2005). However, see chapter 3 for an updated review on green exercise. In relation to mood, a meta-analysis by Barton and Pretty (2010) found exercise in all natural environments resulted in significant improvements in mood; however, these were most pronounced for environments with open water. Improvements were observed after acute exposure/activity (during the first 5 minutes) with diminishing, but still positive returns thereafter.

Within urban settings, a positive association has been found between exercising in UGS and improved mood (Kondo, Fluehr, McKeon, & Branas, 2018). Walking in UGS has been shown to improve mood compared to walking in built urban environments (Mayer, Frantz, Bruehlman-Senecal, & Dolliver, 2009; Song et al., 2014; Song, Ikei, Igarashi, Takagaki, & Miyazaki, 2015; Song et al., 2013) or indoors (Brooks et al., 2017). In addition, walking in UGS leads to more positive emotions than negative emotions compared to walking in built urban environments (Aspinall, Mavros, Coyne, & Roe, 2015).

The evidence on blue space is somewhat limited due to the relatively smaller number of studies, and heterogeneity of study designs and outcome measurements (Gascon, Zijlema, Vert, White, & Nieuwenhuijsen, 2017). In a review of the health benefits associated with blue space, a positive association was observed between exposure to physical activity, mainly for beach and coastal areas (Gascon et al., 2017). The evidence would seem to indicate that exercising in blue spaces supports health and well-being through decreasing perceived and physiological stress (Happy City, University of Virginia, Street Plans Collaborative and Space Syntax, 2017).

The positive affect observed during and after participating in exercise is a critical influential factor in determining if an individual will engage in exercise in the future (Thompson Coon et al., 2011; Williams et al., 2008). It is, therefore, an important consideration in the intention-behaviour gap for promoting exercise as a public health and clinical exercise intervention. The positive affective responses associated with exercising in natural environments may be important not only for physical activity participation, but also exercise adherence (Kinnafick & Thøgersen-Ntoumani, 2014; Lacharité-Lemieux, Brunelle & Dionne, 2015). In particular, positive affect may be an important motivational factor for populations with low levels of exercise adherence (Martin & Sinden, 2001). Designing and promoting accessible and safe natural environments as part of interventions to address the major public health issues in relation to physical inactivity, increased sedentary lifestyles, rising obesity and mental health difficulties should be a key consideration for policy makers, urban planners and health professionals.

Natural environments and chronic stress

Chronic stress is considered a psychosocial risk factor in the development of chronic health conditions such as cardiovascular diseases (CVD), cancer and auto-immune diseases (Cohen, Janicki-Deverts, & Miller, 2007). It is related to greater levels of anxiety and depression which are associated with increased mortality rates (Hammen, 2005). The long-term impact of stress can result in allostatic load, or wear and tear, which manifests as chronic underactivity of the allostatic systems; autonomic nervous system (ANS), the hypothalamus-pituitary-adrenal (HPA) axis, metabolic, immune and cardiovascular systems (McEwen, 1998).

Our environments can provide resources to help us cope with and manage a stress response (Berto, 2014). Positive changes in affect are central in our recovery from psycho-physiological stress (Berto, 2014). Eight main qualities (PSDs – Perceived Sensory Dimensions) of UGS have been implicated in restoration and reducing stress: serene, nature, rich in species, space, prospect, refuge, social and culture (Grahn, 1991; Grahn & Stigsdotter, 2010; Grahn, Stigsdotter & Berggren-Bärring, 2005). Gatersleben and Andrews (2013) found that walking in natural environments which are more accessible and have a high degree of prospect (clear line of vision) were perceived as less dangerous, elicited less fear and were more restorative than walking in natural environments with a high degree of refuge (hiding places). Data from the same study also showed that natural environments with high refuge and low prospect had the potential to increase stress and attention fatigue.

Cross-sectional studies exploring the role of residential urban environments on stress have found that greater levels of green space in urban residential environments are associated with decreased cortisol and perceived stress (Gidlow, Randall, Gillman, Silk, & Jones, 2016; Roe et al., 2013; Thompson et al., 2012). Cortisol is a hormone produced by the body as a result of HPA axis activation and is a primary indicator of the stress response (Michaud, Matheson, Kelly, & Anisman, 2008). Studies indicating a negative association between neighbourhood natural environment and cortisol may point to a possible salutogenic interaction between the natural environment and the HPA axis.

In experimental studies, improvements in self-reported stress has been reported in participants exposed to natural urban settings compared to built settings (Kondo et al., 2018). However, in contrast to the evidence related to chronic stress, the evidence to date with regards to acute responses to urban versus nature exposure and physiological indicators of stress is mixed. Most studies found no difference in physiological stress as measured by cortisol concentrations between pre and post urban nature exposure (Beil & Hanes, 2013; Gidlow et al., 2016; Grazuleviciene et al., 2016; Tyrväinen et al., 2014).

Research on nature-based rehabilitation for those with stress-related mental health disorders showed that 68% of participants returned to workplace related activities after engaging in an 8, 12 or 24-week horticultural programme, with a longer rehabilitation period associated with a higher rate of returning to work (Grahn, Pálsdóttir, Ottosson & Jonsdottir, 2017). Furthermore, the PSDs of serene, nature, space, prospect and refuge were considered equally important for a nature-based rehabilitation environment programme for those with stress-related mental health disorders (Pálsdóttir, Stigsdotter, Persson, Thorpert & Grahn, 2017).

Clinical populations: natural environments, mental health and pain

As those who live in urban environments are at higher risk of mental-health disorders (Galea, Uddin, & Koenen, 2011; Lederbogen et al., 2011; Peen, Schoevers, Beekman, & Dekker, 2010), natural environments can have a central role in the response to the health challenges of urbanisation. In the largest study of its kind (at the time of writing), residential greenness was found to be associated with lower prevalence rates of a major depressive disorder (Sarkar, Webster, & Gallacher, 2018). The beneficial effects of residential greenness were most pronounced for women, adults under 60 years of age, and those living in neighbourhoods with high levels of deprivation and high urbanicity. Previous research has also found that pregnant women in greener quintiles were 18–23% less likely to report depressive symptoms than those in the least green quintile (for within 100 m of green space buffer zone). The green space-depressive symptoms association was significant for women with lower education or who were active. Physical activity partially mediated the association of green space (McEachan et al., 2016). Other studies have reported similar findings (Beyer et al., 2014; Maas et al., 2009; Triguero-Mas et al., 2015).

Engemann et al. (2018) observed a dose-respondent effect between the amount of residential green space in early childhood and the subsequent risk of developing schizophrenia, independent of urbanisation and sex. There was a tendency towards a protective effect for those who lived in closer proximity to green spaces in their earlier years. An observational study exploring the real time effects of natural features in the built environment on mental well-being, found the beneficial impacts of nature lasted several hours (Bakolis et al., 2018). These benefits were strongest for those with highest levels of impulsivity, a trait which predicts future risk of mental health disorders (Dalley & Robbins, 2017; Martel, Levinson, Lee, & Smith, 2017; Tu, Kuan, Li, & Su, 2017).

In relation to blue space and mental health outcomes, a positive association exists for both residential living and exposure to outdoor blue spaces (inland and coastal waters) and mental health and well-being benefits, although there are limited studies and heterogeneity in study designs (Gascon et al., 2017). While the evidence for the effect of natural environments on mental health outcomes is largely cross-sectional, there are some exceptions (e.g. Alcock, White, Wheeler, Fleming, & Depledge, 2014), with further research required to determine causal pathways.

Natural environments have also been linked with affective states through reducing anxiety, stress and perceived pain in those experiencing pain in controlled laboratory environments (Lohr & Pearson-Mims, 2000; Tanja-Dijkstra et al., 2018; Vincent, Battisto, Grimes, & McCubbin, 2010) and clinical settings (Beukeboom, Langeveld, & Tanja-Dijkstra, 2012; Diette, Lechtzin, Haponik, Devrotes, & Rubin, 2003; Miller, Hickman, & Lemasters, 1992; Park & Mattson, 2008; 2009a; 2009b; Tanja-Dijkstra et al., 2017; Ulrich, 1984). Specifically, an increase in positive affect and reduced negative affect is experienced through the diversion of patients' attention to a more pleasant stimulus using nature. Within clinical settings, a nature mural and nature sounds reduced perceived pain in patients undergoing a flexible bronchoscopy (Diette et al., 2003). Live plants in post-operative patients' rooms lowered anxiety, fatigue, pain ratings, cardiovascular responses and analgesic intake compared to rooms with no plants (Park & Mattson, 2008; 2009a; 2009b). Dental patients exposed to coastal nature virtual reality (VR) reported reduced experienced and recalled pain compared to those exposed to urban VR or receiving standard care, with effects maintained up to one week later (Tanja-Dijkstra et al., 2017). While there is a tendency towards small sample sizes in addition to small effect sizes, such studies may provide initial support for using nature as an intervention for managing anxiety, stress and perceived pain in specific clinical procedures, in addition to impacting health and clinical outcomes for patients in recovery.

Green care: nature as a therapeutic intervention

With an increased emphasis and use of green and blue spaces as "health-supporting" environments, the focus has primarily been health promotion initiatives aimed at the general population. While UGS alongside other natural environments can be considered potential settings for such initiatives (e.g., green gyms), they are also potential settings for other health interventions such as "green care" initiatives (WHO, 2017).

Green care is defined as a "nature-based therapy or treatment interventions – specifically designed, structured and facilitated for individuals with a defined need" (Bragg & Atkins, 2016, p.13). Given the increased burden on health care systems, there is a greater need for community-based and voluntary-led local involvement in healthcare (NHS England, 2014). The Five Year Forward View, a policy document issued by the UK's National Health Service (NHS), outlined the need to develop partnerships with local communities and voluntary organisations to support the broader provision and delivery of healthcare (NHS England, 2014). In addition, the UK's 25 Year Environment Plan identifies the need to build on existing work with environmental voluntary sector organisations to support positive mental health outcomes for those with mild to moderate mental health conditions (HM Government, 2018).

Green care social prescribing

Social prescribing is a model that that can address these aims through the provision of non-medical interventions via primary care referral pathways and delivered by community and voluntary-led organisations. Social prescribing programmes work alongside the patients' existing medical treatment to address the wider determinants of health and to support the health and well-being for those with mild to moderate mental health difficulties, LTC's (long-term conditions), dementia and learning disabilities (Bragg & Leck, 2017). There is strong evidence for the efficacy of nature-based interventions in addressing health and social care issues (Bragg & Atkins, 2016). Three different elements that define green care programmes (natural environment, social context and engaging in meaningful activities) interact to generate positive health outcomes for the users of such services (Bragg & Atkins, 2016). Green care social prescribing includes initiatives such as green exercise, care farming, animal assisted therapy, social and therapeutic horticulture, horticultural therapy.

Woodlands for Health (Ireland) is one example of a green care social prescribing initiative where people with mental health problems referred by medical practitioners take part in forest walks and talks in nature. A programme evaluation found significant improvements in participants' mood (by 75%), sleep quality (by 66%), reduction in suicidal ideation (by 82%), in addition to decreased agitation, anxiety, thoughts of guilt, hopeless and self-esteem (Iwata et al., 2016). A commitment has subsequently been made by the Health Services Executive (HSE) in conjunction with the partner organisations to roll out this programme on a national level.

Considerations in maximising the positive affect-nature relationship: urbanisation, natural environments and subpopulations

Policy-makers are beginning to advocate changing the built environment to promote health (Ding & Gebel, 2012; National Institute for Health and Clinical Excellence, 2008; WHO, 2016) and the WHO has emphasised the importance of creating healthy urban areas which offer "a physical and built environment that encourages, enables and supports health, recreation and well-being" (WHO,

2012). Within this context there is a greater need to understand how natural environments including UGS can be designed to support positive health outcomes (Hunter et al., 2015). UGS are often underused (Hunter et al., 2015) and it cannot be assumed that the provision of green space alone will increase physical activity (Foster, Hillsdon, & Thorogood, 2004; Hillsdon, Panter, Foster, & Jones, 2006; Maas, Verheij, Spreeuwenberg, & Groenewegen, 2008). In addition, not all UGS can be considered accessible, safe and inclusive of all populations.

The UN Sustainable Development Goal 11.7 proposes that by 2030, the aim is to "provide universal access to safe, inclusive and accessible, green and public spaces, in particular for women and children, older persons and persons with disabilities". There is evidence that unequal access to green space leads to health inequalities and disparities (Jennings, Floyd, Shanahan, Coutts, & Sinykin, 2017), with some researchers proposing that green space may be "equigenic". That is, equal access to green spaces may help restrict the impact that socioeconomic inequalities and disadvantage can have on mental health (Mitchell, Richardson, Shortt, & Pearce, 2015). Despite the growing literature in this area, there remains a need to better understand how UGSs differentially support and benefit subpopulations (Kabisch, Qureshi, & Haase, 2015).

Women

Within the natural environment-health relationship gender differences must be considered, as gender would seem to affect both the perception and use of UGS (Cohen et al., 2007; Sang, Knez, Gunnarsson, & Hedblom, 2016; Schipperijn et al., 2010). Personal safety can be a significant factor for women in determining whether they access/use green space, as women are less likely to exercise in spaces where they have a concern about safety or where they will be alone (Foster et al., 2004; O'Brien, 2005). Women are also less likely than their male counterparts to use green spaces that display neglect (O'Brien, 2005; Virden & Walker, 1999), and have a greater preference for green spaces that are well-managed and display overt law enforcement (Ho et al., 2005; O'Brien, 2005; Virden & Walker, 1999). In addition, the social quality of green spaces may be important, as social environment has been found to be strongly associated with females' health status. In comparison, males' health status was more related to the physical environment (Molinari, Ahern, & Hendryx, 1998; Poortinga, Dunstan, & Fone, 2007). The fact that males and females may experience and use UGS differently may have implications for UGS design and health outcomes. Specifically, quality, safety and the social environment needs to be reflected in UGS design to support positive health outcomes for females.

Older persons

As people get older they may have more leisure time to spend in natural environments (Gauthier & Smeeding, 2003). Older residents were found to spend a greater amount of time on nature-based activities than younger residents living close to UGS, with urban green associated with improved mental health (Sang et al., 2016). As "awareness of nature experiences" and actual nature experiences (time and frequency of park interaction) increased, health anxiety decreased (Dzhambov & Dimitrova, 2014). Better general and mental health has also been reported for older urban allotment gardeners compared to non-gardeners (Soga, Gaston, & Yamaura, 2017).

The health and well-being of older people can be improved by facilitating physical activity and social connectedness within their communities (HM Government, 2018; WHO, 2017). As older people are more vulnerable to the health challenges associated with urbanisation (Tenkate, 2009), designing appropriate interventions within urban environments to improve mobility and facilitate social cohesion could help to prevent social isolation and physical frailty in this subpopulation (WHO, 2017). UGS have the potential to promote and support the health and well-being of older adults if they offer attractive spaces to facilitate social interaction and build social capital (Bowling et al., 2003); incorporate accessible, walkable, obstacle-free and well-lit paths with way-finding cues (Department of Health and Human Services, 2014; Zhai & Baran, 2017); provide age-sensitive amenities; and are a high quality safe environment (Sugiyama & Thompson, 2008). Considering 30% of over 65s in the UK are currently affected by loneliness, with costs to the economy of 40 billion per annum (Pretty et al., 2017), designing UGS to meet the needs of older people is critical in supporting positive health outcomes for this subpopulation (Sugiyama & Thompson, 2008).

Children

Less than 10% of the current child population report playing in natural environments compared with previous generations (Natural England, 2009). This may be explained in part by changes in modern lifestyles (greater amount of time indoors), demographic changes (urbanisation), parental safety concerns, and increased use of technologies and "screen time" (Biddle, Gorely, & Stensel, 2004; Louv, 2007; Taylor, Kuo, Spencer, & Blades, 2006; Wells & Lekies, 2006). Reduced contact with nature has been linked to greater incidence of attention disorders, depression, cognitive disabilities, diabetes and obesity in children (Louv, 2005), and is a risk factor for poor mental health in childhood (Amoly et al., 2014). In the UK, one in ten children will develop a mental ill-health condition each year (McGinnity, Meltzer, Ford, & Goodman, 2005).

Playing in natural environments has been found to promote social interaction (Bixler, Floyd, & Hammitt, 2002), increase positive feelings towards other children (Moore, 1996), reduce bullying and violent behaviour in youth (Malone & Tranter, 2003), and is associated with lower emotional symptoms and peer-relationship problems (Amoly et al., 2014). Use of, or living in a natural environment, is also associated with lower emotional, social and behavioural difficulties (Amoly et al., 2014; Faber Taylor & Kuo, 2009), reduced aggressive behaviours (Younan et al., 2016), and lower SBP (Systolic Blood Pressure) in children (Markevych et al., 2014).

Childhood nature engagement is related to positive health behaviours (e.g., physical activity) which are more likely to be maintained into adulthood, thus supporting health and well-being across the life course (Chan, 2013; Van Landeghem, Curtis, & Abrams, 2002). Developing connectedness with nature in childhood is also a predictor of natural environment engagement and pro-environmental behaviour as adults (Chawla, 2006; Wells & Lekies, 2006). The UK's 25 Year Environmental Plan identified the need to increase nature contact in children both within and outside of school environments through the creation of nature friendly school grounds, developing nature friendly school programmes for children in the most disadvantaged areas, encouraging more pupil trips to natural spaces, and supporting children from all backgrounds to engage with nature through promoting and increasing young people's environmental social action (HM Government, 2018).

Disabilities

People with learning disabilities experience greater levels of social disadvantage, social exclusion, health inequalities and lower life expectancy than the general population (Emerson & Hatton, 2008; Emerson et al., 2012, 2011). Green care interventions such as care farms, also known as social farming, green care farming, farming for health (Leck, Upton, & Evans, 2015), have the potential to support those with learning disabilities by acting as a space of capability (Fleuret & Atkinson, 2007) through using agricultural landscapes and practices to improve health and well-being (Hassink, 2003). Care farming is a well-established practice in mainland Europe (Haubenhofer, Elings, Hassink, & Hine, 2010), and although quantitative research has been limited by small sample sizes and short follow-up periods, improvements in mental health have been found for patients with mental ill-health (Pedersen, Martinsen, Berget & Braastad, 2012) and in behaviour for dementia patients (Bruin et al., 2009; De Bruin et al., 2012; Schols & van der Schriek-van Meel, 2006). Improvements in mood, confidence, independence, and positive well-being have also been reported in people with learning disabilities through qualitative research methods (Crowley, O'Sullivan, & O'Keefe, 2017; Rotheram, McGarrol, & Watkins, 2017). By offering meaningful work, choice, autonomy and the potential to develop social skills and relationships through green care provision, care farms act as enabling, inclusive and accessible spaces which positively impact well-being. However, reduced funding to the disability sector in the UK (Care Farming, 2015) and Ireland (Crowley et al., 2017), in addition to insecure care contracts, lack of recognition, over-regulation and increased bureaucracy are considered significant threats to care farming (Care Farming, 2016; Crowley et al., 2017).

Conclusion

Notwithstanding the methodological limitations and heterogeneity of study designs in the natural environment-health research, there is a significant and growing evidence base that provides support for a positive relationship between natural environments and psychological well-being. This has prompted governments and policy makers to invest in initiatives and strategies to address the demographic and societal shifts, and their subsequent impact on population health. The UN Sustainable Development Goal 11.7 emphasises the need to provide safe and accessible green spaces for all, inclusive of subpopulations by 2030 (United Nations General Assembly (UNGA), 2015). In the UK, the 25 Year Environmental Plan aims to help improve the health and well-being of the population by promoting the use of green spaces to combat loneliness in older populations, encourage children to have greater engagement with the natural world, increase physical activity for children and adults in outdoor settings, use green space for preventative and therapeutic initiatives to improve mental health, and create greener towns and cities (HM Government, 2018). The "Global Age-Friendly Cities Guide" issued by the World Health Organisation (WHO) identifies UGS as an important age-friendly construct with regards to the demographic changes of urbanisation and an increased older population (WHO, 2007), and the WHO "Urban Green Spaces: A Brief for Action" outlines how UGS can improve urban settings and the health and well-being of urban residents (WHO, 2017).

Within the nature-health relationship, natural environments have the potential to impact on population health by facilitating restoration through promoting positive affect, decreasing negative affect, impacting clinically relevant affective states, acting as a buffer for stressful life events, and promoting positive mental health outcomes. In addition, the therapeutic value of nature may have relevance for both healthcare and community contexts, where there is initial support for the application of nature-based interventions to reduce anxiety, stress, perceived pain and support clinical outcomes. Within the broader community, green care provision and social prescribing have received considerable support at policy level and have the potential for a much wider impact across a range of population groups. Despite this, many people underestimate the extent to which natural environment exposure can promote positive affect. While there is a need for a more robust interdisciplinary evidence base with a focus on causal pathways to support policy implementation, there is also a need to understand in greater depth how UGS can be optimally designed, used and promoted to best support population health. This should be inclusive of subpopulations, disadvantaged communities, and those most in need of restoration to ensure equitable health outcomes for all population groups in the face of significant demographic and societal changes.

References

Alcock, I., White, M. P., Wheeler, B. W., Fleming, L. E., & Depledge, M. H. (2014). Longitudinal effects on mental health of moving to greener and less green urban areas. *Environmental Science & Technology, 48*(2), 1247–1255.

Amoly, E., Dadvand, P., Forns, J., López-Vicente, M., Basagaña, X., Julvez, J., … & Sunyer, J. (2014). Green and blue spaces and behavioral development in Barcelona schoolchildren: The BREATHE project. *Environmental Health Perspectives, 122*(12), 1351.

Aspinall, P., Mavros, P., Coyne, R., & Roe, J. (2015). The urban brain: Analysing outdoor physical activity with mobile EEG. *British Journal of Sports Medicine, 49*(4), 272–276.

Bakolis, I., Hammoud, R., Smythe, M., Gibbons, J., Davidson, N., Tognin, S., & Mechelli, A. (2018). Urban mind: Using smartphone technologies to investigate the impact of nature on mental well-being in real time. *BioScience, 68*(2), 134–145.

Barton, J., Hine, R., & Pretty, J. (2009). The health benefits of walking in greenspaces of high natural and heritage value. *Journal of Integrative Environmental Sciences, 6*(4), 261–278.

Barton, J., & Pretty, J. (2010). What is the best dose of nature and green exercise for improving mental health? A multi-study analysis. *Environmental Science & Technology, 44* (10), 3947–3955.

Beil, K., & Hanes, D. (2013). The influence of urban natural and built environments on physiological and psychological measures of stress—A pilot study. *International Journal of Environmental Research and Public Health, 10*(4), 1250–1267.

Berto, R. (2011). The attentional vantage offered by perceiving fascinating patterns in the environment. *Advances in Environmental Research, 6*, 503–516.

Berto, R. (2014). The role of nature in coping with psycho-physiological stress: A literature review on restorativeness. *Behavioral Sciences, 4*(4), 394–409.

Berto, R., Baroni, M. R., Zainaghi, A., & Bettella, S. (2010). An exploratory study of the effect of high and low fascination environments on attentional fatigue. *Journal of Environmental Psychology, 30*(4), 494–500.

Beukeboom, C. J., Langeveld, D., & Tanja-Dijkstra, K. (2012). Stress-reducing effects of real and artificial nature in a hospital waiting room. *The Journal of Alternative and Complementary Medicine, 18*(4), 329–333.

Beyer, K. M., Kaltenbach, A., Szabo, A., Bogar, S., Nieto, F. J., & Malecki, K. M. (2014). Exposure to neighborhood green space and mental health: Evidence from the survey of the health of Wisconsin. *International Journal of Environmental Research and Public Health, 11*(3), 3453–3472.

Biddle S, Gorely T, Stensel D. (2004). Health-enhancing physical activity and sedentary behaviour in children and adolescents. *Journal of Sports Sciences, 22*, 679–701.

Bixler, R. D., Floyd, M. F., & Hammitt, W. E. (2002). Environmental socialization: Quantitative tests of the childhood play hypothesis. *Environment and Behavior, 34*(6), 795–818.

Blair, S. N. (2009). Physical inactivity: The biggest public health problem of the 21st century. *British Journal of Sports Medicine, 43*(1), 1–2.

Bowler, D. E., Buyung-Ali, L. M., Knight, T. M., & Pullin, A. S. (2010). A systematic review of evidence for the added benefits to health of exposure to natural environments. *BMC Public Health, 10*(1), 456.

Bowling, A., Gabriel, Z., Dykes, J., Dowding, L. M., Evans, O., Fleissig, A., … & Sutton, S. (2003). Let's ask them: A national survey of definitions of quality of life and its enhancement among people aged 65 and over. *The International Journal of Aging and Human Development, 56*(4), 269–306.

Bragg, R., & Atkins, G. (2016). *A review of nature-based interventions for mental health care*. London: Natural England. Available online at: http://publications.naturalengland.org.uk/publication/4513819616346112.

Bragg, R., & Leck, C. (2017). Good practice in social prescribing for mental health: The role of nature-based interventions. Natural England Commissioned Reports, Number 228. York.

Brooks, A. M., Ottley, K. M., Arbuthnott, K. D., & Sevigny, P. (2017). Nature-related mood effects: Season and type of nature contact. *Journal of Environmental Psychology, 54*, 91–102.

Bruin, S. R. D., Oosting, S. J., Kuin, Y., Hoefnagels, E. C., Blauw, Y. H., Groot, L. C. D., & Schols, J. M. (2009). Green care farms promote activity among elderly people with dementia. *Journal of Housing for the Elderly, 23*(4), 368–389.

Cacioppo, John T., Mary Elizabeth Hughes, Linda J. Waite, Louise C. Hawkley, and Ronald A. Thisted. (2006). Loneliness as a specific risk factor for depressive symptoms: Cross-sectional and longitudinal analyses. *Psychology and Aging, 21*(1), 140.

Care Farming, UK. (2016). Care farming in the UK and Ireland: State of play 2015.

Chan, M. (2013). Linking child survival and child development for health, equity, and sustainable development. *The Lancet, 381*(9877), 1514–1515.

Chawla, L. (2006). Learning to love the natural world enough to protect it.

Chodzko-Zajko, W. J., Proctor, D. N., Singh, M. A. F., Minson, C. T., Nigg, C. R., Salem, G. J., & Skinner, J. S. (2009). Exercise and physical activity for older adults. *Medicine & Science in Sports & Exercise, 41*(7), 1510–1530.

Choi, S., Lee, S., Matejkowski, J., & Baek, Y. M. (2014). The relationships among depression, physical health conditions and healthcare expenditures for younger and older Americans. *Journal of Mental Health, 23*(3), 140–145.

Cohen, S., Janicki-Deverts, D., & Miller, G. E. (2007). Psychological stress and disease. *Journal of American Medical Association, 298*(14), 1685–1687.

Cox, D. T., Shanahan, D. F., Hudson, H. L., Plummer, K. E., Siriwardena, G. M., Fuller, R. A., ... & Gaston, K. J. (2017). Doses of neighborhood nature: The benefits for mental health of living with nature. *BioScience, 67*(2), 147–155.

Crowley, C., O'Sullivan, S., & O'Keefe, B. (2017) An evaluation of Kerry Social Farming 2017. KSF.

Dadvand P., de Nazelle A., Triguero-Mas M., Schembari, A., Cirach, M., Amoly, E., Figueras, F., Basagaña, X., Ostro, B., & Nieuwenhuijsen, M. (2012). Surrounding greenness and exposure to air pollution during pregnancy: An analysis of personal monitoring data. *Environmental Health Perspectives, 120*(9), 1286–1290.

Dalley, J. W., & Robbins, T. W. (2017). Fractionating impulsivity: Neuropsychiatric implications. *Nature Reviews Neuroscience, 18*(3), 158.

De Bruin, S., Oosting, S., Tobi, H., Enders-Slegers, M. J., van der Zijpp, A., & Schols, J. (2012). Comparing day care at green care farms and at regular day care facilities with regard to their effects on functional performance of community-dwelling older people with dementia. *Dementia, 11*(4), 503–519.

Department for Communities and Local Government. (2010). *English Housing Survey*. London: Crown, 1999.

Department of Health and Human Services. 2014. Dementia-friendly environments. Available online at: www.health.vic.gov.au/dementia/changes/gardens.htm

Diette, G. B., Lechtzin, N., Haponik, E., Devrotes, A., & Rubin, H. R. (2003). Distraction therapy with nature sights and sounds reduces pain during flexible bronchoscopy: A complementary approach to routine analgesia. *Chest Journal, 123*(3), 941–948.

Ding, D., & Gebel, K. (2012). Built environment, physical activity, and obesity: What have we learned from reviewing the literature? *Health & Place, 18*(1), 100–105.

Dzhambov, A. M., & Dimitrova, D. D. (2014). Elderly visitors of an urban park, health anxiety and individual awareness of nature experiences. *Urban Forestry & Urban Greening, 13*(4), 806–813.

Ekkekakis, P., & Petruzzello, S. J. (2000). Analysis of the affect measurement conundrum in exercise psychology I. Fundamental issues. *Psychology of Sport and Exercise, 1*, 71–88.

Emerson, E., & Hatton, C. (2008). CEDR research report 2008 (1): People with learning disabilities in England.

Emerson, E., Hatton, C., Robertson, J., Roberts, H., Baines, S., Evison, F., & Glover, G. (2012). People with learning disabilities in England 2011. Improving health and lives learning disabilities observatory.

Emerson, E., Madden, R., Graham, H., Llewellyn, G., Hatton, C., & Robertson, J. (2011). The health of disabled people and the social determinants of health. *Public Health, 125* (3), 145–147.

Engemann, K., Pedersen, C. B., Arge, L., Tsirogiannis, C., Mortensen, P. B., & Svenning, J. C. (2018). Childhood exposure to green space–A novel risk-decreasing mechanism for schizophrenia? *Schizophrenia Research, 199*, 142–148,,

Faber Taylor, A., & Kuo, F. E. (2009). Children with attention deficits concentrate better after walk in the park. *Journal of Attention Disorders, 12*(5), 402–409.

Fleuret, S., & Atkinson, S. (2007). Wellbeing, health and geography: A critical review and research agenda. *New Zealand Geographer, 63*(2), 106–118.

Fortier, M. S., Duda, J. L., Guerin, E., & Teixeira, P. J. (2012). Promoting physical activity: Development and testing of self-determination theory-based interventions. *The International Journal of Behavioral Nutrition and Physical Activity, 9*, 20. doi:http://dx.doi.org/10.1186/1479-5868-9-20

Foster, C., Hillsdon, M., & Thorogood, M. (2004). Environmental perceptions and walking in English adults. *Journal of Epidemiology & Community Health, 58*(11), 924–928.

Galea, K. S., Hurley, J. F., Cowie, H., Shafrir, A. L., Jiménez, A. S., Semple, S., & Coggins, M. (2013). Using PM2. 5 concentrations to estimate the health burden from solid fuel combustion, with application to Irish and Scottish homes. *Environmental Health, 12*(1), 50.

Galea, S., Uddin, M., & Koenen, K. (2011). The urban environment and mental disorders: Epigenetic links. *Epigenetics, 6*(4), 400–404.

Gascon, M., Zijlema, W., Vert, C., White, M. P., & Nieuwenhuijsen, M. J. (2017). Outdoor blue spaces, human health and well-being: A systematic review of quantitative studies. *International Journal of Hygiene and Environmental Health, 220*(8), 1207–1221.,,

Gatersleben, B., & Andrews, M. (2013). When walking in nature is not restorative—The role of prospect and refuge. *Health & Place, 20*, 91–101.

Gauthier, A. H., & Smeeding, T. M. (2003). Time use at older ages: Cross-national differences. *Research on Aging, 25*(3), 247–274.

Gidlow, C. J., Jones, M. V., Hurst, G., Masterson, D., Clark-Carter, D., Tarvainen, M. P., & Nieuwenhuijsen, M. (2016a). Where to put your best foot forward: Psycho-physiological responses to walking in natural and urban environments. *Journal of Environmental Psychology, 45*, 22–29.

Gidlow, C. J., Randall, J., Gillman, J., Silk, S., & Jones, M. V. (2016b). Hair cortisol and self-reported stress in healthy, working adults. *Psychoneuroendocrinology, 63*, 163–169.

Grahn, P. (1991). Om parkens betydelse (About the meaning of parks). *Diss. Alnarp: Swedish University of Agricultural Sciences.*

Grahn, P., Pálsdóttir, A. M., Ottosson, J., & Jonsdottir, I. H. (2017). Longer nature-based rehabilitation may contribute to a faster return to work in patients with reactions to severe stress and/or depression. *International Journal of Environmental Research and Public Health, 14*(11), 1310.

Grahn, P., Stigsdotter, U., & Berggren-Bärring, A. M. (2005). A planning model for designing sustainable and healthy cities. The importance of people's need of recreational en-vironments in an urban context. Presented at Inspiring Global Environmental Standards & Ethical Practices. National Association of Environmental Professionals, NAEP 30th Annual Conference,Alexandria, VA: NAEP.

Grahn, P., & Stigsdotter, U. K. (2010). The relation between perceived sensory dimensions of urban green space and stress restoration. *Landscape and Urban Planning, 94*(3-4), 264–275.

Grazuleviciene, R., Vencloviene, J., Kubilius, R., Grizas, V., Danileviciute, A., Dedele, A., .. & Nieuwenhuijsen, M. J. (2016). Tracking restoration of park and urban street settings in coronary artery disease patients. *International Journal of Environmental Research and Public Health, 13*(6), 550.

Hammen, C. (2005). Stress and depression. *Annual Review of Clinical Psychology, 1*, 293–319.

Happy City, University of Virginia, Street Plans Collaborative and Space Syntax (2017). Happier by design. Available online at: https://thehappycity.com/wp-content/uploads/2017/04/STC-reportfinal-version-v.5.pdf.

Hartig, T. (2004). Restorative Environments. *Encyclopedia Applied Psychology, 3*, 273–279.

Hartig, T., Evans, G. W., Jamner, L. D., Davis, D. S., & Gärling, T. (2003). Tracking restoration in natural and urban field settings. *Journal of Environmental Psychology, 23*(2), 109–123.

Hartig, T., Mitchell, R., De Vries, S., & Frumkin, H. (2014). Nature and health. *Annual Review of Public Health, 35*, 207–228.

Hassink, J. (2003). Combining agricultural production and care for persons with disabilities: A new role of agriculture and farm animals. In *Farming and rural systems research and extension. Local identities and globalisation, Fifth IFSA European Symposium, Florence, Italy, 8-11 April 2002* (pp. 332–341).

Haubenhofer, D. K., Elings, M., Hassink, J., & Hine, R. E. (2010). The development of green care in western European countries. *EXPLORE: the Journal of Science and Healing, 6*(2), 106–111.

Hidalgo, M. C., Berto, R., Galindo, M. P., & Getrevi, A. (2006). Identifying attractive and unattractive urban places: Categories, restorativeness and aesthetic attributes. *Medio Ambiente Y Comportamiento Humano*, 7(2), 115–133.

Hillsdon, M., Panter, J., Foster, C., & Jones, A. (2006). The relationship between access and quality of urban green space with population physical activity. *Public Health, 120*(12), 1127–1132.

HM Government. (2018). The 25 Year Environment Plan.

Ho, C. H., Sasidharan, V., Elmendorf, W., Willits, F. K., Graefe, A., & Godbey, G. (2005). Gender and ethnic variations in urban park preferences, visitation, and perceived benefits. *Journal of Leisure Research, 37*(3), 281–306.

Holt-Lunstad, J., Smith, T. B., Baker, M., Harris, T., & Stephenson, D. (2015). Loneliness and social isolation as risk factors for mortality: A meta-analytic review. *Perspectives on Psychological Science, 10*(2), 227–237.

Hopper, I., Billah, B., Skiba, M., & Krum, H. (2011). Prevention of diabetes and reduction in major cardiovascular events in studies of subjects with prediabetes: Meta-analysis of randomised controlled clinical trials. *European Journal of Cardiovascular Prevention & Rehabilitation, 18*(6), 813–823.

HSE. (2016). *Work Related Stress, Anxiety and Depression Statistics in Great Britain 2016*. London, UK: Health and Safety Executive.

Hunter, R. F., Christian, H., Veitch, J., Astell-Burt, T., Hipp, J. A., & Schipperijn, J. (2015). The impact of interventions to promote physical activity in urban green space: A systematic review and recommendations for future research. *Social Science & Medicine, 124*, 246–256.

Iwata, Y., Dhubháin, Á. N., Brophy, J., Roddy, D., Burke, C., & Murphy, B. (2016). Benefits of group walking in forests for people with significant mental ill-health. *Ecopsychology, 8*(1), 16–26.

Jennings, V., Floyd, M. F., Shanahan, D., Coutts, C., & Sinykin, A. (2017). Emerging issues in urban ecology: Implications for research, social justice, human health, and well-being. *Population and Environment, 39*(1), 69–86.

Kabisch, N., Qureshi, S., & Haase, D. (2015). Human–Environment interactions in urban green spaces—A systematic review of contemporary issues and prospects for future research. *Environmental Impact Assessment Review, 50*, 25–34.

Kaplan, R. (2001). The nature of the view from home: Psychological benefits. *Environment and Behavior, 33*(4), 507–542.

Kaplan, R., & Kaplan, S. (1989). *The Experience of Nature: A Psychological Perspective*. Cambridge: CUP Archive.

Kellert, S. R., & Wilson, E. O. (Eds.). (1995). *The Biophilia Hypothesis*. Washington, DC: Island Press.

Keniger, L. E., Gaston, K. J., Irvine, K. N., & Fuller, R. A. (2013). What are the benefits of interacting with nature? *International Journal of Environmental Research and Public Health, 10*(3), 913–935.

Kinnafick, F. E., & Thøgersen-Ntoumani, C. (2014). The effect of the physical environment and levels of activity on affective states. *Journal of Environmental Psychology, 38*, 241–251.

Kondo, M. C., Fluehr, J. M., McKeon, T., & Branas, C. C. (2018). Urban green space and its impact on human health. *International Journal of Environmental Research and Public Health, 15*(3), 445.

Korpela, K., & Hartig, T. (1996). Restorative qualities of favorite places. *Journal of Environmental Psychology, 16*(3), 221–233.

Lacharité-Lemieux, M., Brunelle, J. P., & Dionne, I. J. (2015). Adherence to exercise and affective responses: Comparison between outdoor and indoor training. *Menopause, 22*(7), 731–740.

Leck, C., Upton, D., & Evans, N. (2015). Growing well-beings: The positive experience of care farms. *British Journal of Health Psychology, 20*(4), 745–762.

Lederbogen, F., Kirsch, P., Haddad, L., Streit, F., Tost, H., Schuch, P., & Meyer-Lindenberg, A. (2011). City living and urban upbringing affect neural social stress processing in humans. *Nature, 474*(7352), 498–501.

Lee, J., Park, B. J., Tsunetsugu, Y., Ohira, T., Kagawa, T., & Miyazaki, Y. (2011). Effect of forest bathing on physiological and psychological responses in young Japanese male subjects. *Public Health, 125*(2), 93–100.

Lohr, V. I., & Pearson-Mims, C. H. (2000). Physical discomfort may be reduced in the presence of interior plants. *HortTechnology, 10*(1), 53–58.

Louv, R. (2005). Last child in the woods: Saving our kids from nature deficit disorder.

Louv, R. (2007). Leave no child inside. *Orion Magazine, 57*(11).

Luanaigh, C. Ó., & Lawlor, B. A. (2008). Loneliness and the health of older people. *International Journal of Geriatric Psychiatry, 23*(12), 1213–1221.

Maas, J., Verheij, R. A., de Vries, S., Spreeuwenberg, P., Schellevis, F. G., & Groenewegen, P. P. (2009). Morbidity is related to a green living environment. *Journal of Epidemiology & Community Health, 63*(12), 967–973.

Maas, J., Verheij, R. A., Spreeuwenberg, P., & Groenewegen, P. P. (2008). Physical activity as a possible mechanism behind the relationship between green space and health: A multilevel analysis. *BMC Public Health, 8*(1), 206.

Malone, K., & Tranter, P. J. (2003). School grounds as sites for learning: Making the most of environmental opportunities. *Environmental Education Research, 9*(3), 283–303.

Markevych, I., Thiering, E., Fuertes, E., Sugiri, D., Berdel, D., Koletzko, S., … & Heinrich, J. (2014). A cross-sectional analysis of the effects of residential greenness on blood pressure in 10-year old children: Results from the GINIplus and LISAplus studies. *BMC Public Health, 14*(1), 477.

Martel, M. M., Levinson, C. A., Lee, C. A., & Smith, T. E. (2017). Impulsivity symptoms as core to the developmental externalizing spectrum. *Journal of Abnormal Child Psychology, 45*(1), 83–90.

Martin, K. A., & Sinden, A. R. (2001). Who will stay and who will go? A review of older adults' adherence to randomized controlled trials of exercise. *Journal of Aging and Physical Activity, 9*(2), 91–114.

Mayer, F. S., Frantz, C. M., Bruehlman-Senecal, E., & Dolliver, K. (2009). Why is nature beneficial? The role of connectedness to nature. *Environment and Behavior, 41*(5), 607–643.

McEachan, R. R. C., Prady, S. L., Smith, G., Fairley, L., Cabieses, B., Gidlow, C., Wright, J., Dadvand, D., Van Gent, D., & Nieuwenhuijsen, M. J. (2016). The association between green space and depressive symptoms in pregnant women: moderating roles of socioeconomic status and physical activity. *Journal of Epidemiology and Community Health, 70*(3), 253–259.

McEwen, B. S. (1998). Stress, adaptation, and disease: Allostasis and allostatic load. *Annals of the New York Academy of Sciences, 840*(1), 33–44.

McGinnity, Á., Meltzer, H., Ford, T., & Goodman, R. (2005). *Mental health of children and young people in Great Britain, 2004.* H. Green (Ed.). Basingstoke: Palgrave Macmillan.

McMahan, E. A., & Estes, D. (2015). The effect of contact with natural environments on positive and negative affect: A meta-analysis. *The Journal of Positive Psychology, 10*(6), 507–519.

McMichael, A. J. (2000). The urban environment and health in a world of increasing globalization: Issues for developing countries. *Bulletin of the World Health Organization, 78*(9), 1117–1126.

Michaud, K., Matheson, K., Kelly, O., & Anisman, H. (2008). Impact of stressors in a natural context on release of cortisol in healthy adult humans: A meta-analysis. *Stress, 11*(3), 177–197.

Miller, A. C., Hickman, L. C., & Lemasters, G. K. (1992). A distraction technique for control of burn pain. *Journal of Burn Care & Research, 13*(5), 576–580.

Mitchell, R. J., Richardson, E. A., Shortt, N. K., & Pearce, J. R. (2015). Neighborhood environments and socioeconomic inequalities in mental well-being. *American Journal of Preventive Medicine, 49*(1), 80–84.

Molinari, C., Ahern, M., & Hendryx, M. (1998). The relationship of community quality to the health of women and men. *Social Science & Medicine, 47*(8), 1113–1120.

Moore, R. (1996). Compact nature: The role of playing and learning gardens on children's lives. *Journal of Therapeutic Horticulture, 8*, 72–82.

Murphy, M. H., Nevill, A. M., Murtagh, E. M., & Holder, R. L. (2007). The effect of walking on fitness, fatness and resting blood pressure: A meta-analysis of randomised, controlled trials. *Preventive Medicine*, *44*, 377e385. doi:http://dx.doi.org/10.1016/j.ypmed.2006.12.008

NHS England, Care Quality Commission, Health Education England, Monitor, Public Health England, Trust Development Authority (2014). *NHS five year forward view*. London: NHS England. Available online at: www.england.nhs.uk/ourwork/futurenhs/

National Institute for Health and Clinical Excellence (2008) Physical activity and the environment. NICE guideline (NG90).

Natural England. (2009). *Childhood and Nature: A Survey on Changing Relationships with Nature across Generations*. Cambridgeshire: Author, 32 p.

Natural England. (2010). *Monitor of engagement with the natural environment: The national survey on people and the natural environment. Annex, summary data tables from the 2015-2016 survey*. Sheffield: Natural England.

Newbury, J. Arseneault, L., Caspil, A., Moffitt, T. E., Odgers, C. L., & Fisher, H. L. (2016). Why are children in urban neighborhoods at increased risk for psychotic symptoms? Findings from a UK longitudinal cohort study. *Schizophrenia Bulletin*, *42*(6), 1372–1383.

Nisbet, E. K., & Zelenski, J. M. (2011). Underestimating nearby nature: Affective forecasting errors obscure the happy path to sustainability. *Psychological Science*, *22*(9), 1101–1106.

O'Brien, E. A. (2005). Publics* and woodlands in England: Well-being, local identity, social learning, conflict and management. *Forestry*, *78*(4), 321–336.

Pálsdóttir, A. M., Stigsdotter, U. K., Persson, D., Thorpert, P., & Grahn, P. (2017). The qualities of natural environments that support the rehabilitation process of individuals with stress-related mental disorder in nature-based rehabilitation. *Urban Forestry & Urban Greening*, *29*, 312–321.,,

Park, B. J., Tsunetsugu, Y., Kasetani, T., Hirano, H., Kagawa, T., Sato, M., & Miyazaki, Y. (2007). Physiological effects of shinrin-yoku (taking in the atmosphere of the forest)—Using salivary cortisol and cerebral activity as indicators—. *Journal of Physiological Anthropology*, *26*(2), 123–128.

Park, S. H., & Mattson, R. H. (2008). Effects of flowering and foliage plants in hospital rooms on patients recovering from abdominal surgery. *HortTechnology*, *18*(4), 563–568.

Park, S. H., & Mattson, R. H. (2009a). Therapeutic influences of plants in hospital rooms on surgical recovery. *HortScience*, *44*(1), 102–105.

Park, S. H., & Mattson, R. H. (2009b). Ornamental indoor plants in hospital rooms enhanced health outcomes of patients recovering from surgery. *The Journal of Alternative and Complementary Medicine*, *15*(9), 975–980.

Pedersen, I., Martinsen, E. W., Berget, B., & Braastad, B. O. (2012). Farm animal-assisted intervention for people with clinical depression: A randomized controlled trial. *Anthrozoös*, *25*(2), 149–160.

Peen, J., Schoevers, R. A., Beekman, A. T., & Dekker, J. (2010). The current status of urban-rural differences in psychiatric disorders. *Acta Psychiatrica Scandinavica*, *121*(2), 84–93.

Peron, E., Berto, R., & Purcell, A. T. (2002). Restorativeness, preference and the perceived naturalness of places. *Medio Ambiente Y Comportamiento Humano*, *3*(1), 19–34.

Poortinga, W., Dunstan, F. D., & Fone, D. L. (2007). Perceptions of the neighbourhood environment and self rated health: A multilevel analysis of the caerphilly health and social needs study. *BMC Public Health*, 7(1), 285.

Pretty, J., Peacock, J., Hine, R., Sellens, M., South, N., & Griffin, M. (2007). Green exercise in the UK countryside: Effects on health and psychological well-being, and implications for policy and planning. *Journal of Environmental Planning and Management, 50*(2), 211–231.

Pretty, J., Peacock, J., Sellens, M., & Griffin, M. (2005). The mental and physical health outcomes of green exercise. *International Journal of Environmental Health Research, 15*(5), 319–337.

Pretty, J., Rogerson, M., & Barton, J. (2017). Green mind theory: How brain-body-behaviour links into natural and social environments for healthy habits. *International Journal of Environmental Research and Public Health, 14*(7), 706.

Roe, J. J., Thompson, C. W., Aspinall, P. A., Brewer, M. J., Duff, E. I., Miller, D., & Clow, A. (2013). Green space and stress: Evidence from cortisol measures in deprived urban communities. *International Journal of Environmental Research and Public Health, 10*(9), 4086–4103.

Rosenberg, E. L. (1998). Levels of analysis and organisation of affect. *Review of General Psychology, 2*, 247–270.

Rotheram, S., McGarrol, S., & Watkins, F. (2017). Care farms as a space of wellbeing for people with a learning disability in the United Kingdom. *Health & Place, 48*, 123–131.

Sang, Å. O., Knez, I., Gunnarsson, B., & Hedblom, M. (2016). The effects of naturalness, gender, and age on how urban green space is perceived and used. *Urban Forestry & Urban Greening, 18*, 268–276.

Sarkar, C., Webster, C., & Gallacher, J. (2018). Residential greenness and prevalence of major depressive disorders: A cross-sectional, observational, associational study of 94 879 adult UK Biobank participants. *The Lancet Planetary Health, 2*(4), e162-e173.

Schipperijn, J., Ekholm, O., Stigsdotter, U. K., Toftager, M., Bentsen, P., Kamper-Jørgensen, F., & Randrup, T. B. (2010). Factors influencing the use of green space: Results from a Danish national representative survey. *Landscape and Urban Planning, 95* (3), 130–137.

Schols, J. M., & van der Schriek-van Meel, C. (2006). Day care for demented elderly in a dairy farm setting: Positive first impressions. *Journal of the American Medical Directors Association*, 7(7), 456–459.

Soga, M., Gaston, K. J., & Yamaura, Y. (2017). Gardening is beneficial for health: A meta-analysis. *Preventive Medicine Reports, 5*, 92–99.

Song, C., Ikei, H., Igarashi, M., Miwa, M., Takagaki, M., & Miyazaki, Y. (2014). Physiological and psychological responses of young males during spring-time walks in urban parks. *Journal of Physiological Anthropology, 33*(1), 8.

Song, C., Ikei, H., Igarashi, M., Takagaki, M., & Miyazaki, Y. (2015). Physiological and psychological effects of a walk in urban parks in fall. *International Journal of Environmental Research and Public Health, 12*(11), 14216–14228.

Song, C., Joung, D., Ikei, H., Igarashi, M., Aga, M., Park, B. J., .. & Takagaki, M. & Miyazaki, Y. (2013). Physiological and psychological effects of walking on young males in urban parks in winter. *Journal of Physiological Anthropology, 32*(1), 1.

Staats, H., Kieviet, A., & Hartig, T. (2003). Where to recover from attentional fatigue: An expectancy-value analysis of environmental preference. *Journal of Environmental Psychology, 23*(2), 147–157.

Sugiyama, T., & Thompson, C. W. (2008). Associations between characteristics of neighbourhood open space and older people's walking. *Urban Forestry & Urban Greening*, 7(1), 41–51.

Tanja-Dijkstra, K., Pahl, S., White, M. P., Auvray, M., Stone, R. J., Andrade, J., May, J., Mills, I & Moles, D. R. (2018). The soothing sea: a virtual coastal walk can reduce experienced and recollected pain. *Environment and Behavior, 50*(6), 599-625.

Tate, D. F., Jeffery, R. W., Sherwood, N. E., & Wing, R. R. (2007). Long-term weight losses associated with prescription of higher physical activity goals. Are higher levels of physical activity protective against weight regain?– *The American Journal of Clinical Nutrition, 85*(4), 954–959.

Taylor, A. F., Kuo, F. E., Spencer, C., & Blades, M. (2006). Is contact with nature important for healthy child development? State of the evidence. In C. Spencer & M. Blades (Eds.), *Children and Their Environments: Learning, Using and Designing Spaces* (pp. 124): Cambridge, UK: Cambridge University Press.

Tenkate, T. (2009). The anatomy of a silent crisis-human impact report: Climate change. *Environmental Health, 9*(1/2), 97.

Thompson Coon, J., Boddy, K., Stein, K., Whear, R., Barton, J., & Depledge, M. H. (2011). Does participating in physical activity in outdoor natural environments have a greater effect on physical and mental wellbeing than physical activity indoors? A systematic review. *Environmental Science & Technology, 45*(5), 1761–1772.

Thompson, C. W., Roe, J., Aspinall, P., Mitchell, R., Clow, A., & Miller, D. (2012). More green space is linked to less stress in deprived communities: Evidence from salivary cortisol patterns. *Landscape and Urban Planning, 105*(3), 221–229.

Triguero-Mas, M., Dadvand, P., Cirach, M., Martínez, D., Medina, A., Mompart, A., & Nieuwenhuijsen, M. J. (2015). Natural outdoor environments and mental and physical health: Relationships and mechanisms. *Environment International*, 77, 35–41.

Tu, P. C., Kuan, Y. H., Li, C. T., & Su, T. P. (2017). Structural correlates of trait impulsivity in patients with bipolar disorder and healthy controls: A surface-based morphometry study. *Psychological Medicine, 47*(7), 1292–1299.

Tyrväinen, L., Ojala, A., Korpela, K., Lanki, T., Tsunetsugu, Y., & Kagawa, T. (2014). The influence of urban green environments on stress relief measures: A field experiment. *Journal of Environmental Psychology, 38*, 1–9.

Ulrich, R. (1984). View through a window may influence recovery. *Science, 224*(4647), 224–225.

Ulrich, R. S. (1983). Aesthetic and affective response to natural environment. In I. Altman & J. Wohlwill (Eds.), *Behavior and the Natural Environment* (pp. 85–125). Boston, MA: Springer.

Ulrich, R. S., Simons, R. F., Losito, B. D., Fiorito, E., Miles, M. A., & Zelson, M. (1991). Stress recovery during exposure to natural and urban environments. *Journal of Environmental Psychology, 11*(3), 201–230.

United Nations. (2015a). World population ageing 2015. United Nations, New York.

United Nations General Assembly (UNGA). (2015). Transforming our world: The 2030 agenda for sustainable development. *A/RES/70/1*, 35.

Van Den Berg, A. E., Koole, S. L., & Van der Wulp, N. Y. (2003). Environmental preference and restoration:(How) are they related? *Journal of Environmental Psychology, 23*(2), 135–146.

Van Landeghem K., Curtis D., Abrams M., 2002. Reasons and strategies for strengthening childhood development services in the healthcare system.

Vincent, E., Battisto, D., Grimes, L., & McCubbin, J. (2010). The effects of nature images on pain in a simulated hospital patient room. *HERD: Health Environments Research & Design Journal, 3*(3), 42–55.

Virden, R. J., & Walker, G. J. (1999). Ethnic/racial and gender variations among meanings given to, and preferences for, the natural environment. *Leisure Sciences, 21*(3), 219–239.

Vos, T., Allen, C., Arora, M., Barber, R. M., Bhutta, Z. A., Brown, A., .. & Coggeshall, M. (2016). Global, regional, and national incidence, prevalence, and years lived with disability for 310 diseases and injuries, 1990–2015: A systematic analysis for the Global Burden of Disease study 2015. *The Lancet, 388*(10053), 1545–1602.

Wells, N. M., & Lekies, K. S. (2006). Nature and the life course: Pathways from childhood nature experiences to adult environmentalism. *Children Youth and Environments, 16*(1), 1–24.

Williams, D. M., Dunsiger, S., Ciccolo, J. T., Lewis, B. A., Albrecht, A. E., & Marcus, B. H. (2008). Acute affective response to a moderate-intensity exercise stimulus predicts physical activity participation 6 and 12 months later. *Psychology of Sport and Exercise, 9*(3), 231–245.

Wilson, E. O. (1984). *Biophilia.* Cambridge (Mass.): Harvard Press.

World Health Organization. (2007). *Global age-friendly cities: A guide.* Geneva, Switzerland: Author.

World Health Organization. (2012). *Action Plan for Implementation of the European Strategy for the Prevention and Control of Noncommunicable Diseases 2012–2016.* Copenhagen: Author.

World Health Organization. (2013). *Mental health action plan 2013–2020.* World Health Organisation.

World Health Organization. (2014). *Healthy cities: Promoting health and equity-evidence for local policy and practice.* World Health Organisation.

World Health Organization. (2015). *World report on ageing and health.* World Health Organization

World Health Organization. (2016). *Urban Green Spaces and Health–A Review of Evidence.* Geneva, Switzerland: Author.

World Health Organization. (2017a). *Urban green spaces: A brief for action.* Copenhagen.

World Health Organization. (2017b). *Urban green space interventions and health: A review of impacts and effectiveness.* World Health Organization.

Younan, D., Tuvblad, C., Li, L., Wu, J., Lurmann, F., Franklin, M., ... & Chen, J. C. (2016). Environmental determinants of aggression in adolescents: Role of urban neighborhood greenspace. *Journal of the American Academy of Child & Adolescent Psychiatry, 55*(7), 591–601.

Zhai, Y., & Baran, P. K. (2017). Urban park pathway design characteristics and senior walking behavior. *Urban Forestry & Urban Greening, 21*, 60–73.

8

A REMEDY FOR BOREDOM

Natural environments as a psychological resource

Eric R. Igou and Wijnand A. P. van Tilburg

You are 11 years old and waiting in the car. Your mother asked you to wait for 20 minutes in the car in a parking lot downtown while she had to run some errands for the weekend. She said she would be back at 2pm. Time has passed. It's approaching 2pm. You have nothing to do. Nothing in the car looks interesting and the radio is not working. The parking lot is grey and smelly. It's 2:15pm, no mother in sight. You are bored. You step out of the car and look at the pavement. You identify patterns in tiles and step with your feet on those that seem to be similar to each other and you avoid those that do not. This keeps you busy for a few minutes. Then boredom creeps back into your chest. There is nothing you can do. It's 2:30pm. Still, no mother is in sight. Again, you look at the pavement and try to think how to make this look interesting. Then you hear her steps. Your mother approaches the car with five shopping bags. There will be food for the weekend and probably some chocolate, you hope. But, more importantly, it's finally time to get out of there. You are moving. You envisage yourself with your friends kicking a soccer ball on the green grass at home. Boredom will be left behind, for a while at least, possibly until next weekend.

Boredom strikes at some point or another. For some people it strikes more frequently, for others less frequently. For some people it strikes more intensely, for others less intensely. It is remarkable that given the possibly universal familiarity with boredom, this experience and its consequences have received relatively little attention in the psychological literature. That said, philosophical and empirical research to this date concurs that boredom is an unpleasant state and that people long to reduce boredom and the meaninglessness that it conveys. Below we will first summarize some of the most important findings on boredom and its consequences. Afterwards, we will describe and explain how exposure to natural environments may help in overcoming boredom and its potential consequences.

Boredom

Boredom is unpleasant (Van Tilburg & Igou, 2012, 2017a). This insight is not new. It has long been stated that boredom is an unpleasant state that conveys a sense of meaninglessness (e.g., Schopenhauer, 2010; Fromm, 1955, 1963, 1973, 1991; Heidegger, see Thiele, 1997). From Fromm's perspective, for example, boredom indicates alienation from the self and others, fueling destructive behaviors such as aggression and violence (1973). Similarly, a range of philosophers including Sartre, Kierkegaard, and Kuhn focused on the meaninglessness and the existential challenges that result from boredom (see Martin, Sadlo, & Stew, 2006). Sociological accounts of boredom seem to concur (Barbalet, 1999).

Up until the 1990s, relatively little attention had been given to boredom in psychological research. Since then, boredom has become a more popular research topic (for more details see Van Tilburg & Igou, 2017a). A recent definition of boredom is the one offered by Eastwood, Frischen, Fenske, and Smilek (2012). They define boredom as 'the aversive experience of wanting, but being unable, to engage in satisfying activity' (p. 482). Beyond that definition, boredom can be described as a state of low arousal (Smith & Ellsworth, 1985), it is distinctive in the way it is expressed (see Wallbott, 1998), it comprises a lack of perceived meaning and challenge, and comes with a desire to disengage from current activities or alter them (Sansone, Weir, Harpster, & Morgan, 1992; Van Tilburg & Igou, 2011b, 2012, 2016, 2017b; Van Tilburg, Igou, & Sedikides, 2013).

Most research on boredom has been correlative in nature. That is, individual differences in boredom have been related to other psychological or sociological variables (e.g., Blaszczynski, McConaghy, & Frankova, 1990; Dahlen, Martin, Ragan, & Kuhlman, 2004; Kass, Vodanovich, & Callander, 2001; Watt & Vodanovich, 1999). Proneness to boredom (Farmer & Sundberg, 1986), for example, seems to be associated with social and psychological dysfunctions, such as eating disorders and pathological gambling (e.g., Blaszczynski et al., 1990) and negative emotions, such as depression, fear, anxiety, loneliness, and hopelessness (e.g., Fahlman, Mercer, Gaskocski, Eastwood, & Eastwood, 2009).

To understand the impact of boredom, one needs to look more closely at the characteristics of this experience. Our early work highlighted lack of meaning and low perceived challenge as crucial components of the boredom experience (Van Tilburg & Igou, 2011b). Eastwood et al. (2012) conceptualize boredom more in terms of attention. That is, people are not able to focus on a task at hand or on internal states; they are aware of this lack of focus, and attribute it to the surrounding environment. Both approaches seem valid as recent research on the distinctiveness of boredom suggests. In comparing boredom to a range of other negative states, we (Van Tilburg & Igou, 2017a) could characterize the unique experience of boredom as a relatively mild negative experience, low in arousal, associated with low perceived challenge, with little if any perceived meaning, and characterized by low levels of attention. In particular, lack of meaning and attention distinguish boredom from other negative emotions.

Boredom's qualities hint at ways in which people can cope with such experiences. One can distinguish at least two broad ways of dealing with boredom. One way to re-establish or 'repair' a sense of meaning is characterized by a search for sources of meaning and meaningful engagement (Van Tilburg & Igou, 2011b; Van Tilburg et al., 2013), in the hope of overcoming the meaningless state of boredom. This form of meaning-regulation can be described as symbolic in that sources of meaning are approached to symbolize meaningfulness of one's activities and life in general (e.g., Van Tilburg & Igou, 2011a, 2013).

Our own research shows, for example, that boredom boosts people's social identity (Van Tilburg & Igou, 2011b) and political beliefs (Van Tilburg & Igou, 2016) via meaning search. Similarly, boredom promotes feelings of nostalgia (Van Tilburg et al., 2013) and prosocial engagement (Van Tilburg & Igou, 2016), which are both important sources of meaning in life. Consistent with this notion, we found that boredom affects evaluations of heroes via meaning search (Coughlan, Igou, Van Tilburg, Kinsella, & Ritchie, 2017).

Another way of managing experiences of boredom and the lack of meaning that boredom signals, is to re-direct one's attention by withdrawing from or distracting oneself from the current situation. That is, when sources of meaning are not directly available to people, then people choose stimulating and exciting alternatives (Leary, Rogers, Canfield, & Coe, 1986; Martin et al., 2006; Sansone et al., 1992; Van Tilburg & Igou, 2012), which offer distraction from the lack of meaning that people experience (e.g., Fahlman, Mercer-Lynn, Flora, & Eastwood, 2011; Moynihan et al., 2015; Van Tilburg & Igou, 2012). In the literature, this avoidant psychological process is referred to as pre-symbolic meaning regulation (e.g., Wisman, 2006; Wisman & Koole, 2003). This search for alternative stimulation and withdrawal from threats of meaninglessness, such as boredom, is consistent with the notion that the pursuit of stimulation and challenge are associated with boredom (Barbalet, 1999; Todman, 2003; Van Tilburg & Igou, 2012, 2017a). In line with this reasoning, we found, for example, that boredom increases impulsiveness (Moynihan, Igou, & Van Tilburg, 2017) and preference for unhealthy, but tasty, food (Moynihan et al., 2015). Search for meaningful activities and withdrawing one's mind from the boring situations are both consistent with a meaning-regulation approach to boredom (e.g., Van Tilburg & Igou, 2011b, 2012, 2016, 2017b) and with an attention-regulation approach to boredom (e.g., Eastwood et al., 2012).

The characteristics of boredom have implications for activities and situations that either reduce or enhance the boredom experience. Below, we explore the effects of nature on boredom experiences and physical activities in these natural settings. Very recently, we (Van Tilburg & Igou, 2019) examined some effects of nature on boredom. Would boredom increase or decrease the evaluation of natural environments? Would natural environments affect the sense of boredom that people experience? If natural environments affected boredom, could this have implications for physical activities in natural environments?

Positive effects of natural environments and the case of boredom

Nature as a resource

A common belief in many cultures is that nature has a positive effect on human beings as reflected, for example, in popular and scientific versions of the biophilia hypothesis (Wilson, 1984; see Fromm, 1973), pantheism, and nature connectedness. This common belief has, to some degree, been backed up by research that has focused on nature as a psychological and physical resource regarding its positive effects on attention and memory (for an overview see Chapter 6; also Kaplan & Kaplan, 1989;), stress reduction (e.g., Bowler, Buyung-Ali, Knight, & Pullin, 2010; Hartig, Mitchell, de Vries, & Frumkin, 2014; Ulrich et al., 1991; Warrington, Brick, Lanhart, & Cloak, 2017), and resilience, also with regard to physical activity (e.g., Berto, 2014; Capaldi, Passmore, Nisbet, Zelenski, & Dopko, 2015; see also Chapters 9 and 17 for overviews). Beyond the general effects that nature seems to have on psychological well-being, recently attention shifted towards physical activities in natural environments, which include green environments (e.g., forest) and water activities in nature (and its psychological state 'blue minds'; see Donnelly et al., 2016). For example, across many studies, it was found that natural environments alleviated negative affective states and increased revitalization in association with physical activities (e.g., Thompson Coon et al., 2011). In addition, it was reported that natural environments increase performance in physical activities (e.g., DeWolfe, Waliczek, & Zajicek, 2011; Pennebaker & Lightner, 1980). Both well-being and performance are important given that they are likely to influence motivation for and commitment to such activities, which are in turn important for general health benefits (see Chapter 2).

Nature as a resource in the case of boredom

It is surely possible that some people are not interested in nature or can even be bored by seeing nature or being in natural environments. It is said, for example, that Friedrich Schiller, a famous German poet, did not indulge nature as much as many of his colleagues, rather he preferred to discuss the newest writing, whether he was strolling through natural environment or not. Simply put, nature is not everyone's cup of tea. We want to state clearly here that we do not want to exaggerate the potential positivity of nature as if the effects were universal and very strong. Nature is often romanticized by people in urban areas because of unfavorable urban stimuli and because 'the grass is often greener on the other side'. Keeping in mind that nature, whether green or blue, is certainly not the sole solution of all problems, or even a many, we pose that on average nature could have positive effects for people, such as on their thoughts, on their feelings, on their behaviors, and on their physical and/or psychological health (Capaldi et al., 2015).

In our research (Van Tilburg & Igou, 2019), we examined whether visual displays of nature compared to displays of urban environments reduce the experience of boredom. In two studies using an online research platform (Mechanical Turk) with participants in the United States of America, we found evidence that displays of nature substantially reduce the experience of boredom. Further, these studies demonstrate that the effects of boredom are due to high brightness, deep color saturation, and highly contrasting colors that are typically found in real and in depictions of natural environments. Specifically, in one of our studies we found that the perceived higher brightness, saturation, and contrast associated with nature displays, relative to displays of urban environments, accounted for the difference in boredom that these environments elicited. We followed this up in a second study where we manipulated these features. Specifically, we showed participants a large range of nature and urban environments and asked them to judge each on boredom. Unbeknownst to the participants, we subtly manipulated the original displays to increase or reduce their brightness, saturation, and contrast (see samples online at https://tinyurl.com/chapterimagesGREENEX). The same displays caused less boredom when brightness was high rather than low, when saturation was high rather than low, and when contrast was high rather than low, and this was especially the case for urban environments. Consistently, people expressed a greater desire to spend time in these natural environments compared to the urban environments.

What these studies showed, then, was that nature displays reduce boredom relative to urban environments, and that the high levels of brightness, saturation, and contrast that people attribute to nature are at least partly the reason why nature reduces boredom. Strikingly, and consistent with our earlier work on boredom (e.g., Van Tilburg & Igou, 2011b, 2012, 2016, 2017b; Van Tilburg et al., 2013), by alleviating boredom these natural displays indirectly contributed to higher levels of meaning in life. That is, due to the link that exists between boredom and meaning in life, natural displays indirectly contributed to more meaning in life. This research thus shows that nature can serve as a resource in providing a sense of meaning in life by reducing negative experiences such as boredom. Plausibly, the basic color features that we investigated and manipulated—brightness, saturation, and contrast—engage people's attention (Boynton & Olson, 1990), preventing the mind from straying and becoming bored due to under-stimulation (Van Tilburg & Igou, 2012). Although, in-vivo effects of nature on boredom have yet to be tested, our research promotes the idea that exposure to nature has these positive effects. The implications for physical activities in natural environments are clear and important. Moreover, these studies suggest a way of reducing boredom in urban environments where nature is difficult to find: use bright, saturated, and contrasting colors.

Implications for physical activities in natural environments

Boredom is a momentary experience and some people are more prone to boredom than others. Given that boredom seems to be reduced by exposure to nature, and given that natural environments are often associated with physical activities, exposure to nature might very well affect physical activities via the reduction of boredom and increase of meaning in life. How could positive effects of exposure to nature increase physical activities in natural environments?

Reduction of boredom

The sources of boredom are theoretically unlimited. That is, boredom can be rooted in many activities. Natural environments can counteract boredom, in general, but perhaps also the boredom stemming from the physical activities that nature facilitates. As a result, physical activities would be perceived as less aversive, which in turn should increase likelihood of engagement in these activities. If a person plans to engage or does engage in physical activities, boredom may also arise from sources that are not directly related to the actual physical activity. For example, due to time constraints the person engaged in the physical activity may have to think about the rather boring workday schedule for the next day. Also in this case, natural environments may reduce or buffer against boredom with positive effects for the physical activity and the accompanying thoughts. In short, natural environments seem to have the capacity to reduce the averseness of the boredom experience. This reduction may thus increase the frequency and quality of performance of activities that either seemed boring or occurred in a context that originally caused boredom.

Maintaining meaning in life and side effects

Our research (Van Tilburg & Igou, 2019) shows that natural environments can reduce boredom, and that through this effect people's sense of meaning in life is more or less retained or re-established. Given the importance of perceptions of meaningfulness in actions and life in general (e.g., Heine, Proulx, & Vohs, 2006), exposure to nature is thus likely to have positive effects on variables that are associated with perceptions of meaning in life. For example, perceiving life as meaningful is strongly linked to motivation (e.g., Steger, Frazier, Oishi, & Kaler, 2006; Van Tilburg & Igou, 2011a) and mental health (e.g., Isaacs et al., 2017). We thus assume that the protective indirect impact of natural environments on meaning in life will have positive effects on variables such as these. Further, perceptions of meaning in life can become linked to nature and to activities in natural environments, which in turn facilitate physical activities in such environments with their known positive health effects (e.g., Ulrich et al., 1991). If via the reduction of boredom physical activities in natural environments become more likely, then the original effect on boredom not only transfers to increasing meaning in life, but also to, for example, resilience (see Chapter 9), reducing stress and increasing abilities in emotion regulation (see Chapter 11), and potentially increasing memory span and attention and other crucial cognitive processes (see Chapter 6).

Future research and practice

Given the prevalence of boredom in everyday life, our research examines the exposure to nature as a promising antidote to boredom. Our research is a first step in this direction. More research needs to be conducted to confirm the positive effects of nature that we found on the experience of boredom and on the effect on meaning maintenance via the reduction of boredom.

Importantly, the effects of exposure to nature on physical activities via boredom reduction have yet to be examined. It needs to be confirmed that exposure to nature affects physical activities via the reduction in boredom and maintenance of meaning in life. This relationship needs to be tested in green and in blue natural environments. Further, it needs to be tested for proneness to boredom, casual and intense physical activities, and for a range of health measures, with some assessing mental health and others assessing physical health.

References

Barbalet, J. M. (1999). Boredom and social meaning. *British Journal of Sociology, 50*, 631–646. doi:10.1111/j.1468-4446.1999.00631.x

Berto, R. (2014). The role of nature in coping with psycho-physiological stress: A literature review on restorativeness. *Behavioral Sciences, 4*, 394–409. doi:10.3390/bs4040394

Blaszczynski, A., McConaghy, N., & Frankova, A. (1990). Boredom proneness in pathological gambling. *Psychological Reports, 67*, 35–42. doi:10.2466/pr0.1990.67.1.35

Bowler, D. E., Buyung-Ali, L. M., Knight, T. M., & Pullin, A. S. (2010). A systematic review of evidence for the added benefits to health of exposure to natural environments. *BMC Public Health, 10*, 456. doi:10.1186/1471-2458-10-456

Boynton, R. M., & Olson, C. X. (1990). Salience of chromatic basic color terms confirmed by three measures. *Vision Research, 30*, 1311–1317. doi:10.1016/0042-6989(90)90005-6

Capaldi, C. A., Passmore, H.-A., Nisbet, E. K., Zelenski, J. M., & Dopko, R. L. (2015). Flourishing in nature: A review of the benefits of connecting with nature and its application as a wellbeing intervention. *International Journal of Wellbeing, 5*, 1–16. doi:10.5502/ijw.v5i4.449

Coughlan, G., Igou, E. R., Van Tilburg, W. A. P., Kinsella, E. L., & Ritchie, T. D. (2017). From boredom to perceptions of heroes: A meaning-regulation approach to heroism. *Journal of Humanistic Psychology*. doi:10.1177/0022167817705281

Dahlen, E. R., Martin, R. C., Ragan, K., & Kuhlman, M. M. (2004). Boredom proneness in anger and aggression: Effects of impulsiveness and sensation seeking. *Personality and Individual Differences, 37*, 1615–1627. doi:10.1016/j.paid.2004.02.016

DeWolfe, J., Waliczek, T. M., & Zajicek, J. M. (2011). The relationship between levels of greenery and landscaping at track and field sites, anxiety, and sports performance of collegiate track and field athletes. *Horttechnology, 21*, 329–335.

Donnelly, A. A., MacIntyre, T. E. Warrington, G., O'Sullivan, N., Harrison, A., Gordon B. R., Igou, E. R, Jones, M., Gidlow, C., Cloak, R., Lahart, I., Brick, N., & Lane, A. M. (2016). Environmental influences on elite sport athletes well being: From gold, silver and bronze to blue green and gold. *Frontiers in Psychology*, 7, 1167. doi:10.3389/fpsyg.2016.01167

Eastwood, J. D., Frischen, A., Fenske, M. J., & Smilek, D. (2012). The unengaged mind: Defining boredom in terms of attention. *Perspectives on Psychological Science*, 7, 482–495. doi:10.1177/1745691612456044

Fahlman, S. A., Mercer, K. B., Gaskocski, P., Eastwood, A. E., & Eastwood, J. D. (2009). Does a lack of life meaning cause boredom? Results from psychometric, longitudinal, and experimental analyses. *Journal of Social and Clinical Psychology, 28*, 307–340. doi:10.1521/jscp.2009.28.3.307

Fahlman, S. A., Mercer-Lynn, K. B., Flora, D. B., & Eastwood, J. D. (2011). Development and validation of the multi-dimensional boredom scale. *Assessment, 20*, 68–85. doi:10.1177/1073191111421303

Farmer, R., & Sundberg, N. D. (1986). Boredom proneness – The development and correlates of a new scale. *Journal of Personality Assessment, 50*, 4–17. doi:10.1207/s15327752jpa5001_2

Fromm, E. (1955). *The sane society*. New York. NY: Rinehart.

Fromm, E. (1963). *The dogma of Christ and other essays*. New York, NY: Holt, Rinehart and Winston.

Fromm, E. (1973). *The anatomy of human destructiveness*. New York, NY: Holt McDougal.

Fromm, E. (1991). *Die Pathologie der Normalität*. Weinheim, Germany: Beltz Verlag.

Hartig, T., Mitchell, R., de Vries, S. & Frumkin, H. (2014). Nature and health. *Annual Review of Public Health, 35*, 207–228. doi:10.1146/annurev-publhealth-032013-182443

Heine, J. S., Proulx, T., & Vohs, K. D. (2006). The meaning maintenance model: On the coherence of social motivations. *Personality and Social Psychology Review, 10*, 88–110. doi:10.1207/s15327957pspr1002_1

Isaacs, K., Mota, N. P., Tsai, J., Harpaz-Rotem, I., Cook, J. M., Kirwin, P. D., Krystal, J. H., Southwick, S. M., & Pietrzak, R. H. (2017). Psychological resilience in U.S. military veterans: A 2-year, nationally representative prospective cohort study. *Journal of Psychiatric Research, 84*, 301–309. doi:10.1016/j.jpsychires.2016.10.017

Kaplan, R., & Kaplan, S. (1989). *The experience of nature: A psychological perspective*. Cambridge, UK: Cambridge University Press.

Kass, S. J., Vodanovich, S. J., & Callander, A. (2001). State-trait boredom: The relationship to absenteeism, tenure, and job satisfaction. *Journal of Business and Psychology, 16*, 317–327. doi:10.1023/A:1011121503118

Leary, M. R., Rogers, P. A., Canfield, R. W., & Coe, C. (1986). Boredom and interpersonal encounters: Antecedents and social implications. *Journal of Personality and Social Psychology, 51*, 968–975. doi:10.1037/0022-3514.51.5.968

Martin, M., Sadlo, G., & Stew, G. (2006). The phenomenon of boredom. *Qualitative Research in Psychology, 3*, 193–211. doi:10.1191/1478088706qrp066oa

Moynihan, A. B., Igou, E. R., & Van Tilburg, W. A. P. (2017). Boredom increases impulsiveness: A meaning-regulation perspective. *Social Psychology, 48*, 293–309. doi:10.1027/1864-9335/a000317

Moynihan, A. B., Van Tilburg, W. A. P., Igou, E. R., Wisman, A., Donnelly, A. E., & Mulcraire, J. B. (2015). Eaten up by boredom: Consuming food to escape awareness of the bored self. *Frontiers in Psychology, 6*, 369. doi:10.3389/fpsyg.2015.00369

Pennebaker, J. W., & Lightner, J. M. (1980). Competition of internal and external information in an exercise setting. *Journal of Personality and Social Psychology, 39*, 165–174. doi:10.1037/0022-3514.39.1.165

Sansone, C., Weir, C., Harpster, L., & Morgan, C. (1992). Once a boring task always a boring task? Interest as a self-regulatory strategy. *Journal of Personality and Social Psychology, 63*, 379–390. doi:10.1037/0022-3514.63.3.379

Schopenhauer, A. (2010). *Aphorismen zur Lebensweisheit.* Wiesbaden, Germany: Marix Verlag.

Smith, C. A., & Ellsworth, P. C. (1985). Patterns of cognitive appraisal in emotion. *Journal of Personality and Social Psychology, 48*, 813–838. doi:10.1037/0022-3514.48.4.813

Steger, M. F., Frazier, P., Oishi, S., & Kaler, M. (2006). The meaning in life questionnaire: Assessing the presence of and search for meaning in life. *Journal of Counselling Psychology, 53*, 80–93. doi:10.1037/0022-0167.53.1.80

Thiele, L. P. (1997). Postmodernity and the routinization of novelty: Heidegger on boredom and technology. *Polity, 29*, 489–551.

Thompson Coon, J., Boddy, K., Stein, K., Whear, R., Barton, J., & Depledge, M. H. (2011). Does participating in physical activity in outdoor natural environments have a greater effect on physical and mental wellbeing than physical activity indoors? A systematic review. *Environmental Science & Technology, 45*, 1761–1772. doi:10.1021/es102947t

Todman, M. (2003). Boredom and psychotic disorders: Cognitive and motivational issues. *Psychiatry: Interpersonal and Biological Processes, 66*, 146–167. doi:10.1521/psyc.66.2.146.20623

Ulrich, R. S., Simons, R. F., Losito, B. D., Fiorito, E., Miles, M. A., & Zelson, M. (1991). Stress recovery during exposure to natural and urban environments. *Journal of Environmental Psychology, 11*, 231–248. doi:10.1016/S0272-4944(05)80184-7

Van Tilburg, W. A. P., & Igou, E. R. (2011a). On the meaningfulness of existence: When life salience boosts adherence to worldviews. *European Journal of Social Psychology, 41*, 740–750. doi:10.1002/ejsp.819

Van Tilburg, W. A., & Igou, E. R. (2011b). On boredom and social identity: A pragmatic meaning-regulation approach. *Personality and Social Psychology Bulletin, 37*, 1679–1691. doi:10.1177/0146167211418530

Van Tilburg, W. A. P., & Igou, E. R. (2012). On boredom: Lack of challenge and meaning as distinct boredom experiences. *Motivation and Emotion, 36*, 181–194. doi:10.1007/s11031-011-9234-9

Van Tilburg, W. A. P., & Igou, E. R. (2013). On the meaningfulness of behavior: An expectancy x value approach. *Motivation and Emotion, 37*, 373–388. doi:10.1007/s11031-012-9316-3

Van Tilburg, W. A., Igou, E. R. (2016). Going to political extremes in response to boredom. *European Journal of Social Psychology*. doi:10.1002/ejsp.2205

Van Tilburg, W. A. P., & Igou, E. R. (2017a). Boredom begs to differ: Differentiation from other negative emotions. *Emotion, 17*, 309–322. doi:10.1037/emo0000233

Van Tilburg, W. A. P., & Igou, E. R. (2017b). Can boredom help? Increased prosocial intentions in response to boredom. *Self and Identity*. doi:10.1080/15298868.2016.1218925

Van Tilburg, W. A., Igou, E. R. (2019). Unnaturally bored: Nature alleviates boredom. *Unpublished Manuscript.*

Van Tilburg, W. A., Igou, E. R., & Sedikides, C. (2013). In search of meaningfulness: Nostalgia as an antidote to boredom. *Emotion, 13*, 450–461. doi:10.1037/a0030442

Wallbott, H. G. (1998). Bodily expression of emotion. *European Journal of Social Psychology, 28*, 879–896.

Watt, J. D., & Vodanovich, S. J. (1999). Boredom proneness and psychosocial development. *Journal of Psychology, 133*, 303–314. doi:10.1080/00223989909599743

Wilson, E. O. (1984). *Biophilia*. Cambridge, MA: Harvard University Press.

Wisman, A. (2006). Digging in terror management theory: To 'use' or 'lose' the symbolic self? *Psychological Inquiry, 17*, 319–327. doi:10.1080/10478400701369468

Wisman, A., & Koole, S. (2003). Hiding in the crowd: Can mortality salience promote affiliation with others who oppose one's worldviews? *Journal of Personality and Social Psychology, 84*, 511–526. doi:10.1037/0022-3514.84.3.511

9

GROWING RESILIENCE THROUGH CONNECTING WITH NATURE

Stephen Smith, Evan Hunt, Moya O'Brien and Deirdre MacIntyre

The importance of establishing contact and, subsequently, a deeper connection with nature has long been underestimated in terms of the maintenance of wellbeing and boosting of resilience. Increases in urbanization and the digital colonization of humans' daily lives has resulted in people becoming more and more detached from this essential fount of wellbeing. The outdoors is no longer the central hub of all children's play, with advances in technology and elevated parental concerns around child safety resulting in children playing in settings which are increasingly artificial and devoid of any natural stimuli. This trend is particularly noteworthy given the wealth of research which outlines the extent of the positive impact that nature can exert upon children's physical and mental health and wellbeing (Chawla, 2015; Tillmann et al., 2018).

This chapter will set about examining the development of childhood resilience through nature connectedness. Firstly, the dearth of contact between children and nature will be outlined in terms of the potential impact it is yielding upon the health and wellbeing of young people in modern society. Next, the constructs of resilience and nature connectedness (see Chapter 1) will be defined and the current thinking in relation to the theories and mechanisms which may link the two constructs will be explored. In this chapter, we will emphasize the research pertaining to the value of children engaging with nature rather than merely exposing them to natural stimuli. Finally, a variety of strategies and suggestions around the most effective ways in which to develop nature connectedness, and in turn promote resilience through this connection will be suggested, in addition to recommendations for future research directions in the area.

For thousands of years, people have sought out nature as a source of healing, wisdom, clarity and perspective. Shamans seek wilderness to explore the innermost layers of the psyche, Yogis enter the forest to enhance their brain functioning and decrease stress. Christian Fathers retreat to the desert in search of a simpler and purer existence, and young males from the Native American community embark upon nature vision quests as rites of passage in order to gain an understanding of their purpose in life and to obtain the strength they need to pursue this purpose. These continued nature-based quests are informed by these groups' positive past experiences in nature, which have elucidated nature's capacity to heal and calm, remove mental trivia and remind one of what truly matters in life (Walsh, 1999).

As urbanization and the digital revolution gather pace, it has begun to feel as though humans are living subjects in an uncontrolled global experiment, wherein the vast majority of our time is spent within environments which are almost entirely artificial. This trend towards the increased immersion of the human race in manmade environs cannot be seen more clearly than when one examines the national and worldwide statistics pertaining to urban growth. Human survival was previously dependent upon a capacity to live off the land and hunt for sustenance, with just 30% of the worldwide population comprising urban dwellers up until as recently as 1950 (United Nations, UN, 2018). However, a seismic shift has been observed in the distribution of the population across the globe within the intervening century. A recent report revealed that 55% of the worldwide population is located within urban centers (UN, 2018), with an even greater proportion of Irish residents (63%) being located in urban areas (Central Statistics Office, 2017). Not only have instances of urban centers increased dramatically across the world, but these urbanized areas are now substantially more populated than ever before, with the number of cities with a population greater than 1 million people rising from 12 cities in 1900 to 548 worldwide in 2018 (UN, 2018). These trends of urbanization are anticipated to persist into the future, with 68% of the world's population projected to be urban dwellers by 2050 (UN, 2018). Urban growth of this nature demands vast expanses of land in which to occur and this sprawling expansion of urban areas has led to the corresponding loss of green space and natural sites, which, in turn has prompted a reduction in the level of contact and sense of connectedness people feel with the natural environment.

Nowhere is this chasm between humans and the natural world more apparent than amongst the millennial generation. Young people have been shown to spend half as much time in outdoor environments as their parents a generation before them (just over 4 hours on average as compared to the 8.2 hours average of their parents) (Press Association, 2016). Another noteworthy survey investigating children's outdoor recreation time revealed that 75% of children in the UK spend less time in the outdoors than prison inmates. It is hardly surprising then that four out of five children in the UK labeled themselves as not having a sense of connectedness with nature (Royal Society for the Protection of Birds, 2013). In his bestselling publication *Last Child in The Woods* (2005), Richard Louv summarized the modern day childhood quite adeptly when he declared children to be overprotected, overscheduled and over stimulated, spending less and less time in nature. Children's free time has become increasingly structured and regimented, with parents seemingly determined to fill almost every waking hour of the day with formalized activities (art class, swimming lessons, music lessons etc.), so as to know where their child is at all times. Whilst these activities are beneficial in and of themselves, the increasingly scheduled nature of children's recreational activities has eroded opportunities to engage in free outdoor play. Free play had previously been identified as a critical agent in children's development and learning (Fromberg & Bergen, 2006). However, a growing culture of parental caution regarding the potential for accidents during episodes of free outdoor play, namely potential hazards, interactions with strangers or incidents with cars, has made parents increasingly reticent to permit their children to embark on a solo adventure into nature, despite an awareness of the beneficial nature of these experiences (Singer et al., 2009; Kernan & Devine, 2010).

Intriguingly, a corpus of research literature has indicated that this growing distance between children and nature is mirrored within the cultural media to which children are exposed (films, books, songs etc.) throughout their childhood. For example, Grice (1975) suggested that culture provides a keen insight into the broader psyche of society at large, as the cultural communicators tailor their content and messages to maximize its relevance to the interests of the intended audience. In the light of this theory, the decline in the prominence of natural environments, animals, and nature-related concepts in the Disney animated movies, which was highlighted by Prévot-Julliard et al. (2015), provides a telling insight into the decline in interest and enthusiasm in relation to the natural world amongst young people. Similar findings were yielded upon examining the winners of the children's Caldecot book awards between 1938–2008, whereby depictions of animals and natural scenes within leading instances of children's literature were shown to be in decline and being replaced by stories which were based in urban settings (Williams et al., 2012). Kesebir and Kesebir (2017) also revealed that the endangerment of nature-related constructs within modern culture had also spread to the medium of music. Through an analysis of the prevalence of nature-related lyrics within the top 100 songs for every year between 1950–2011, it was found that references to nature tailed off significantly as one moved closer to the modern day. From this body of research, it is clear that script writers, authors and musicians do not turn to nature-based concepts as the most effective means through which to reach the younger generation. The increasing absence of nature from such creative endeavors merely serves to perpetuate and accentuate the divide between child and nature and signals a concerning decline in the use of what was previously a crucial cog in the creation of bonds and generation of knowledge among young people in relation to the natural world.

Perhaps an even more startling discovery emerged from a paper by Flood (2015) pertaining to the selection process of terms to be introduced into the updated version of the *Oxford Junior Dictionary*. The paper underlined the continued deviation from natural world towards an increasingly technologically dominated society, by calling attention to the omission of nature-centric terms such as canary, clover, pasture and blackberry in favor of more technologically based words such as blog, attachment, voicemail and Blackberry. This selection most accurately encapsulates the direction in which society is going – one in which a blackberry is not instantly recognized as a delicious, juicy snack which grows in the wild amidst the brambles but rather as a mobile device which a person uses to organize their work calendar and respond to the array of emails they receive on a daily basis. The removal of natural constructs from reliable sources of information such as dictionaries is of particular concern as children's knowledge regarding flora and fauna has already been exhibited to be on the wane. A survey conducted by researchers in Cambridge (Balmford et al., 2002) using a cohort of 4- to 11-year-old children shone a light upon this issue by revealing that the children possessed a more extensive knowledge of the various Pokémon types (80% identification accuracy) than of living organisms such as badgers or oak trees (50% identification accuracy). It follows that one might express fear that the removal of nature-related terms from a vital information source such as a dictionary might limit the dictionary's potential as a learning resource in relation to nature-related concepts and, thus, further exacerbate the existing blind spots which young people exhibit in terms of their knowledge of the natural world.

The reduction in outdoor play and engagement with nature amongst the millennial generation has coincided with a boom in the area of smart technology and young people have increasingly gravitated towards seeking their thrills via a multitude of online media. Where once young people invested their time into outdoor activities such as learning to surf the waves, they now pass vast proportions of their time surfing the web. For instance, Rideout, Foehr, and Roberts (2010) exhibited the extent of young people's online connectivity with their findings revealing that US children are condensing 8 hours of online time into just 5.5 hours by virtue of technological multitasking (e.g. watching television whilst playing video games/browsing on a handheld device). These findings suggest that young people are inundated with exhilarating content and should bring about a situation whereby young people are more connected to their peers than ever before by virtue of the 24/7 round the clock availability that goes hand in hand with social media sites and instant messaging applications.

However, Turkle (2012) painted a decidedly different picture with respect to the knock-on effects of the increase in online activity exhibited by the young people of today. She wrote of how the ubiquity of social media had brought about a sanitization of experience. Interactions have, in many cases, been condensed down into likes or retweets, leaving many people feeling as though the majority of their online activity is distinctly lacking in substance and does little to sate their innate human need for connection. Turkle believed that basing a significant amount of one's social interaction around social media activity was akin to replacing one big gulp of deep experience with little sips of empty, mindless interaction. Kaschak (2017) reinforces this outlook by asserting that once one places an excessive dependence on the role of symbols or pixels in replicating the impact of physical experience, loneliness results.

It is important to clarify at this stage that our intention is not to propagate the views of luddites by engaging in scaremongering designed to demonize the digital age or to curtail the technological adroitness of young people. Nor do we wish to lay the blame for the disconnection which exists between young people and nature at the feet of the youth themselves. It is obvious that technology does not simply represent an opiate of the masses, but also constitutes a vital functional tool of the modern world. As the human race becomes increasingly engulfed in a digitally led society, the next generation must remain abreast of the latest technological advances in preparation for the society which awaits them. In fact, one of the foremost priorities in the field of environmental research concerns the identification of the most effective methods through which the immense potential of technology can be harnessed, with a view to boosting the depth and quality of human experiences within natural environments. Chapter 15 details the progress in the area of technological nature, technologies that in various ways mediate, augment, or simulate the natural world (Kahn et al., 2009). Continued work in this area represents a pivotal strand of nature-based research as it is only through the identification of evidence-based recommendations for the inclusion of technology within the experience of the natural world that research of this nature can hope to retain relevance within our evolving society.

Yet, even with the marked progress noted in research pertaining to the promising potential of innovations in technological nature, the adage of the authors is that it is imperative that a balance be struck, and that time is retained for the purity of experience that accompanies time spent in the outdoors. At present, it is apparent that this equilibrium is not being achieved amongst the younger generation, with this imbalance perhaps being encapsulated most strikingly by the aforementioned selection process for the *Oxford Junior Dictionary*. Digital literacy is seemingly being prioritized to the detriment of nature-related knowledge, resulting in an ever widening disconnect between young people and the natural world around them. Within this detachment, the assessments presented by both Turkle and Kaschak pertaining to the inability of digitally based interactions and recreation to provide a comparable degree of depth or mental nourishment as in-person experiences appear to be unfolding before our eyes, with increased reliance on online media correlating with a sharp rise in physical and mental issues noted among young people.

The media is awash with coverage relating to the adverse impact of society's increased inclination towards an indoor, sedentary lifestyle upon physical health worldwide. A recent World Health Organization (WHO) news release (2019) revealed that just one in every five adolescents is steadily achieving the recommended guidelines for physical activity of 60 minutes moderate to vigorous physical activity daily. This shortfall in physical activity among the majority of young adults has correlated with a notable spike in rates of diabetes (Mayer-Davis et al., 2017), obesity and a raft of physical health concerns. Yet, perhaps the most insidious aspects of the schism between children and nature are to be found in the roots of the growing mental health crisis which is afflicting young people across the globe. According to the WHO, mental health problems have been shown to affect between 10–20% of children and adolescents worldwide. However, one particularly noteworthy finding in the context of this chapter emerges in the form of the mean age of onset of mood and anxiety disorders, which has to this point been shown to range between 14–25 years (Kessler et al., 2007; Cía et al. 2018). This data suggests that a window of opportunity may exist within childhood wherein protective factors can be embedded into the lives of young people. It is our postulation that nature contact, and the subsequent fostering of a deep seated connection with the natural world may play a crucial preventative role at this stage in life by aiding the development of a collection of crucial adaptive skills which can aid positive coping and adaptation in the face of adversity.

In fact, many researchers have portrayed the natural world as a vessel through which young people can cultivate their own positive personal development and establish connections with others, whilst also re-establishing their own bond with nature itself. Some have even ventured so far as to indicate that the physical, mental and spiritual health of young people could be dependent upon the rekindling of the human-nature connection. Such beliefs are receiving increasing support from an expanding evidence base across a variety of disciplines ranging from philosophy and sociology to environmental science and psychology, which exhibits the potential for positive health benefits (physical and mental) to be reaped through the strengthening of one's contact and connection with nature. However, these promising findings have been undermined by a lack of integration across disciplines, owing to an absence of clarity and accuracy in the definition of terms and a tendency for those from each discipline to stick rigidly to the terms of reference of their own perspective and discipline (see Chapter 2). More specifically, two of the most fundamental challenges to be overcome within this field are the lack of commonality in the language utilized in discussing ideas and concepts, and an absence of universal assessment methods to evaluate the impact of interventions from a multitude of scientific and academic disciplines.

Therefore, prior to any detailed examination of the promising findings relating mental and physical health outcomes to a strong sense of connectedness to nature, it is first vital to outline the definitions of both "resilience" (see Figure 9.1) and "nature connectedness" as these concepts will be addressed throughout the chapter.

What is Resilience?

Conflation & Confusion

Resilience has been conflated and confounded with, for example, grit and mental toughness and debate continues as to whether it best viewed as a state or trait (Bryan et al., 2017).

Original Derivation of "Resilience"

Comes from the Latin word "resilio" meaning to jump back and can be defined as the ability to rebound from adversity.

Positive Adaptation

However, the concept of rebounding from adversity does not fully encompass the construct.
Masten (2001) defined resilience as the *process of positive adaptation in the face of adversity and the ability to take advantage of new opportunities.*

Natural Resilience

The term resilience is also present within references to the natural environment wherein it refers to the ability of a system to persist in the face of perturbations.

FIGURE 9.1 What do we mean by resilience?

Resilience – why is it important?

Resilience is a construct which has received considerable attention across a variety of research domains from neurobiology to environmental science to psychology, and has accordingly been subject to an array of theoretically diverse conceptualizations. This lack of unanimity in definition has resulted in the concept of resilience becoming clouded by confusion and uncertainty as to its meaning. In spite of this absence of consensus amongst the multitude of definitions which have been posited, two core elements emerge as being central to the majority of efforts to define resilience, namely, positive adaptation and response to adversity (Fletcher & Sarkar, 2013). Within the current chapter (see also Chapters 8 and 10), the term resilience will refer to *the process of positive adaptation in the face of adversity and the ability to take advantage of new opportunities* (Masten, 2001). This definition is clear and unequivocal, whilst also addressing another of the longstanding issues which has dogged resilience research – the state-trait debate. Much of the early research broached the topic of resilience from the trait perspective, wherein resilience was portrayed as a personality trait which assisted individuals in coping with adversity by inoculating them against the potential impacts of adversity or trauma (Connor & Davidson, 2003; Ong et al., 2006). However, more recent research has shifted away from this perspective, and, instead, has come to view resilience in terms of being a continual process which can be nurtured and developed across the duration of the life span (Bryan et al., 2017; Shatté et al., 2017). Cyrulnik (2009) analogized the cultivation of resilience to knitting an item of clothing, in order to detail the complex nature of the developmental process of resilience, stating that: "Resilience is a sweater knitted from developmental, emotional and social strands of wool ... We are forced to knit ourselves, using people and things we meet in our emotional and social environments" (p. 51).

From the state perspective, resilience is believed to be honed through daily exchanges and interactions with one's environment and successful navigations of challenging experiences and events. The positive adaptation and response to adversity is seen as the critical component of what it means to be resilient. It also vital to emphasize that the adversity referred to can vary markedly, from novel, minor challenges to severe instances of trauma in one's life. Rutter (2012) labeled these moments as turning points in an individual's life, while Cyrulnik (2009) referred to them as part of the fabric one uses to knit their resilience. Masten's definition of resilience elucidates the dynamism and evolving nature of resilience, wherein one's biology and development interact within a social context over time to grow and craft one's resilience. As resilience is based upon a number of variables (available psychological and personal resources, context and the nature of the challenge presented) as well as one's personality, resilience can be seen to fluctuate across time points and contexts (Southwick et al., 2014). Consider the expression "the straw that broke the camel's back" which is prominent in everyday parlance pertaining to one's capacity to cope with stressors that crop up in life. This emphasizes the essence of resilience by highlighting the manner in which one's capacity to cope fluctuates depending upon one's emotional state, the ready availability of social supports and the physical resources which an individual possesses when confronted with adversity or challenge.

Theoretical explanations of resilience have deconstructed the quality of resilience into its component parts with some viewpoints citing the promotion of influential protective factors, such as secure attachments and a stable childhood, as essential to the construction of resilience. Other approaches have focused upon a collection of internal resources or skills as the foundation of the cultivation of resilience in humans. One of the foremost theories relating to resilience proposes that the quality of resilience is rooted in the nurturing of a specific set of skills, namely emotional regulation, impulse control, causal analysis, self-efficacy and realistic optimism (Shatté et al., 2017). The aforementioned skills possess the potential to mediate one's experience of stress and bring about a productive response to adversity and setbacks. One of the most encouraging aspects of this perspective lies in the fact that the skills that underpin resilience can be learnt and taught. By virtue of the malleability of these skills, psychological resilience can be developed through targeted development of evidence-based factors associated with resilience such as realistic optimism, problem-solving capabilities, self-regulatory capacities and interpersonal skills, and natural environments offer the ideal context in which to foster these resilience-relevant skills from an early age.

What do we mean by nature connectedness?

The starting point for any conversation surrounding what it means to be connected to nature and how this connection may benefit individuals and society more broadly must first centre upon the establishment of a definition of the entity that humans are endeavoring to build a connection to i.e. *what is nature?* This query is one which has proved to be a complex one to address. Ives et al. (2017) posit their definition of nature as being "*places, landscapes and ecosystems that are not completely dominated by people, but also include non-human organisms, species and habitats*". This definition emphasizes the importance of limited human influence being evident within those scenes which are considered to be "natural". Bratman et al. (2012) adopts a similar definitional template of the construct of nature, but does outline the existence of a spectrum when considering natural scenes, wherein these scenes can be range from being "largely nonhuman to heavily human influenced" (see Chapter 2) This is a crucial point of consideration as the aforementioned issue of urban sprawl has impinged markedly upon the availability of predominantly nonhuman environments for vast swathes of the global population. Examples of scenes which are perhaps most synonymous with the most classical representations of nonhuman natural environments include forests, riverbanks, beaches and open green fields. However, as urban expansion has continued apace, a multitude of human influenced nature spaces, ranging from kempt parks and gardens to water features and flowerbeds, have been constructed in an effort to retain some element of the natural world within the expanse of concrete jungle. The conceptualization of nature as existing upon this spectrum allows the impact of built nature spaces to also be considered in the context of exposure to nature.

The construct of nature contact has been expanded to encompass the wide range of forms in which nature contact can be experienced, with variation in the nature contact experience emerging based upon the spatial scale of the natural scene, proximity, the sensory medium through which the natural elements are experienced (visual, tactile, auditory) etc. (Frumkin et al., 2017). This differentiated approach to considering one's contact with nature has enabled researchers to conceptualize nature contact as existing upon a spectrum, wherein nature contact experiences can be analyzed based upon the frequency with which they are experienced (everyday frequentation of a green school or work environment vs. once off 3 day trekking activity) and also, the expansiveness or extent of the natural elements within which the contact experience is occurring (a potted plant in one's office vs. an excursion to a sizeable forest). In essence, the conceptualization of nature contact as existing upon a spectrum means that not all nature experiences are created equal, and the extent of the benefits extracted from exposure to the natural environment can be influenced significantly by both spatial and temporal factors (Frumkin et al., 2017).

In addition to the outlined practical considerations which can impact upon the extent of the beneficial effects of the nature experience, the degree to which one engages with the natural elements within their environs can also play a considerable role in dictating just how substantial the ameliorative effect of one's nature-based experience is deemed to be. The manner in which humans interact with the natural world can be understood via a graded scale of conscious engagement, ranging from instance of being passively present within natural surroundings to more immersive and concerted efforts to engage and connect with the natural world. This concept of conscious engagement with nature has been subject to a growing research interest across disciplines and has been examined through the utilization of a range of related terms (e.g. nature exposure, nature contact, nature engagement). Nature engagement can account for the cognitive, affective and tactile processes that mediate our immersion in natural stimuli (see Chapter 2). In essence, what truly underlies a young person's interaction with nature is the degree to which they feel connected to it.

Nature connectedness is among the terms employed to characterize this phenomenon of one's subjective sense of affinity towards and connection with nature (Capaldi et al., 2014; Ives et al., 2017). Other terms include nature-relatedness (Nisbet et al., 2009), connectedness to nature (Mayer & Frantz, 2004), commitment to nature (Davis et al., 2011) and inclusion of the self in nature (Schultz, 2002). Each of these terms assesses slightly different expressions of the same underlying construct (see Chapters 1 and 2). For the purposes of this chapter, the term "nature connectedness" will be utilized as an all-encompassing umbrella term as per Capaldi et al. (2014) and Ives et al. (2017), wherein a connection to nature was seen to encompass five subthemes: material connection, experiential connection, cognitive connection, emotional connection and philosophical connection. Nature connectedness has been construed as an individual trait which pertained to an individual's "experiential sense of oneness with the world" (Mayer & Frantz, 2004). The concept has also been categorized more in terms of being a temporary state, which has been shown to partially mediate the effects of nature contact upon individual wellbeing (Mayer et al., 2009).

Assessment of nature connection

A prerequisite to determining the extent of the influence one's connection to nature can exert upon their psychological wellbeing is the capacity to accurately measure said sense of connectedness to the natural world. Generally, the assessment of an individual's connection to nature has been carried out primarily through the use of subjective measures, wherein people are requested to self-report their connection and exposure to nature, in addition to their overall wellbeing. Such measures (e.g. the Connectedness to Nature Scale (Mayer & Frantz, 2004)) revolve around the assessment of the feelings, behaviors and attitudes that one exhibits within, and towards, the natural world. However, a multitude of relevant measures have been developed and adopt alternative approaches to examining and assessing the intricacies of the human-nature relationship, including Schultz's Inclusion of the Self in Nature assessment, Diessner et al.'s Engagement with Natural Beauty Scale (2008), and Nisbet et al.'s Nature Relatedness Scale (2009) amongst others.

However, in more recent times, the prevalence of more objective, physiological measures in the assessment of the human-nature relationship has been steadily rising. Stellar et al. (2015) investigated how experiences of awe in the natural environment impacted one levels of inflammatory cytokines, and determined that natural environments possessed the potential to contribute to regular experiences of awe which are associated with healthier, reduced levels of inflammatory cytokines. As part of the H2020 PHENOTYPE research (Gidlow et al., 2016), levels of hair cortisol concentration were utilized as a physiological marker of the degree of stress experienced by participants within natural and urban surroundings. Other physiological markers which have recently come to be utilized in the context of human-nature connection research include heart rate variability, galvanic skin response, immune function and oxytocin levels (Tsunetsugu et al., 2007; Valtchanov et al., 2010).

Oxytocin measurement is of particular pertinence to the current chapter, as this hormone is associated with social connection and bonding in humans. Could it be that humans experience connection to natural stimuli or species in the natural world in a manner which is comparable to the interpersonal connection noted among humans? The continued inclusion of oxytocin measurement in future human-nature connection research studies could assist in explaining the manner in which the human-nature connection develops and grows across the life course, and, therefore, is worthy of further exploration as a key marker of the human-nature connection.

A more exhaustive overview of the assessment measures and primary methodological considerations whilst investigating the human-nature connection can be found in Chapter 2, as well as in Tam's (2013) review which offers a detailed insight into the key concepts and assessment measures in this field of research.

Assessment of children's nature connectedness

Upon examination, a prevalent and noteworthy theme which emerges across the range of tools utilized to gain an insight into the sense of connectedness adults hold towards the natural world is the age specific nature of investigatory methods. Most prominent assessment tools require the respondent to be capable of differentiating between an affinity towards nature, which is based in emotion, and intellectual interest in components of the natural world, which is rooted in cognition (Picard et al., 2004). Equally, many of these tools demand the completion of scaled response items, which fail to allow for absolute thinking patterns (all or nothing) that characterize how a young person sees the world

(Oshio et al., 2016). With these major issues considered, it becomes clear that the aforementioned tools typically availed of in the assessment of nature connectedness in adults are unfit for purpose when it comes to the surveying of younger respondents.

Thus, given the link between nature connectedness in children and an array of positive psychological and environmental outcomes, increased exigency has been attached to the development of an assessment tool which can accurately quantify the level of connection which exists between the natural environment and a young respondent. To date, no one reliable means to this has been identified. Sobko et al. (2018) have recently developed the Connectedness to Nature Index for Parents of Preschool Children (CNI-PPC), which seeks to measure connectedness to nature among very young children who are unable to provide their own responses to the items being examined. Initial testing of the CNI-PPC among an urban population indicated that the tool does appropriately tap into four distinct dimensions allied with nature connectedness (enjoyment of nature, empathy for nature, sense of responsibility, and awareness of nature), which suggests that the CNI-PPC may well represent a promising tool with which to examine nature connectedness in young people moving forward.

The development of the child-nature relationship

While advancements in researchers' capacity to more accurately capture the extent of nature connectedness exhibited by preschool children signals a significant leap forward for research in this area, progress in relation to measurement has merely served to accentuate the growing chasm which is unfolding between young people and the natural world. For example, a study (2013) commissioned by the Royal Society for the Protection of Birds examining the extent to which a cohort of in excess of 1,000 8- to 12-year-old children in the UK deemed themselves to be connected to nature found that just 20% of children reported a connection with nature. Thus, findings such as these emphasize the need for researchers to gain a clearer understanding of the manner in which the child-nature connection develops throughout these key formative years.

Firstly, it is necessary to acknowledge that, as with the formation of any relationship in a child's life, the development of children's connection to nature is marked by complexity and can only occur in the presence of consistent exposure to nature over time (Giusti et al., 2018). One recently proposed framework illustrates the stages which occur throughout the process of growing a connection with nature, postulating that a child's relationship with nature is cultivated by first being in nature, then nourished further by being with nature, and finally being for nature (see Figure 9.2).

This framework and accompanying assessment tool, the Assessment Framework for Children's Human Nature Situations (ACHUNAS), highlight the

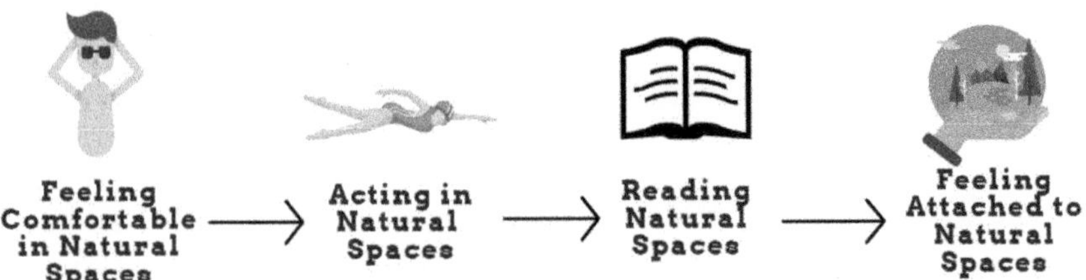

FIGURE 9.2 Framework for the Development of Nature Connectedness in Children

significance of children's emotions and thinking as key contributors in the construction of a child-nature connection. ACHUNAS assesses the specific features within the environment in which the nature contact occurs, in terms of its capacity to provide "significant nature situations" (SNS). Giusti and colleagues provided 16 different constituent elements which may be present in SNS, ranging from challenging or awe inspiring components to thought provoking or restorative experiences. Debate has persisted within the literature with respect to whether simply providing children with the opportunity to make contact with the natural elements is sufficient to fortify the affiliation a child feels towards the natural world. When viewed through the prism of the ACHUNAS tool, it becomes increasingly apparent that fostering a lasting connection to nature requires more than mere exposure to natural landscapes from an early age. Regular contact with nature is now viewed as the human-nature connection in its embryonic stage. The development of a meaningful bond with the natural world involves a lifelong process whereby people consistently and actively engage with their surroundings, take time to understand the intricacies of the world around them and cultivate an inbuilt consideration of the environmental impact of their lifestyle and choices.

Thus, the process of promoting the child-nature connection should reflect this trajectory accordingly, by allowing for a multifaceted approach to building children's bond to nature. Undeniably, there is still considerable merit in encouraging children to embark upon solitary pursuits in the outdoors (free play and exploration in a forest, digging for worms amidst the clay and, even, experiencing the sting of nettle or a bee). Such activities create opportunities for valuable learning experiences about both about the natural world and oneself (O'Malley, 2014), and act as the foundations for the construction of a lasting bond between individuals and the natural environment.

However, given that our aim is to identify the means through which nature connectedness and resilience can be promoted through exploits in the outdoors, it is the view of the authors that such results may only be yielded by blending free play with more explicit and structured activities within nature. Young people require scaffolding and support from informed adults in order to truly maximize the value of their contact with the natural world. Adults must tailor certain nature-based activities towards the explicit teaching of the key skills required in the development of resilience, whilst also prompting reflection upon the key takeaway messages and the emotions experienced throughout the duration of the activity itself. The need for a more structured approach to nature-based learning explains the recent upsurge in popularity experienced by nature schools, forest schools and other similar outdoor learning initiatives (discussed further in Chapter 14), as parents seek to maximize the benefits their children reap from reconnecting with the outdoors.

Growing resilience through the natural world

By now, a substantial body of research has underlined the ameliorative impact of immersing young people in natural surroundings on a regular basis. Nature-based scenes have been shown to instill an unrestricted sense of independence and autonomy in young people, offering a scope for exploration, calculated risk-taking and practical problem-solving opportunities not commonly found in alternative settings. Furthermore, challenges that arise within the natural environment often create ready-made opportunities for the formation of meaningful social connections to peers, the enhancement of interpersonal skills, and the development a sense of empathy and compassion with others and the broader natural environment (Abbott-Chapman & Robertson, 2009; Ives et al., 2017). Other positive effects of exposure to natural environments include the enhancement of human vitality (Ryan et al., 2010) and the experience of transcendent emotions such as awe (Shiota et al., 2007), which have been linked to increased levels of humility, prosocial behavior and generosity (Piff et al., 2015; Stellar et al., 2017).

Prominent interest groups such as the Guides, Scouts and other nature-centric youth organizations have identified nature's capacity for character building in young people, leading to said groups providing a collection of strategies designed to strengthen nature connectedness in young people through the cultivation of a selection of key skills such as active coping, increased hardiness and the experience of mastery. However, these groups have consistently fallen short of joining the dots between the development of these distinct skills and the broader process of growing one's overall levels of resilience.

It is our belief that fortifying the sense of connection young people feel towards the natural world represents an ideal means through which to develop young people's resilience. By spending time in natural spaces, young people become more psychologically literate and emotionally adept, as the environment demands attentiveness towards the present moment. This "here and now" focus aids children's ability to label emotions and sensations in the moment and challenges young people to regulate their emotions and cope with unexpected occurrences as they arise. Sustained present moment focus acts as a psychological reset button for the young person as it redirects attention away from draining stressors towards restorative experiences of positive emotion, hope, awe, gratitude and transcendence. Experiences of this type boost one's sense of positivity whilst also generating memories which the individual can take with them and recount and call upon at a later date when they may need a psychological fillip to buoy their mood.

As well as offering a protective buffer to unexpected stressors which may arise in the day to day, nature-based experiences provide opportunities to enhance key resilience-related skills by also offering a medium through which a range of negative emotions and mild to moderate threat may be experienced (exposure to unknown species and wildlife or coping with unexpected instances of inclement or volatile weather conditions). Such opportunities to navigate periods of adversity are vital in the developmental process in helping to foster one's capacity to think flexibly, self-regulate emotions and cultivate an optimistic explanatory style, all skills which are indelibly tied to the building of psychological resilience in young people.

Based upon the ACHUNAS model of fostering a connection to nature, the importance of adults being actively involved in the process of optimizing the nature experience for young people should not be understated. The role of the adult can range from one of (i) mentor, wherein they guide a young person's reflections on a nature-based event, (ii) the promoter of positive emotion which involves the creation of positive narratives around the experience via storytelling (see Box 9.1), or (iii) role model of resilience-relevant behaviors such as calculated risk-taking, flexible thinking, empathy and the management of their emotions within the natural environment. The presence of an adult who can pose questions throughout the course of the learning experience, and prompt a child to think about their emotional response to the flora and fauna within the environment can yield considerable benefits in terms of the level of engagement children exhibit with the natural surroundings and signal a more advanced way of developing their connection to nature. Essentially, young people require more than mere exposure to natural stimuli in order for a deeply ingrained connection to nature to evolve and the qualities of resilience to be nurtured. The influence and input of experienced and knowledgeable mentors provide requisite cultural meaning and context to their nature-based experiences, help to selectively direct their attention and focus towards significant components of the natural environment, and assist in deepening their understanding about the safe and dangerous elements present within any given natural scene (Chawla et al., 2014).

Table 9.1 outlines a selection of activities designed to target several critical resilience-related components and maximize the beneficial impact of nature-based experiences upon young people.

TABLE 9.1 Structured activities to build psychological literacy within nature-based contexts

Component of resilience being developed	*Recommended nature-based activities*
Building self-awareness & self-regulation in natural environments When one engages their senses, it is necessary to be in the moment as they are required to focus on specific sensations. Such instances demand that an individual is capable of maintaining control over thoughts, resisting impulses to think about other things and to retain a focus upon the events which are panning out in the present moment. This is a mindful manner in which to interact with the world. An array of nature-based activities require individuals to connect with the present moment in order to fully appreciate and enjoy the experiences in question. This means nature can be utilized as a vessel through which individuals can learn in a practical manner about a range of psychological constructs ranging from impulse control, self-awareness and cause and effect (i.e. if you touch a nettle, you get stung, or if you plant and nourish a seed, it grows into a beautiful flower).	Activities which provide a substantial level of sensory stimulation: • *Jumping in puddles* • *Making a mud pie* • *Walking on a beach barefoot* • *Picking and eating wild berries* • *Running into the ocean* • *Stargazing/cloud gazing.* Activities which demand an awareness of how one's actions impact the environment and require the young person to manage their emotions and conduct in order to maximize their experience: • *Bird watching* • *Animal watching* • *Helping to clean up a local river or picking up rubbish from the streets of your town.*
Developing a sense of compassion and empathy towards natural surroundings Empathy is crucial component of resilience, as it is something individuals require to be capable of forgiving others, and is essential to being able to be compassionate to oneself. Self-compassion is a fundamental aspect of resilience as only when one is not excessively prone to engaging in unnecessary self-criticism can they transform a negative occurrence into a positive learning experience from which they can take valuable lessons into their future endeavors.	Activities which require young people show care and compassion for elements within the natural environment: • *Take time to visit a nearby lake and feed the ducks (research the most suitable food to give them)* • *Rescue a spider from the bath or a bird with a broken wing* • *Build a birdhouse for birds within the region* • *Volunteer with a local animal rescue shelter.*

(*Continued*)

TABLE 9.1 (Cont.)

Component of resilience being developed	*Recommended nature-based activities*
Nature presents a multitude of scenarios wherein people are provided with opportunities to assist the safe and successful growth and development of natural species. These opportunities can be capitalized upon to teach and cultivate valuable skills in young people.	
Cultivating a sense of connection to place The cultivation of a connection to the natural world can help to establish a person-place connection and develop a keener understanding of how humans and the natural world are two interdependent entities in young people. This can enhance the likelihood of young people experiencing relevant emotions such as wonder, awe and the appreciation of nature's beauty.	Activities which generate and fortify young people's affiliation to a specific space within the natural environment or deepen their understanding of the natural environment: • *Construct your own special place in nature by building a hut a fort or a den* • *Investigate your local environment and use what you learn to draw a map of the area marking in habitats, animals, trees etc.* • *Identify a favorite space in nature (beach, forest, lake) and compile a photographic portfolio which documents visits to the designated place in all seasons/weather conditions.*
Generating positive emotion within natural settings In many cases, the experience of positive emotion in natural environments does not require any concerted effort. Rather, the spontaneity of occurrences within nature can mean that events which resonate with the individual emerge organically provided that the observer is diligent and mentally present. However, it is also possible to harness one's natural surrounding with a view to experiencing positive emotion. By seeking out awe inspiring sights and breathtaking nature-based experiences, we can create memories that we can recount and call upon to sustain and energize us in harder times – each time reawakening the positive emotions attached to the initial event.	Activities which are designed to promote feelings of joy, awe, contentment and appreciation of the beauty of the natural world: • *Notice three good things in nature every day* • *Engage in the act of photographing hope in nature e.g. growth of an animal or plant in a field* • *Evoke a sense of awe via planned activities* • *Hike to a viewing point to take in a breathtaking vista/waterfall.*

(*Continued*)

TABLE 9.1 (Cont.)

Component of resilience being developed	*Recommended nature-based activities*
Opportunity for experiences of mastery and accomplishment Natural environments provide children with optimal conditions for play, exploration and growth. Areas such as forests, beaches and lakes are not tailored to the needs of humans and, therefore, retain the rugged terrain, threats and risks that have been eliminated from the modern playground. These rough edges provide challenges which young people need to surmount through showing bravery, commitment and perseverance. When these challenges are conquered, young people receive much needed boosts to their self-efficacy, confidence and resilience.	Activities which challenge young people within their natural environment and provide them with an opportunity to face fears, overcome setbacks and reach targets: • *Set a goal such as a hike to the top of a difficult trail* • *Climb to the top of a tree unharnessed* • *Complete a mud run or an alternative physical challenge in nature* • *Pitch a tent, set up camp and spend a fulfilling night reconnecting with nature beneath the stars.*
Fostering realistic optimism about the world Everywhere one looks in nature, beacons of hope and optimism are visible. These messages can be exhibited to young people in many different ways. Nature can be availed of as a valuable storytelling aid through which young people can come to recognize the transience of one's problems and understand that beauty and vitality can blossom even in the harshest of surroundings. The transitions from caterpillar to butterfly, winter to summer and rainstorm to rainbow perfectly capture a key life lesson: negatives rarely persist forever and are often followed by joy and vibrancy.	Activities which display the changeability of circumstance, the transience of adversity and the presence of beauty and positivity amidst harsh natural surroundings: • *Going out in all seasons and finding good in the change of seasons* • *Use natural phenomena as metaphors which help to provide context in our lives e.g. watch the clouds go by to exhibit how problems in our lives will come and go, identify the presence of a rainbow following a torrential downpour or highlight the resilience of the snowdrop, which flourishes in spite of inhospitable conditions* • *Demonstrate the hatching of birds' eggs in a nest or the transition of a caterpillar into a butterfly.*
Making meaning from the natural world (see Chapter 5) The provision of an opportunity to play freely within natural settings is a reliable method to promote exploration and discovery in young people. Unstructured play of this nature enables young people	Activities which foster feelings of awe and transcendence and demand that a young person partakes in activities which serve the "greater good" for society: • *Write a story based on nature and your connection to it including the theme of*

(*Continued*)

TABLE 9.1 (Cont.)

Component of resilience being developed	*Recommended nature-based activities*
to work through routine issues that they encounter in their daily life and make sense of occurrences which they may already have experienced. In addition, the untethered nature of the environment and the activity provide optimal conditions for young people to enter the much sought after state of flow. Equally, establishing a genuine connection to the natural world can serve to assist us in comprehending our role within the world beyond our primal needs and wants. Simple occurrences within nature can promote feelings of transcendence and awe in people of all ages, and such experiences have been linked to a reduction in self-centeredness, an increased likelihood of prosocial behavior and a boost to one's overall life satisfaction.	*hope, never giving up, bouncing back, a positive ending, nature's beauty, new life* • *Engage in a mindful walking meditation in a nearby natural space (forest, lakeside, beach)* • *Get involved with a cause which serves the restoration and protection of nature e.g. tree planting, the Green schools committee with your school etc.*

BOX 9.1 STORYTELLING AS A MEANS TO ENHANCE NATURE CONNECTEDNESS AND RESILIENCE

Storytelling is an immensely powerful vessel through which to engage young people, increase their awareness of the world around them and set about building their personal strengths and emotional competencies (Fox-Eades, 2006). It has long been accepted that stories possess the capacity to transcend cultural divides, and transfer key messages to the recipients. Many of the stories and fairytales with which young people are regaled centre around nature-based constructs or settings (animal protagonists, forest/river settings etc.) and the personal growth of the central characters. A quick reflection upon some of the most prominent fairytales from one's own childhood – the Three Billy Goats Gruff, Jack and the Beanstalk, Little Red Riding Hood to name but a few – reveal a consistent strand of humans' intrinsic connection to nature. The literary device of pathetic fallacy (wherein inanimate objects/systems such as the setting or weather will mirror the mood of the protagonist) is regularly utilized to symbolize the lasting connection between humans and the natural world. Equally, it is commonplace that the protagonist will be required to harness resources from the natural environment in order to obtain the desired outcome to the story. These narrative techniques are utilized to emphasis and reinforce humans' inherent need for a close and meaningful connection to the natural world in order to lead a successful life.

Furthermore, narratives of resilience can be readily created through nature-based systems or cycles – the leaves of a tree growing after harsh winter period, a starfish which is capable of regenerating lost limbs or the beautiful snowdrops thriving amidst the snow. Such examples can be utilized to generate a sense of hope in the face of adversity and develop an understanding of the transience of many of the problems one might encounter in life. Relating these messages of strength and optimism from nature to occurrences in our own life can create a sense of oneness between humans and nature, can enhance a child's sense of place, and build their personal resources in terms of their capability to persevere and problem solve in hard times.

Future directions in nature-based resilience building

This chapter has provided considerable detail on a collection of the foremost challenges in the fields of research in relation to the constructs of nature connectedness and resilience, both of which retain an interdisciplinary interest. Research pertaining to these constructs is continually undercut by a lack of common purpose across research disciplines, the absence of universally accepted definitions which would allow for coherent, cross-disciplinary research, and the presence of a multitude of assessment methods which tend to emphasize different components of the same overarching concepts (see Chapter 2). Until a sense of clarity is reached regarding these issues, the research will remain flawed and incomplete as a sense of unanimity and agreement is inconceivable within these parameters.

Even with this absence of consensus within the field considered, the substantial benefits that can result from the immersion of young people in nature at an early age are apparent and are sufficiently striking to demand further investigation. As acceptance of this positive relationship prevails, the debate regarding the optimal methods through which to harness the benefits of the natural environment in the psychological development of young people becomes a growing priority, with particular emphasis being placed upon three specific areas: the role of technology and technological nature in child development, the potential efficacy of green schoolyards as compared with grey schoolyards in cultivating resilience in young people, and the utility of outdoor education initiatives in building psychological capacities in young people. By zoning in on these three areas, researchers are displaying a recognition of the importance of weaving nature-based experiences into children's typical day and harnessing the power of the juggernaut that is technological advance to enhance the experience as opposed to rendering it taboo in the field of nature connectedness research. It is only through embracing the realities of modern day childhood that the promising potential exhibited within nature connectedness relevant research can be translated into the desired tangible impacts upon young people's mental health and the future conservation of the planet.

Technology, nature and the development of psychological resilience

As indicated throughout the chapter, our primary aim has been to investigate the ways in which young people can re-establish their connection to the natural world within the context of their daily lives. Technology (see also Chapter 15) is now so firmly embedded into the fabric of society and the daily routines of our target group that there is little to be gained from demonizing the behemoths of social media, instant messaging and online entertainment. Instead, the focus of researchers must shift towards the identifying how technology can be availed of to enhance the quality of child-nature interactions and contribute positively to resilience building in natural contexts.

The explosion of the mobile application market has seen a rapid and exponential rise in use among children and teenagers, with a range of previously niche topics now becoming accessible to everyone at the touch of a button. Where once such technological advancements may have been scoffed at by nature enthusiasts as a means to idly whittle away time, the medium has instead led to the creation of a wealth of valuable resources which can be used to supplement and add value to excursions into the outdoors. Available applications range from those which provide helpful bucket lists outlining a varied range of suggested outdoor activities for young people, those detailing picturesque walks and hiking routes present in one's locality, or handy learning aids which can assist in deepening a young person's knowledge in relation to tree species, bird watching, rock types or stargazing.

Perhaps the key to channeling the benefits that technology can introduce into the child-nature relationship may lie in accurately pinpointing where individual children's passion lies in relation to the natural world. Upon identifying this, applications of the ilk of those outlined above can be used to foster a sense of deeper connection to nature by adding value to the relevant nature-based activities. For example, for those who enjoy interacting through the completion of adventurous, risk-taking activities, a mobile application such as the 50 Things app developed by the National Trust may provide ideas for excursions that may suit their needs. Equally, for more inquisitive children, applications may augment the benefits that can be obtained from a nature walk by providing a child with the chance to build autonomy and leadership skills through the use of an application which allows for the creation of interactive maps of the intended walking routes prior to one embarking on an outdoor excursion. Alternatively a young person can be provided with access to an extensive bird watching/stargazing/animal or plant spotting guide at the touch of a button (e.g. ForestXplorer, Star Chart apps).

Indeed, the ubiquity of mobile phones means that the majority of young adults carry a camera with them everywhere they go, including during any nature-based activities upon which they embark. Having young people photograph examples of hope, resilience or beauty within nature can fortify the sense of connection young people feel to the natural world, heighten engagement with an experience, and boost one's overall sense of enjoyment of a positive event (Diehl et al., 2016).

The greening of schoolyards and urban areas

Given the intense urbanization which can be seen within modern society, opportunities for young people to interact with the natural environment through unrestricted and playful exploration of a forest or an expansive field appear to be ever dwindling. As a result of these trends, an array of ideas has been postulated regarding how best to rekindle a closer bond between child and the natural world. Among the most prominent of these proposed initiatives is the suggestion to engage in a widespread greening of school playgrounds (Chawla et al., 2014). The renovation of schoolyards to include more natural elements has been shown to promote physical activity and reduce daily sedentary behavior in young people, two factors which are closely tied to desirable physical and psychological outcomes in youth (Janssen & LeBlanc, 2010; Tremblay et al., 2011). A selection of the positive psychological impacts which have so far been linked to the greening of schoolyards include elevated instances of prosocial behavior and positive emotion, and reduced levels of anger and perceived stress whereby the green schoolyards appear to exert a buffering effect between disclosed adversity and the perception of stress it exerts upon the young person's life (Corraliza et al., 2012; Chawla et al., 2014; Carrus et al., 2015). Given the promising evidence base which has been generated in relation to the capacity of green schoolyards to help foster critical components required to develop resilience in youths, we would strongly recommend that research continues in this area to help further illuminate and better understand the mechanisms which underscore this growing phenomenon.

Further to the outlined physical and psychological benefits associated with the incorporation of natural elements into the schoolyard, the greening of playgrounds in urban areas also appears to possess considerable utility in terms of its potential contribution to standards of living within urban hotspots worldwide. The Schoolyard Oasis Resilience Project in Paris was launched in 2017 as part of the city's resilience strategy and outlined a core aim of transforming circa 800 schoolyards within the city perimeters into a green space by 2040. The strategy signals an ambitious leap forward in terms of efforts to redress the concretization of the city (just 9.5% of space within Paris is dedicated to public parks and gardens, the lowest percentage of any European city (World Cities Culture Forum, n.d.)) and curtail the hurtling impact of urbanization on Parisian temperatures, which in recent times, have been approaching unsustainable levels (Clement, 2018). By revamping each of these schoolyards, the intentions of the initiative extend beyond solely providing a cool and comfortable environment within which children can spend their recess periods interacting with natural stimuli, to something impactful at a broader, societal level. By 2050, the project goal is that these 800 schoolyards will be havens of community engagement and recreation after school hours, and oases of respite for the most vulnerable individuals (homeless, elderly) in society should another heat wave comparable to the infamous extremities of June 2017 revisit the city. It is hoped that increasing the presence of vegetation within the city via these 800 hubs of trees, plants and greenery may contribute to the development of a microclimate within the city which may aid the overall cooling of the city.

Plans for the mass greening of urban spaces are not restricted to Parisian context – plans for the development of Liuzhou Forest City, China, as part of a broader eco-city initiative in the country are well underway. Liuzhou, designed to house 30,000 residents, will be engulfed in greenery, comprising 1 million plants of more than 100 species, which will absorb up to 10,000 tons of carbon dioxide and 57 tons of pollutants, and produce approximately 900 tons of oxygen annually (Lant, 2017). This should yield a beneficial knock-on effect in terms of reducing average air temperatures, improving the local air quality, decreasing noise pollution and broadening biodiversity in the region.

With the impact of climate change and unrestricted sprawling urbanization becoming all the more palpable on the global stage, the array of actions taken to aid the adaptation of urban areas towards incorporating natural elements and stimuli (ranging from the Sky gardens of Seoul and Singapore to the afforestation of New Orleans and Cairo) will surely account for a considerable proportion of the research being conducted within this field over the coming years.

Greener educational and recreational practices

Though the precise mechanisms which underlie the relationship between connectedness to the natural environment and the building of one's resilience have not yet been clarified, what is clear is that active engagement with the natural environment yields a beneficial impact upon humans, and, more specifically, young people. Intuitively, engagement with nature presents considerable opportunities for young people to cultivate a sense of deep connection with the world around them through the exploration of novel stimuli, experience a wealth of positive emotions (wonder and awe, joy, hope etc.), and hone their problem-solving capacities to overcome challenges and accomplish stretch goals. While the aforementioned plans to transform schoolyards into nature-based havens will contribute to an increased exposure to natural stimuli among students, Rogers and Lucas (2016) indicate that another means through which to harness the ameliorative impact of the natural environment on the resilience and wellbeing of young people is to allocate dedicated time slots within school timetables in which students should engage in tailored outdoor educational excursions (Chapter 14 delves further into the "greening" of learning environments). The evidence base supporting this assertion continues to grow, with investigations into the efficacy of specifically designed outdoor education ventures continuing to yield highly promising findings in terms of their potential resilience building qualities in young people (Ewert & Yoshino, 2008; Gillespie & Allen-Craig, 2009; Mutz & Müller, 2016).

Within this chapter, a number of outdoor activities based upon experiential learning have been proposed as a means through which to boost resilience and coping in young people. Continued research regarding learning of this nature would be helpful in further refining best practice in the area of outdoor education and learning, and it is highly important to take steps to concretize the promising findings which have resulted from research into such programs to date. Further investigation of the most effective forms of outdoor education represents a priority issue in nature-based research, in order to ensure that practitioners can identify best practice in terms of outdoor and adventure education methods and use these to build a mutually beneficial bond between young people and the natural environment.

Conclusion

Though uncertainties remain around the measurement of the concept of nature connectedness in young people, intuitively it is known that the children obtain significant physical and psychological benefits from being present within and developing a connection to the natural world. Though the child-nature disconnect has never been more pronounced, children remain innately drawn to natural stimuli and their bond with the natural world can be readily rekindled in the presence of the appropriate guidance and facilitation by significant adults in their lives.

The onus now rests on parents, guardians and educators to play their requisite roles in restoring a sense of connection to the natural world. This is vital not just for the ameliorative impact it could yield upon children's resilience, but also in equipping the next generation with the sense of duty, respect and affiliation required for them to act as responsible, safe guardians of the planet moving into the future.

References

Abbott-Chapman, J., & Robertson, M. (2009). Adolescents' favorite places: redefining the boundaries between private and public space. *Space and Culture, 12*(4), 419–434.

Balmford, A., Clegg, L., Coulson, T., & Taylor, J. (2002). Why conservationists should heed Pokémon. *Science, 295*(5564), 2367.

Bratman, G. N., Hamilton, J. P., & Daily, G. C. (2012). The impacts of nature experience on human cognitive function and mental health. *Annals of the New York Academy of Sciences, 1249*(1), 118–136.

Bryan, C., O'Shea, D., & MacIntyre, T. (2017). Stressing the relevance of resilience: a systematic review of resilience across the domains of sport and work. *International Review of Sport and Exercise Psychology, 12*(1), 1–41.

Central Statistics Office (2017). Census 2016 *summary results: Part 1.* Retrieved from https://www.cso.ie/en/media/csoie/newsevents/documents/census2016summaryresultspart1/Census2016SummaryPart1.pdf

Capaldi, C. A., Dopko, R. L., & Zelenski, J. M. (2014). The relationship between nature connectedness and happiness: a meta-analysis. *Frontiers in Psychology, 5*, 976.

Carrus, G., Passiatore, Y., Pirchio, S., & Scopelliti, M. (2015). Contact with nature in educational settings might help cognitive functioning and promote positive social behavior. *Psyecology 6*, 191–212.

Chawla, L. (2015). Benefits of nature contact for children. *Journal of Planning Literature, 30*(4), 433–452.

Chawla, L., Keena, K., Pevec, I., & Stanley, E. (2014). Green schoolyards as havens from stress and resources for resilience in childhood and adolescence. *Health Place*, *28*, 1–13.

Cía, A. H., Stagnaro, J. C., Gaxiola, S. A., Vommaro, H., Loera, G., Medina-Mora, M. E., ... Kessler, R. C. (2018). Lifetime prevalence and age-of-onset of mental disorders in adults from the Argentinean Study of Mental Health Epidemiology. *Social Psychiatry and Psychiatric Epidemiology*, *53*(4), 341-350.

Clement, M. (2018, 16th August). Green space in every schoolyard: the radical plan to cool Paris. *The Guardian*. Retrieved from: www.theguardian.com/cities/2018/aug/16/could-greening-every-paris-schoolyard-cool-the-city

Connor, K. M., & Davidson, J. R. (2003). Development of a new resilience scale: the Connor-Davidson resilience scale (CD-RISC). *Depression and Anxiety*, *18*(2), 76–82.

Corraliza, J. A., Collado, S., & Bethelmy, L. (2012). Nature as a moderator of stress in urban children. *Procedia – Social and Behavioral Sciences*, *38*, 253–263.

Cyrulnik, B. (2009). *Resilience: how your inner strength can set you free from the past*. London: Penguin Books.

Davis, J. L., Le, B., & Coy, A. E. (2011). Building a model of commitment to the natural environment to predict ecological behavior and willingness to sacrifice. *Journal of Environmental Psychology*, *31*(3), 257–265.

Diehl, K., Zauberman, G., & Barasch, A. (2016). How taking photos increases enjoyment of experiences. *Journal of Personality and Social Psychology*, *111*(2), 119.

Diessner, R., Solom, R. D., Frost, N. K., Parsons, L., & Davidson, J. (2008). Engagement with beauty: appreciating natural, artistic, and moral beauty. *The Journal of Psychology*, *142*(3), 303–332.

Ewert, A., & Yoshino, A. (2008). A preliminary exploration of the influence of short-term adventure-based expeditions on levels of resilience. *Journal of Experiential Education*, *30*(3), 262–266.

Fletcher, D., & Sarkar, M. (2013). Psychological resilience: a review and critique of definitions, concepts, and theory. *European Psychologist*, *18*(1), 12.

Flood, A. (2015, 13th January). Oxford Junior Dictionary's replacement of 'natural' words with 21st-century terms sparks outcry. *The Guardian*. Retrieved from www.theguardian.com/books/2015/jan/13/oxford-junior-dictionary-replacement-natural-words on 12th March, 2019.

Fox-Eades, J. (2006). *Classroom tales: Using storytelling to build social, emotional and academic skills across the primary curriculum*. London: Jessica Kingsley.

Fromberg, D. P., & Bergen, D. (2006). *Play from birth to twelve: contexts, perspectives, and meanings*. London: Routledge.

Frumkin, H., Bratman, G. N., Breslow, S. J., Cochran, B., Kahn, Jr, P. H., Lawler, J. J., ... Wood, S. A. (2017). Nature contact and human health: a research agenda. *Environmental Health Perspectives*, *125*(7), 075001.

Gidlow, C. J., Randall, J., Gillman, J., Silk, S., & Jones, M. V. (2016). Hair cortisol and self-reported stress in healthy, working adults. *Psychoneuroendocrinology*, *63*, 163–169.

Gillespie, E., & Allen-Craig, S. (2009). The enhancement of resilience via a wilderness therapy program: a preliminary investigation. *Journal of Outdoor and Environmental Education*, *13*(1), 39–49.

Giusti, M., Svane, U., Raymond, C. M., & Beery, T. H. (2018). A framework to assess where and how children connect to nature. *Frontiers in Psychology*, *8*, 2283.

Grice, H. P. (1975). Logic and conversation. In P. Cole & J. L. Morgan (Eds.), *Syntax and semantics: speech acts* (pp. 41–58). New York, NY: Academic Press.

Ives, C. D., Giusti, M., Fischer, J., Abson, D. J., Klaniecki, K., Dorninger, C., ... Raymond, C. M. (2017). Human–Nature connection: a multidisciplinary review. *Current Opinion in Environmental Sustainability, 26,* 106–113.

Janssen, I., & LeBlanc, A. G. (2010). Systematic review of the health benefits of physical activity and fitness in school-aged children and youth. *International Journal of Behavioral Nutrition and Physical Activity,* 7(1), 40.

Kahn, Jr, P. H., Severson, R. L., & Ruckert, J. H. (2009). The human relation with nature and technological nature. *Current Directions in Psychological Science, 18*(1), 37–42.

Kaschak, E. (2017, 18th July). Loneliness and Dis-Connection. *Psychology Today.* Retrieved from www.psychologytoday.com/us/blog/she-comes-long-way-baby/201707/loneliness-and-dis-connection

Kernan, M., & Devine, D. (2010). Being confined within? Constructions of the good childhood and outdoor play in early childhood education and care settings in Ireland. *Children & Society, 24,* 371–385.

Kesebir, S., & Kesebir, P. (2017). A growing disconnection from nature is evident in cultural products. *Perspectives on Psychological Science, 12*(2), 258–269.

Kessler, R. C., Amminger, G. P., Aguilar-Gaxiola, S., Alonso, J., Lee, S., & Ustun, T. B. (2007). Age of onset of mental disorders: A review of recent literature. *Current Opinion in Psychiatry, 20*(4), 359.

Lant, K. (2017, 28th June). China has officially started building the world's first 'Forest City'. Retrieved from www.sciencealert.com/china-has-officially-started-construction-on-the-world-s-first-forest-city

Louv, R. (2005). *Last child in the woods: saving our children from nature-deficit disorder.* London: Atlantic Books.

Masten, A. S. (2001). Ordinary magic: resilience processes in development. *American Psychologist, 56*(3), 227.

Mayer, F. S., & Frantz, C. M. (2004). The connectedness to nature scale: a measure of individuals' feeling in community with nature. *Journal of Environmental Psychology, 24*(4), 503–515.

Mayer, F. S., Frantz, C. M., Bruehlman-Senecal, E., & Dolliver, K. (2009). Why is nature beneficial? The role of connectedness to nature. *Environment and Behavior, 41,* 607–643

Mayer-Davis, E. J., Lawrence, J. M., Dabelea, D., Divers, J., Isom, S., Dolan, L., ... Pihoker, C. (2017). Incidence trends of type 1 and type 2 diabetes among youths, 2002–2012. *New England Journal of Medicine, 376*(15), 1419–1429.

Mutz, M., & Müller, J. (2016). Mental health benefits of outdoor adventures: results from two pilot studies. *Journal of Adolescence, 49,* 105–114.

Nisbet, E. K., Zelenski, J. M., & Murphy, S. A. (2009). The nature relatedness scale: linking individuals' connection with nature to environmental concern and behavior. *Environment and Behavior, 41*(5), 715–740.

O'Malley, S. (2014). *(Re) connecting children with nature? A sociological study of environmental education in Ireland* (Doctoral dissertation).

Ong, A. D., Bergeman, C. S., Bisconti, T. L., & Wallace, K. A. (2006). Psychological resilience, positive emotions, and successful adaptation to stress in later life. *Journal of Personality and Social Psychology, 91*(4), 730.

Oshio, A., Mieda, T., & Taku, K. (2016). Younger people, and stronger effects of all-or-nothing thoughts on aggression: moderating effects of age on the relationships between dichotomous thinking and aggression. *Cogent Psychology, 3*(1), 1244874.

Picard, R. W., Papert, S., Bender, W., Blumberg, B., Breazeal, C., Cavallo, D., ... Strohecker, C. (2004). Affective learning: a manifesto. *BT Technology Journal, 22*(4), 253–269.

Piff, P. K., Dietze, P., Feinberg, M., Stancato, D. M., & Keltner, D. (2015). Awe, the small self, and prosocial behavior. *Journal of Personality and Social Psychology, 108*(6), 883.

Press Association. (2016, July, 27). Children spend only half as much time playing outside as parents did. *The Guardian.* Retrieved from https://www.theguardian.com/environment/2016/jul/27/children-spend-only-half-the-time-playing-outside-as-their-parents-did.

Prévot-Julliard, A. C., Julliard, R., & Clayton, S. (2015). Historical evidence for nature disconnection in a 70-year time series of Disney animated films. *Public Understanding of Science, 24*(6), 672–680.

Rideout, V. J., Foehr, L. G., & Roberts, D. F. (2010). *Generation M^2: media in the lives of 8- to 18-year-olds.* Menlo Park, CA: Kaiser Family Foundation.

Rogers, P., & Lucas, N. (2016, winter). Feature: the time is right to prioritize well-being in higher education. *Bringing Theory to Practice Newsletter.* Retrieved from www.bttop.org/news-events/feature-time-right-prioritize-well-being-higher-education

Royal Society for the Protection of Birds. (2013). *Connecting with nature: Finding our how connected to nature the UK's children are.* Bedfordshire: RSPB.

Rutter, M. (2012). Resilience as a dynamic concept. *Development and Psychopathology, 24*(2), 335–344.

Ryan, R. M., Weinstein, N., Bernstein, J., Brown, K. W., Mistretta, L., & Gagne, M. (2010). Vitalizing effects of being outdoors and in nature. *Journal of Environmental Psychology, 30,* 159–168

Schultz, P. W. (2002). Inclusion with nature: The psychology of human-nature relations. In P. Schmuck & W. P. Schultz (Eds.), *Psychology of sustainable development* (pp. 62–78). Norwell, MA: Kluwer Academic.

Shatté, A., Perlman, A., Smith, B., & Lynch, W. D. (2017). The positive effect of resilience on stress and business outcomes in difficult work environments. *Journal of Occupational and Environmental Medicine, 59*(2), 135.

Shiota, M. N., Keltner, D., & Mossman, A. (2007). The nature of awe: elicitors, appraisals, and effects on self-concept. *Cognition and Emotion, 21*(5), 944–963.

Singer D. G., Singer J. L., Agostino, H. D., & Delong R. (2009). Children's pastimes and play in sixteen nations: is free-play declining? *American Journal of Play, 1,* 283–312.

Sobko, T., Jia, Z., & Brown, G. (2018). Measuring connectedness to nature in preschool children in an urban setting and its relation to psychological functioning. *PLoS One, 13*(11), e0207057.

Southwick, S. M., Bonanno, G. A., Masten, A. S., Panter-Brick, C., & Yehuda, R. (2014). Resilience definitions, theory, and challenges: interdisciplinary perspectives. *European Journal of Psychotraumatology, 5*(1), 25338.

Stellar, J. E., Gordon, A. M., Piff, P. K., Cordaro, D., Anderson, C. L., Bai, Y., ... Keltner, D. (2017). Self-transcendent emotions and their social functions: compassion, gratitude, and awe bind us to others through prosociality. *Emotion Review, 9*(3), 200–207.

Stellar, J. E., John-Henderson, N., Anderson, C. L., Gordon, A. M., McNeil, G. D., & Keltner, D. (2015). Positive affect and markers of inflammation: discrete positive emotions predict lower levels of inflammatory cytokines. *Emotion, 15*(2), 129.

Tam, K. P. (2013). Dispositional empathy with nature. *Journal of Environmental Psychology, 35,* 92–104.

Tillmann, S., Tobin, D., Avison, W., & Gilliland, J. (2018). Mental health benefits of interactions with nature in children and teenagers: a systematic review. *Journal of Epidemiology and Community Health*, *72*(10), 958–966.

Tremblay, M. S., LeBlanc, A. G., Kho, M. E., Saunders, T. J., Larouche, R., Colley, R. C., … Gorber, S. C. (2011). Systematic review of sedentary behaviour and health indicators in school-aged children and youth. *International Journal of Behavioral Nutrition and Physical Activity*, *8*(1), 98.

Tsunetsugu, Y., Park, B. J., Ishii, H., Hirano, H., Kagawa, T., & Miyazaki, Y. (2007). Physiological effects of Shinrin-yoku (taking in the atmosphere of the forest) in an old-growth broadleaf forest in Yamagata Prefecture, Japan. *Journal of Physiological Anthropology*, *26*(2), 135–142.

Turkle, S. (2012, 21st April) The flight from conversation. *The New York Times*. Retrieved from www.nytimes.com/2012/04/22/opinion/sunday/the-flight-from-conversation.html on 5th November, 2018.

United Nations: Department of Economic and Social Affairs – Population Division (2018). World urbanization prospects: the 2018 revision.

Valtchanov, D., Barton, K. R., & Ellard, C. (2010). Restorative effects of virtual nature settings. *Cyberpsychology, Behavior, and Social Networking*, *13*(5), 503–512.

Walsh, R. (1999). Asian contemplative disciplines: common practices, clinical applications, and research findings. *Journal of Transpersonal Psychology*, *31*(2), 83–108.

Williams, Jr, J. A., Podeschi, C., Palmer, N., Schwadel, P., & Meyler, D. (2012). The human-environment dialog in award-winning children's picture books. *Sociological Inquiry*, *82*(1), 145–159.

PART III

Case studies

10

FROM TRACKS TO TRAILS

Case studies in green exercise

Tadhg E. MacIntyre, Greig Oliver, Andree Walkin, Giovanna Calogiuri, Aoife A. Donnelly, Susan Gritzka and Maire-Treasa Ni Cheallaigh

One aspect that has been overlooked in the study of human-nature interactions is the voice of the participant in green exercise. As outlined in Chapter 4, green exercise research has grown in the past 15 years to provide a greater understanding of physical activity in natural settings, largely focusing on green natural settings (Barton et al., 2016).

Outdoor recreation through green exercise offers opportunities to experience health and well-being benefits including relaxation and restoration, energy-boosting, increasing self-esteem and feelings of self-efficacy (Bowler et al., 2010; Hansmann, Hug, & Seeland, 2007; Hartig et al., 2014; Irvine et al, 2013; O'Brien & Morris, 2014) as well as an enhanced sense of place and connection with nature through engagement with the natural environment. It is this complex interplay between athlete and nature that we explore in this chapter.

In the UK, the benefits of green exercise have been widely recognised within the public health domain (Coutts, Forkink, & Weiner, 2014; Marmot, 2010) and partnerships have developed between health and environmental sectors. There are many examples, such as Scottish Natural Heritage (2015), volunteer-led walking groups, health walks in community contexts (Marselle, Irvine, & Warber, 2014), green gym programmes (Pretty et al., 2007) and green prescribing (Carpenter, 2013). In the Irish context, strides to catch up are being made with a Coillte (Irish Forestry Agency) sponsored programme called Woodlands for Health and Mental Health Ireland, Sport Ireland (e.g. Get Ireland Walking) and Waterways Ireland are collaborating with our research group, GO GREEN, on the design and implementation of new initiatives (e.g., O'Sullivan et al., 2016).

The design of such programmes targeting both young and old requires an understanding of the role of a multitude of factors (see Chapter 2) including probing the role of childhood experience in supporting green exercise as a lifetime habit. For instance, Ward Thompson, Aspinall, and Montarzino (2008) found that UK adults' frequency of visits to greenspace was predicted by the frequency of visits during childhood. Accordingly, Calogiuri (2016) found that recall of childhood experiences of nature was a predictor of Norwegian adults engaging in green exercise during a regular week. Other studies have found corresponding effects of childhood nature experience on attitudes towards outdoor recreation activities (Bixler, Floyd, & Hammitt, 2002; Calogiuri 2016). Taken together, these studies support the hypothesis that "environmental socialisation" and early years development of engaging with nature has an important influence on human-nature relationships in adult life and efforts need to be made to engage our children (Bixler et al., 2002).

When we thinking of feeling "at home," we tend to think about where we live and sleep, and where we feel most safe and secure, but as it turns out, we may also attach those feelings to places we identify strongly with or feel a connection. Brown and Raymond (2007) noted that "visitors" recorded similar factor loadings on each of the place-identity and dependence items as "residents." This suggests that the concept of "home" or "place" extends beyond a person's place of residence to places visited and this factor will be explored further in this chapter.

Another topic of interest, recovery, as Sonnentag (2018) alludes to, is an experience of unwinding, recuperating or restoring physical or mental resources. Recovery, by being engaged in natural environments, seems particularly suited to replenishing depleted resources (Sonnentag, Venz, & Casper, 2017). Exposure to natural stimuli, whether being physically present within nature, being surrounded by nature, or looking at nature images, is related to enhanced recovery (Bratman, Hamilton, & Daily, 2012; Hartig et al., 2014). Interestingly, the less built environment elements that are present, the higher the recovery potential of a specific environment.

Theories from environmental psychology accounting for the benefits of green exercise have focused on a narrow set of variables, namely attention (Attention Restoration Theory, Kaplan & Kaplan, 1989), and stress reduction (Stress Reduction Theory, Ulrich et al., 1991) while other psychological factors such as resilience have been overlooked in the research. Resilience is a plausible outcome from outdoor exercise as participants overcome challenges of the conditions, the weather, terrain and the physical effort of green exercise (Bryan, O'Shea, & MacIntyre, 2017).

Lived experiences of outdoor sport experiences have largely been autobiographical and informed by an environmental psychology perspective. We know little of the motives, perceived benefits and developmental trajectory of people who regularly engage in green exercise (see Table 10.1). As a result, this study will seek to explore the lived experiences of a pre-selected sample of participants in outdoor activities. Psychological constructs from physical activity, positive psychology and sport psychology can arguably further elucidate our understanding of the biophilic experiences among regular participants in outdoor physical

TABLE 10.1 Participant characteristics

Name	*Gender*	*Sporting experience*
Jessie Barr	F	2012 Olympian (400m), World University finalist (400m hurdles)
Niamh Briggs	F	Six Nations Rugby Grand Slam winner (63 caps)
Felix Jones	M	Former Ireland rugby international (13 caps)
Cathal Sheridan	M	Former Munster rugby player (35 caps)
Giles Warrington	M	Olympic team physiologist (2004–2016) and recreational athlete
Keith Wood	M	Former international rugby player: Ireland (58 caps) and British & Irish Lions (5 caps)

activity in natural green spaces. Thus, the overall aim of this chapter is to explore the lived experiences of participants in green exercise through a mixed-methods approach with explicit permission to waive anonymity (Education and Health Sciences Faculty Ethical Approval No. 2016 _11_20 EHS).

The participants were six athletes (four males, two females; Mean age = 39.6; *SD* = 11.1) and comprised both active and retired professional athletes from track and field.

The participants were invited to complete online surveys to measure well-being and mental health (*WHO-5 Well-Being Index*, Topp et al., 2015), the individual's connectedness to the natural world (Connectedness to Nature Scale (CNS), Mayer & Frantz, 2004), and attitudes towards the environment (*NEP The New Ecological Paradigm Scale*, Dunlap et al., 2000).

This survey-based approach was designed to explore previously established links between connectedness to nature, well-being and psychological recovery and connecting with nature (e.g. Capaldi et al., 2015) with in this case a unique focus upon athletes. A semi-structured interview guide (see Table 10.2) was developed by the lead author with other members of the research team based on prior qualitative research.

Table 10.3 displays the overall mean and standard deviations for the WHO-5, CNS and NEP inventories.

A *WHO-5 Well-being Index* score can range from 0–100, with 0 representing the lowest and 100 representing the best achievable well-being (Topp et al., 2015). The participants all spoke positively about green exercise and scored on average 76.67 on the WHO-5, which is indicative of high levels of well-being. In the literature a mean score of 70 is provided for the general population (Ellervik et al., 2014) and the EU-27 average for adults is 62 (European Foundation for the Improvement of Living and Working Conditions, 2017).

The CNS original studies by Mayer and Frantz (2004) found a CNS mean score of 3.65 ±.64 (Study 1, *N* = 60) and 3.52 ±.56 (Study 4, *N* = 135) in an

TABLE 10.2 Interview guide structure

Interview section	*Aim*	*Exemplar questions*
I Introduction	To explain the focus of the study and address any initial questions in advance of the discourse.	Do you have any questions before we commence?
ii. Rapport Building	To develop trust with the participant by referring back to their prior experiences.	Please tell me about your career achievements and personal milestones.
iii. Identification of Adversity	To examine coping strategies, experience of post-traumatic growth and coping with daily hassles.	What adversities have you faced in your sporting career and how have you coped and thrived in response?
iv. Green and Blue Exercise Participation	To explore frequency, type (individual/ group), intensity of exercise.	What activities do you do outdoors?
v. Place Attachment	To explore place-blindness, emotions associated with different natural spaces.	Do you have a favourite natural space?
vi. Access to Nature	To address barriers to engaging with nature.	Are there any other barriers or risks to being active in nature?
vii. Environmental Sustainability	To explore attitudes towards the environment and sustainability.	What are your views on sustainability and the environment?
viii. Technological Nature	To probe if they augment authentic nature with tech nature.	Do you need to be in nature for it to impact upon you?
ix. Additional comments	To provide an opportunity to discuss any other issues that they would like to raise.	Anything else you would like to add on how blue or green natural spaces can benefit health?
x. Closure	To ensure any anxieties or concerns are addressed before ending the interview.	The next step will be approval of the transcript.

TABLE 10.3 Overall mean and standard deviation of questionnaire based findings ($N = 7$)

Questionnaire	*M*	*SD*
WHO-5 Well-being Index	76.67	5.89
Connectedness to Nature Scale (CNS)	3.00	.67
NEP: New Ecological Paradigm	3.51	.16

American adult sample. Surprisingly, our sample scored lower (M = 3.00, SD =.67) on the personal trait connectedness to nature compared to the aforementioned normative data. However, an overall mean score of 3.51 ±.16 for NEP can be considered as a good endorsement of a pro-ecological world view (Dunlap et al., 2000).

Table 10.4 provides an overview of sample items and their scoring on both questionnaires CNS and NEP.

The subsequent section discusses the results of the themes that emerged from the interviews. The meta-themes were (1) Early Childhood, (2) Role Models (3) Sport, (4) Access to Nature, (5) Weather, (6) Emotional Response, (7) Restorative Space, (8) Well-Being, and (9) Environmental Concern (see Figure 10.1).

Early childhood

In this study, reflecting research cited earlier about our childhoods shaping our adult experiences, all the interviewees recalled memorable early-life experiences in green space.

It's debatable whether Keith Wood's mother was an influence on his early outdoor experience as he says that she "used to tell me to get out of the

TABLE 10.4 Overall mean and standard deviation of CNS and NEP sample items

Items	*M*	*SD*
CNS[a] ($N = 7$)		
(1) I often feel a sense of oneness with the natural world around me.	4.43	.53
(2) I think of the natural world as a community to which I belong.	4.00	.82
(3) I recognise and appreciate the intelligence of other living organisms.	4.14	1.21
NEP[b] ($N = 7$)		
(6) Humans are seriously abusing the environment.	4.43	.79
(9) Despite our special abilities, humans are still subject to the laws of nature.	4.43	.98
(15) If things continue on their present course, we will soon experience a major ecological catastrophe.	4.29	.76

FIGURE 10.1 Qualitative themes: green exercise

house!" Keith said that the family garden provided a myriad of opportunities for nature engagement: "Our garden was wild, so we spent all of our time in a couple of acres, not gardening, messing, playing, digging holes, making huts, making whatever." Olympian Jessie Barr described her family as active, "we'd always be outside playing, racing each other. We'd often play in the fields when the grass was long, we'd be making tunnels through them and getting bitten to bits, but we loved it." The running theme was unstructured play, "the blue and the green were very important, swimming in the sea all throughout the summer and playing a lot of outdoor unstructured sports all year round, just fun and play."

Role models

The encouragement and commitment shown by parents has not been forgotten and was a big influence on our participants' habits. Niamh explained: "My dad definitely has been a huge influence on my career, when I started playing I had to be ferried often, so he's in the car, he bringing me here, there and everywhere."

Similarly Jessie's parents have left a legacy in her life:

> They always wanted us to be outdoors, they were very active themselves, we've always had dogs so I mean going outside and going for long walks was kind of instilled in us from a young age and wanting to be outdoors.

Even when Jessie and brother Thomas excelled in international athletics reaching Olympic standard, the encouragement was the same as when they were fledgling athletes: "My parents never put any pressure on us, they never expected anything, the only expectation was that we enjoy it, and when the enjoyment is gone then we would need to reconsider why we are doing it." Inspiration to experience, explore or just be surrounded by nature was influenced from different sources. Giles Warrington explained: "I would have read a lot about Tom Crean and I'm a bit of a geek on the history of polar exploration by Shackleton and Scott," while another participant had an unlikely role model in Keith Wood's love of gardening and being in that space comes from watching television gardener Monty Don, "the way he talks about the garden, I don't have his love and attention to detail but there's a way you want to get out there when you hear him talk."

Sport

In high performance sport, the expectations and pressures on elite athletes are on the increase, without a similar focus on resources (MacIntyre et al., 2017). During the height of competition, Jessie Barr finds solace in training in a natural setting away from the track:

> I have that love of being and running on a trail and being in nature. I'm not judging times, I don't wear a watch, I just go and run and judge by how I feel. These sessions are hard, and as exhausted as you would be afterwards, I'd always really look forward to it as it was just a different challenge in that environment.

Similarly for rugby player Keith Wood he recalled that the lure of tranquillity put perspective into his sporting life when competing at the 2003 World Rugby Cup:

> In the height of the big matches ... I took a pillow and a blanket and travelled out onto a headland rather than sit in the team-room. I'd sit on the rocks and listen to the waves crashing, I just thought it was something remarkable, and a damn sight bigger than yourself. When you become a little bit too focused on yourself, it's kind of cool to focus on something that's infinitely more powerful.

Preparations for international competitions would prove claustrophobic for Niamh Briggs and she chose to go outdoors for short periods of time, and felt she could return carrying a little less stress and more focused: "If I go outside for 15 or 20 minutes, I find that I come back a bit de-stressed and re-focused." The contrast in indoor and outdoor training is obvious to the athletes, as Felix explains: "When I exercise in the gym, I would be very much goal-driven, testing myself, trying to really push a limit on myself, whereas when I am outdoors and I'm out for a run it's pretty much for pure pleasure."

Access to nature

Not only accessibility to natural environments, but also the extent to which they are supportive for physical activity (e.g. being large enough, attractive, and containing features such as trails that allow exercising), are known to be crucial factors for people to engage in green exercise (Calogiuri, 2016; Lackey & Kaczynski, 2009; Lee & Maheswaran, 2011). Outdoor settings, as Currie, Lackova, and Dinnie (2016) suggested, can relieve stress of everyday life, and access to the natural environment is improving with bespoke initiatives proliferating. As Giles Warrington explains:

> Running trails are being developed, simple methods where you can grade your exercise, you don't need to go to a fancy gym, you don't need to be an expert on physical activity, you can just go out and do it.

Keith Wood, who led the team that developed the sport and recreation facility at Clarisford Park in County Clare, which is a ParkRun venue, would like to see similar initiatives as the benefits are numerous:

> Park Run is a phenomenal concept for runners, I want a Park Walk, I want something where people don't have to feel that they are timed, they don't have to get a better time. If you're active, it is the biggest silver bullet for mental health, for a whole variety of different elements. You may or may not lose weight, that's not the point, the point is that, it's the best drug of all if you can be active.

Agreeing with Ferrer-i-Carbonell and Gowdy (2007) that having environmental awareness benefits well-being, the positive effects of engaging with nature can link into each individual's environmental concern as Jessie Barr outlines:

> We went out for a walk to the Clare Glens and we were blown away by it, you don't have to pay to use it and I actually just feel that people don't realise just how many nice things we have on our doorstep. I think there are a lot of places people just don't realise we have so we need to increase awareness of our natural spaces, our hidden gems that shouldn't be hidden.

This aligns with the concept of "place-blindness" (Louv, 2012) whereby individuals tend to perceive far away settings (e.g. coastal or tourist destinations) as being a preferred option to access nature, often overlooking local and indigenous natural spaces.

Social well-being is often understated as a controlling variable in pursuing green space, and the support of an outdoors buddy goes a long way (Howell et al., 2011; Howell, Passmore, & Buro, 2013), as alluded to by Jessie Barr:

> I think the most daunting thing is the idea of doing something on your own so try to bring someone with you. Just see what we have on this grander scale and just doing it once and seeing how you feel.

Keith Wood agrees: "If you're on your own, find a buddy to go with you, if you're active with someone, share the load a little, that's pretty cool."

In contrast to being present in a build-up environment, people are substantially happier when they are in nature (MacKerron & Mourato, 2013), bespoke green initiatives, and close to water. Blueways, a Waterways Ireland initiative, is one example. Waterways Ireland are an all-island agency responsible for the development of inland waterways for recreational purposes. "Not only is it good for us, but it's good for our local economies," something Keith Wood, an advocate of sustainable tourism, discussed further: "Ireland, because the state or state agencies are in control of the waterways and control of the forests and the mountains, it's a kind of cool place. We can be the centre for health sustainable tourism, green tourism."

Giles Warrington made a salient point: "The outdoors targets the whole lifecycle from the very young to the very old and we should take advantage of that." However, cycleways need significant infrastructure, especially in Ireland, as he concludes:

> Cities like Copenhagen and Amsterdam, who have large populations have excellent cycle paths everywhere and cycling becomes a way of life. In Ireland, there are certain places you wouldn't go on for love or money because of the fear of getting knocked down so I think just simple initiatives need to be put in place.

In agreement, Niamh Briggs states: "I think we have so many unbelievable beaches, lakes, so water sports could be a huge thing here, I don't think we thrive on them enough."

Giles Warrington has the final word by highlighting that:

> People are living longer but the irony is they are living longer but the quality of their health is probably less, so they have more years spent in poor health, so if we can live longer but be more physically active, and physically and mentally well, and focus on our wellness that can only benefit everybody.

If you live in Ireland, you talk about the weather. Colloquially, weather is often suggested as a barrier to going outdoors for exercise, but interestingly, our interviewees were pragmatic in their approach to the varied conditions of the Irish climate. For example, Keith Wood stated: "I'm a believer in the saying that there isn't bad weather, there's just bad clothing," while another re-adjusted his schedule around the weather. The challenge of our changeable climate was a stimulus for physical activity for Giles and others. He said in Ireland "you can usually find a stormy beach even on a summer's day."

Similarly, Felix Jones explained that: "I'm happy out if it's lashing rain. I prefer running in the rain … I like swimming in cold water, I like swimming in the sea, there's very few things that I don't enjoy being outside." On the other hand, for Niamh Briggs, the seasonal variation was a driver for activity:

> When the summer months come in I'll try and get out there as often as I can … There are days when the sea is rough, it's cool and you don't mind it, and there are days when it is calm and that's what you are looking for.

Similarly, for Cathal Sheridan: "Rain would be a barrier I would like to go for that early in the morning whereas if I'm doing that and if it's absolutely teaming down outside and I need to come back in." Weather conditions are perceived as both a facilitator and barrier among our sample.

Emotional response to nature

Being immersed in nature can promote positive emotions and prompt reduction of negative emotions (Bowler et al., 2010; Irvine et al., 2013), which can be overlooked if we don't have access to green spaces. This effect is largest when comparing natural environments with urban settings, which contain stress-inducing stimuli such as traffic and other noises (Bowler et al., 2010).

For example, Cathal reflected, "When I retired, not having that outlet into nature had a massive effect on me. I think it's detrimental not being able to get outside and get moving." When we talk about our favourite smells, we often mention the smell of the sea or summertime grass cutting. One athlete spoke very pragmatically, saying he was actively savouring his surroundings. Nature can range along an engagement spectrum from viewing nature to immersion (e.g. attending to the stimuli) and this complexity leads to idiosyncratic responses. For instance, Felix stated:

> I can't say that I have a heightened sense of trees and grass, but that's not to say that I don't enjoy the smell of cut grass in the summer … I like the tangible things about being in nature.

Athlete Jessie Barr admitted the barrier of cold winter mornings had to be overcome before experiencing the benefits of being immersed, even for athletes:

> When it's colder in the winter, I'm cursing the dog because I just don't want to go for a walk but I always feel better once I'm out … and I come back with a feeling of refreshment… ready to tackle the day.

This conveys that pre-exercise anxiety is commonplace even for recovery bouts in outdoor natural spaces (Ekkekakis, 2017).

Engagement in nature gave many of our interviewees a space for reflection as rugby player Cathal Sheridan expressed:

> Being in nature is a massive de-stressor, and even if I'm not stressed it takes away the potential stress, it's very good just for a bit of clarity in your own mind … I've made most of my big life decisions in the outdoors.

Restorative space

Agreeing with Korpela, Kyttä, and Hartig (2002) that children could relate to a favourite place (Sommer, 1990), all the participants had "special places" where they felt restoration. Jessie Barr can recount experiences close to her home:

> I would have spent a lot of time on the fields overlooking a lovely little cove near home, picnicking on the side of the cliffs, probably quite dangerous when I think about it, right on the edge of the cliffs eating our ice-cream, swinging our legs but that's just reminds me of being like carefree.

Similarly, Niamh Briggs, regularly takes in natural surroundings when she returns home:

> I love the fact that I can hear it, and what I associate with the sounds of the countryside, the beach, the water, and the views, I just think that it brings me back to a sense of calm.

Cathal Sheridan recounts many a visit to his restorative space close to home:

> I sound a bit corny, you feel quite close to nature at that point, you feel quite small when you realise how big everything is and then maybe if you've got worries or anxieties, they start to dissipate a bit as you realise that maybe they are not as big as I initially thought.

Well-being and stress and coping

Our interviewees are stimulated in natural environments, As Giles Warrington states:

> I think we go through cycles and challenges within our life and I have found that when there are periods where I feel my mental health and well-being is under stress, I would always turn to exercise in the outdoors – the

> sound of the river, the sound of the birds and being immersed in nature just sets me up for the day.

Ulrich et al's (1991) *Stress Reduction Theory* predicts greater positive changes in emotional state and activity levels as well as sustained attention; Giles Warrington alludes to other benefits:

> It's not just being in the green or blue, it's your awareness and being in the moment, the now, taking a pause in the day and being aware of what's going on around you. You don't have to be exercising, it's listening to the sounds, it's listening to everything that's going on, it's that awareness and that paying attention rather than just glossing over things so I think that's so crucial and its understated.

Jessie Barr also finds comfort in nature, saying:

> Once I got involved in high-level sport there was always a goal to my exercise, I was not into physical activity, I hated going on walks. When I got my dog, I was accountable and actually it was the best thing for me. Suddenly I was finding nice trails, I just really enjoyed exercising for the sake of it, not for a goal not to get fitter, not as I need to qualify for this competition, but just because of my little dog. She came at the completely right time because I probably wouldn't have engaged in nature the way I did and I probably realised how much you know how important it was going to be to me … it's like a reset for me.

The recent Bryan et al. (2017) review of resilience conveyed that resilience focused on being an adaptive process to adversity, allied to coping strategies through sport-related life. Cathal spoke of learning about the true importance of sport:

> I probably didn't spend enough time reflecting and actually fully dealing with things in the correct manner. The beauty in sport is that it's not always about how successful you are, it's about the friendships you develop and about how much you actually genuinely need people, even though as an athlete and as a performer you try and pretend to be very independent. I think everyone needs people, everyone needs support and I think sport is fantastic for that.

Felix Jones elaborated by saying:

> It's such a bubble, you don't realise how well you are treated until you leave it. The transition out of playing matures you for sure, and gets you to see the bigger picture that rugby is only a game.

On the other hand, Felix Jones is well aware of the adversity:

> There is a stigma surrounding mental health in professional sport. In rugby, a lot of players have come in straight out of school, they have just come straight into a routine, and a lot of those life skills you don't actually get to learn.

In an effort to assist coping strategies, Giles Warrington conveyed his awareness of mental recovery:

> We spend so much time talking about athletes and athlete recovery, but the focus tends to be all on the physical side when it needs to be more holistic as stress is multi-factorial, and mental recovery and self-reflection are a critical part of the recovery process and I think that athletes' coaches should factor this into their down-time.

However, Niamh Briggs says the interpretation of mental health can often be mis-leading: "We also need to differentiate between mental health, good and bad, and just a bad day."

Giles Warrington cautiously concludes: "We can get so immersed in our work and the demands of that, and we can forget about self-care. We talk about athlete burn-out and over-training, but burn-out applies to everybody."

Environmental concern

As people who engage in outdoor recreation, the participants are aware of the ecosystem benefits and the need for greater access, as Cathal points out: "I think infrastructure-wise we actually need to make places more accessible, make it easier for families, for kids, for dogs." There are inherent risks to the natural environment from recreation. Giles explains:

> We just need to take care of this very scarce resource and appreciate what we have because it won't be there unless we do, so I think it is sustainable but I think there has to be great growing awareness there has to be initiatives put in place driven at a governmental level to make sure that we do cherish this wonderful resource that we have.

Recycling and awareness of pro-environmental behaviours are key to sustainability. Niamh Briggs notes that "in theory, we should all be, you know, looking after the environment in terms of our recycling and what we do." Thus, the perils of unsustainable consumerism, exploitation of our wilderness and degrading our biodiversity are familiar to our participants for whom nature is not merely a playground but an integral part of who they are.

Limitations

Although the study gave particular insight into the psychological benefits for sportspeople that consistently connect with nature, there were a number of limitations. Although the interviews were retrospective, the majority of the participants had retired from their respective high performance domains with only two active high-level participants. Thus the generalisability is greater for retired athletes than active ones, although the lessons learned clearly resonate with all. A possible confound is the possibility that the sample participants, although at varying ages, were experiencing different stages of transition within their particular sport (Park, Lavallee, & Tod, 2013). This may have impacted upon their well-being and mental health.

From a quantitative perspective, the small sample did not allow the calculation of inferential statistics and only comparisons with expected norms were made. Notwithstanding these limitations, the study offers valuable insights that can be further explored in the sporting environment in future research.

Future research directions

We need to explicitly evaluate the benefits of restorative places and psychological recovery strategies both among elite sporting samples in addition to recreational exercisers. Restorative spaces, if recognised and utilised, can be used both strategically and opportunistically as a place to rewind, reflect and prepare. Typically in sport, recovery strategies have been limited (Gill, Beaven, & Cook, 2006) to acute physical recovery methods (e.g. ice baths, compression garments and active pool recovery), with a paucity of research conducted on mental recovery (Kellmann et al., 2018). An important application would be to use the recovery strategies (e.g. either direct or indirect nature contact) in longitudinal research with those athletes with a high risk of mental health disorder (e.g. in transition phases, Park et al., 2013; or injured athletes, Schinke et al., 2017). Similarly, recovery experiences may be useful for sport-science support staff as a workplace based recovery strategy (Sonnentag et al., 2017). As mentioned earlier, high performance sport is increasingly placing more demands on performers, and interventions to ameliorate long term stress and distress are required (MacIntyre et al., 2017; Schinke et al., 2017). Mixed-methods could be applied appropriately to explore the periodised nature of their recovery-stress cycles. Specifically, a combination of diary studies, qualitative interviews, focus groups coupled with monitoring using standardised inventories could, using a quasi-experimental design, provide insightful research to promote sustainable performance and well-being.

Survey findings conveyed that the participants had high levels of well-being, were highly connected to nature but had idiosyncratic views on the issue of sustainability. The qualitative findings have provided useful insights into the relationship of green exercise and well-being, highlighting the synergistic positive effect on sporting individuals when engaged with nature. The role of nature as a means of coping has been illuminated and the possibility that the challenge of outdoor nature experiences promotes resilience was recounted. Access to nature is largely viewed as beneficial and our participants gave examples of innovations that could facilitate access for the wider population.

References

Barton, J., Bragg, R., Wood, C., & Pretty, J. (Eds.). (2016). *Green exercise: Linking nature, health and well-being*. London: Routledge.

Bixler, R. D., Floyd, M. F., & Hammitt, W. E. (2002). Environmental socialization: Quantitative tests of the childhood play hypothesis. *Environment and Behavior, 34*(6), 795–818.

Bowler, D. E., Buyung-Ali, L. M., Knight, T. M., & Pullin, A. S. (2010). A systematic review of evidence for the added benefits of health of exposure to natural environments. *BMC Public Health, 10*, 456. doi:10.1186/1471-2458-10-456

Bratman, G. N., Hamilton, J. P., & Daily, G. C. (2012). The impacts of nature experience on human cognitive function and mental health. *Annals of the New York Academy of Sciences, 1249*(1), 118–136.

Brown, G., & Raymond, C. (2007). The relationship between place attachment and landscape values: Toward mapping place attachment. *Applied Geography, 27*(2), 89–111.

Bryan, C., O'Shea, D., & MacIntyre, T. (2017). Stressing the relevance of resilience: A systematic review of resilience across the domains of sport and work. *International Review of Sport and Exercise Psychology*, 1–41. doi:10.1080/17500984X.2017.1381140

Calogiuri, G. (2016). Natural environments and childhood experiences promoting physical activity, examining the mediational effects of feelings about nature and social networks. *International Journal of Environmental Research in Public Health, 13*(4), 439. doi:10.3390/ijerph13040439

Capaldi, C. A., Passmore, H.-A., Nisbet, E. K., Zelenski, J. M., & Dopko, R. L. (2015). Flourishing in nature: A review of the well-being benefits of connecting with nature and its application as a positive psychology intervention. *International Journal of Wellbeing, 5*, 1–16.

Carpenter, M. (2013). From 'healthful exercise' 'to 'nature on prescription': The politics of urban green spaces and walking for health. *Landscape and Urban Planning, 118*, 120–127.

Coutts, C., Forkink, A., & Weiner, J. (2014). The portrayal of natural environment in the evolution of the ecological public health paradigm. *International Journal of Environmental Research and Public Health, 11*(1), 1005–1019.

Currie, M., Lackova, P., & Dinnie, L. (2016). Greenspace matters: Exploring the links between greenspace, health and well-being with conservation volunteers and the ways in which gender is enacted (or not) in the space. *Landscape Research, 41*(6), 641–651.

Dunlap, R. E., Van Liere, K. D., Mertig, A. G., & Jones, R. E. (2000). New trends in measuring environmental attitudes: Measuring endorsement of the new ecological paradigm: A revised NEP scale. *Journal of Social Issues, 56*(3), 425–442.

Ellervik, C., Kvetny, J., Christensen, K. S., Vestergaard, M., & Bech, P. (2014). Prevalence of depression, quality of life and antidepressant treatment in the Danish General Suburban Population Study. *Nordic Journal of Psychiatry, 68*(7), 507–512. doi: 10.3109/08039488.2013.877074. Epub 2014 Jan 29.

Ekkekakis, P. (2017). People have feelings! Exercise psychology in paradigmatic transition. *Current Opinion in Psychology, 16*. doi:10.1016/j.copsyc.2017.03.018

European Foundation for the Improvement of Living and Working Conditions. (2017). *European Quality of Life Survey 2016: Quality of life, quality of public services, and quality of society*. Luxembourg: Publications Office of the European Union.

Ferrer-i-Carbonell, A., & Gowdy, J. M. (2007). Environmental degradation and happiness. *Ecological Economics*, *60*(3), 509–516.

Gill, N. D., Beaven, C. M., & Cook, C. (2006). Effectiveness of post-match recovery strategies in rugby players. *British Journal of Sport Medicine*, *40*(3), 260–263.

Hansmann, R., Hug, S. M., & Seeland, K. (2007). Restoration and stress relief through physical activities in forests and parks. *Urban Forestry & Urban Greening*, *6*(4), 213–225.

Hartig, T., Mitchell, R., De Vries, S., & Frumkin, H. (2014). Nature and health. *Annual Review of Public Health*, *35*, 207–228.

Howell, A. J., Dopko, R. L., Passmore, H.-A., & Buro, K. (2011). Nature connectedness: Associations with well-being and mindfulness. *Personality and Individual Differences*, *51*, 166–171. doi:10.1016/j.paid.2011.03.037

Howell, A. J., Passmore, H.-A., & Buro, K. (2013). Meaning in nature: Meaning in life as a mediator of the relationship between nature connectedness and well-being. *Journal of Happiness Studies*, *14*, 1681–1696.

Irvine, K. N., Warber, S. L., Devine-Wright, P., & Gaston, K. J. (2013). Understanding urban green space as a health resource: A qualitative comparison of visit motivation and derived effects among park users in Sheffield, UK. *International Journal of Environmental Research and Public Health*, *10*, 417–442.

Kaplan, R., & Kaplan, S. (1989). *The experience of nature: A psychological perspective*. Cambridge, UK: Cambridge University Press.

Kellmann, M., Bertollo, M., Bosquet, L., Brink, M., Coutts, A. J., Duffield, R., … Kallus, K. W. (2018). Recovery and performance in sport: Consensus statement. *International Journal of Sports Physiology and Performance*, *13*(2), 240–245.

Korpela, K., Kyttä, M., & Hartig, T. (2002). Restorative experience, self-regulation, and children's place preferences. *Journal of Environmental Psychology*, *22*(4), 387–398.

Lackey, K. J., & Kaczynski, A. T. (2009). Correspondence of perceived vs. objective proximity to parks and their relationship to park-based physical activity. *International Journal of Behavioral Nutrition and Physical Activity*, *6*. doi:Artn 53. doi:10.1186/1479-5868-6-53

Lee, A. C., & Maheswaran, R. (2011). The health benefits of urban green spaces: A review of the evidence. *Journal of Public Health*, *33*(2), 212–222. doi:10.1093/pubmed/fdq068

Louv, R. (2012). *The nature principle: Reconnecting with life in a virtual age*. Chapel Hill, NC: Algonquin Books.

MacIntyre, T. E., Jones, M., Brewer, B. W., Van Raalte, J., O'Shea, D., & McCarthy, P. J. (2017). Mental health challenges in elite sport: Balancing risk with reward. *Frontiers in Psychology*, *8*, 1892. doi:10.3389/fpsyg.2017.01892

MacKerron, G., & Mourato, S. (2013). Happiness is greater in natural environments. *Global Environmental Change*, *23*, 992–1000.

Marmot, M. (2010). *Fair society, healthy lives: The marmot review- strategic review of health inequalities in England post-2010*. London: The Marmot Review Team.

Marselle, M. R., Irvine, K. N., & Warber, S. L. (2014). Examining group walks in nature and multiple aspects of well-being: A large-scale study. *Ecopsychology*, *6*(3), 134–147.

Mayer, F. S., & Frantz, C. M. (2004). The connectedness to nature scale: A measure of individuals' feeling in community with nature. *Journal of Environmental Psychology*, *24*, 503–515. doi:10.1016/j.jenvp.2004.10.001

O'Brien, L., & Morris, J. (2014). Well-being for all? The social distribution of benefits gained from woodlands and forests in Britain. *Local Environment*, *19*(4), 356–383.

O'Sullivan, N., Donnelly, A., MacIntyre, T. E., & Warrington, G. (2016). Investigating the impact of green exercise on population health and well-being in a small community in Ireland – A novel approach using a natural laboratory ecosystem. *Nternational Journal of Environment and Health*, *18*(1), 34–40.

Park, S., Lavallee, D., & Tod, D. (2013). Athletes' career transition out of sport: A systematic review. *International Review of Sport and Exercise Psychology*, *6*, 22–53.

Pretty, J., Peacock, J., Hine, R., Sellens, M., South, N., & Griffin, M. (2007). Green exercise in the UK countryside: Effects on health and psychological well-being, and implications for policy and planning. *Journal of Environmental Planning and Management*, *50*(2), 211–231.

Schinke, R. J., Stambulova N. B., Si, G., & Moore, Z. (2017). International society of sport psychology position stand: Athletes' mental health, performance, and development. *International Journal of Sport and Exercise Psychology*. doi:10.1080/1612197X.2017.1295557

Scottish Natural Heritage (Producer). (2015, 09/06/16). Our natural health service: An action plan. Retrieved from www.snh.gov.uk/docs/A1889716.pdf.

Sommer, B. (1990). Favorite places of Estonian adolescents. *Children's Environmental Quarterly*, 7, 32–36.

Sonnentag, S. (2018). *Job-stress recovery: Core findings, future research topics, and remaining challenges*. Work Science Center Thinking Forward Report Series. Atlanta, GA: Georgia Institute of Technology.

Sonnentag, S., Venz, L., & Casper, A. (2017). Advances in recovery research: What have we learned? What should be done next? *Journal of Occupational Health Psychology*, *22*(3), 365–380.

Topp, C. W., Østergaard, S. D., Søndergaard, S., & Bech, P. (2015). The WHO-5 Well-Being Index: A systematic review of the literature. *Psychotherapy and Psychosomatics*, *84*(3), 167–176.

Ulrich, R. S., Simons, R. F., Losito, B. D., Fiorito, E., Miles, M. A., & Zelson, M. (1991). Stress recovery during exposure to natural and urban environments. *Journal of Environmental Psychology*, *11*(3), 201–230.

Ward Thompson, C., Aspinall, P., & Montarzino, A. (2008). The childhood factor: Adult visits to green places and the significance of childhood experience. *Environment and Behavior*, *40*(1), 111–143.

11

IMMERSION, WATERSPORTS AND BLUEWAYS AND THE BLUE MIND

Case studies in blue exercise

Tadhg E. MacIntyre, Andree Walkin, Giovanna Calogiuri, Greig Oliver, Aoife A. Donnelly, Susan Gritzka and Giles Warrington

The concept of "blue mind" coined by Wallace J. Nichols (2014) which has popularized water-based activities as a pathway to well-being and health provides a fitting backdrop for this chapter. The term refers to a "mildly meditative state characterized by calm, peace, unity and a sense of general happiness and satisfaction with life in the moment" (p. 6). Researchers have been concerned with the impact of being close to water on different scales. For example, BlueHealth2020 (www.bluehealth2020.eu) is a pan-European research project investigating the links between environment, climate and health with a specific focus on blue-natural spaces (Grellier et al., 2017). Their findings from their systematic review of 35 studies suggest a positive association between greater exposure to outdoor blue spaces and benefits to both mental health and well-being and levels of physical activity (*N*=13 studies). Support for benefits to general health including cardiovascular health was less prominent and the findings were highly limited by the heterogeneity among the published studies (Gascon et al., 2017). Further evidence suggests that in the UK up to 270m recreational visits are made to marine environments in England annually, with walking a predominant activity on beaches (Elliott et al., 2018). In Norway, activities by or on the sea are the second most common form of nature recreations, with around 30% of adults reporting that they engage in these activities fairly often (Calogiuri et al., 2016). This is significant as almost half of the EU population lives less than 50 km from the sea and the majority is concentrated in urban areas along the coast water (Eurostat, 2011). In its many forms, water and blue natural space is largely accessible with vast potential for the promotion of sustainable recreation, restoration and well-being. EU research continues to emerge in this domain with the advent of the SOPHIE (Seas, Oceans & Public Health in Europe) project, for example, as part of a nomothetic approach (www.sophie2020.eu).

On the idiographic scale, however, few studies had explored the lived experiences of those who were highly active in sport and adventure in blue natural spaces. This chapter, in parallel with the previous chapter articulating a green-exercise focused narrative, prioritizes the participants voice using a mixed-methods methodology, fusing standardized survey instruments with semi-structured interviews.

Prior research has been grounded in theoretical accounts from environmental psychology which have been concerned with attention restoration and stress recovery, which are a narrow set of outcomes given the corpus of evidence on the psychological benefits of human-nature interactions (Frumkin et al., 2017; van den Bosch et al., 2017). Organizational psychology offers interesting perspectives regarding psychological recovery, for example, which are integrated with the construct of resilience and provide additional testable hypotheses. Recovery, as Sonnentag et al. (2017) allude to, refers to the process of psychological unwinding, recuperating, or restoring physical or mental resource that counteracts the stress process triggered by job demands and other stressors. This perspective based on psychological resources theory (Hobfoll, 1989) can illuminate our understanding of nature as a restorative place. Integral to the psychological resources approach is the construct of resilience which has been largely overlooked in our understanding of human-nature interactions. This is somewhat surprising given that resilience is integral to biological systems in general, including ecosystems (see Chapter 9). Exploring resilience as an outcome of the positive and adaptive response to the challenge of extreme sports in nature offers an opportunity to explore how stress, psychological resources, coping and psychological growth interact (Bryan et al., 2017).

The concept of connectedness with nature or the similar concept of nature relatedness was also of concern to our investigations. Individuals with higher self-reported nature connectedness (see also Chapter 1) typically benefit more from interacting with nature. A novel approach in our study was the consideration of pro-environmental behavior and environmental concern.

The topic of environmental sustainability has been emerging as a major social issue in the present century not only in environmental sciences but also in public health (see Chapter 16). Connectivity with nature and place attachment (an emotional, cognitive, and functional bond with a place) have emerged as key psychological components fostering sustainable behavior (Geng et al., 2015; Restall & Conrad, 2015). Studies have found significant associations of both our relationship with nature (e.g. Mayer & Frantz, 2004; Nisbet et al., 2009) and place attachment (e.g. Halpenny, 2010; Scannell & Gifford, 2010) with environmental concerns and commitment to pro-environmental behaviors.

The overall aim of our research was to explore the lived experiences of participants in activities, both sporting and adventure, in blue natural spaces. Lived experiences of athletes from extreme sports have been previously reported using the lens of environmental psychology (Brymer et al., 2009), whereas in this mixed-methods approach, we augmented the participants story with survey findings using standardized instruments. A pre-selected sample (three males and four females) drawn from participants in a range of activities such as long distance open-water swimming, white-water and ultra-endurance kayaking and big wave surfing (See Table 11.1) volunteered to participate in the study. To validate the case-study approach all waived the right to anonymity which was part of the institutional ethical approval (EHS Ethical Approval No. 2016 _11_20 EHS).

The online survey measured well-being and mental health (*WHO-5 Well-Being* Index; Topp et al., 2015), individuals' connectedness to the natural world (*Connectedness to Nature Scale*, Mayer & Frantz, 2004) and attitudes towards the environment (*New Ecological Paradigm Scale*, NEP scale, Dunlap, 2008). The aforementioned measures have been used extensively in both the environmental psychology literature and in health and exercise settings and there is extensive comparative data available (see Chapters 1 and 2). The scores in the original studies by Mayer and Frantz (2004) reported a *CNS* mean score of 3.65 ±.64 (Study 1, N = 60) and 3.52 ±.56 (Study 4, N = 135) in an adult sample from the United States. Our sample (see Table 11.2) scored higher (M = 3.71, SD =.62) on the personal trait connectedness to nature compared to the aforementioned normative data. Similarly, the overall mean score of 3.70 for NEP can be considered as a good

TABLE 11.1 Participant name, gender, nationality and sporting experience

Name	*Gender*	*Nationality*	*Sporting experience*
Easkey Britton	F	Irish	Former international professional surfer and big wave surfer
Chris Bryan	M	Irish	International competitor in long distance open-water swimming
Rosie Foley	F	Irish	Channel swimmer and former Ireland rugby international (36 caps)
Sandra Hyslop	F	British	Professional white-water and extreme kayaker
Jim Kennedy	M	Irish	Ultra-endurance competitor
Tehillah McGuinness	F	South African	International professional surfer and big wave surfer
Humphrey Murphy	M	Irish	Expedition white-water kayaker

TABLE 11.2 The means and standard deviation for the participants on key inventories

Inventory	*Mean*	*SD*
Connectedness to Nature Scale (CNS)	3.71	.62
NEP: New Ecological Paradigm	3.70	.69
WHO-5 Well-being Index	78	12.48

endorsement of a pro-ecological world view (Dunlap, 2008). The mean score for well-being was 78 which is higher than the EU-27 average of 62 (European Foundation for the Improvement of Living and Working Conditions, 2017).

Specific item analyses provide further support for this contention (see Table 11.3) but given the descriptive snapshot that this data provides caution must be used in interpreting these findings. On the other hand, the qualitative interviews provide a rich personal narrative revealing the interaction between nature, well-being and a sustainable environment.

Qualitative analysis

The meta-themes that emerged from the qualitative analysis were as follows: (1) Early Childhood, (2) Challenge of Outdoors, (3) Emotional Response to Nature, (4) Nature for Coping, (5) Restorative Spaces, and (6) Environmental Concern (see Figure 11.1).

Early childhood

The influence of childhood engagement in nature has been noted in previous research (Asah et al., 2011; Calogiuri, 2016; Ward Thompson et al., 2008) and in Chapter 9. Two major themes emerged under this theme in our analysis of the interviews: Positive (sub-themes: outdoor play, sport and influencers) and negative (sub-themes: running). Jim Kennedy reflected on the importance of his early childhood experiences growing up by the river Lee in Cork city: "It was pre-TV if your heads can imagine that. There were maybe 20 to 30 kids in the streets so outside for us was just the natural thing, we didn't know any better, we would run everywhere." Interestingly, Sandra Hyslop, a fellow kayaker states that she hated running: "It's just really uncomfortable for me to do," showing the multiple trajectories for individuals engaging in outdoor play during their formative years.

TABLE 11.3 Overall mean and standard deviation of CNS and NEP on sample items

Items	*Mean*	*SD*
CNS[a] ($N = 8$)		
(1) I often feel a sense of oneness with the natural world around me.	4.50	.76
(2) I think of the natural world as a community to which I belong.	4.25	.89
(3) I recognize and appreciate the intelligence of other living organisms.	4.25	.89
NEP[b] ($N = 8$)		
(6) Humans are seriously abusing the environment.	4.63	.52
(9) Despite our special abilities, humans are still subject to the laws of nature.	4.50	.53
(15) If things continue on their present course, we will soon experience a major ecological catastrophe.	4.50	.53

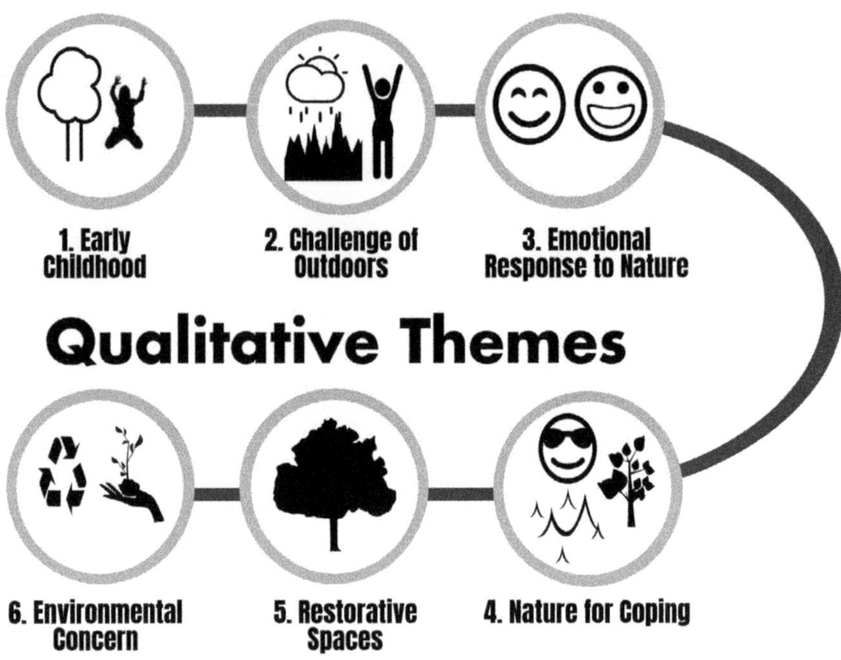

FIGURE 11.1 Qualitative themes: blue exercise

Sandra Hyslop, who won the Adidas Sickline extreme kayak race (e.g. kayak race on category Class 5 white-water on river Oetz), noted both negative and positive contributions of early childhood experience:

> We always used to go hillwalking as a family and dad was really into caving which we didn't enjoy quite so much but that was the weekend thing as a family, we used to go hillwalking or caving.

She continued "I just always like water … I can't remember not being able to swim." In England, she recalled that she wanted to join the swim club at six years of age but they refused as they didn't take people until they were eight years old. A major life event was to provide an opportunity for Sandra:

> We moved to America when I was seven and they are pretty big on swimming in the States so I joined the swim club there so I started and used to go every day in the summer … so it was probably pretty serious swim training from about age eight I guess and that probably built the fitness and confidence in the water.

Similarly, for Irish surfer Easkey Britton, childhood experiences were key for her introduction to competition at a similar age:

> I'm a lifelong surfer and I've been competing since the age of eight and have surfed professionally, it's something that is a huge part of my life. From an early age surfing and the sea has been a huge part of who I am and this has continued to influence me daily.

Tehillah sums up her early introduction to competition in the same sport concisely: "Surfing chose me, I didn't choose surfing." Big wave surfing differs from other competition events in that participants engage in tow-in-surfing and thus the waves are typically of a greater magnitude. However, she described that at eight years old before she started surfing that she got into long distance running: "that was like my dream to be in the Olympics." Rosie Foley describes how as a child she would try any sport with Anthony and her younger sister Orla: "Any sport that was on the TV, we were doing on the front lawn."

Sibling support was influential for Tehillah McGuinness who noted:

> I think I was quite a tomboy – I mean growing up we are all incredibly close – my mum kind of had us in pairs – so my brother and I when we were younger we were a year apart so I would do everything with him and his friends.

In swimming, the inspirational role of coaches was also noted by Chris Bryan:

> The coach who was at Ennis Swimming Club, Sean O'Sullivan, was the father of my best friend I regularly stayed with them at Spanish Point [coastal town 35km from Ennis, Co. Clare]. He would have been a major influence. You could see the passion they had that really then helped me, kind of, glue to the open-water swimming scene.

Britton found her influence in a fellow female sportsperson who inspired her to take her sport to the next level:

> Sarah Gerhardt … was one of the first women to pioneer one of the wave spots called Mavericks in the 1990s … so this was the first time we would have seen a woman in a wetsuit in cold water.

Challenge of outdoors

The common challenge among the extreme sport (e.g. first descents, big wave surfing, extreme kayaking races) and ultra-endurance activities (e.g. Channel swims and Devizes to Westminster race) is not perhaps in their threat to individual survival, nor their specific psychological task demands and physiological requirements, but in the nature contact. For example, the Devizes to Westminster kayak race is known as a rite of passage for members of the elite forces (e.g.

Special Boat Service) and while an ultra-endurance event, the 77 portages, 125 miles of both river and canal (much of it in darkness) spans the Wiltshire and Berkshire countryside. Arguably, blue mind experience and immersion in water is a common theme across the settings

Fruhauf et al. (2017) found that challenge in the extreme sport of freeriding for some participants provided an opportunity to explore and stretch their personal limits. Extreme sports create an opportunity for participants to self-determine their own level of challenge. This theme resonated with Easkey Britton who said:

> You're always on the edge of challenge because of the environment and definitely big wave surfing you're in extreme situations all the time so plenty of adversity in that sense … there is a lot of fear as well as attraction as we are drawn to water environments.

Humphrey Murphy juxtaposed two of his feats – expedition kayaking and Everest. Interestingly, he is one of approximately 50 Irish people who have successfully climbed Mount Everest, ascending via the Northeast ridge route in 2005. Humphrey noted:

> Everest was a relatively straightforward one of all of them. The Everest trip, in a way there was something artificial about that because of the level of structure there is around it and in terms of signature trips.

Whereas he says of kayaking:

> Caucasus and Siberia and they were again going out to do rivers that were very challenging but again very remote in so far as you step into gorges for a week at a time and really didn't have much of an option than to stay in them and kayak down them.

Fellow kayaker Sandra recounts how coupling the physical and technical challenges is the toughest aspect for her, so competition scenarios create an added pressure:

> what's nice is the challenge. You've got to be on the athletic edge physically pushing as hard as you can and still have enough to nail the technical aspects. I did the white-water grand prix one year – that's definitely the most scared I've been ever been racing.

Stress can be ameliorated by taking on challenges in new ways as Sandra explains:

> When I started kayaking we used to love just swimming down the rapids … if you'll happily swim down it then why wouldn't you

> kayak it – the worst that can happen is that you'll swim and so I think that's why being a strong swimmer is huge for your white-water confidence.

While swimming in white-water has its own challenges, open-water swimming on the other hand provides a unique environment as Channel swimmer Rosie Foley recalls: "I was reared in the water in Killaloe so I don't mind the blackness and that darkness." Rosie's extreme feat was the Channel swim (22 miles at its narrowest point) with a duration of 15 hours, 53 minutes.

Emotional response to nature

Our participants' emotions from interacting with nature were predominantly positive with only one potential negative outcome. As a result, only two major themes, positive and negative, emerged under this meta-theme in our analysis of the interviews: positive (sub-themes: positive emotions, calmness, variation, stress reduction, vitality, therapeutic and awe) and negative (sub-theme: disruption).

Firstly, Sandra extols the virtues of being on the water: "Pretty much whatever the river is like once you're in the boat I'm pretty much always happy." She reflects that "just being on the water is awesome." Activity in nature as a source of positive emotions aligns with the literature base (Lumber et al., 2017).

Another kayaker Jim refers to the inherent vitality of nature:

> Where the sea meets the land is probably the most powerful place in the world. That line. That coastal line where the white waves, that's probably the most, besides volcanoes, or earthquakes, that's probably the most incredibly natural forceful place in the world, a powerful place in the world. It's an amazing area.

The contrasting experiences recounted by our participants convey how nature offers a myriad of experiences with different emotional outcomes as Sandra explains:

> It kind of depends on the river which offers like different rewards. I guess you're getting the adrenaline rush if you are in the harder stuff and kind of that sense of achievement when you make it through the rapid.

For kayaker Humphrey geography is no barrier: "When I am in a particular environment be it the sea or a mountain environment or an air sport environment … it evokes certain reactions within me regardless of whether that's in Ireland Kerry or the Himalayas." He explains how we can disrupt the positive emotional response in certain situations:

> Green spaces and blue spaces are unquestionably therapeutic whether we want them to be or not however if we do a sort of boot camp approach to the outdoors if we are shouting at people to do more trying to get them to go further or faster and so on we actually we undermine the meanings of those environments and we create a negative environment.

Nature for coping

Nature has long been established as providing a role in coping, both in human geography (e.g. therapeutic landscapes, Bell et al., 2018) and in explanatory accounts of human-nature interactions (e.g. stress reduction theory, Ulrich et al., 1991) and within the literature on psychological recovery (Sonnentag et al., 2017). Three themes emerged from our analyses: emotional regulation (sub-themes: absorption, competition) blue and green spaces (sub-theme: relaxation) and sense of loss (sub-themes: bereavement, injury). Perception of awe has unique beneficial effects for mood, according to a recent review by Lumber et al. (2017).

Our participants similarly conveyed this idea of emotional regulation through nature expressed by open-water swimmer Chris Bryan: "the beach in Sri Lanka. It has really, really strong currents. I really enjoy the rough seas as well. I swam there every day last year. It humbles me." The sense of flow, which has been evident in prior research (Brymer et al., 2009) appears to be linked to the multi-modal memorable experiences as Easkey describes:

> Obviously, the emotional connection has to be there. I think it can be very powerful, especially memory. I think memory get formed or shaped in water from experiences with being immersed in water. As a surfer you can recall that exact moment even though it only lasts a few seconds and it could be years and years ago whereas you can't really remember so clearly what you did yesterday.

Swimmer Rosie Foley elaborates on how nature promotes relaxation: "I can physically relax in seconds, that's what I can do when I get into nature. I just let my mind go." According to Rosie, "the emotions are just pure relaxation and just that lovely feeling of this is where I'm supposed to be. This relaxes me, this gets everything out of me." This cleansing metaphor highlights the de-stressing effect of human-nature interactions.

One clear example of this is how Rosie, whose brother Anthony Foley passed away in 2016, coped with the bereavement:

> When I'm swimming I can cry when I'm swimming I can do whatever the hell I want when I'm swimming and it's me on my own and its fine and I'm not upsetting anyone else … that's how it helps me cope.

Restorative spaces

Three major themes emerged under this topic in our analysis of the interviews: Blue Spaces (sub-themes: imaginary, local, connectedness, reflections, favourite natural space), Blue and Green Spaces (sub-themes: beauty and connectedness) and finally, Green Spaces (sub-themes: soundscape). Blue natural spaces are different to green, with potentially greater salutogenic effects, and discrete pathways (Gascon et al., 2017).

Not surprisingly, given that more than two-thirds of our participants had extreme sport experiences in water sports, their preference for blue natural spaces were typically higher among our participants. Rugby international, and later a Channel swimmer, Rosie Foley said:

> I'm more blue, I think, I'm more blue but it's funny like I'm drawn to places where there is water … Lough Derg to me would equate in a sense to the channel and I always felt that it was on my own backyard this is what I've spent so much time on the lake I love it here.

Rosie lives adjacent to the Lough Derg Blueway (a series of bespoke multi-recreational trails on Ireland's third largest lake over 24 miles in length, totalling 50 square miles) and thus the connection to water is not unexpected. Similarly, Jim Kennedy has access to a body of water on his doorstep:

> Where we kayak, we have a site, and you take four steps from it and you're in the sea, it's on the sea, on a tiny little slip about 25–30 feet high so most beautiful, spectacular place for what we do.

Another kayaker, Sandra, outlines how it's neither the challenge nor the competition that defines the experience but the engagement and absorption with the activity in nature:

> I think I guess some people in the white-water community find me a bit strange cause I am perfectly happy paddling on flat water for an hour and it's not as good probably as the white-water but … I just like being on the water and I can enjoy great flatwater.

This connectedness with nature is echoed by a lucid description from Humphrey Murphy: "the outdoors is a more real place than most else in my life." Open-water swimmer Chris explains:

> I used to go out to Killaloe [Lough Derg Blueway] quite a lot … And again it was that combination of cold water and just, eh, getting away from it all, that it was actually the one time that I could stop and frame my thoughts. So that was actually really valuable to me.

Sandra echoes these sentiments: "I love getting out in nature, if you are by yourself enjoying some space and getting away from everything." Experiences in nature appear to have a restorative function for our interviewees – they provide energy to the participant and instil a sense of recovery.

This restorative function of nature was mirrored in their description of their favourite places. As Easkey alluded: "I travel a lot and coming home has always had the restorative aspect and back home to Donegal where I grew up and that has that kind of energy." Jim's favourite place is idyllic but imaginary: "I have never actually physically seen it. But it's a tiny little beach, it's about 50 feet wide, and there's shells on the left-hand side and there's a slope on the beach, and I know it intimately."

The interviewees display a unique cognitive flexibility in how they access nature and optimize their interactions as surfer Easkey Britton conveys:

> If I go to say London for work, within a few hours or a few days I feel like claustrophobic and I need to be near the sea – nature yes definitely beautiful forests, yes, I love the forests but the sea that's kind of what mentally does it for me.

Aesthetics of nature resonate clearly with our participants, supporting the findings of Lumber et al. (2017). As the quote from Tehillah stated:

> When we moved from Jeffreys Bay to the UK, as I said we moved from living right – basically I stood up in bed and opened my window and I could see the sea … And we moved from that to a little village where you wake up and see sheep in the field, it was green and, as beautiful as that was, it was different and for me it kind of evokes different emotions.

The ubiquitous influence of nature, whether blue or green, is integral to Easkey's connection with nature: "I'm also passionate about overcoming that sense of separation and disconnect I suppose we have between land and sea, nature and culture, and ourselves and nature." For Rosie "the green has brought us some great places around the world I have to say so if we are walking the dogs or walking with the kids or we are going cycling." At some level it may be artificial to categorize interviewees as linked to blue or green spaces by their predominant physical activity – their narrative appears to be far richer than such a dichotomy can describe.

Environmental concern

Interestingly, marine social scientist and surfer Easkey Britton, currently employed on the aforementioned SOPHIE project, showed her research insights in her comment: "I think the real barrier or issue is even when we do access it, it's the quality of the environment … I think we are at crisis point when it comes to the health of our oceans."

Our participants were well-placed to have an opinion on the challenge of the sustainability of their outdoor activities. None more so than Jim Kennedy, who as an adventure tourism provider described how he could see the beauty of it:

> we are actually passionate, most people like us come into the business for the passion, of nature, of our business, so that's what's happened, and we're like-minded people who are pushing adventure tourism at a very high level, very professional level, but one of the benefits of that, we're educating people, and sustainability, how to look after the sea, learn how to respect the waters, the walkways, the rivers, the trees, everything.

Sandra too was aware of the apparent contradictions in desiring to protect the wilderness and accessing it, sometimes by helicopter.

> I definitely love being outdoors but I would definitely be hypocritical to say how much I care about it, I like to buy a lot of plane tickets I drive to a lot of rivers … it's not something I feel 100% awesome about.

Cultural differences in attitudes towards sustainability have been shown in recent surveys. For example, the Eurobarometer survey (2017) suggests that when asked about the top five issues, compared to the EU average (56%), Irish people rated air pollution as a lower priority issue (47%, lowest among EU-27) with similar discrepancies for items relating to the depletion of natural resources (EU-27 36%, IE 28%) and the loss of natural ecosystems (EU-27 26%; IE 19%). Among sport participants, their values and attitudes may also be different depending upon their sport. Sandra gives the example of energy:

> Kayakers are always super anti-hydro … cause dams ruin rivers but then the part of me that has looked into different energy forms and stuff, like really hydroelectricity is quite a good renewable energy source compared to fossil fuels.

According to Tehillah McGuinness:

> Everyone has an obligation but I think out there so many people have an opportunity with the kind of audience they have to be able to really push these things and get people involved … maybe not so much self-promotion but more taking care of the planet.

This concept of personal responsibility was clearly expressed by the former pro-surfer: "I think if we all take it upon ourselves I think hopefully that should make a difference … we have a huge responsibility to kind of to protect it and to encourage people."

The theme of education resonates with secondary school teacher Rosie Foley: "why not start to educate? From a very young age they want to know everything so we talked about plastic and the planet." The participants' insights paralleled their scores on the NEP test items with the ecosystem services of outdoor recreation (i.e. the non-material benefits that humans obtain from natural and semi-natural ecosystems, Millennium Ecosystem Assessment, 2005) providing both challenges and solutions. Surfer Tehillah sums this up succinctly: "the ocean is kind of what pays our bills in a way. We are earning money through being able to enjoy the ocean." Our findings on environmental concern support the findings from analyses of large-scale survey data that contend that engaging with nature can have an impact on an individual's environmental concern (Brymer & Schweitzer, 2013; Ferrer-i-Carbonell & Gowdy, 2007).

Limitations

Although the current study is based on a small sample of participants, the findings suggest that blue exercise has psychological benefits for the participants ranging from evoking positive emotions and developing resilience and life coping skills to helping them adopt a strong affinity to and connection with nature and the natural environment. An uncontrolled factor is the possibility that the sample participants were experiencing different stages of transition within their particular extreme sport career. From a qualitative perspective, research argues that interviewers' work can be flawed by individual perceptions, inferring that recall biases can persist. From a quantitative perspective, the small sample did not facilitate the use of inferential statistics. Generalizability is limited to extreme sport athletes and yet this study offers valuable insights into the lived experiences of extreme sports participants.

Future research directions

This exploratory study gives us an insight into the individuals behind the extreme sport mindset and highlights extreme sport individuals' positive attitudes towards nature and the environment. Constructs such as resilience clearly resonate with this sample of extreme sport participants and future research could use longitudinal designs to explore the dynamic emotional responses to nature interactions. Research is proliferating on the concept of recovery within the elite sport context (Frank et al., 2018; Kellmann & Beckmann, 2018) and developing interventions to help athletes employ nature as a means of psychological recovery would be a worthy pursuit for researchers and practitioners (Donnelly et al., 2016).

The role of early childhood experiences highlighted by our interviewees provides a fitting backdrop to the development of both blue and green infrastructure to facilitate recreation and sport activity in natural spaces. The concept of Blueways, which are water and land-based routes with supporting infrastructure, provide an opportunity for early access to sport activities in nature. It is worth recalling how access to a safe environment to take on a variety of challenges was integral to the development of our athletes' mindset.

Conclusions

Our disparate sample displayed commonalities in their mindset, their well-being, connectivity with nature and attitudes towards the environment. Their differences paled in significance relative to their overlapping values, goals and response to interacting with nature in the context of extreme sports. Interestingly, kayaker Sandra Hyslop said during her interview that her dream when she was about 5 or 6 "was to swim the Channel (e.g. English Channel) – still haven't done it yet … one day!"

References

Asah, S. T., Bengston, D. N., & Westphal, L. M. (2011). The influence of childhood: Operational pathways to adulthood participation in nature-based activities. *Environmental Behavior, 44*(4), 545–569.

Bell, L. B., Foley, R., Houghton, F., Maddrell, A. & Williams, A. M. (2018). From therapeutic landscapes to healthy spaces, places and practices: A scoping review. *Social Science & Medicine, 196*, 123–130.

Bryan, C., O'Shea, D. & MacIntyre, T. (2017). Stressing the relevance of resilience: A systematic review of resilience across the domains of sport and work. *International Review of Sport and Exercise Psychology*, 1–41. doi:10.1080/17500984X.2017.1381140

Brymer, E., Downey, G. & Gray, T. (2009). Extreme sports as a precursor to environmental sustainability. *Journal of Sport Tourism, 14*(2–3), 1–12.

Brymer, E. & Schweitzer, R. (2013). Extreme sports are good for your health: A phenomenological understanding of fear and anxiety in extreme sport. *Journal of Health Psychology, 18*, 477–487. doi:10.1177/1359105312446770

Calogiuri, G. (2016). Natural environments and childhood experiences promoting physical activity examining the mediational effects of feelings about nature and social networks. *International Journal of Environmental Research in Public Health, 13*, 439.

Calogiuri, G., Patil, G. G., & Aamodt, G. (2016). Is green exercise for all? A descriptive study of green exercise habits and promoting factors in adult Norwegians. *International Journal of Environmental Research in Public Health, 13*(11), 1165. doi:10.3390/ijerph13111165

Donnelly, A. A., MacIntyre, T. E., O'Sullivan, N., Warrington, G., Harrison, A. J., Igou, E. R., … Lane, A. M. (2016). Environmental influences on elite sport athletes well-being: From gold silver and bronze to blue green and gold. *Frontiers in Psychology, 7*, 1167. doi:10.3389/fpsyg.2016.01167

Dunlap, R. E. (2008). The New Environmental Paradigm Scale: From marginality to worldwide use. *Journal of Environmental Education, 40*, 3–18.

Elliott, L. R., White, M. P., Grellier, J., Rees, S. E., Waters, R. D., & Fleming, L. E. (2018). Recreational visits to marine and coastal environments in England: Where, what, who, why, and when? *Marine Policy*. doi:10.1016/j.marpol.2018.03.013.

Eurobarometer Environment. (2017). *Special Eurobarometer 468: Attitudes of European Citizens towards the Environment.* Brussels: EC.

Eurostat. (2011). *Europe in figures. Eurostat yearbook 2011.* Luxembourg: Publications Office of the European Union.

European Foundation for the Improvement of Living and Working Conditions. (2017). *European quality of life survey 2016: Quality of life, quality of public services, and quality of society.* Luxembourg: Publications Office of the European Union.

Ferrer-i-Carbonell, A. & Gowdy, J. M. (2007). Environmental degradation and happiness. *Ecological Economics*, *60*(3), 509–516.

Frank, R., Nixdorf, I. & Beckmann, J. (2018). Stress, underrecovery and health problems in athletes. In M. Kellmann & J. Beckmann (Eds.), *Sport, Recovery and Performance: Interdisciplinary Insights* (pp. 119–131). Abingdon: Routledge.

Frühauf, A., Hardy, W. A., Pfoestl, D., Hoellen, F. G., & Kopp, M. (2017). A qualitative approach on motives and aspects of risks in freeriding. *Frontiers in Psychology*, *8*, 1998. doi: 10.3389/fpsyg.2017.01998.

Frumkin, H., Bratman, G. N., Breslow, S. J., Cochran, B., Kahn, P.H., Lawler, J.J., et al. (2017). Nature contact and human health: A research agenda. *Environmental Health Perspectives*, *125*(7), 075001. doi:10.1289/EHP1663

Gascon, M., Zijlema, W., Vert, C., White, M. P., & Nieuwenhuijsen, M. J. (2017). Outdoor blue spaces, human health and well-being: A systematic review of quantitative studies. *International Journal of Hygeine and Environmental Health*, *4*. doi:10.1016/j.ijheh.2017.08.004

Geng, L., Xu, J., Ye, L., Zhou, W. & Zhou, K. (2015). Connections with nature and environmental behaviors. *PLoS ONE*, *10*(5), e0127247. doi:10.1371/journal.pone.0127247

Grellier, J., White, M. P., Albin, M., Bell, S., Elliott, L. R., Gascón, M., … Fleming, L. E. (2017). BlueHealth: A study programme protocol for mapping and quantifying the potential benefits to public health and well-being from Europe's blue spaces. *BMJ Open*, 7, e016188. doi:10.1136/bmjopen-2017-016188

Halpenny, E. A. (2010). Pro-environmental behaviours and park visitors: The effect of place attachment. *Journal of Environmental Psychology*, *30*(4), 409–421.

Hobfoll, S. E. (1989). Conservation of resources a new attempt at conceptualizing stress. *American Psychologist*, *44*, 513–524.

Kellmann, M. & Beckmann, J. (2018). Sport, recovery and performance: A concluding summary. In M. Kellmann & J. Beckmann (Eds.), *Sport, Recovery and Performance: Interdisciplinary Insights* (pp. 260–265). Abingdon: Routledge.

Lumber, R., Richardson, M. & Sheffield, D. (2017). Beyond knowing nature: Contact emotion compassion meaning and beautyare pathways to nature connection. *PLoS ONE*, *12*(5), e0177186.

Mayer, F. S. & Frantz, C. M. (2004). The connectedness to nature scale: A measure of individuals' feeling in community with nature. *Journal of Environmental Psychology*, *24*, 503–515. doi:10.1016/j.jenvp.2004.10.001

Millennium Ecosystem Assessment (Program). (2005). *Ecosystems and Human Well-Being.* Washington, DC: Island Press.

Nichols, W. J. (2014). *Blue Mind.* New York: Little, Brown and Company.

Nisbet, E. K., Zelenski, J. M., & Murphy, S. A. (2009). The nature relatedness scale: Linking individuals' connection with nature to environmental concern and behavior. *Environmental Behavior*, *41*(5), 715–740.

Restall, B. & Conrad, E. (2015). A literature review of connectedness to nature and its potential for environmental management. *Journal of Environmental Management*, *159*, 264–278.

Scannell, L. & Gifford, R. (2010). The relations between natural and civic place attachment and pro-environmental behavior. *Journal of Environmental Psychology, 30*(3), 289–297.

Sonnentag, S., Venz, L., & Casper, A. (2017). Advances in recovery research: What have we learned? What should be done next? *Journal of Occupational Health Psychology, 22*(3), 365–380.

Topp, C. W., Østergaard, S. D., Søndergaard, S. & Bech, P. (2015). The WHO-5 well-being index: A systematic review of the literature. *Psychother Psychosom, 84*, 167–176.

Ulrich, R. S., Simons, R. S., Losito, B. D., Fiorito, E., Miles, M. A., & Zelson, M. (1991). Stress recovery during exposure to natural and urban environments. *Journal of Environmental Psychology, 11*, 201–230.

van den Bosch, M., Ward-Thompson, C. & Grahn, P. (2017). Preventing stress and promoting mental health. In M. van den Bosch & W. Bird (Eds.), *Oxford Textbook of Nature and Public Health: The Role of Nature in Improving the Health of a Population* (pp. 108–115). Oxford: Oxford University Press.

Ward Thompson, C., Aspinall, P., & Montarzino, A. (2008). The childhood factor: Adult visits to green places and the significance of childhood experience. *Environment and Behavior, 40*(1), 111–143.

12

WHY OUTDOORS?

A systematic approach to examine and value the social benefits of outdoor sports

Barbara Eigenschenk and Mike McClure

Introduction

The European White Paper on Sport (Commission of the European Communities, 2007, p.7) highlights that "sport makes an important contribution to economic and social cohesion and more integrated societies." However, while there is information within member states as to what the social benefits of sport are, such as "The Social Benefits of Sport – An Overview to Inform the Community Planning Process" of Coalter (2005), the partners involved in the project were not aware of any pan-European evidence on the social benefits of outdoor sports or even sport in general.

Low levels of physical activity are increasingly causing concern in member states and are highlighted by the EU Special Eurobarometer 472 on Sport and Physical Activity (Directorate-General for Communication, 2018). This document highlights that the proportion of Europeans that never exercise or play sport has increased from 42% to 46% in the past five years.

The White Paper also highlights the importance of evidence-based policies to encourage increased participation. In Europe there is an agreed system for measuring the economic impact of sport – the Satellite Accounts system (Directorate-General for Education, Youth, Sport and Culture (European Commission), 2013), but this only takes account of the hard data on sales, consumption of goods and services and employment. It does not take into account the value that sport and in particular outdoor sports can make to individual and societal development.

The Benefits of Outdoor Sports for Society (BOSS) project aims to bridge these gaps by collating and publishing evidence that outdoor sports bring clear benefits at an individual and societal level and providing empirical evidence for the value of these social benefits in economic terms.

This project is focusing on outdoor sports rather than sports in general as European Network of Outdoor Sports (ENOS) members were aware of anecdotal evidence on the benefits of outdoor sports. However, the methodology developed will be able to be applied to the overall sport sector. Reasons for focusing on outdoor sports also include:

1. The outdoors is recognised by the European Commission as a key way to engage people with health enhancing physical activity as the EU Special Eurobarometer 472 shows that at least 40% of those participating do so in the outdoors. Therefore, the use of the natural environment is important for European citizens.
2. Outdoor sports are very accessible and in many cases are free at the point of use, making them affordable for those who are economically disadvantaged.
3. Outdoor sports suit those who prefer non-organised or self-organised activities and this is a trend that is highlighted within the EU Special Eurobarometer 472 and therefore has the capacity to effectively deliver social benefits.
4. Outdoor sports are cross-sectoral, linking sport, tourism, heritage, local development, health and environment and therefore have the potential to accrue a much greater range of benefits from a wider cross section of society.
5. There is an established network for outdoor sports at a European level, ENOS. The Charter for Outdoor Sports (2013) developed by ENOS highlights the connectivity between social responsibility and environmental respect that outdoor sports can generate.
6. Local or national actions have already been started such as the 2014 Outdoor Recreation Action Plan for Northern Ireland and, in France, there is a specific national policy about the sustainable practice of outdoor sport for all that was created in 2003. However, only the coordinated production and analyses of data from all over Europe (taking into account cultural and environmental considerations) can provide a solid base for the systematic development of appropriate opportunities that will maximise the social benefits associated with outdoor sports.
7. There is an extensive range of organisations across Europe that have an interest in one or more outdoor sports and a multi-outdoor sports development approach through cooperation and partnership will bring additional benefits and economies of scale that cannot be achieved alone.
8. Outdoor sports can also improve rural development by creating employment, opportunity and infrastructure in rurally deprived areas.

The BOSS project provides a multi-disciplinary, coordinated, sequential and stepped approach to the development of a methodology which will provide evidence for policy and interventions that support actions at a local level to increase health enhancing physical activity in the outdoors. This approach is consistent with the EU Physical Activity Guidelines (2008) and the Global Advocacy Council for Physical Activity (2010) document: Investments that work for Physical Activity, which complements the Toronto Charter for Physical Activity: A Global Call to Action.

Structure of BOSS – a multi-disciplinary approach

The ENOS network has brought together a multi-disciplinary and multi-cultural team to ensure greater objectivity and diversity to the project. Within the team there are:

1. Representatives from seven different EU countries as well as from pan-European organisations.
2. Academics with expertise in systematic reviews, sports development and education, economic modelling and social return on investment calculations.
3. Policy makers at a regional and national level who are focused on outdoor sport development, management and promotion.
4. Practitioners who work at a grass roots level for delivery of outdoor sports opportunities and initiatives.
5. Network coordinators who bring together stakeholders from the outdoor and tourism industries at a European level.

Co-ordination

The project is being coordinated and led by the French National Outdoor Resource Centre (CREPS Rhone Alpes) and is utilising the skills and expertise of the various partners in a coordinated manner.

Stepped sequential approach

The project was undertaken through a systematic staged approach that involved three key stages and an overarching dissemination plan (see Figure 12.1).

Stage 1

A systematic review of existing studies across Europe was carried out. This was led by partners from Technical University Munich (TUM) and at the time of publication this element of the project has been completed (Eigenschenk et al., 2019). The process for gathering this data was carried out, in an innovative manner, by searching national databases in each partner country as well as large scale international databases. An agreed search string was developed that included three forms of keywords: an element of nature or outdoor combined with forms

FIGURE 12.1 Structure of the BOSS project

of physical, active exercise and the description of effects. The search string was translated into the participating partner languages and a timeframe of 15 years from March 2002 to March 2017 was set. This provided studies in a range of languages and from a large variety of backgrounds and sources. Evidence that a very broad range of benefits can be accrued from outdoor sports was therefore collated and translated into English. This evidence has been categorised into five broad areas and also a category for those "additional" benefits that did not fit with these categories:

1. Physical health
2. Mental health and wellbeing
3. Education and life-long learning
4. Active citizenship
5. Crime and anti-social behaviour
6. Additional benefits

Stage 2

The second stage involves bringing together an expert group to develop an appropriate methodology and model to assess the economic value of these identified benefits. This stage is being led by the Sports Industry Research Centre at Sheffield Hallam University who have been instrumental in the measurement of the social impact of sport in the UK. The group will also identify and include external experts in the field of Social Value to provide a check and challenge function, thereby ensuring that the model developed is robust.

Stage 3

The other partners from across the seven member states will provide a minimum of five case studies each of "live" projects or programmes that can be used to test the model. A steering group led by The National Sports Academy in Bulgaria along with The Union des Centres de Plein Air (UCPA) in France who have expertise in sports education and development will then select the 12 most appropriate case studies for testing. This will ensure there is variety in terms of geographical, type of outdoor sport, environment and participant profile so that the model can be tested in a variety of settings and in a practical manner. This testing phase is essential to ensure the veracity and practicability of the methodology developed.

On completion of the testing phase, evaluation and modifications can be applied to the methodology to facilitate the creation of a toolkit/methodological approach that can be practically used by other projects and organisations.

Dissemination

Throughout the lifespan and especially at key stages of the project, the results, reports, data and ultimately the toolkit will be disseminated widely through the BOSS (www.outdoorsportsbenefits.eu) and ENOS (www.outdoor-sports-network.eu) websites and database. This element of the project will be led by Sport Northern Ireland and the European Outdoor Group (a consortium of the equipment manufacturers and outdoor businesses in Europe). Both these organisations have a strong marketing element and are well renowned at an EU level for their involvement in outdoor sports.

Details and results from stage 1

One of the preliminary tasks of the partnership was to agree a definition for outdoor sports. This was a challenging task, as there are a plethora of sports and activities that use the natural and semi-natural environment as venues for their activities. The partnership had to be cognisant of this and that these may involve the use of one or more of the elements of land, water or air. For the purposes of this project, outdoor sports are defined as activities:

- that are normally carried out with a (strong) **relation to nature** and landscape and the **core aim is dealing with natural elements** rather than with an object
- where the **natural setting** is perceived by users, as at most, only minimally modified by human beings*
- that are perceived as (at least minimally) **physical demanding**
- that are based on man or natural element power and are not motorised during the sport itself
- that may use some form of tool (for example a surf board, bicycle, skis etc.) or just involve the human body
- that have their roots in natural places but may use artificial structures designed to replicate the natural environment.

* does not have to be wild, just perceived as natural.

From all databases and partner searches, a total number of 20,950 hits came up in the primary searches. After deletion of duplicates, this reduced to 17,560 studies that were then screened for inclusion or exclusion. The studies were initially screened by title and abstract and then, if required, the researchers consulted the full text as a second step for confirmation. After the national selection process, the studies were additionally verified by TUM team.

Within this process a total of 133 studies have been selected. Standardised forms were developed to extract relevant data from the selected studies. This data extraction was made from the full texts and included the following data: full reference, title in English, methodological design, country, sample description (age, number of participants, population), description of study and interventions, type of sport, key findings, description of social benefits and outcomes, quantification of results and methods used.

The publication dates showed that interest in the field of outdoor sports research appears to have increased over the selection period of the last 15 years (see Figure 12.2). This verifies the statement of Dickson, Gray, and Mann who explained: "As the empirical and anecdotal evidence in the outdoor adventure field begins to unfold, the proliferation of evidenced-based research grows exponentially" (2008, p. iv).

An analysis of the origin of the data shows that most of the selected studies emanated from English speaking countries with over a quarter of studies from the U.S.A. (26.3%). This is not surprising as there is a long interest and research tradition in the field of outdoor sports from these countries. The total from European countries was 72 studies (over 54%).

In terms of the quality of the evidence base, an important aspect is the methodological design of the studies. 6% of the studies followed the approach of a systematic review or meta-analyses. 27.8% have compared effects of an intervention to a control group, either with a randomised controlled trial design or a case-control design. 11.3% compared effects of an intervention over time with an ex-post facto or pre-post design and 14.3% analysed cross-sectional measurements or surveys. Most of the studies (40.6%) followed a qualitative approach with a case report, qualitative evaluation, narrative, non-systematic literature reviews or theoretical papers.

The benefits of outdoor sports for society

The compilation of studies provides a great resource and overview on the range of benefits of outdoor sports for individuals, groups and for society. Benefits have been grouped to six broad categories including additional benefits that were not foreseen in the research process (see Figure 12.3).

The majority of studies (73 articles) deal with the effect of outdoor sports on mental health benefits followed by the positive effects on education and lifelong learning (55 studies) and physical health (45 studies). 23 studies came up in the research process that focus on active citizenship and only 11 studies highlighted the effect of outdoor sports on crime reduction and anti-social behaviour as a central theme. 44 studies were listed as additional benefits.

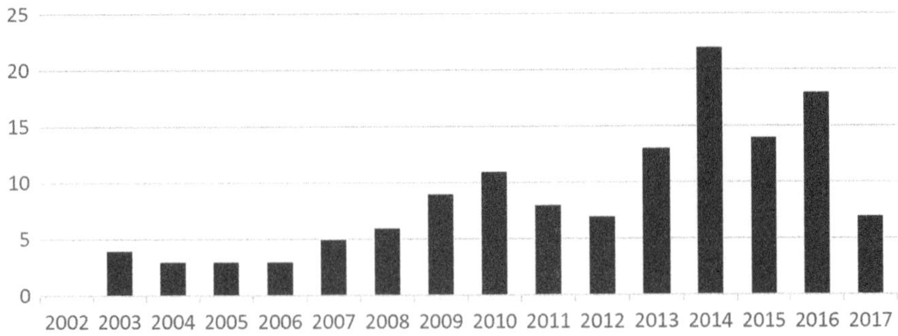

FIGURE 12.2 Publication dates of selected studies (note: studies from 2017 have only been included up to March 2017)

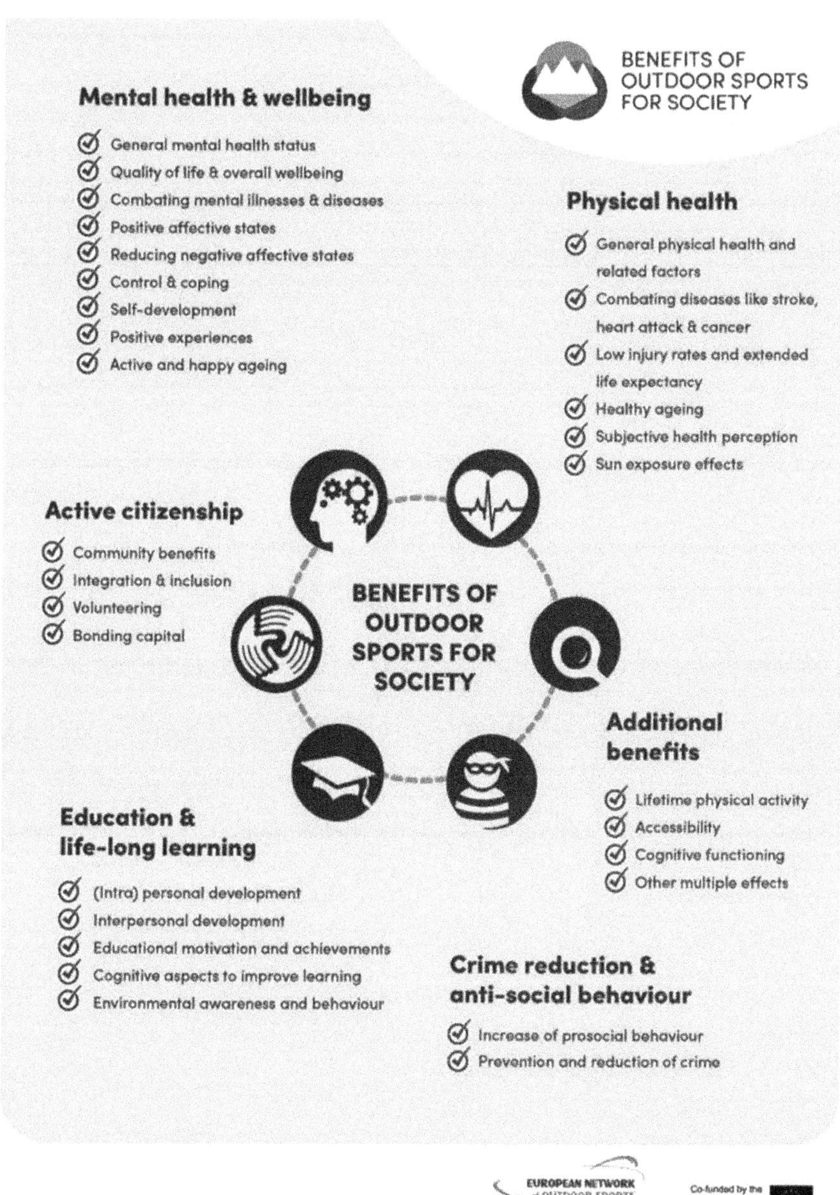

FIGURE 12.3 Overview of the benefits of outdoor sports for society

Following are a range of insights from these studies and research fields as well as implications for therapeutic and educational practice. The snapshots of benefits highlighted are good examples of the information that has been extracted during the literature research.

Physical health benefits

Outdoor sports are associated with a range of positive health benefits in like manner to physical activity in general. This starts with general health related factors such as increased fitness and better cardiovascular function, as well as reduced blood pressure, obesity, resting heart rate and a positive influence on other health markers. Consequently, those health enhancing effects result in a reduced risk for several major conditions or diseases such as heart attack, stroke, cancer and type 2 diabetes. Blond, Rasmussen, Østergaard, and Grøntved (2016) highlighted that Danish cyclists had 11 to 18% fewer heart attacks, which rises to a 26% lower risk of developing coronary artery disease when participants started and then maintained active biking. For the activity of hiking, Hakim et al. (1999) (in Kux & Wolfgang, 2014) show a 50% reduction in the risk of coronary artery disease. High levels of leisure-time physical activity were also associated with lower risks of 13 cancer types, including oesophageal (-42%), liver (-27%), lung (-26%), kidney (-23%), stomach (-22%), endometrial (-21%), myeloid leukemia (-20%), myeloma (-17%), colon (-16%), head and neck (-15%), rectal (-13%), bladder (-13%) and breast cancer (-10%) (Moore et al., 2016).

While outdoor sports are often discussed in the context of injuries and a high risk of cases of death, this cannot be confirmed through this research. On the contrary, inactivity is identified as a much greater risk for premature deaths and a shorter life-expectancy (de Moor, 2015).

Besides the reduction in risk of diseases, outdoor sports also lead to a better subjective overall health perception and physical quality of life. In the context of healthy ageing, outdoor sports help the elderly to maintain their physical performance, especially with improved balance. Furthermore, exposure to sunlight has been shown to help to maintain the level of vitamin D (25OHD level) especially in the elderly (De Rui et al., 2014), and outdoor activities are highlighted as helping to prevent multiple sclerosis (Dalmay et al., 2010) and the onset and progression of myopia (Russo et al., 2014).

Mental health and wellbeing benefits

Most published articles identified through the systematic review focused on the benefits to mental health of being active in nature. The studies identified the need to deal with mental disorders but also the various opportunities that outdoor sports create that can help to prevent and alleviate mental health problems. Green and blue environments were shown to have especially positive effects that go beyond the benefits of being physically active. Several research teams show the positive effects of being active in a natural environment on general mental health and psychological stability as well as overall wellbeing, quality of life, happiness and life satisfaction (see also Chapter 4 on the green exercise concept of Rogerson & Barton). The research of Mitchell (2013) concludes that there is a correlation between regular activity in a natural environment setting and a lower risk of poor mental health. Each additional physical activity session in the natural environment per week could be associated with a 6% lower risk of poor mental health. Bratman, Hamilton, Hahn, Daily, and Gross (2015) show one possible explanation of the positive effect of green exercise on a reduced risk of mental illness. A 90-minute walk in a natural setting decreased both self-reported rumination and neural activity in an area of the brain linked to risk of mental illness, whereas no such effects appeared in the urban walks.

Outdoor sports are not only presented as having the potential to help in the prevention of mental illnesses, they are also used in the treatment of them, with prominent examples including Alzheimer's disease (de Moor, 2015), dementia (Mapes, 2016) or major depressive disorders.

Based on relevant literature and various qualitative statements from case studies, Mapes (2016) gives a narrative insight on the benefits of green exercise for people with dementia. Those include physical benefits like better eating and sleeping patterns, better fitness and mobility and fewer falls, but also psychological and wellbeing benefits like increased happiness, an improved emotional state through reduced stress, agitation, anger, apathy and depression, and a higher level of self-esteem. Furthermore, social benefits like improved interaction with other people, the reconnection with places and activities they love, as well as a sense of belonging, helps patients to lead better quality lives.

Outdoor sports are also used as therapeutic treatment for children with autism. The study of Stuhl and Porter (2015) summarises the effects of three different surf camp programmes on the improvement of social skills. The surfing programme is shown to significantly improve outcomes for assertion and empathy, responsibility and engagement, positive functioning, physical health, emotional wellbeing, resilience, self-esteem, vitality, friendship, social trust, and enjoyment in the outside environment.

Education and life-long learning benefits

The previous example shows that some of the benefits highlighted are cross cutting and cannot be placed in just one category. In many instances, issues of mental health and wellbeing sometimes are combined with other benefits for education and the development of personal and social skills.

As outdoor sports provide an environment that leads to an intense contact with oneself and others, there are many benefits for personal development, especially for young people. The experience-based pedagogy sector provides evidence on various different educational benefits from outdoor sports including experience-based lessons within the school or college curriculum, or expedition programmes of Friluftsliv in Norway, or crossing the Alps by foot. Within this field, the pilot study of Henstock, Barker, and Knijnik (2013) shows the impact of a sailing programme on at risk or disengaged young people. Participation in the sailing voyage had a positive effect on development of social relationships and networking skills, general self-concept, motivation to study, and sense of purpose for learning.

The intense contact and relation to nature in outdoor sports is also highlighted as having positive effects on environmental attitudes of people. A longer-term programme seems to be most effective but some educational programmes aim to develop this through more condensed interventions. The five-day extra-curricular outdoor sports programme "Ticket2nature" is a good example of a concentrated outdoor sport intervention with children. Evaluations of the programme show a positive short-term effect on the students' environmental attitudes. It is noteworthy that interventions seemed most effective for children from urban areas and for students who had a lower level of academic attainment (Limmer & Roth, 2016).

Outdoor activities are also seen to be effective for either the treatment of or improving the education of a range of people with special needs including children with disabilities, veterans, ADHD sufferers, drug addicts and young people with autism, or who are at risk or perceived as disorderly.

Faber Taylor and Kuo (2008) analyse the effects of 20-minute walks in different environments on attention in children with ADHD. Their results show that the children concentrated significantly better after a walk in the park compared to a downtown or a neighbourhood walk and achieved results that are comparable with medication by methylphenidate (commonly branded as Ritalin). The authors conclude that walking in natural settings can enhance attention not only in the general population but also in those with ADHD.

Active citizenship benefits

Outdoor sports provide opportunities and places for social contacts and relations and help in the inclusion or (re-)integration of special groups. Furthermore, outdoor sports are associated with community benefits like the construction and maintenance of local community life, identity and pride. Donoghue, O'Connell, and Kenny (2016) showed that older people (50+) who participated in regular walking, report greater participation in social activities and lower loneliness scores than those who are less physically active.

Zabriskie, Lundberg, and Groff (2005) showcase how outdoor adaptive sports programmes such as skiing and horse riding can increase a sense of community participation for disabled people. The ethnographic study of Beaumont and Brown (2015) describes how shared experiences of local surfers can play a positive cultural role, for individuals and for the construction and maintenance of local community life.

Crime reduction and (anti-)social behaviour benefits

Only 11 studies focused on the benefits of crime reduction and (anti-)social behaviour and the evidence base is primarily qualitative and anecdotal reports from the field. However, the studies found give valuable insights into how outdoor sports can be used to increase prosocial behaviour, to prevent youth delinquency or how to improve the behaviour and habits of adults with drug addiction or other social exclusion factors.

An example from a surf therapy programme describes the effects of an intervention for children and young people in foster care institutions (Matos et al., 2017). Results suggest that surf therapy had a number of positive intra and interpersonal effects in vulnerable, at risk young people. These include improved effort and perseverance, problem-solving, time management, social competencies, interpersonal relationships and emotional regulation. The children's tutors reported a statistically significant decrease in the emotional symptoms, behavioural problems and in a scale that assessed difficulties.

Additional benefits

There were a number of examples of studies and programmes that show that participating in outdoor sports can have positive effects that surpass those of physical activity alone. In this context, Thompson Coon et al. (2011) have conducted a systematic review of the comparative effects of participating in indoor and outdoor activity that confirms these effects. The benefits of exercising in natural environments were that participants had greater feelings of revitalisation and positive engagement, decreases in tension, confusion, anger and depression. The authors highlighted however another important aspect of outdoor sports was that as participants reported greater enjoyment and satisfaction with the activity, they then declared a greater intention to repeat the activity at a later date. Outdoor sports are seen by this and other studies as positively influencing long-term adherence to physical activity.

Conclusions and further outlook

The results of the literature review back up the common knowledge and the feeling of many practitioners about the positive effects of outdoor sports. As a conclusion it can be summarised that:

- Outdoor sports effectively combine the positive outcomes of physical activity and being in nature.
- Mental health and wellbeing are significantly improved by participation in outdoor sports, and there are a wide range of physical health benefits for individuals. However, outdoor sports are also effective for intra and interpersonal development and contribute to other social benefits such as active citizenship and crime reduction.
- Connecting people with nature and resulting improved environmental education and awareness are a key facet of outdoor sports.
- Outdoor sports provide a broad range of sport and recreational activities and opportunities that both engage and provide benefits to people of all ages, social or economic background and ability.

- Outdoor sports have few limitations to participation and are great for providing life-long physical activity.

This overview highlights that there are numerous positive benefits for both individuals and communities from outdoor sports. However, it has to be admitted that the evidence base is not equally strong for all types of benefits. While the evidence base on health benefits is becoming more scientifically verified, there still seems to be a lack of evidence for the social benefits associated with personal and social development.

This chapter has focused on the benefits identified from outdoor sports literature (stage 1 of the project). However, as previously highlighted, information on all selected studies (stage 1), the details of the model developed (stage 2) and results from the testing of this model in real life projects (stage 3) will be published on the BOSS and ENOS websites.

References

Beaumont, E. & Brown, D.H.K. (2015). 'Once a Local Surfer, Always a Local Surfer': Local Surfing Careers in a Southwest English Village. *Leisure Sciences*, 37(1), pp.68–86.

Blond, K., Rasmussen, M., Østergaard, L. & Grøntved, A. (2016). Prospective Study of Bicycling and Risk of Coronary Heart Disease in Danish Men and Women. *Circulation*, 134(18), pp.1409–1411.

Bratman, G.N., Hamilton, J.P., Hahn, K.S., Daily, G.C. & Gross, J.J. (2015). Nature Experience Reduces Rumination and Subgenual Prefrontal Cortex Activation. *Proceedings of the National Academy of Science*, 112(28), pp.8567–8572.

Coalter, F. (2005). *The Social Benefits of Sport. An Overview to Inform the Community Planning Process*. Research Report no. 98. Sportscotland. Retrieved from: https://sportscotland.org.uk/../thesocialbenefitsofsport.doc

Commission of the European Communities. (2007). *European White Paper on Sport*. Retrieved from https://eur-lex.europa.eu/legal-content/EN/TXT/?uri=celex:52007DC0391

Dalmay, F., Bhalla, D., Nicoletti, A., Cabrera-Gomez, J.A., Cabre, P., Ruiz, F., et al. (2010). Multiple Sclerosis and Solar Exposure Before the Age of 15 Years: Case–Control Study in Cuba, Martinique and Sicily. *Multiple Sclerosis Journal*, 6(8), pp.899–908.

de Moor, D. (2015). *Walking Works: Making the Case to Encourage Greater Uptake of Walking as a Physical Activity and Recognise the Value and Benefits of Walking for Health*. London, UK: Ramblers and Macmillan Cancer Support.

De Rui, M., Toffanello, E.D., Veronese, N., Zambon, S., Bolzetta, F., Sartori, L., et al. (2014). Vitamin D Deficiency and Leisure Time Activities in the Elderly: Are All Pastimes the Same?. *PLoS One*, 9(4), p.e94805.

Dickson, T., Gray, T. & Mann, K. (2008). *Australian Outdoor Adventure Activity. Benefits Catalogue*. n.p: University of Canberra.

Directorate-General for Communication. (2018). *EU Special Eurobarometer 472 on Sport and Physical Activity*. Retrieved from https://data.europa.eu/euodp/data/dataset/S2164_88_4_472_ENG

Directorate-General for Education, Youth, Sport and Culture (European Commission). (2013). *Sport Satellite Accounts, a European Project*. Retrieved from https://publications.europa.eu/en/publication-detail/-/publication/d44cae16-23bc-4cee-8bc8-f1411c447464.

Donoghue, O., O'Connell, M. & Kenny, R.A. (2016). *Walking to Wellbeing: Physical Activity, Social Participation and Psychological Health in Irish Adults Aged 50 Years and Older.* Dublin, Ireland: TILDA (The Irish Longitudinal Study on Ageing).

Eigenschenk, B., Thomann, A., McClure, M., Davies, L., Gregory, M., Dettweiler, U. & Inglés, E. (2019). Benefits of Outdoor Sports for Society. A Systematic Literature Review and Reflections on Evidence. *International Journal of Environmental Research and Public Health*, 16, E937. doi:10.3390/ijerph16060937

EU Physical Activity Guidelines. (2008). *Recommended Policy Actions in Support of Health-Enhancing Physical Activity*. Brussels. Retrieved from http://ec.europa.eu/assets/eac/sport/library/policy_documents/eu-physical-activity-guidelines-2008_en.pdf

Faber Taylor, A. & Kuo, F.E. (2008). Children with Attention Deficits Concentrate Better after Walk in the Park. *Journal of Attention Disorders*, 12(5), pp.402–409.

Global Advocacy Council for Physical Activity. (2010). The Toronto Charter for Physical Activity: A Global Call for Action. *The Journal of Physical Activity and Health*, 7(3), pp.370–S373.

Henstock, M., Barker, K. & Knijnik, J. (2013). 2, 6, Heave! Sail Training's Influence on the Development of Self-Concept and Social Networks and Their Impact on Engagement with Learning and Education. A Pilot Study. *Australian Journal of Outdoor Education*, 17(1), pp.32–46.

Kux, S. & Wolfgang, H. (2014). *Health Benefits of Non-Motorized Outdoor Recreation: A Summary of Published Findings*. Burnaby, BC: School of Resource and Environmental Management, Simon Fraser University.

Limmer, M., & Roth, R. (2016). Effects of a 5-Day Outdoor Sports Intervention on Environmental Attitudes in Children. In A. Baca (Hrsg.), *Book of Abstracts – 21. Annual Congress of the European College of Sport Science: Crossing Borders through Sport Science* (p. 520). Vienna: European College of Sport Science.

Mapes, N. (2016). Green Exercise and Dementia. In J. Barton, R. Bragg, C. Wood & J. N. Pretty (Eds.), *Green Exercise: Linking Nature, Health and Well-Being* (pp. 150–160). London: Routledge.

Matos, M.G., Santos, A., Fauvelet, C., Marta, F., Evangelista, E.S., Ferreira, J., et al. (2017). Surfing for Social Integration: Mental Health and Well-Being promotion through Surf Therapy among Institutionalized Young People. *Journal of Community Medicine and Public Health Care*, 4(1), pp.1–6. doi:10.24966/CMPH-1978/100026

Mitchell, R. (2013). Is Physical Activity in Natural Environments Better for Mental Health Than Physical Activity in Other Environments? *Social Science & Medicine*, 91, pp.130–134.

Moore, S.C., Lee, I.-M., Weiderpass, E., Campbell, P.T., Sampson, J.N., Kitahara, C.M. et al. (2016). Association of Leisure-Time Physical Activity With Risk of 26 Types of Cancer in 1.44 Million Adults. *JAMA Internal Medicine*, 176(6), pp. 816–825. Published online.

Russo A., Semeraro F., Romano M.R., Matropasqua R., Dell'Omo R. & Castagliola C. (2014). Myopia Onset and Progression: Can It be Prevented? *International Ophthalmology*, 34, pp. 693–705.

Stuhl, A. & Porter, H. (2015). Riding the Waves: Therapeutic Surfing to Improve Social Skills for Children with Autism. *Therapeutic Recreation Journal*, 49(3), pp.253–256.

The European Network of Outdoor Sports. (2013). *Charter for outdoor sports*. Retrieved from www.outdoorsportsnetwork.eu/charter

Thompson Coon, J., Boddy, K., Stein, K., Whear, R., Barton, J. & Depledge, M.H. (2011). Does Participating in Physical Activity in Outdoor Natural Environments Have a Greater Effect on Physical and Mental Wellbeing than Physical Activity Indoors? A Systematic Review. *Environmental Science & Technology*, 45(5), pp.1761–1772.

Zabriskie, R.B., Lundberg, N.R. & Groff, D.G. (2005). Quality of Life and Identity: The Benefits of a Community-Based Therapeutic Recreation and Adaptive Sports Program. *Therapeutic Recreation Journal*, 39(3), pp. 176–191.

13

'DOING' ADVENTURE

The mental health benefits of using occupational therapy approaches in adventure therapy settings

Mike Rogerson, Sinéad Kelly, Simone Coetzee, Jo Barton and Jules Pretty

This chapter considers how occupational therapy approaches could be applied and used skilfully within adventure therapy settings, due to the shared principles, aims and preferred methods of improving health in both disciplines. Here we focus on how the challenges and demands presented by specific occupations within adventure therapy can ameliorate states of mental distress and accompanying symptoms. Occupational therapy provides the means to use participation and collaboration to overcome everyday occupational barriers, while adventure therapy provides alternative spaces and means for these barriers to be faced. This combination of participation, collaboration and adventure is a new opportunity for both disciplines to consider their roles and the benefits of a partnership in promoting wellbeing in a unique, person-centred and effective way.

Adventure therapy

Outdoor recreation has, in the last decade, been recognised for its positive influence on health and wellbeing (Frances, 2006). The term *outdoor recreation* encapsulates a variety of activities, including but not limited to: walking, hill walking, rock climbing, camping, kayaking, canoeing, ropes courses and abseiling, which take place in diverse natural environments (Bowen & Neill, 2013). Outdoor recreation activities are often utilised within *adventure therapy* to help people cope with a diverse range of issues, including psychosocial difficulties (Bowen & Neill, 2013). *Adventure therapy* is often referred to alongside adjacent, alternative terms, such as wilderness therapy, ecotherapy, therapeutic outdoor programming, bush adventure therapy, outdoor behavioural therapy, adventure based counselling, wilderness adventure therapy and more recently, nature based/green therapy (Richards, Carpenter, & Harper, 2011). There is continuing debate in relation to the interchangeability of terms (Crisp, 1996; Hine, Pretty, & Barton, 2009); in this current chapter, we use the term *adventure therapy* to refer to the overall therapeutic use of challenging activities that take place in natural outdoor environments (Bowen & Neill, 2013).

Common underlying principles

Clear links exist between the principles, aims and approaches of occupational therapy and adventure therapy. A core tenet of occupational therapy is that the activity choices that people make can influence their health (Creek, 2014; Pretty, Rogerson, & Barton, 2017). Occupational therapists are specifically concerned with the meaning that individuals place on their chosen occupations (Duncan, 2011), and view individuals holistically rather than one-dimensionally (College of Occupational Therapists, 2015). This is represented within models of practice and approaches to interventions, which provide occupational therapists with the methods needed to treat a person holistically (Turpin & Iwama, 2011). A biopsychosocial approach to health ensures that biological, psychological and sociological factors, which are unique to every individual, are considered when providing interventions and support, to promote engagement with their regular environments. Parallel to this, adventure therapy uses a 'deliberate, strategic combination of adventure activities and therapeutic change processes with the goal of making lasting changes in the lives of participants' (Gillis & Ringer, 1999). Likewise emphasis is placed on enabling participants to engage in meaningful experiences using holistic processes (Gass, Gillis, & Russell, 2012). This emphasis of adventure therapy is also concurrent with occupational therapists Christiansen and Townsend's view of enablement (Christiansen & Townsend, 2003), which highlights the importance of providing people with the necessary tools for more independent participation.

Further linkage comes via experiential learning, which includes reflection on the action of doing (Wolf & Mehl, 2011). Experiential learning is a key component of adventure therapy, assisting individuals to cope with and grow from personal struggles (Bowen & Neill, 2013; Kolb, 2014; Luckner & Nadler, 1997; Panicucci, 2007), and this concept is not dissimilar to Wilcock's notions of *doing, being, becoming and belonging*, which are integral elements of principles of occupational therapy (Wilcock, 1999; Wilcock & Hocking, 2015).

Adventure therapy can be of use in improving a range of aspects of an individual's functionality and health and wellbeing. As well as general discussion about such usage, this chapter focuses particularly on beneficial engagement for individuals experiencing mental distress (Clough, Mackenzie, Mallabon, & Brymer, 2016; Epstein, 2004; Ewert & Yoshino, 2011), because mental health problems are one of the leading causes of overall global disease burden (Vos et al., 2015), and are often a prominent factor directly requiring attention from occupational therapists. The term mental distress can cover a broad range of diagnoses, with post-traumatic stress disorder, schizophrenia, anxiety and depression being amongst the most common.

Low self-esteem, mood, and a lack of confidence can lead to difficulties in relation to engaging and participating in meaningful activities within individuals' everyday lives. Although occupational therapists have worked with people experiencing mental ill-health for decades (Paterson, 2014), there is little evidence of the use of adventure therapy as a therapeutic tool. However, adventure therapy offers great scope for the purposes of occupational therapy assessments (Gass et al., 2012), and serves as an extensive platform for occupational therapy's approach of using meaningful activity as a means of intervention.

Psychological impacts of outdoor settings

Occupational therapy based in outdoor environments is a growing research area, which has, at this point, built only a relatively small base of evidence. The environment, however, is a key aspect when considering any therapeutic intervention, as each environment brings different challenges, meanings and opportunities to an individual. Outdoor settings can be unpredictable and more difficult to adapt to different needs, but they do offer a therapeutic element of their own, as documented by Kaplan (Kaplan, 1995), Fieldhouse and Sempik (Fieldhouse & Sempik, 2014), Gonzales (Gonzalez, Hartig, Patil, Martinsen, & Kirkevold, 2010) and many others. Research evidence across a range of domains suggests that outdoor nature environments can be psychologically restorative (Li & Sullivan, 2016; Pretty et al., 2017; Rogerson & Barton, 2015; Tang et al., 2017), improving mood and self-esteem (Barton, Griffin, & Pretty, 2012; Barton, Hine, & Pretty, 2009; Barton & Pretty, 2010; Barton, Wood, Pretty, & Rogerson, 2016; Rogerson, Gladwell, Gallagher, & Barton, 2016; Thompson Coon et al., 2011), and improving recovery from acute mental stress (Brown, Barton, & Gladwell, 2013; Gladwell et al., 2012).

Reduction of stress

Stress Reduction Theory is partly derived from psycho-evolutionary theory (Plutchik, 1980a, 1980b) and is based on historical human-environment interactions and relationships. It suggests that, when there is an absence of threat, nature environments invoke positive primary emotional responses, which promote recovery from stress (Ewert, Overholt, Voight, & Wang, 2011; Herzog & Strevey, 2008; Ulrich, 1984, 1981; Ulrich et al., 1991). This is important for wellbeing as primary emotions are related to secondary and tertiary emotions (Plutchik, 1980a), which can also be termed 'affect'. Natural environments also provide positive distractions from daily stresses and invoke feelings of interest, pleasantness and calm, thereby further reducing stress symptoms and promoting positive affect (Ewert et al., 2011; Herzog & Strevey, 2008; Ulrich, 1984, 1981; Ulrich et al., 1991). Studies supporting this theory report reductions in stress measures, such as blood pressure, heart rate and stress hormones, following exposure to nature (Hartig, Evans, Jamner, Davis, & Gärling, 2003; Herzog & Strevey, 2008; Laumann, Gärling, & Stormark,

2003; Ulrich et al., 1991). After viewing a psychologically stressful video, simply viewing scenes of nature improves recovery of parasympathetic activity, compared to viewing urban scenes (Ulrich et al., 1991).

Improved attention

In addition to Stress Reduction Theory, Attention Restoration Theory proposes that humans can attend to 'softly fascinating' elements of nature environments using minimal attentional resource, and that this provides opportunity for restoration of depleted attentional resources, which is accompanied by affective (e.g. mood) improvements (Berman, Jonides, & Kaplan, 2008; Corbetta & Shulman, 2002; Fan, McCandliss, Fossella, Flombaum, & Posner, 2005; Kaplan, 1995; Kaplan & Berman, 2010; Rogerson & Barton, 2015; Tang et al., 2017). Pointing further towards the relevance of person-environment interaction, Green Mind Theory outlines that the human brain, body and behaviour are linked to physical and social environments, and that these reciprocally influence one another (Pretty et al., 2017). In these ways, adventure therapy can function as a vehicle via which the natural environment can become an additional factor for managing mental distress and associated symptoms. Furthermore, when cases of mental distress are accompanied or contributed to by psychological burn-out, restoration of attentional resources might aid a participant's ability to mentally engage in activities requiring concentration, thereby increasing the likelihood that their potential efficacy will be realised. Many people also regard the natural environment as an escape from the reality of difficult circumstances at home (Kyriakopoulos, 2011), which can further function to facilitate mind-sets conducive to occupational therapy. Indeed, participants have reported that a wilderness setting itself encouraged their engagement in an intervention, and that being away in this environment provided space to reflect and process emotions (Scheinfeld, Rochlen, & Buser, 2011). This body of research clearly evidences the therapeutic health benefits of engaging in activities in outdoor green settings, which can easily be harnessed within occupational therapy practice.

Gavin, a young man in his late twenties, came across the community market garden on the outskirts of London when he enrolled in an evening course there. He had been feeling low up until that point, having been involved in construction work that felt wrong for him physically, socially and emotionally. He was consequently unemployed and struggling with depression, having lost confidence in his abilities and sense of direction.

The market garden, on first sight left him 'blown away by the views'. He remarked how he struggled at first with the social side of working alongside other community garden volunteers due to his lack of confidence and the different nature of the garden to a building site. But he slowly realised how he started to like the person he recognised developing inside himself, more confident with the work he was doing in the garden and more able to relate to people due to the shared intention of the growing work. He felt the 'peace and quiet' of the garden and the work itself had slowly changed him and given him a sense of purpose in life.

(Case study adapted from Coetzee, 2016)

Opportunities offered by the outdoor adventure environment

Offering an approach to understanding relationships between individuals, tasks and environments (both social and physical), the ecological dynamics perspective views each of the individual, the environment and the task as a system comprising a complex arrangement of factors termed 'constraints' (Brymer & Davids, 2012). For example, within the 'individual' system, cognitive, affective and physiological states, physical flexibility, and limb length all represent 'constraints'. Ecological dynamics considers how these complex systems can constrain or promote processes and shape behaviours relating to human wellbeing (Brymer & Davids, 2014; Brymer, Davids, & Mallabon, 2014; Yeh et al., 2015). Resonating with this perspective, adventure therapy activities afford opportunities for individuals to tackle and master new and novel challenges and skills, in an alternative contextual setting, either as an individual or as part of a group (Granerud & Eriksson, 2014).

Pretty et al.'s Green Mind Theory posits that a greener, calmer mind centres on activities that bring immersive-attentiveness; and that engagement with nature and other people while participating in craft or skill based activities supports this sense of immersive-attentiveness (Pretty et al., 2017). Survey responses relating to outdoor therapy experiences indicate that although overcoming specific barriers in that environment with a therapist is important, the being in the outdoor environment is sometimes the most important underlying component of the therapy (Revell, Duncan, & Cooper, 2014). This seems concurrent with Brymer et al.'s interpretation of the ecological dynamics perspective that, comparatively, nature environments and adventure activities more readily offer 'challenging, complex, varied, and intense affordances whereby individuals are invited to experience a broad range of perceived pleasurable and non-pleasurable emotions and to experience undertaking action despite these emotions' (Brymer et al., 2014). A great deal can be experienced and learnt about personal transition through coping with the challenges posed in nature, and the change in seasons through time (Fieldhouse & Sempik, 2014; Granerud & Eriksson, 2014). In this way, adventure therapy can be used to create scenarios that encourage and enable individuals to behave in ways that access beneficial processes and outcomes.

Building mental resilience through adventure therapy can significantly contribute to the efficacy of occupational therapy in enhancing individual *mental capital* – an individual's cognitive and emotional skill and reserve, that directs how they are able to contribute to society and the quality of life that they experience (Collins et al., 2011; Duncan & Creek, 2014). It is difficult to ascertain from the literature which specific adventure activities might be most beneficial. Koperski, Tucker, Lung, and Gass (2015) found that no one specific activity or environment accounted for positive outcomes within adventure therapy, and Clough et al. emphasise that even extreme adventure activities often have positive impacts on psychological and overall wellbeing, and should be included as a viable mental health intervention (Clough et al., 2016). This indicates an aspect of intersectionality to the adventure therapy arena and occupational range, similar to that of other green care environments, allowing people with differing needs to access and apply different occupations to their lives (Coetzee, 2016).

The social components of adventure therapy

Occupational therapy views restriction of occupational engagement and social connectedness as an occupational injustice that requires addressing in order to reduce further exclusion and prevent the additional mental distress this could cause (Stadnyk, Townsend, & Wilcock, 2010). Wellbeing can be negatively impacted when individuals are excluded from engaging in activities that are meaningful to them, for example due to weight restrictions on certain adventure activities (Moxham, Liersch-Sumskis, Taylor, Patterson, & Brighton, 2015); or exclusion due to inaccessible activities or environments (Bryant, Pettican, & Coetzee, 2017). Within green care settings, nature engenders a sense of equality with others at the location, as there is often a common goal to be achieved (Bryant et al., 2017; Coetzee, 2016; Granerud & Eriksson, 2014). In adventure therapy settings, care should be taken to consider occupational justice issues, removing barriers to social and occupational participation where they might arise due to access and activity complexity.

Social interaction is an often-documented, prominent and critically important characteristic of adventure therapy. A sense of social inclusion can be a simultaneously occurring by-product of shared experiences, mutual encouragement, social reassurance and learning to take collaborative approaches to the activities (Cotton & Butselaar, 2013; Kelley, Coursey, & Selby, 1997; Vella, Milligan, & Bennett, 2013). Vella et al. reported that the social support developed through outdoor recreational activity was a lasting and highly important aspect of the intervention for individuals with PTSD (Vella et al., 2013). In line with Voruganti's biopsychosocial approach (Voruganti et al., 2006), a combination of physical activity, nature and social support is important for positive and sustained health changes (Barton et al., 2012; Granerud & Eriksson, 2014), and these key aspects of occupational therapy are well catered for by an adventure therapy approach.

Although little-discussed in the literature, it should also be considered that social and other connected elements of adventure therapy have the potential to impact negatively on social anxieties; for example, if intra-group personalities are not well suited, where recipients have particular mental health difficulties, or if participants are challenged to do something that is too difficult or overwhelming for them, creating a poor occupational fit between the demand and the person's capabilities (Amini et al., 2014). Meeting fellow participants prior to the adventure therapy intervention can help to reduce social anxieties (Kyriakopoulos,

2011), and many of those who have participated in adventure therapy studies have reported that they enjoyed belonging to a group, and that their relationships with fellow participants were of more importance than their relationship with the therapist (Bryson, Feinstein, Spavor, & Kidd, 2013; Revell et al., 2014). Despite this, the prospect of achieving goals collaboratively set between therapist and participant is also positive, particularly for those who find initiation or the idea of what to engage in, difficult (Levack, 2003); one study reported that the therapeutic relationship was most valued by participants who appreciated the therapist's ability to offer adaptation and choice (Koperski et al., 2015). The idea of co-occupation (Pickens & Pizur-Barnekow, 2009; Pierce, 2009), a concept highlighting the positive relationship between two people collaboratively involved in shaping the action of one another, is useful when considering occupational therapy within green care or adventure settings (Coetzee, 2016). In the context of adventure therapy, activities offer great scope for co-occupation, for example, in rock climbing with another person. One-to-one and group interactions appear to be of equal importance for sustained results in managing interpersonal difficulties (Roberts, Stroud, Hoag, & Massey, 2017). The building of trust is an important component within adventure therapy. Both Kyriakopoulos and Scheinfeld et al. found that mutual trust was increased through social interactions that occur within cooperative group activities in adventure therapy (Kyriakopoulos, 2011; Scheinfeld et al., 2011).

Experiential processes and coping

The experiential nature of adventure therapy is complex and unique, therefore the impacts of these experiences can be attributed to any of several different variables, as depicted in Figure 13.1.

Kyriakopoulos highlighted that engaging in adventure therapy encouraged participants to *challenge themselves* rather than avoid activities that have the potential to be unsuccessful in some way (Kyriakopoulos, 2011). A disequilibrium is created during these challenging activities, which needs to be resolved by the participant to promote positive outcomes (Levack, 2003). Resonating strongly with Brymer et al.'s ecological dynamics perspective-based interpretation (Brymer & Davids, 2012, 2014; Brymer et al., 2014; Yeh et al., 2015), the implication is that engaging in challenging outdoor activities includes a satisfactory level of risk, can enhance confidence and motivation, and increases one's capacity to cope, through overcoming the physical, mental and social demands associated with the activities (Bryson et al., 2013; Cotton & Butselaar, 2013; Moxham et al., 2015; Revell et al., 2014). Developing *reflective skills* and the *ability to share emotional experiences* have also been identified as important by those who have utilised adventure therapy for mental wellbeing (Kelley et al., 1997; Revell et al., 2014; Scheinfeld et al., 2011). Some participants also rely upon parallel services such as counselling and social support for encouragement and assistance with reflection and sharing

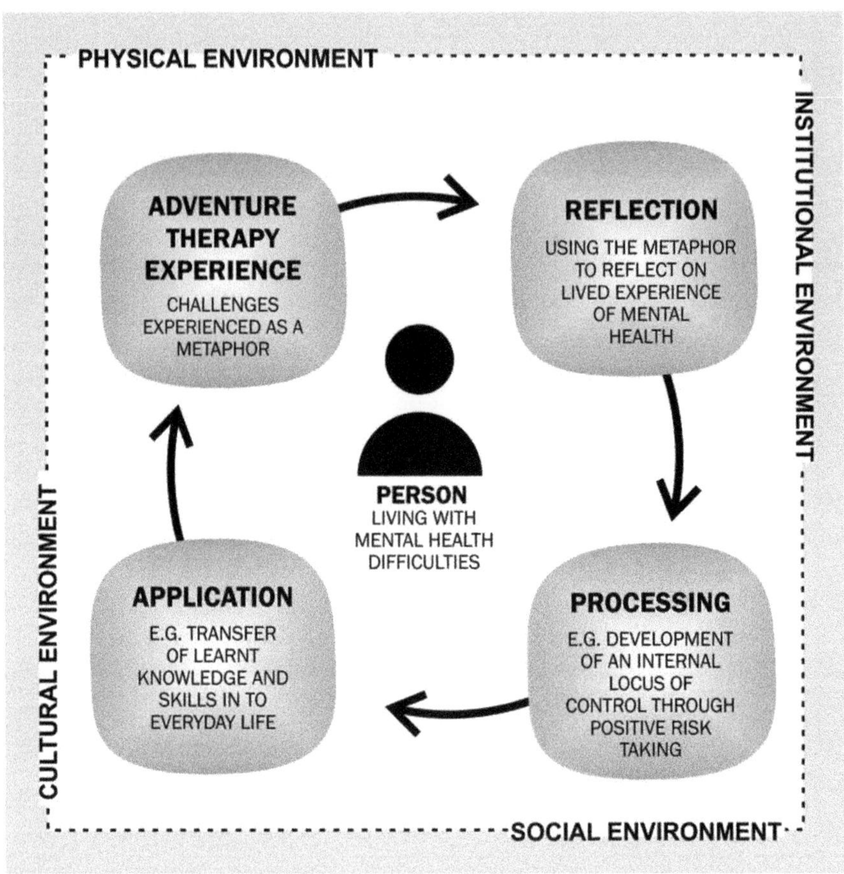

FIGURE 13.1 The experience of adventure therapy, considering the multiple environments involved and the process of reflection and application to everyday life (illustration by Rebecca Licorish)

(Cotton & Butselaar, 2013; Kyriakopoulos, 2011), suggesting a need to ensure that adventure therapy experiences are adequately dovetailed with other appropriate support, and that experiences are reflected upon in conditions that suit participants.

Experiencing positive stress during adventure activities can enable participants to develop coping strategies to manage their emotions within these activities (Koperski et al., 2015). Activities that enable positive risk taking and simulate challenging experiences people may face in their daily lives can be approached through adventure therapy settings, and in so doing, may help to build a more confident internal locus of control (Kelley et al., 1997). Kyriakopoulos referred to this as making isomorphic connections between the adventure activity and personal experiences in the lives of the participants (Kyriakopoulos, 2011). Creating a sense of occupational fit through meeting challenges in situations where people feel safe to push their own physical and mental boundaries highlights the occupational importance of adventure therapy and what it has to offer people from a wellbeing perspective. It can range from the first steps to the 'just-right' challenge or occupational stress, to providing sufficient positive stress or challenge, giving an improved locus of control and ultimately better coping skills.

It is of course important that adventure therapy interventions are tailored to the needs, goals and diagnoses of specific individuals; for example, 'challenge' did not play a large part in an intervention for adults living with PTSD, which achieved reduced stress levels (Vella et al., 2013). Psychological wellbeing can be positively impacted, upon successful completion of well-designed activities that consider the person's needs and capabilities (Clough et al., 2016; Levack, 2003). This is concurrent with literature from a range of disciplines; however it specifically fits within the realms of the Person – Environment – Occupation Performance model in occupational therapy (Baum & Christiansen, 2015). Further, for occupational therapists using a philosophy of enablement (Townsend & Polatajko, 2013), adventure therapy settings provide varied and novel opportunities for challenge-related processes and personal development for the recipient.

Collaboration towards wellbeing and resilience

Adventure therapy, informed by occupational therapy theoretical and practice frameworks, could offer a much richer experience, along with potentially more enduring benefits beyond the bounds of the adventure therapy setting, for those experiencing mental distress and associated symptoms (see Figure 13.2). This approach may be more appealing or more suited to some individuals than routes taken by those accessing occupational therapy in more traditional settings. Accepting adventure therapy as a novel approach to working with people with mental distress broadens the scope and skills of occupational therapists and has the potential, if used in collaboration with members of wider communities, to benefit many groups of people and individuals at risk of mental distress, particularly those who feel marginalised (Duncan & Creek, 2014).

Challenging aspects of adventure therapy can give individuals a chance to overcome obstacles in a supportive environment to experience successes, which in turn, tackle negative thoughts and increase more positive attitudes to participation (Barton et al., 2012). Adventure therapies provide an opportunity for participants to experience challenges in controlled situations, allowing them to implement decision-making, planning and judgement at a safe and comfortable pace. Occupational therapists aim to use occupation in collaboration with people to enhance their autonomy and sense of empowerment. That is, upon considering their respective sets of principles, aims and approaches together, the combination of adventure therapy's focus on utilising the transformational impact of engaging in outdoor challenge and occupational therapy's principles of collaboration towards autonomy and building self-efficacy through meaningful activity can be of great importance and use within the future promotion of wellbeing in the mental health arena.

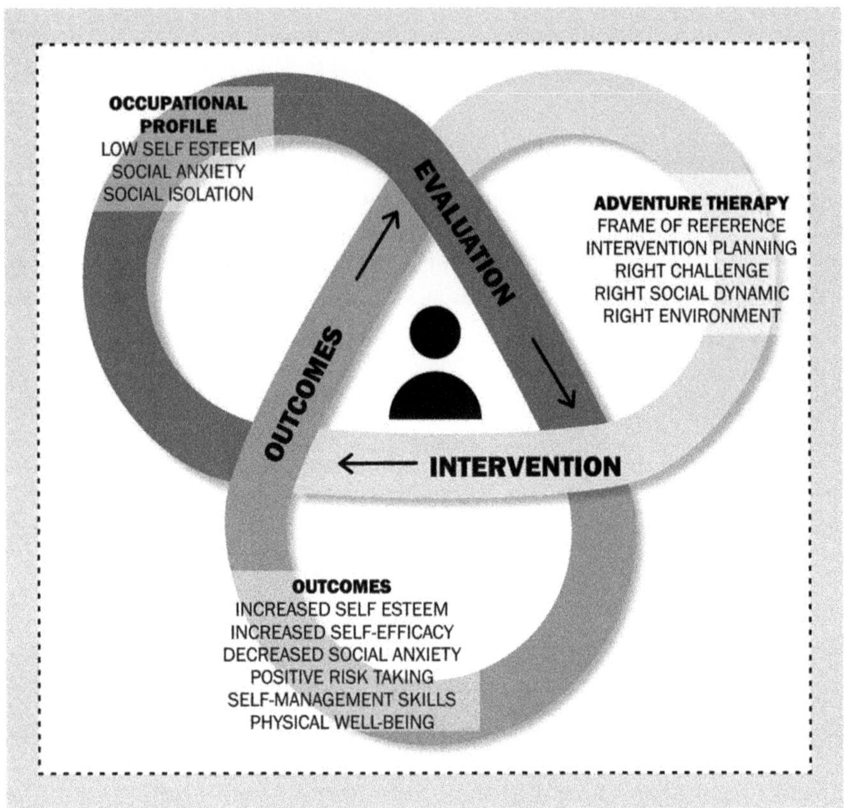

FIGURE 13.2 Adventure therapy providing therapeutic occupational challenge within the occupational therapy process (illustration by Rebecca Licorish)

References

Amini, D., Kannenberg, K., Bodison, S., Chang, P., Colaianni, D., Goodrich, B., & Lieberman, D. (2014). Occupational therapy practice framework: Domain & process 3rd edition. *American Journal of Occupational Therapy, 68*, S1–S48.

Barton, J., Griffin, M., & Pretty, J. (2012). Exercise-, nature- and socially interactive-based initiatives improve mood and self-esteem in the clinical population. *Perspectives in Public Health, 132*(2), 89–96.

Barton, J., Hine, R., & Pretty, J. (2009). The health benefits of walking in greenspaces of high natural and heritage value. *Journal of Integrative Environmental Sciences, 6*(4), 261–278.

Barton, J., & Pretty, J. (2010). What is the best dose of nature and green exercise for improving mental health? A multi-study analysis. *Environmental Science & Technology, 44*(10), 3947–3955.

Barton, J., Wood, C., Pretty, J., & Rogerson, M. (2016). Green exercise for health: A dose of nature. In J. Barton, R. Bragg, C. Wood, & J. Pretty (Eds.), *Green Exercise: Linking Nature, Health and Well-Being* (pp. 262–266). Abingdon: Taylor & Francis Ltd.

Baum, C.M., & Christiansen, C.H. (2015). The person-environment-occupatinal-performance (peop) model. In C. Christiansen, C.M. Baum, & J. Bass-Haugen (Eds.), *Occupational Therapy: Performance, Participation and Wellbeing* (pp. 49–56). Thorofare, NJ: Slack.

Berman, M.G., Jonides, J., & Kaplan, S. (2008). The cognitive benefits of interacting with nature. *Psychological Science, 19*(12), 1207–1212.

Bowen, D.J., & Neill, J.T. (2013). A meta-analysis of adventure therapy outcomes and moderators. *The Open Psychology Journal, 6*(1), 28–53.

Brown, D.K., Barton, J.L., & Gladwell, V.F. (2013). Viewing nature scenes positively affects recovery of autonomic function following acute-mental stress. *Environmental Science & Technology, 47*(11), 5562–5569.

Bryant, W., Pettican, A., & Coetzee, S. (2017). Designing participatory action research to relocate margins, borders and centres. In D. Sakellariou & N. Pollard (Eds.), *Occupational Therapies without Borders: Integrating Justice with Practice* (pp. 73–81). Edinburgh, London, New York, Oxford, Philadelphia, Sydney, Toronto: Elsevier.

Brymer, E., & Davids, K. (2012). Ecological dynamics as a theoretical framework for development of sustainable behaviours towards the environment. *Environmental Education Research, 19*(1), 45–63.

Brymer, E., & Davids, K. (2014). Experiential learning as a constraint-led process: An ecological dynamics perspective. *Journal of Adventure Education & Outdoor Learning, 14*(2), 103–117.

Brymer, E., Davids, K., & Mallabon, L. (2014). Understanding the psychological health and well-being benefits of physical activity in nature: An ecological dynamics analysis. *Ecopsychology, 6*(3), 189–197.

Bryson, J., Feinstein, J., Spavor, J., & Kidd, S. A. (2013). An examination of the feasibility of adventure-based therapy in outpatient care for individuals with psychosis. *Canadian Journal of Community Mental Health, 32*(2), 1–11.

Christiansen, C., & Townsend, E. (2003). *Introduction to Occupation: The Art of Science and Living* (1st ed.). Upper Saddle River, NJ: Pearson.

Clough, P., Mackenzie, S. H., Mallabon, L., & Brymer, E. (2016). Adventurous physical activity environments: A mainstream intervention for mental health. *Sports Medicine, 46*(7), 963–968.

Coetzee, S. (2016). *"Connecting People and the Earth": The Occupational Experience of People with Different Capabilities Participating in an Inclusive Horticultural Social Enterprise*. Brunel University London. Retrieved from: http://bura.brunel.ac.uk/handle/2438/14754 [Accessed July 7, 2017].

College of Occupational Therapists. (2015). *Code of ethics and professional conduct*. London: College of Occupational Therapists. Retrieved from: www.rcot.co.uk/sites/default/files/CODE-OF-ETHICS-2015_0.pdf

Collins, P.Y., Patel, V., Joestl, S.S., March, D., Insel, T.R., Daar, A.S., … Fairburn, C. (2011). Grand challenges in global mental health. *Nature, 475*(7354), 27–30.

Corbetta, M., & Shulman, G.L. (2002). Control of goal-directed and stimulus-driven attention in the brain. *Nature Reviews Neuroscience, 3*(3), 201–215.

Cotton, S., & Butselaar, F. (2013). Outdoor adventure camps for people with mental illness. *Australasian Psychiatry, 21*(4), 352–358.

Creek, J. (2010). *The Core Concepts of Occupational Therapy: A Dynamic Framework for Practice*. London: Jessica Kingsley Publishers.

Creek, J. (2014). The knowldege base of occupational therapy. In W. Bryant, J. Fieldhouse, & K. Bannigan (Eds.), *Creek's Occupational Therapy and Mental Health* (pp. 27–47). Oxford: Elsevier Churchill Livingstone.

Crisp, S. (1996). International models of best practice in wilderness and adventure therapy: Implications for Australia an investigation of selected innovative mental health programs for adolescents using wilderness and adventure activities as a primary therapeutic Modalit.

Duncan, E. (2011). *Foundations for Practice in Occupational Therapy-E-BOOK*. Edinburgh: Elsevier Health Sciences.

Duncan, E.M., & Creek, J. (2014). Working on the margins: Occupational therapy and social inclusion. In W. Bryant, J. Fieldhouse, & K. Bannigan (Eds.), *Creek's Occupational Therapy and Mental Health* (5th ed., pp. 457–473). Oxford: Elsevier.

Epstein, I. (2004). Adventure therapy: A mental health promotion strategy in pediatric oncology. *Journal of Pediatric Oncology Nursing, 21*(2), 103–110.

Ewert, A., Overholt, J., Voight, A., & Wang, C. C. (2011). Understanding the transformative aspects of the wilderness and protected lands experience upon human health.

Ewert, A., & Yoshino, A. (2011). The influence of short-term adventure-based experiences on levels of resilience. *Journal of Adventure Education and Outdoor Learning, 11*(1), 35–50.

Fan, J., McCandliss, B.D., Fossella, J., Flombaum, J.I., & Posner, M.I. (2005). The activation of attentional networks. *NeuroImage, 26*(2), 471–479.

Fieldhouse, J., & Sempik, J. (2014). Green care and occupational therapy. In W. Bryant, J. Fieldhouse, & K. Bannigan (Eds.), *Creek's Occupational Therapy in Mental Health* (5th ed., pp. 309–327). Oxford: Elsevier.

Frances, K. (2006). Outdoor recreation as an occupation to improve quality of life for people with enduring mental health problems. *British Journal of Occupational Therapy, 69*(4), 182–186.

Gass, M.A., Gillis, H., & Russell, K.C. (2012). *Adventure Therapy: Theory, Research, and Practice* (1st ed.). New York, NY: Routledge.

Gillis, H., & Ringer, T. (1999). Adventure as therapy. In J.C. Miles & S. Priest (Eds.), *Adventure Programming* (pp. 29–37). State College: Venture Publishing.

Gladwell, V., Brown, D., Barton, J.L., Tarvainen, M., Kuoppa, P., Pretty, J., … Sandercock, G. (2012). The effects of views of nature on autonomic control. *European Journal of Applied Physiology, 112*(9), 3379–3386.

Gonzalez, M.T., Hartig, T., Patil, G.G., Martinsen, E.W., & Kirkevold, M. (2010). Therapeutic horticulture in clinical depression: A prospective study of active components. *Journal of Advanced Nursing, 66*(9), 2002–2013.

Granerud, A., & Eriksson, B.G. (2014). Mental health problems, recovery, and the impact of green care services: A qualitative, participant-focused approach. *Occupational Therapy in Mental Health, 30*(4), 317–336.

Hartig, T., Evans, G.W., Jamner, L.D., Davis, D.S., & Gärling, T. (2003). Tracking restoration in natural and urban field settings. *Journal of Environmental Psychology, 23*(2), 109–123.

Herzog, T.R., & Strevey, S.J. (2008). Contact with nature, sense of humor, and psychological well-being. *Environment and Behavior, 40*(6), 747–776.

Hine, R., Pretty, J., & Barton, J. (2009). Research project: Social, psychological and cultural benefits of large natural habitat & wilderness experience: A review of current literature. Report for the Wilderness Foundation. Report for the Wilderness Foundation. Colchester: University of Essex.

Kaplan, S. (1995). The restorative benefits of nature: Toward an integrative framework. *Journal of Environmental Psychology, 15*(3), 169–182.

Kaplan, S., & Berman, M.G. (2010). Directed attention as a common resource for executive functioning and self-regulation. *Perspectives on Psychological Science, 5*(1), 43–57.

Kelley, M., Coursey, R., & Selby, P. (1997). Therapeutic adventures outdoors: A demonstration of benefits for people with mental illness. *Psychiatric Rehabilitation Journal, 20*(4), 61–73.

Kolb, D.A. (2014). *Experiential Learning: Experience as the Source of Learning and Development*. Pearson FT Press.

Koperski, H., Tucker, A.R., Lung, D.M., & Gass, M.A. (2015). The impact of community based adventure therapy on stress and coping skills in adults. *Practitioner Scholar: Journal of Counseling and Professional Psychology, 4*(1), 1–16.,

Kyriakopoulos, A. (2011). How individuals with self – Reported anxiety and depression experienced a combination of individual counselling with an adventurous outdoor experience: A qualitative evaluation. *Counselling and Psychotherapy Research, 11*(2), 120–128.

Laumann, K., Gärling, T., & Stormark, K.M. (2003). Selective attention and heart rate responses to natural and urban environments. *Journal of Environmental Psychology, 23*(2), 125–134.

Levack, H. (2003). Adventure therapy in occupational therapy: Can we call it spiritual occupation? *New Zealand Journal of Occupational Therapy, 50*(1), 22.

Li, D., & Sullivan, W.C. (2016). Impact of views to school landscapes on recovery from stress and mental fatigue. *Landscape and Urban Planning, 148*, 149–158.

Luckner, J.L., & Nadler, R.S. (1997). *Processing the Experience: Strategies to Enhance and Generalize Learning*. Dubuque, IA: Kendall/Hunt.

Moxham, L., Liersch-Sumskis, S., Taylor, E., Patterson, C., & Brighton, R. (2015). Preliminary outcomes of a pilot therapeutic recreation camp for people with a mental illness: Links to recovery. *Therapeutic Recreation Journal, 49*(1), 61.

Panicucci, J. (2007). Cornerstones of adventure education. In D. Prouty, J. Panicucci, & R. Collinson (Eds.), *Adventure Education: Theory and Applications* (pp. 33–48). Leeds: Human Kinetics.

Paterson, C.F. (2014). A short history of occupational therapy in mental health. In W. Bryant, J. Fieldhouse, & K. Bannigan (Eds.), *Creek's Occupational Therapy and Mental Health* (5th ed., pp. 2–14). Oxford: Elsevier.

Pickens, N.D., & Pizur-Barnekow, K. (2009). Co-occupation: Extending the dialogue. *Journal of Occupational Science, 16*(3), 151–156.

Pierce, D. (2009). Co-occupation: The challenges of defining concepts original to occupational science. *Journal of Occupational Science, 16*(3), 203–207.

Plutchik, R. (1980a). A general psychoevolutionary theory of emotion. *Emotion: Theory, Research, and Experience, 1*(3), 3–33.

Plutchik, R. (1980b). Measurement implications of a psychoevolutionary theory of emotions. In K.R. Blankstein, P. Pliner, & J. Polivy (Eds.), *Assessment and Modification of Emotional Behavior* (pp. 47–69). New York, NY: Plenum Press.

Pretty, J., Rogerson, M., & Barton, J. (2017). Green mind theory: How brain-body-behaviour links into natural and social environments for healthy habits. *International Journal of Environmental Research and Public Health, 14*(7), 706.

Revell, S., Duncan, E., & Cooper, M. (2014). Helpful aspects of outdoor therapy experiences: An online preliminary investigation. *Counselling and Psychotherapy Research, 14*(4), 281–287.

Richards, K., Carpenter, C., & Harper, N. (2011). *Looking at the Landscape of Adventure Therapy: Making Links to Theory and Practice*. Taylor & Francis.

Roberts, S.D., Stroud, D., Hoag, M.J., & Massey, K.E. (2017). Outdoor behavioral health care: A longitudinal assessment of young adult outcomes. *Journal of Counseling & Development, 95*(1), 45–55.

Rogerson, M., & Barton, J. (2015). Effects of the visual exercise environments on cognitive directed attention, energy expenditure and perceived exertion. *International Journal of Environmental Research and Public Health, 12*(7), 7321–7336.

Rogerson, M., Gladwell, V.F., Gallagher, D.J., & Barton, J.L. (2016). Influences of green outdoors versus indoors environmental settings on psychological and social outcomes of controlled exercise. *International Journal of Environmental Research and Public Health, 13*(4), 363.

Scheinfeld, D.E., Rochlen, A.B., & Buser, S.J. (2011). Adventure therapy: A supplementary group therapy approach for men. *Psychology of Men & Masculinity, 12*(2), 188.

Stadnyk, R., Townsend, E.A., & Wilcock, A. (2010). Occupational justice. In C. Christiansen & E.A. Townsend (Eds.), *Introduction to Occupation: The Art and Science of Living* (Vol. 2, pp. 329–358). Upper Saddle River, NJ: Pearson.

Tang, I.-C., Tsai, Y.-P., Lin, Y.-J., Chen, J.-H., Hsieh, C.-H., Hung, S.-H., ... Chang, C.-Y. (2017). Using functional Magnetic Resonance Imaging (fMRI) to analyze brain region activity when viewing landscapes. *Landscape and Urban Planning, 162*, 137–144.

Thompson Coon, J., Boddy, K., Stein, K., Whear, R., Barton, J., & Depledge, M.H. (2011). Does participating in physical activity in outdoor natural environments have a greater effect on physical and mental wellbeing than physical activity indoors? A systematic review. *Environmental Science & Technology, 45*(5), 1761–1772.

Townsend, E.A., & Polatajko, H.J. (2013). Enabling: Occupational therapy's core competency. In E.A. Townsend & H.J. Polatajko (Eds.), *Enabling Occupation II: Advancing an Occupational Therapy Vision for Health, Well-Being and Justice through Occupation* (pp. 87–133). Ottawa: Canadian Association of Occupational Therapists.

Turpin, M.J., & Iwama, M.K. (2011). *Using Occupational Therapy Models in Practice E-Book: A Fieldguide*. Edinburgh: Elsevier Health Sciences.

Ulrich, R. (1984). View through a window may influence recovery. *Science, 224*(4647), 224–225.

Ulrich, R.S. (1981). Natural versus urban scenes some psychophysiological effects. *Environment and Behavior, 13*(5), 523–556.

Ulrich, R.S., Simons, R.F., Losito, B.D., Fiorito, E., Miles, M.A., & Zelson, M. (1991). Stress recovery during exposure to natural and urban environments. *Journal of Environmental Psychology, 11*(3), 201–230.

Vella, E.J., Milligan, B., & Bennett, J.L. (2013). Participation in outdoor recreation program predicts improved psychosocial well-being among veterans with post-traumatic stress disorder: A pilot study. *Military Medicine, 178*(3), 254–260.

Voruganti, L.N., Whatham, J., Bard, E., Parker, G., Babbey, C., Ryan, J., ... MacCrimmon, D.J. (2006). Going beyond: An adventure-and recreation-based group intervention promotes well-being and weight loss in schizophrenia. *The Canadian Journal of Psychiatry, 51*(9), 575–580.

Vos, T., Barber, R.M., Bell, B., Bertozzi-Villa, A., Biryukov, S., Bolliger, I., ... Dicker, D. (2015). Global, regional, and national incidence, prevalence, and years lived with disability for 301 acute and chronic diseases and injuries in 188 countries, 1990–2013: A systematic analysis for the Global Burden of Disease Study 2013. *The Lancet, 386*(9995), 743–800.

Wilcock, A.A. (1999). Reflections on doing, being and becoming. *Australian Occupational Therapy Journal, 46*(1), 1–11.

Wilcock, A.A., & Hocking, C. (2015). *An Occupational Perspective of Health* (3rd ed.). Thorofare, NJ: Slack.

Wolf, M., & Mehl, K. (2011). Experiential learning in psychotherapy: Ropes course exposures as an adjunct to inpatient treatment. *Clinical Psychology & Psychotherapy*, *18*(1), 60–74.

Yeh, H.-P., Stone, J.A., Churchill, S.M., Wheat, J.S., Brymer, E., & Davids, K. (2015). Physical, psychological and emotional benefits of green physical activity: An ecological dynamics perspective. *Sports Medicine*, *46*(7), 947–953.

14

GREENING EDUCATION

Education outside the classroom in natural settings as a school-based health promotion approach for child and youth populations

Peter Bentsen, Glen Nielsen, Mads Bølling, Lærke Mygind, Matt P. Stevenson and Erik Mygind

Education and the school system have increasingly gained attention as a domain for public health and health promotion interventions that aim to increase physical activity amongst children and young people by enhancing the use of green and blue environments (van den Bosch & Bird, 2018). Interventions are understood broadly as programmes, pedagogies, services, products, and policies (Bowen et al., 2009; Pressley et al., 2006), developed, evaluated, and implemented to improve outcomes within an identified context and/or population (Craig et al., 2008).

The aim of this chapter is to describe, exemplify, and advocate for *education outside the classroom* (EOtC) as an 'add-in' holistic school-based health promotion approach for child and youth populations. Based on theory, empirical research, and illustrative practical cases, we argue that EOtC in natural settings is a promising approach for health promotion. We draw on Danish *udeskole* (literally meaning 'outdoor school') as an illustrative example of EOtC. In recent decades, Scandinavian countries have often been perceived as 'countries of reference' concerning EOtC, including education taking place in natural settings, in school and pre-school systems, i.e. kindergarten to 16 years of age (Rea & Waite, 2009). Further, there is a long-standing commitment and increasingly widespread provision of these education practices in the North European region (Barfod, Ejbye-Ernst, L. Mygind, & Bentsen, 2016; Bentsen, Jensen, E. Mygind, & Randrup, 2010). The Danish concept of *udeskole* denotes a specific approach to EOtC, which emerged as a way to engage children and young people with the outdoors and promote their learning, but in the proces also their health and active living.

This chapter 1) situates EOtC in natural settings within policy and research related to children's physical activity, health, and well-being and the school as a health promoting setting; 2) illustrates the nature of EOtC by presenting case studies and projects; 3) highlights the benefits of EOtC in natural settings by summarising the existing body of research; and 4) advocates for the unique potential of this 'add-in' holistic approach to school-based health promotion. Thus, this chapter aims to provide a source of inspiration for developing state-of -the-art interventions to support the practice of EOtC in order to promote children's physical activity, movement, and positive experiences in green and blue spaces as a key strategy for both education and public health.

Why are natural settings important for increasing children's physical activity?

In the past few decades, childhoods have changed dramatically, with some children spending as little as 2% of their leisure time in natural environments (Wheeler, Cooper, Page, & Jago, 2010). During the same period, there has been an increase in childhood obesity rates, with associated health problems (Ng et al., 2014), and an increase in the amount of children diagnosed with mental health disorders (Merikangas et al., 2010).

The extent to which the disconnection with the natural world and the rise in health problems are related remains unknown. However, there is mounting evidence that exposure to natural environments can have a positive impact on diverse indicators of mental, physical, and social health (L. Mygind et al., 2019), including well-being (McMahan & Estes, 2015), stress reactivity (Lederbogen et al., 2011), cognition (Ohly et al., 2016), inattention-hyperactivity protection (Kuo & Faber Taylor, 2004), immune system function (Kuo, 2015), and physical activity (Pietilä et al., 2015). Therefore, a change in lifestyle and living conditions towards greater exposure to natural environments represents a sensible intervention to improve childhood health, well-being, and skills related to learning, with few, if any, negative consequences.

In a recent analysis, Kuo (2015) identified 21 pathways linking natural environments with human health. Kuo argued that these pathways may contribute cumulatively, pointing to increased immune function as a central pathway that subsumes most others. Kuo further noted that certain pathways linking nature to health, such as increased physical activity, may only occur under certain conditions or in specific contexts. One promising context for increasing physical activity through contact with natural environments, particularly in children, is in education settings.

Fjørtoft (2001) argued that natural environments are particularly suited for promoting physical activity by offering children dynamic and challenging landscapes. Fjørtoft suggested children of this age (5–7 years in the study) relate to environments in terms of their functionality (Heft, 1988) and affordances (Gibson, 2014), and that natural environments differ in these aspects from purposefully built play areas. For example, rather than perceiving a tree on pure aesthetics, children are likely to assess the tree based on whether its branches are climbable. Thus, they seek out affordances within their environment, including opportunities to be physically active, such as climbing. Indeed, it was found that children perceive and even name areas of their environment based on affordances from vegetation and topography (Fjørtoft, 2004). It was further argued that although built outdoor playgrounds are designed with the intention of promoting physical development, the range of possibilities for action is more narrow than a natural, non-designed environment (Fjørtoft, 2004). It is through meeting the need for challenges and exploration that natural environments are believed to promote physical activity (Fjørtoft, 2004) as well as motor skills, which are important for future physical activity levels.

Affordances for physical activity in natural environments may also stimulate creative problem-solving, which is highly related to academic success (Wallace & Russ, 2015). If children view environments in terms of functionality, non-designed environments should stimulate divergent thinking (Studente, Seppala, & Sadowska, 2016), where many solutions to one situation are considered. Although this is yet to be explored in children, several studies have shown that reasoning and problem-solving skills can be enhanced after exposure to natural environments in adults (Chow & Lau, 2015; Ferraro, 2015; Studente et al., 2016). These additional benefits may augment the well-established association between physical activity and cognition (Fedewa & Ahn, 2011).

Why are schools and classrooms key settings for nature-based physical activity interventions?

The environment (including natural settings) has recently been prioritised as a significant component in health promotion models and concepts (World Heath Organization, WHO, 2004, 2010b, 2016a). These models and concepts have been used to inform the development of health promotion practices and have been influential in the shaping of the theoretical designs and implementation strategies of the settings movement (e.g. recent innovations as healthy cities, health promoting schools and health promoting worksites). The shaping of health promoting settings at work, in hospital, in schools, and in local communities has therefore been significantly supported by the WHO.

The WHO, as well as many national health organisations, regard schools as an important setting for a wide range of public health and health promotion initiatives because children spend a large proportion of their waking hours at school (Strum, 2005; WHO, 2004) and because children from all socioeconomic and cultural backgrounds can be reached (Inchley et al., 2016). However, school-based health promotion initiatives are often extra-curricular activities or 'add-ons' to schools' main objectives (i.e. academic learning) and everyday practice (Norris et al., 2015; Simovska, Nordin, & Madsen, 2016). Initiatives are often an extra task on top of other teaching obligations or take time away from curricular activities, which can act as a barrier to the implementation of such initiatives. This may be one reason why the results of some school-based health promotion interventions are mixed (Pucher, Boot, & De Vries, 2013). Aligning health promotion and interventions with the main objectives defined by the schools may legitimise implementation and feasibility of such interventions. In this way, teachers and students may experience them as 'add-ins' rather than 'add-ons'.

Recently, there have been calls towards holistic settings-based physical activity interventions that integrate and align with school curricula and consider the core mandates, constraints, and essential procedures of education and school systems (ASCD, 2015; Norris et al., 2015; Webster, Russ, Vazou, Goh, & Erwin, 2015). Such interventions often aim to promote learning, health, and development of the whole child simultaneously. Thus, there is a growing need to develop, implement, and evaluate educational practices that integrate physical activity and natural settings into school hours in a school setting required to deliver increasingly higher academic goals. This form of 'add-in' or 'integration within education systems' is in many ways, a response to or form of the Health in All Policies initiative being undertaken in the health sector globally (WHO, 2010a).

EOtC is an example of such an 'add-in' holistic school-based health promotion approach, that changes the physical classroom to whatever is chosen by the teacher (Barfod et al., 2016), such as cultural or natural environments, the school grounds, but mostly green space close to the school, or a forest further away (Bentsen, Schipperijn, & Jensen, 2013). In this way, the approach allows for use of different pedagogies of the teachers' choice, in order to promote physical activity, along with learning, social relations, and well-being. In a Scandinavian school context, EOtC refers to curriculum-based education outside of school in natural as well as cultural settings on a regular basis, *udeskole* (Bentsen, Mygind, & Randrup, 2009). EOtC activities are characterised by teachers using the local environment in their teaching, and involve innovative teaching methods, child-led approaches to problem-solving, experimentation, cooperation, physical activity, and play (Beames, Higgins, & Nicol, 2012; Waite, Bølling, & Bentsen, 2016).

What is *udeskole* and how is it practised in Danish schools?

School-based teaching in the local outdoor environment as an integrated part of the school system is a relatively new form of teaching and learning in Scandinavia. It is called *udeskole* in Danish, *uteskole* in Norwegian and *utomhuspedagogik* in Swedish. The concept has been described in a Norwegian context by Jordet (1998), in a Swedish context by Dahlgren and Szczepanski (1998) and in a Danish context by Mygind (2005). *Udeskole* targets children aged 6–16, and is characterised by *compulsory* educational activities outside of school on a *regular* basis, e.g. one day weekly or fortnightly. The concept of *udeskole* is characterised by regular, compulsory, curriculum-based EOtC in schools and is not fully captured by concepts like forest school, fieldwork, outdoor visits, outdoor adventure education, school ground, or community projects (cf. Davis, Rea, & Waite,

2006; Rickinson et al., 2004). In Scandinavia, *udeskole* practice has increased in the past decade. In Denmark, for example, there has been an increase from a few schools and teachers practising *udeskole* at the turn of the century to more than 290 schools in 2007 (approximately 14% of all schools in the country) (Bentsen et al., 2010), with continued growth reaching approximately 18% in 2014 (Barfod et al., 2016). *Udeskole* can take place in both natural and cultural settings, e.g. forests, parks, local communities, factories, farms, galleries, and theatres (Jordet, 1998, 2007). However, in Denmark *udeskole* has mainly been practised in natural settings. The term *nature class* has also been used and could be understood as a concept subsumed under *udeskole* (E. Mygind, 2005). *Udeskole* activities are characterised by making use of the local environment when teaching specific subjects and curriculum areas by, for example, measuring and calculating the volume of trees in mathematics, writing poems in and about nature when teaching languages, or visiting historically significant places or buildings in history education (Bentsen et al., 2009). Teaching and learning activities are often cross-disciplinary, where academic subject matter is considered in its real, concrete form to facilitate understanding (Bentsen & Jensen, 2012).

EOtC is not a statutory requirement of the Danish school system and the decision to take teaching outdoors rests with the individual teacher and school. *Udeskole* is not mentioned in the Danish national curriculum; however, outdoor teaching and learning are mentioned indirectly in the overall aims, and directly under some of the subjects; e.g. biology, geography, and physical education. A new school reform was initiated in Danish schools in August 2014, which included support for the use of movement and physical activity, and variation of teaching methods with the aim of promoting more positive and healthy school days for children (Danish Ministry of Education, 2014). Beside physical education lessons, the pupils are expected to be physically active 45 minutes daily during lessons and recess. Despite the *udeskole* concept not yet being explicitly recognised, *udeskole* seems to support these new goals (see Box 14.1).

BOX 14.1 EIGHT YEAR OLDS IN THE FOREST: A DANISH EXAMPLE OF EOTC IN NATURAL SETTINGS

The theme was 'signs of spring in the forest', and the class was leaving on their weekly *udeskole* day. The school was located in urban Copenhagen, so there was a half-hour train journey to the forest, *Hareskoven*, where the teaching was to take place.

The day had begun with daily reading time in class. After this, the teacher, Mette, showed examples of signs of spring. She had taken pictures of various herbs, shrubs, and trees and showed these on the smart board, and she also showed the children five common spring flowers in bloom. In the forest, the children were asked to take pictures of spring plants with a digital camera and record spring sounds. These would later, back at the school, be sorted and processed linguistically and conceptually, and used to stimulate creative writing.

The children chatted as they walked 700 metres to the train station. In the train, calm conversation continued between teachers and pupils about various topics including social conflicts, personal relationships, soccer, family events, and everyday observations. At the destination, the children walked about one kilometre to a campfire in the forest.

When they arrived, they had a break where the children could move freely in the area. The two teachers spoke with children who did not explore the area and they prepared to start the project 'signs of spring'. The teachers gathered the group of children around the campfire. The campfire was placed on a small hill, and the windy March weather made it cool to be assembled and sit still. The children sang a song and quickly got into pairs for the photography activity. The children instructed each other in the use of the camera and, with few interactions with the teachers, they started working independently in pairs.

Photographs included sprouting plants, trees, shrubs, children, and teachers. Some children spent a long time finding new motifs, but most had few concepts and plans for the motifs they chose, but took pictures nevertheless. A group of boys finished rather quickly and went over to play with sticks, running around exploring the forest and playing hide and seek, with the camera in their pocket. After an hour, it was lunchtime.

Following lunch, the class gathered again. The teachers had decided that the planned listening task was not appropriate, as there were not many sounds of birds (i.e. signs of spring). Instead, the children were given an identification sheet from the website the Forest in School (www.skoveniskolen.dk). Here, there were pictures of buds and leaves of 24 common trees. The children's task was to find out which trees were in the forest and cross them out on the sheet. The children researched in different ways. Some went to a teacher and investigated whether they could find features that could justify that crosses could be placed. Others went around quickly and put 24 crosses on their sheets, although not necessarily accurately, and then played further in the forest.

After an hour on what had now turned in to a warm March day, the teacher whistled, everyone assembled, and the group went back on the train. The mood was positive. When the children arrived at the school, they wrote in their logbook about the day for half an hour. There was a relaxed atmosphere during the process, and the relationship between children and teachers seemed good.

'Development of *Udeskole*': a joint development and research project by the Danish Ministry of Education and Ministry of Environment

Following the new school reform in 2014 (Danish Ministry of Education, 2014), the Danish Ministry of Education and the Danish Ministry of Environment, in a unique collaboration, decided to support and develop *udeskole* with approximately 12 million DKK (about €1.6 million) over three years by launching a large national development, research, and demonstration project, 'Development of *Udeskole*'. The ministries allied themselves with a consortium of university colleges and *udeskole* experts, and decided upon an action-research development model. The project supports the new school reform, with the aim of generating and disseminating practice-related knowledge about *udeskole* to support the development of *udeskole* and to create a basis for spreading *udeskole* as a teaching method.

This illustrates how *udeskole* has developed from being a bottom-up grassroots movement initiated by individual schools and teachers (Bentsen et al., 2009) to becoming an integral part of a top-down school reform in Danish schools. In most Western countries, including Scandinavia, a neo-liberal focus on performance and measurable outcomes in schools has become well-established (Wiborg, 2013). The top-down approach to development of *udeskole* can be seen as an increase of instrumentalisation of EOtC, where the use of EOtC is encouraged and supported as part of an agenda for strengthening academic performance (Waite et al., 2016).

What does the body of knowledge say about benefits of EOtC?

The interest in links between natural settings, schools, physical activity, and learning has led to research exploring the benefits of engaging children with 'the outdoor classroom'. Research has highlighted that children can benefit from EOtC in several ways. EOtC has been associated with improvements in concentration, increased motivation, a decrease in stress levels, and higher levels of physical activity (Becker, Lauterbach, Spengler, Dettweiler, & Mess, 2017; Dettweiler et al., 2017; L. Mygind, Stevenson, Liebst, Konvalina, & Bentsen, 2018).

Case studies indicated that children accumulate more moderate to vigorous physical activity in EOtC in natural environments compared to typical school days (Dettweiler et al., 2017; Grønningsæter, Hallås, Kristiansen, & Nævdal, 2007; E. Mygind, 2016). Likewise, a case study of a forest school in Scotland showed that the children accumulated a greater total amount of physical activity, at a higher intensity, and with a greater frequency of longer bouts, in comparison to their typical school days (Lovell, 2009). In another UK-based, non-controlled, intervention study with one class, EOtC in natural environments was related to higher levels of moderate to vigorous physical activity than classroom-based learning; and over a two year intervention period, reduced the children's body-mass indexes (BMI) (Aronsson, Tighe

Clark, & Waite, 2014). In a larger controlled study (see Box 14.2), Schneller et al. (2017a) showed that EOtC was associated with boys spending more daily time being moderately and vigorously physically active. No differences were found for girls. However, days with EOtC were associated with higher light physical activity for girls (Schneller, Schipperijn, Nielsen, & Bentsen, 2017b). Schneller et al. (2017a) suggested that implementing EOtC can be a time- and cost-neutral, supplementary way to increase time spent physically active for boys through grades three to six.

Several case studies have indicated that EOtC is related to higher levels of general mental and social well-being (E. Mygind, 2005, 2009). Over a period of eight months, O'Brien and Murray (2007) found positive impacts of forest school on confidence, social skills, motivation, and concentration. In a review of a range of outdoor learning studies, Rickinson et al. (2004) found that effective fieldwork, and residential-based experience in particular, was found to lead to individual growth and improvements in social skills (Rickinson et al., 2004). A one-year Swedish elementary school experiment found that at least one hour of EOtC a day increased mental health among boys, however not among girls (Gustafsson, Szczepanski, Nelson, & Gustafsson, 2012). In an interview-based study of young people's retrospective perceptions of EOtC, Hartmeyer and E. Mygind (2016) found that the participants deemed the unique opportunities for active play, interaction, participation, and pupil-centered tasks in EOtC fundamental to the positive influence of EOtC on social relations elsewhere observed (E. Mygind, 2009; Rickinson et al., 2004).

It is possible that social relations, physical activity, and mental well-being are interrelated as children tend to engage in active play where some children are included and others are excluded (Nielsen, 2011; Nielsen & Stelter, n.d.; Pawlowski, Ergler, Tjørnhøj-Thomsen, Schipperijn, & Troelsen, 2015). Therefore, social relations and social inclusion amongst children in school is likely to be linked to which children, and how many of them, are physically active. Furthermore, positive social relations and inclusion are important to motivation and well-being (Deci & Ryan, 2002; Gutman & Vorhaus, 2012) along with mental health, as a lower number of friends for example is related to depressive symptoms (Schwartz, Gorman, Duong, & Nakamoto, 2008). Finally, physical activity has the capacity to promote school engagement (Owen et al., 2016), and the amount of physical activity in itself may also have an independent effect on cognitive functioning and well-being (Fedewa & Ahn, 2011; Verburgh, Königs, Scherder, & Oosterlaan, 2014); see Figure 14.1.

The Danish 'Rødkilde' udeskole project

The first major Danish *udeskole* research and development project was a case study that took place in Rødkilde School in Copenhagen from 2000 to 2003. Sporadic EOtC had been carried out in Denmark for decades. The Rødkilde project applied a new perspective on EOtC characterised by compulsory EOtC on a regular weekly basis one day every week over three years. A research team

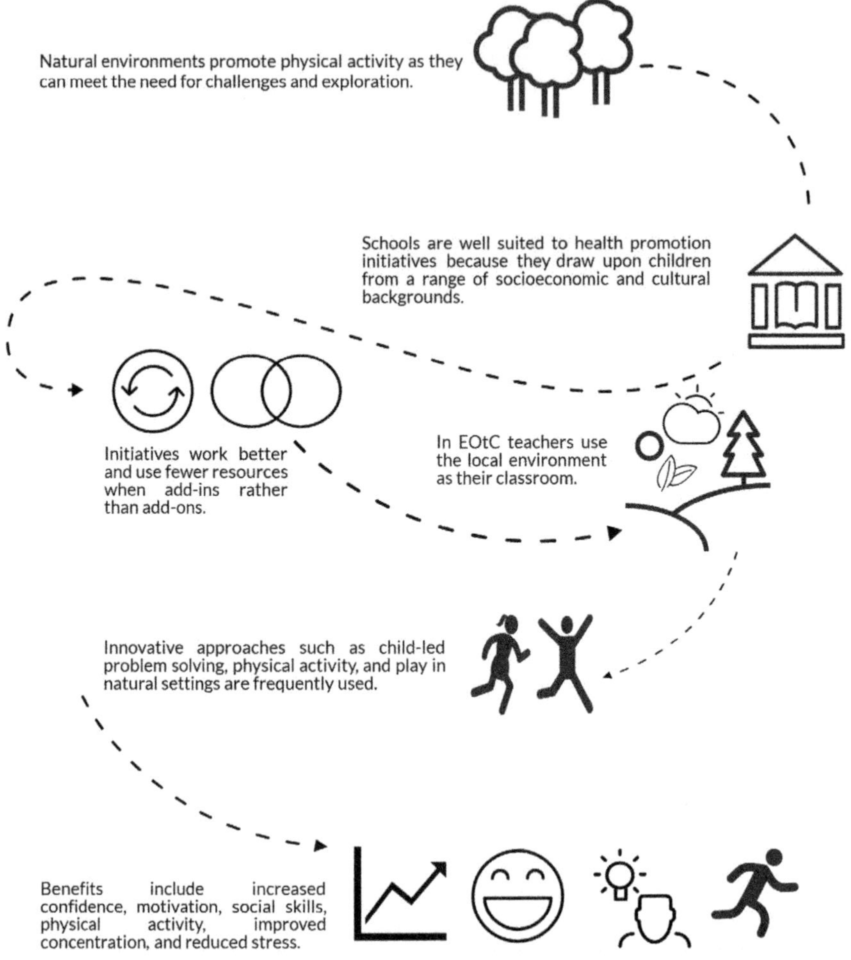

FIGURE 14.1 Outline of rationale for EOtC approach

followed two teachers and their 'Nature Class' (19 pupils; grade level 3–5; age 8–11) while conducting their lessons for 20% of the total school time in a natural setting over three years.

The Rødkilde project was organised as a multi-dimensional and cross-scientific research project that aimed to investigate the impact on physical activity, learning, and social relations, but also the opinions of their parents and the two teachers (Mygind, 2005). The pupils' physical activity levels were measured with an accelerometer, and *udeskole* days in the forest was compared with traditional school days with and without two physical education lessons. The pupils' mean physical activity levels were more than twice as high on forest days measured in summer and winter weeks as compared to traditional school days and equal to a school day including two physical education lessons (Mygind, 2007).

The pupils in the Rødkilde project were asked how they experienced lessons in the classroom and the forest settings. Two almost identical questionnaires, including 26 statements adjusted to each context, were completed by the children four times from 2000 to 2003. Ten statements were categorised as aspects of 'social relations', 14 statements as 'teaching', and finally two related to 'self-perceived physical activity'. The aspects 'social relations', 'teaching', and 'self-perceived physical activity' showed significantly more positive levels in the context of the forest setting. It was concluded that the combination of classroom and outdoor teaching, over a three-year period had a positive effect on the children's social relations, experience with teaching, and self-perceived physical activity level (Mygind, 2009).

Retrospectively, seven years after the Rødkilde *udeskole* project (i.e. 2013), five pupils and two teachers were interviewed to explore the conditions influencing social relations during the three years as 'Nature Class' and the following years in secondary school. A conventional qualitative content analysis was applied and identified six conditions important for the improvement of social relations. Four of them – 'play', 'interaction', 'participation', and 'pupil-centred tasks' – were important conditions for the positive social relations during the 'Nature Class' project. Two conditions – 'cooperation' and 'engagement' – seemed to be consequences of the improved social relations found during the 'Nature Class' period which positively influenced the pupils' abilities to cooperate and the pupils' strong engagement in the subsequent school years (Hartmeyer & E. Mygind, 2016).

In conclusion, the Rødkilde School case study demonstrated a significant and positive impact on physical activity and social relations when integrating *udeskole* one day a week, particularly in natural settings.

BOX 14.2 THE TEACHOUT STUDY: A QUASI-EXPERIMENTAL CROSS-DISCIPLINARY EVALUATION OF THE IMPACTS OF EOTC ON PUPILS' PHYSICAL ACTIVITY, WELL-BEING, AND LEARNING

The TEACHOUT project was a Danish research project running from 2013–2018 in primary and lower secondary school. The study evaluated the impacts of EOtC on school children, and examined 16 participating schools containing 19 EOtC school classes and 19 parallel non-EOTC classes, with a total of 834 children aged 9 to 13 years (Nielsen et al., 2016).

The TEACHOUT research project aimed to achieve research-based knowledge about the strengths and weaknesses of practising teaching outside the classroom and school buildings. The overall question was: *Will the alternative teaching methods in the practice of EOtC increase and improve children's physical activity, academic learning, social interaction, motivation, and attitudes towards schooling? And if so, how?*

TEACHOUT was a quasi-experimental, cross-disciplinary study using a mixed methods research design and consists of three individual PhD projects focusing on physical activity, learning, peer social relations, school motivation, and well-being amongst pupils. An additional PhD project focused on the teachers' role while teaching in different *udeskole* contexts (Nielsen et al., 2016).

The effects of EOtC were mainly analysed by comparing EOtC pupils to non-EOtC (i.e. teaching as usual control) pupils based on their scores on the outcome variables (i.e. school performance, well-being, school motivation, and peer social network relations) at the end of the school year (2015), adjusting for the baseline values from the beginning of the year (2014), and previously known confounding variables. A survey of the pupils' academic performance included information about learning in reading and basic math skills (Otte, Bølling, Stevenson, Ejbye-Ernst, Nielsen, & Bentsen, 2019a; Otte, Bølling, Elsborg, Nielsen, & Bentsen, 2019b), which was compared to pupils who did not receive teaching outside the school buildings. Further, the survey held information about the pupils' perception of their own learning with and without *udeskole*. The TEACHOUT project consisted of a series of quantitative surveys comparing the pupils in EOtC to non-EOtC classes based on the self-determination theory examining psychosocial conditions (Ryan & Deci, 2000). Further, pre and post measures were collected about the pupils' psychosocial well-being using the Strengths and Difficulties Questionnaire (Bølling, Niclasen, Bentsen, & Nielsen, 2019a; Goodman, 1997), the school Academic Self-Regulation Questionnaire (Bølling, Otte, Elsborg, Nielsen, & Bentsen, 2018; Ryan & Connell, 1989) and their friendship relationships (social cognitive mapping network analysis) (Bølling, Pfister, Mygind, & Nielsen, 2019b; Kindermann, 2007).

The impacts of EOtC on physical activity were evaluated by comparing the total as well as context-specific amounts of physical activity of children participating in EOtC to those of children in their parallel non-EOtC classes. Data on physical activity levels were collected over ten-day periods during the school year using accelerometers (Schneller et al., 2017c). The project analyses how physical activity accumulates in various school contexts, for example, on normal school days, on days with physical education lessons, and on *udeskole* days.

Finally, the TEACHOUT project examined and highlighted experienced *udeskole* teachers' intended and implemented practices and classroom management through qualitative case studies with observation and interviews. The project included results from a number of *udeskole* teachers' concrete planning, their use of teaching methods in- and outside the school buildings, and their expectations for the pupils' learning process.

EOtC as a holistic 'add-in' approach to school-based health promotion for child and youth populations?

Holistic and interrelated outcomes

Health and education programmes commonly focus on one specific outcome, such as an increase of pupils' daily amount of physical activity (Dobbins, Husson, DeCorby, & LaRocca, 2013), enhancement of their social competences (Merrill et al., 2017) or mental capacities (Zenner, Herrnleben-Kurz, & Walach, 2014). EOtC is often implemented as a means for pupils to actively supplement their learning processes with experimental and hands-on activities in collaborative peer-feedback processes (James & Williams, 2017; Waite, 2011; Waite et al., 2016). However, as described above, EOtC stands out as it also involves additional health-related and learning supportive outcomes – increased physical activity, psychosocial well-being, and motivation for school. In sum, the range of simultaneous and interrelated outcomes suggests EOtC can be considered a holistic approach (Bentsen & Jensen, 2012) with a variety of potentials with respect to reaching both educational and health-related goals, and should be assessed and evaluated as a multi-component and multi-outcome programme (Tate et al., 2016).

While several aspects of EOtC have their own relevance and contribution to health and education benefits, there may also be interactions between the single concepts and outcomes. Interrelation of the single beneficial aspects of EOtC may be expected. Hence, the impacts of EOtC require consideration not only of the separate beneficial aspects, but of the mutual benefits and interrelatedness of the aspects.

This chain of benefits reflects recent education policy. Academic performance and learning must be considered the core deliverable of modern schooling, which also applies for the Scandinavian countries (Hamre, 2015; Wiborg, 2013). Nevertheless, there is evidence of educational policy that emphasises physical activity, motivation, and social and emotional well-being as supportive for curricular learning, as it for example occurred in Denmark in 2014 with the new school reform (Danish Ministry of Education, 2014).

Health promotion for child and youth populations

More than ever, we need effective and integrated strategies for promoting health in whole child and youth populations. As argued, EOtC is holistic in its nature, as it has the potential to influence various education and health outcomes. However, as a health promotion programme the expected benefits of EOtC must be evaluated critically. As a health programme with intended benefit for a wider population, i.e. a universal approach, it may not provide large effects for individuals. For example, in school-based interventions with an explicit aim to promote mental well-being through social and emotional learning in primary education of the wider group of pupils, studies have only yielded small impacts (Adi, Killoran, Janmohamed, & Stewart-Brown, 2007). Even though EOtC takes a universal approach and is a part of the everyday school curriculum, its emphasis is mainly on academic learning and not on health education. Despite the impacts being potentially small for individuals, the impact of universal approaches for the wider population is considerable (Rose, 1985). Thus, the potential modest impact of EOtC on individual pupils can be outweighed by the impact for the wider population of pupils. Furthermore, mounting evidence that childhood physical activity tracks into later life (Herman et al., 2009; Kristensen et al., 2008; Telama, 2009) indicates long term impacts in adult generations.

An 'add-in' approach

It is becoming increasingly accepted by those seeking to promote physical activity in education that linking these activities with curriculum goals is crucial. On the one hand, this is to improve the implementation and impact of interventions, and on the other hand, to make sure that schools can argue a concern with physical activity and health to teachers, parents, and policy-makers (Norris et al., 2015; Webster et al., 2015). Those involved in school-based health and physical activity promotion at every level need to ensure they work closely with education providers to demonstrate that their cooperation can benefit what schools perceive as their core values: pupils' academic learning, achievement, and well-being (ASCD, 2015).

A key feature of EOtC is its nature of implementation in the existing educational system and teaching practices, i.e. an 'add-in' approach, as for instance, reflected in movement integration in curriculum time (Webster et al., 2015). Educational programmes implemented in addition to the everyday teaching practices, i.e. an 'add-in' approach to education, could likely cause the same beneficial aspects as 'add-on' approaches. However, 'add-on' approaches require additional resources; for example, a) an extended time schedule to create opportunities for extra-curricular programmes, b) staff resources to undertake the implementation, and c) development of a curriculum additional to the existing syllabus. Thus, 'add-on' programmes can be expected to have a minor impact on the wider population, as many pupils will not be influenced by such extracurricular programmes and services due to low programme dissemination and marginalisation of non-student core achievement agendas, such as mental health agendas (Weist et al., 2012). 'Add-in' approaches to educational programmes can meet these challenges (Bentsen, Bonde, Schneller, Danielsen, Bruselius-Jensen, & Aagaard-Hansen, 2018). In the integrative 'add-in' approach, programme content and aim are delivered as an integrated part of the existing everyday teaching practice. The fundamental mechanism of 'add-in' programmes is that the aims of programmes operate in the background of existing syllabus. Thus, programme benefits can be seen as additional and simultaneous to academic performance and learning. For example, in EOtC, physical activity may not be the immediate aim of a teaching session; however, active transportation, walking or biking to and from the site away from the school ground, and the use of learning activities that require students to move will potentially benefit both learning and cardiovascular health (see Box 14.1). A high level of implementation of 'add-in' programmes is expected; as such programmes do not require substantial supplementary time resources. Furthermore, the reduced resistance to implementing the programmes in existing everyday teaching practice and syllabus content ensures better prospects for sustainability.

Conclusion

In this chapter, we have advocated for EOtC as an 'add-in' holistic approach to school-based health promotion for child and youth populations. The compulsory nature of formal education for children and young people makes schools ideally positioned to extend the reach of physical activity interventions to all children and youth. Based on existing research, theory, and case studies, we conclude that schools hold potential as an innovative platform for early intervention to increase children's daily physical activity in natural settings. EOtC in natural settings offers a novel approach in the fields of education and health promotion practice and policy through its 'add-in', holistic, and population-wide health promotion strategy. It is potentially a low-cost and non-invasive solution; however, more research and knowledge on implementation is needed.

While the focus here is EOtC in Danish schools and the cases and examples provided are Danish, similar development, practice, and research can be seen in many other countries and contexts (Dahlgren & Szczepanski, 1998; Davis et al., 2006; Jordet, 2007). This chapter has dealt with a particular type of programme in a particular kind of place: *udeskole* in Danish schools. Hopefully, it has relevance for a wider Scandinavian, European, and worldwide readership, who, we acknowledge, are at different phases in considering the inclusion of EOtC as a means of promoting physical activity and contact with nature in the school curriculum.

References

Adi, Y., Killoran, A., Janmohamed, K., & Stewart-Brown, S. (2007). Systematic review of the effectiveness of interventions to promote mental wellbeing in children in primary education: Report 1: Universal approaches non-violence related outcomes. *ResearchGate*.

Aronsson, J., Tighe Clark, M. & Waite, S. (2014). *Woodland Health for Youth (WHY): An evaluation of physical health benefits derived from outdoor Learning in Natural Environments (LINE) for school-age children*. Retrieved from www.lotc.org.uk/wp-content/uploads/2014/10/Woodland-Health-for-Youth-WHY-project-report.pdf

ASCD. (2015). Statement for the integration of health and education. Retrieved from www.ascd.org/ASCD/pdf/siteASCD/wholechild/Statement-for-the-Integration-of-Health-and-Education_English.pdf

Barfod, K., Ejbye-Ernst, N., Mygind, L., & Bentsen, P. (2016). Increased provision of udeskole in Danish schools: An updated national population survey. *Urban Forestry & Urban Greening, 20*, 277–281.

Beames, S., Higgins, P., & Nicol, R. (2012). *Learning outside the Classroom: Theory and Guidelines for Practice*. New York & London: Routledge.

Becker, C., Lauterbach, G., Spengler, S., Dettweiler, U., & Mess, F. (2017). Effects of regular classes in outdoor education settings: A systematic review on students' learning, social and health dimensions. *International Journal of Environmental Research and Public Health, 14*(5), E485.

Bentsen, P., Bonde, A. H., Schneller, M. B., Danielsen, D., Bruselius-Jensen, M., & Aagaard-Hansen, J. (2018). Danish 'add-in'school-based health promotion: integrating health in curriculum time. *Health Promotion International*, day095. doi:10.1093/heapro/day095

Bentsen, P., & Jensen, F. S. (2012). The nature of udeskole: Outdoor learning theory and practice in Danish schools. *Journal of Adventure Education and Outdoor Learning, 12*(3), 199–219.

Bentsen, P., Jensen, F. S., Mygind, E., & Randrup, T. B. (2010). The extent and dissemination of *udeskole* in Danish schools. *Urban Forestry & Urban Greening, 9*(3), 235–243.

Bentsen, P., Mygind, E., & Randrup, T. B. (2009). Towards an understanding of udeskole: Education outside the classroom in a Danish context. *Education 3-13, 37*(1), 29–44.

Bentsen, P., Schipperijn, J., & Jensen, F. S. (2013). Green space as classroom: Outdoor school teachers' use, preferences and ecostrategies. *Landscape Research, 38*(5), 561–575.

Bølling, M., Otte, C. R., Elsborg, P., Nielsen, G., & Bentsen, P. (2018). The association between education outside the classroom and students' school motivation: Results from a one-school-year quasi-experiment. *International Journal of Educational Research, 89*, 22–35.

Bølling, M., Niclasen, J., Bentsen, P., & Nielsen, G. (2019a). Association of education outside the classroom and pupils' psychosocial well-being: Results from a school year implementation. *Journal of School Health, 89*(3), 210–218.

Bølling, M., Pfister, G. U., Mygind, E., & Nielsen, G. (2019b). Education outside the classroom and pupils' social relations? A one-year quasi-experiment. *International Journal of Educational Research, 94*, 29–41.

Bowen, D. J., Kreuter, M., Spring, B., Cofta-Woerpel, L., Linnan, L., Weiner, D., et al. (2009). How we design feasibility studies. *American Journal of Preventive Medicine, 36*(5), 452–457.

Chow, J. T., & Lau, S. (2015). Nature gives us strength: Exposure to nature counteracts ego-depletion. *The Journal of Social Psychology, 155*(1), 70–85.

Craig, P., Dieppe, P., Macintyre, S., Mitchie, S., Nazareth, I., & Petticrew, M. (2008). Developing and evaluating complex interventions: The new medical Research Council Guidance. *British Medical Journal, 337*(7676), 979–983.

Dahlgren, L. O., & Szczepanski, A. (1998). *Outdoor Education – Literary Education and Sensory Experience. An Attempt at Defining the Identity of Outdoor Education*. Linköping, Sweden: Kinda Education Center, Linköping University.

The Danish Ministry of Education. (2014). Improving the Public School – Overview of reform of standards in the Danish public school (primary and lower secondary education). Retrieved from www.uvm.dk/-/media/filer/uvm/publikationer/engelsksprogede/2014-improving-the-public-schools.pdf

Davis, B., Rea, T., & Waite, S. (2006). The special nature of the outdoors: Its contribution to the education of children aged 3-11. *Australian Journal of Outdoor Education, 10*(2), 3–12.

Deci, E. L., & Ryan, R. M. (2002). *Handbook of Self-Determination Research*. Rochester, NY: University Rochester Press.

Dettweiler, U., Becker, C., Auestad, B. H., Simon, P., & Kirsch, P. (2017). Stress in school: Some empirical hints on the circadian cortisol rhythm of children in outdoor and indoor classes. *International Journal of Environmental Research and Public Health, 14*(5), 475.

Dobbins, M., Husson, H., DeCorby, K., & LaRocca, R. L. (2013). School-based physical activity programs for promoting physical activity and fitness in children and adolescents aged 6 to 18. *Cochrane Database of Systematic Reviews, 2*, CD007651.

Fedewa, A. L., & Ahn, S. (2011). The effects of physical activity and physical fitness on children's achievement and cognitive outcomes: A meta-analysis. *Research Quarterly for Exercise and Sport, 82*(3), 521–535.

Ferraro, F. M., III. (2015). Enhancement of convergent creativity following a multiday wilderness experience. *Ecopsychology*, 7(1), 7–11.

Fjørtoft, I. (2001). The natural environment as a playground for children: The impact of outdoor play activities in pre-primary school children. *Early Childhood Education Journal, 29*(2), 111–117.

Fjørtoft, I. (2004). Landscape as playscape: The effects of natural environments on children's play and motor development. *Children Youth and Environments, 14*(2), 21–44.

Gibson, J. J. (2014). The theory of affordances. In Jen Jack Gieseking, William Mangold, Cindi Katz, Setha Low, & Susan Saegert (Eds.), *The People, Place, and Space Reader* (pp. 56–60): New York: Routledge.

Goodman, R. (1997). The strengths and difficulties questionnaire: A research note. *Journal of Child Psychology and Psychiatry, 38*(5), 581–586.

Grønningsæter, I., Hallås, O., Kristiansen, T., & Nævdal, F. (2007). Fysisk aktivitet hos 11-12-åringer i skulen [Physical activity amongst 11-12 year old in the school; in Norwegian]. *Tidsskrift for Norsk Lægeforening, 127*(22), 2927–2929.

Gustafsson, P. E., Szczepanski, A., Nelson, N., & Gustafsson, P. A. (2012). Effects of an outdoor education intervention on the mental health of schoolchildren. *Journal of Adventure Education and Outdoor Learning, 12*(1), 63–79.

Gutman, L., & Vorhaus, J. (2012). *The Impact of Pupil Behaviour and Wellbeing on Educational Outcomes*. London: Institute of Education, University of London; Childhood Wellbeing Research Centre.

Hamre, B. (2015). Diagnosing, special education and "learnification" in Danish schools. *Nordic Journal of Social Research*. Retrieved from www.forskningsdatabasen.dk/en/catalog/2282493058

Hartmeyer, R., & Mygind, E. (2016). A retrospective study of social relations in a Danish primary school class taught in "udeskole." *Journal of Adventure Education and Outdoor Learning, 16*(1), 78–89.

Heft, H. (1988). Affordances of children's environments: A functional approach to environmental description. *Children's Environments Quarterly, 5*(3), 29–37.

Herman, K. M., Craig, C. L., Gauvin, L., & Katzmarzyk, P. T. (2009). Tracking of obesity and physical activity from childhood to adulthood: The physical activity longitudinal study. *International Journal of Pediatric Obesity, 4*(4), 281–288.

Inchley, J., Currie, D., Young, T., Samdal, O., Torsheim, T., Augustson, L., Mathison, F., Aleman-Diaz, A., Molcho, M., Weber, M., & Barnekow, V. (2016). *Growing up unequal: Gender and socioeconomic differences in young people's health and well-being. Health Behaviour in School-aged Children (HBSC) study: International report from the 2013/2014 survey* (Health policy for children and adolescents, No. 7). Copenhagen: World Health Organization Regional Office for Europe.

James, J. K., & Williams, T. (2017). School-based experiential outdoor education: A neglected necessity. *Journal of Experiential Education, 40*(1), 58–71.

Jordet, A. N. (1998). *Nærmiljøet som klasserom. Uteskole i teori og praksis* [Local community as classroom. Uteskole in theory and practice; in Norwegian]. Oslo, Norway: Cappelen Akademisk Forlag.

Jordet, A. N. (2007). *Nærmiljøet som klasserom. En undersøkelse om uteskolens didaktikk i et danningsteoretisk og erfaringspedagogisk perspektiv* [Local community as classroom; in Norwegian]. Doctoral diss. Oslo, Norway: University of Oslo.

Kindermann, T. A. (2007). Effects of naturally existing peer groups on changes in academic engagement in a cohort of sixth graders. *Child Development, 78*(4), 1186–1203.

Kristensen, P. L., Møller, N. C., Korsholm, L., Wedderkopp, N., Andersen, L. B., & Froberg, K. (2008). Tracking of objectively measured physical activity from childhood to adolescence: The European youth heart study. *Scandinavian Journal of Medicine & Science in Sports, 18*(2), 171–178.

Kuo, F. E., & Faber Taylor, A. (2004). A potential natural treatment for attention-deficit/hyperactivity disorder: Evidence from a national study. *American Journal of Public Health, 94*(9), 1580–1586.

Kuo, M. (2015). How might contact with nature promote human health? Promising mechanisms and a possible central pathway. *Frontiers in Psychology, 6*, 1093. doi:10.3389/fpsyg.2015.01093

Lederbogen, F., Kirsch, P., Haddad, L., Streit, F., Tost, H., Schuch, P., ... Deuschle, M. (2011). City living and urban upbringing affect neural social stress processing in humans. *Nature, 474*(7352), 498–501.

Lovell, R. (2009). *An Evaluation of Physical Activity at Forest School.* PhD thesis. Scotland: University of Edinburgh.

McMahan, E. A., & Estes, D. (2015). The effect of contact with natural environments on positive and negative affect: A meta-analysis. *The Journal of Positive Psychology, 10*(6), 507–519.

Merikangas, K. R., He, J.-P., Burstein, M., Swanson, S. A., Avenevoli, S., Cui, L., ... Swendsen, J. (2010). Lifetime prevalence of mental disorders in US adolescents: Results from the National Comorbidity Survey Replication-Adolescent Supplement (NCS-A). *Journal of the American Academy of Child & Adolescent Psychiatry, 49*(10), 980–989.

Merrill, K. L., Smith, S. W., Cumming, M. M., & Daunic, A. P. (2017). A review of social problem-solving interventions: Past findings, current status, and future directions. *Review of Educational Research, 87*(1), 71–102.

Mygind, E. (Ed.). (2005). *Udeundervisning i folkeskolen. Et casestudie om en naturklasse på Rødkilde Skole og virkningerne af en ugentlig obligatorisk naturdag på yngste klassetrin i perioden 2000–2003* [Outdoor teaching in the public municipality school. A case study of a nature class at Rødkilde School; in Danish]. Copenhagen, Denmark: Museum Tusculanums Forlag and Department of Exercise and Sport Sciences.

Mygind, E. (2007). A comparison between children's physical activity levels at school and learning in an outdoor environment. *Journal of Adventure Education and Outdoor Learning, 7*(2), 61–76.

Mygind, E. (2009). A comparison of children's statements about social relations and teaching in the classroom and in the outdoor environment. *Journal of Adventure Education and Outdoor Learning, 9*(2), 151–169.

Mygind, E. (2016). Physical activity during learning inside and outside the classroom. *Health Behavior and Policy Review, 3*, 455–467.

Mygind, L., Stevenson, M., Liebst, L., Konvalina, I., & Bentsen, P. (2018) Stress response and cognitive performance modulation in classroom versus natural environments: A quasi-experimental pilot study with children. *International Journal of Environmental Research and Public Health, 15*(6), 1098.

Mygind, L., Kjeldsted, E., Hartmeyer, R., Mygind, E., Bølling, M., & Bentsen, P. (2019). Mental, physical and social health benefits of immersive nature-experience for children and adolescents: a systematic review and quality assessment of the evidence. *Health & Place, 58*, 102136.

Ng, M., Fleming, T., Robinson, M., Thomson, B., Graetz, N., Margono, C., … Abera, S. F. (2014). Global, regional, and national prevalence of overweight and obesity in children and adults during 1980–2013: A systematic analysis for the Global Burden of Disease Study 2013. *The Lancet, 384*(9945), 766–781.

Nielsen, G. (2011). *Children's Daily Physical Activity: Patterns and the Influence of Socio-Cultural factors*. (Doctoral dissertation). Copenhagen, Denmark: Department of Exercise and Sport Sciences, University of Copenhagen.

Nielsen, G., Mygind, E., Bølling, M., Otte, C. R., Schneller, M. B., Schipperijn, J., … Bentsen, P. (2016). A quasi-experimental cross-disciplinary evaluation of the impacts of education outside the classroom on pupils' physical activity, well-being and learning: The TEACHOUT study protocol. *BMC Public Health, 16*(1), 1117.

Nielsen, G., & Stelter, R. (n.d.). *Mellen social kreativitet og sportslige kompetencer* [Between Social Creativity and Sporting Competences]. Mellen Soc. Kreat. Og Sportslige Kompet. Btween Soc. Creat. Sport. Competences 10.

Norris, E., Shelton, N., Dunsmuir, S., Duke-Williams, O., & Stamatakis, E. (2015). Physically active lessons as physical activity and educational interventions: A systematic review of methods and results. *Preventive Medicine, 72*, 116–125.

O'Brien, L., & Murray, R. (2007). Forest school and its impacts on young children: Case studies in Britain. *Urban Forestry & Urban Greening, 6*, 249–265.

Ohly, H., White, M. P., Wheeler, B. W., Bethel, A., Ukoumunne, O. C., Nikolaou, V., & Garside, R. (2016). Attention restoration theory: A systematic review of the attention restoration potential of exposure to natural environments. *Journal of Toxicology and Environmental Health, Part B, 19*(7), 305–343.

Otte, C. R., Bølling, M., Stevenson, M. P., Ejbye-Ernst, N., Nielsen, G., & Bentsen, P. (2019a). Education outside the classroom increases children's reading performance: Results from a one-year quasi-experimental study. *International Journal of Educational Research, 94*, 42–51.

Otte, C. R., Bølling, M., Elsborg, P., Nielsen, G., & Bentsen, P. (2019b). Teaching maths outside the classroom: Does it make a difference? *Educational Research, 61*(1), 38–52.

Owen, K. B., Parker, P. D., Van Zanden, B., MacMillan, F., Astell-Burt, T., & Lonsdale, C. (2016). Physical activity and school engagement in youth: A systematic review and meta-analysis. *Educational Psychologist, 51*(2), 129–145.

Pawlowski, C. S., Ergler, C., Tjørnhøj-Thomsen, T., Schipperijn, J., & Troelsen, J. (2015). "Like a soccer camp for boys". A qualitative exploration of gendered activity patterns in children's self-organized play during school recess. *European Physical Education Review, 21*, 275–291.

Pietilä, M., Neuvonen, M., Borodulin, K., Korpela, K., Sievänen, T., & Tyrväinen, L. (2015). Relationships between exposure to urban green spaces, physical activity and self-rated health. *Journal of Outdoor Recreation and Tourism, 10*, 44–54.

Pressley, M., Graham, S., & Harris, K. (2006). The state of educational intervention research as viewed through the lens of literacy intervention. *British Journal of Educational Psychology*, *76*(1), 1–19.

Pucher, K. K., Boot, N. M. W. M., & De Vries, N. K. (2013). Systematic review: School health promotion interventions targeting physical activity and nutrition can improve academic performance in primary- and middle school children. *Health Education*, *113*(5), 372–391.

Rea, T., & Waite, S. (2009). Editorial. International perspectives on outdoor and experiential learning. *Education 3–13*, *37*(2), 1–4.

Rickinson, M., Dillon, J., Teamey, K., Morris, M., Choi, M., Sanders, K., & Benefield, P. (2004). *A Review of Research on Outdoor Learning*. Shrewsbury, UK: Field Studies.

Rose, G. (1985). Sick individuals and sick populations. *International Journal of Epidemiology*, *14*(1), 32–38.

Ryan, R. M., & Connell, J. P. (1989). Perceived locus of causality and internalization: Examining reasons for acting in two domains. *Journal of Personality and Social Psychology*, *57*(5), 749.

Ryan, R. M., & Deci, E. L. (2000). Self-determination theory and the facilitation of intrinsic motivation, social development, and well-being. *American Psychologist*, *55*(1), 68–78.

Schneller, M. B., Bentsen, P., Nielsen, G., Brønd, J. C., Ried-Larsen, M., Mygind, E., & Schipperijn, J. (2017c). Measuring children's physical activity: Compliance using skin-taped accelerometers. *Medicine & Science in Sports & Exercise*, *49*(6), 1261–1269.

Schneller, M. B., Duncan, S., Schipperijn, J., Nielsen, G., & Mygind, E., & Bentsen, P. (2017a). Are children participating in a quasi-experimental education outside the classroom intervention more physically active? *BMC Public Health*, *17*, 523.

Schneller, M. B., Schipperijn, J., Nielsen, G., & Bentsen, P. (2017b). Children's physical activity during a segmented school week: Results from a quasi-experimental education outside the classroom intervention. *International Journal of Behavioral Nutrition and Physical Activity*, *14*, 80.

Schwartz, D., Gorman, A. H., Duong, M. T., & Nakamoto, J. (2008). Peer relationships and academic achievement as interacting predictors of depressive symptoms during middle childhood. *Journal of Abnormal Psychology*, *117*(2), 289.

Simovska, V., Nordin, L. L., & Madsen, K. D. (2016). Health promotion in Danish schools: Local priorities, policies and practices. *Health Promotion International*, *31*(2), 480–489.

Strum, R. (2005). Childhood obesity - what we can learn from existing data on societal trends, part 1. *Preventing Chronic Diseases*, *2*, A12.

Studente, S., Seppala, N., & Sadowska, N. (2016). Facilitating creative thinking in the classroom: Investigating the effects of plants and the colour green on visual and verbal creativity. *Thinking Skills and Creativity*, *19*, 1–8.

Tate, D. F., Lytle, L. A., Sherwood, N. E., Haire-Joshu, D., Matheson, D., Moore, S. M., … Michie, S. (2016). Deconstructing interventions: Approaches to studying behavior change techniques across obesity interventions. *Translational Behavioral Medicine*, *6*(2), 236–243.

Telama, R. (2009). Tracking of physical activity from childhood to adulthood: A review. *Obesity Facts*, *2*(3), 187–195.

van den Bosch, M., & Bird, W. (Eds.). (2018). *Oxford Textbook of Nature and Public Health. The Role of Nature in Improving the Health of a Population*. Oxford: Oxford University Press.

Verburgh, L., Königs, M., Scherder, E. J. A., & Oosterlaan, J. (2014). Physical exercise and executive functions in preadolescent children, adolescents and young adults: A meta-analysis. *British Journal of Sports Medicine, 48*, 973–979.

Waite, S. (2011). Teaching and learning outside the classroom: Personal values, alternative pedagogies and standards. *Education 3-13, 39*(1), 65–82.

Waite, S., Bølling, M., & Bentsen, P. (2016). Comparing apples and pears? A conceptual framework for understanding forms of outdoor learning through comparison of English forest schools and Danish udeskole. *Environmental Education Research, 22*(6), 868–892.

Wallace, C. E., & Russ, S. W. (2015). Pretend play, divergent thinking, and math achievement in girls: A longitudinal study. *Psychology of Aesthetics, Creativity, and the Arts, 9*(3), 296.

Webster, C. A., Russ, L., Vazou, S., Goh, T. L., & Erwin, H. (2015). Integrating movement in academic classrooms: Understanding, applying and advancing the knowledge base. *Obesity Reviews, 16*(8), 691–701.

Weist, M. D., Mellin, E. A., Chambers, K. L., Lever, N. A., Haber, D., & Blaber, C. (2012). Challenges to collaboration in school mental health and strategies for overcoming them. *Journal of School Health, 82*(2), 97–105.

Wheeler, B. W., Cooper, A. R., Page, A. S., & Jago, R. (2010). Greenspace and children's physical activity: A GPS/GIS analysis of the PEACH project. *Preventive Medicine, 51*(2), 148–152.

Wiborg, S. (2013). Neo-liberalism and universal state education: The cases of Denmark, Norway and Sweden 1980–2011. *Comparative Education, 49*(4), 407–423.

World Health Organization. (2004). *The Physical School Environment – An Essential Component of a Health-Promoting School.* Information Series on School Health. Geneva, Switzerland: WHO.

World Health Organization. (2010a). *Global Recommendations on Physical Activity for Health.* Switzerland: World Health Organization.

World Health Organization. (2010b). *Urban Planning, Environment and Health: From Evidence to Policy Action.* Copenhagen: World Health Organization Regional Office for Europe.

World Health Organization. (2016a). *Urban Green Spaces and Health – A Review of Evidence.* Geneva, Switzerland: WHO.

Zenner, C., Herrnleben-Kurz, S., & Walach, H. (2014). Mindfulness-based interventions in schools – A systematic review and meta-analysis. *Frontiers in Psychology, 5*, 503.

PART IV

Future pathways

15

FUTURE-THINKING THROUGH TECHNOLOGICAL NATURE

Connecting or disconnecting

Giovanna Calogiuri, Sigbjørn Litleskare and Tadhg E. MacIntyre

In the recent tome entitled the *Oxford Textbook of Nature and Public Health: The Role of Nature in Improving the Health of a Population*, Peter Kahn (2018) discusses the concept of *technological nature*, a term coined almost a decade previously (Kahn, Severson, & Ruckert, 2009). It refers to technologies that in various ways mediate, augment and simulate our experience of the natural world. In the discourse, Kahn (2018) addresses the question of whether we are on a path to replace real nature with technological nature. Although this author considers that ' … in terms of physical and psychological human health that interaction with technological nature is better than no nature', the increasing advancement and pervasive presence of technological nature is viewed from a somewhat pernicious perspective:

> … as we move to an increasingly technological world with at best technological nature as a substitute for the real thing, we will be shifting the baseline downwards–as we have already–for what can be consider as physically and psychologically healthy humans.
>
> *(Kahn, 2018, p. 163)*

Considering the extent to which the world is progressively becoming disconnected from real or authentic nature due to urbanization (see Chapters 1 and 18), and at the same time the extent to which technological nature is becoming more and more accessible for consumers, a question arises of whether we are doomed to live in what Kahn (2018) defines as a 'massive urban prison' (p. 163), and what can we do to avoid such a destiny. Although we share the concerns expressed above, and acknowledge both the challenges and potential unintended consequences associated with the promotion of technological nature as part of a solution to different health challenges, we believe that there is a promising future yet to be explored. In this chapter, we will explore ways in which technological nature can not only act as a tool to supplement nature experiences for people for whom access to real or authentic nature is limited, but additionally we propose it as a strategy to promote enhanced feelings of connectedness with the natural world which has temporal power beyond the actual nature experience. To explain, we can use technology to review our last visit to a real natural environment (e.g. video or photos), employ it to augment our current nature interaction (e.g. add soundscape to green infrastructure) or utilize virtual reality (VR) to reduce barriers for our next contact with authentic nature.

In this chapter we will focus on so-called immersive virtual environments. This technology, which is what most people are accustomed to think of in relation to VR experiences, can be defined as synthetic sensory information that provide a surrounding and continuous stream of stimuli, creating the illusory perception of being enclosed within and interacting with a real environment (Loomis, Blascovich, & Beall, 1999; Smith, 2015). In particular, we are predominantly interested in a specific form of immersive virtual environment: one that provides a representation of some sort of *natural* environment. We may refer to this as *immersive virtual nature* (IVN).

Firstly, we will present a brief overview of how this tool emerged in the broader landscape of technological nature and has been increasingly present (or accessible) in people's lives. We then summarize evidence that allows us to examine whether or not (and to what extent) it can provide psychophysiological benefits similar to those associated with interacting with real nature. We then describe the concepts of "immersion", "presence" and "cyber sickness", which are known challenges associated with the use of IVN that can not only determine its effectiveness but also (as in the case of cyber sickness) carry some degree of risk for the users. Subsequently, we present a series of contexts in which IVN could be especially useful, as well as propose some insight relative to the potential of this technology in research and in the mission of reconnecting people to real nature.

Technological nature: a very broad concept

Technological nature is quite a broad concept, which encompasses any technology that in various ways mediates, augments and simulates our experience of the natural world. Abiding by the very definition of technology, i.e. the application of scientific knowledge for practical purposes, technological nature has for decades mainly comprised artefacts such as pictures, stuffed animals, or synthetic flowers and foliage plants. Further developments have seen the rise of robot-pets, some less advanced and relatively inexpensive (such as robot-toys) and some far more sophisticated. The advancement of robotics has come to a point in which robot-pets show life-like interactions with humans, using facial recognition technology to make the robot-pet stare in a person's eyes and respond to petting with affectionate motions (see for example PARO Therapeutic Robot www.parorobots.com).

It is only in relatively recent times that we became accustomed to associate the idea of technological nature with *digital* technology. Thanks to digital cameras (today integrated in our own phones), we can take high-resolution images of fascinating landscapes or our favourite pet without having photography training, use them as screen-savers for our phone or computer, and share them instantaneously with friends on social media. Researchers on human-nature interactions have employed what one could call 'hybrid-thinking' to explore emotional responses to nature. For example, a recent study had students take photos of notable natural or built environment features in a two-week long study of individual and social benefits of noticing nature (Passmore & Holder, 2017). Arguably, the most recent development in the field of technological nature, and in our perspective most interesting in terms of potential for reconnecting people with real nature, is the advancement of VR.

VR can be referred to as a computer-generated simulation of a three-dimensional image or environment that allows a certain degree of interaction, creating the illusion of reality. A characteristic of VR is that it creates a high degree (though not necessarily total) disconnection of a person's senses from the external (real) world. Different types of VR exist, including three-dimensional surrounding screens, the Reality Cube and head-mounted devices. The latter, more commonly known as a 'VR mask' or 'VR googles', is a device with a motion sensor that allows a 360° vision of a virtual world while eliminating the visual contact with external reality.

Head-mounted devices are the technology that makes viewing immersive virtual environments and IVN possible. It is thanks to the commercialisation of affordable head-mounted devices (for example, a Google Cardboard can cost less than $20), which allow a person to immerse themselves in a virtual environment by plugging in their own smart-phone, that VR has taken off and become a phenomenon of mass consumption. Relatively inexpensive cameras are also available that take 360° pictures and film 360° videos, which can be in turn shared on online platforms. Today people can be exposed to IVN (even in the form of movies, news and documentaries) from online platforms such as YouTube VR and Google Earth VR. In light of the progressive commercialization and enhanced accessibility of this technology, many argue that the digital world is already on its way towards a 'VR revolution'.

What are we going to earn and what are we going to lose along the way of the VR revolution?

Watching old sci-fiction movies we can realize how people in the past used to imagine the future. It seems like people in the past were expecting huge advancement in the field of transportation and space-travelling, with humans driving flying cars running on waste and riding flying hover-boards, or living in wandering space-ships. Would the people in the past be disappointed or amazed to find out that real incredible technological development has occurred in the field of telecommunications? Something similar can be observed in relation to the development of VR. While old sci-fi movies let us understand how in the past we imagined a future in which VR could perfectly simulate real perceptions, today VR still presents many technical limitations in the extent to which it can give us fully immersive experiences, but at the same time its potential resides in the way it can connect people and places throughout the world.

Some believe that VR will have the same impact on people's lives that the advent of smart-phones (and cell phones before them) had. VR might change the way we look for and assimilate information, as well as the way we communicate long-distance, or the way we organize our travels. Using platforms such as Google Street View and Google Earth we can virtually visit any place on the globe. Already from a physical activity perspective, one can track the entire route of the London Marathon using Google Street View, for example. Assuming that this VR revolution is really happening, we are left to ask ourselves what we are going to earn and what we are going to lose along the way. This question is especially relevant in relation to the way we value and interact with the natural world.

Is virtual nature as good as the real thing?

There is accumulating evidence demonstrating that IVN can provide restorative and pleasant experiences (White et al., 2018). For instance, Yu, Lee, and Luo (2018) looked at participants' physiological and psychological responses to viewing an IVN as compared to a virtual urban environment. Consistent with a large body of literature comparing natural versus urban environments *in vivo* (see e.g. Bowler, Buyung-Ali, Knight, & Pullin, 2010), they found that exposure to the IVN elicited an increase in vigour and a reduction in negative emotions, as opposed to an increase in fatigue and a decrease in the levels of self-esteem observed in relation to exposure to the virtual urban environment. On the other hand, however, unlike trials *in vivo*, no difference between the two virtual environments was observed with respect to physiological measurements (blood pressure, salivary α amylase and heart-rate variability). The authors suggest that this finding could be explained by the fact that VR technology does not provide the full range of stimuli (sounds, smells, temperature, etc.) that a person would experience in a real environment.

Few studies have compared the effects of exposure to IVN with exposure to real nature. Calogiuri et al. (2018) found that participants assigned to an IVN experienced levels of perceived environmental restorativeness equivalent to those assigned to the same natural environment *in vivo*. Chirico and Gaggioli (2019) found that the emotional responses to viewing a natural landscape *in vivo* or in the form of IVN were not statistically significant different. On the other hand, in a systematic review of literature on the effects of green exercise, we found inconclusive evidence concerning the extent to which exposure to real nature (in the form of green exercise) provided more positive psychological or physiological benefits as compared with exposure to virtual nature (Lahart, Darcy, Gidlow, & Calogiuri, 2019). While the studies found no significant difference between IVN and real nature for a number of outcomes, they also found significantly superior effects in favour of real nature for about the same number of outcomes.

In the light of this evidence, it seems like there is still insufficient quality evidence available to support the assumption that IVN can provide health benefits fully comparable to those provided to real nature. It has been suggested by Calogiuri et al. (2018) that differences might exist depending on the type of VR technology used and, especially, on whether the IVN is 'static' (e.g. footages with no or limited change in the viewer's perspective) or 'dynamic' (e.g. videos showing a first-person view of a virtual walk). It has to be noted, however, that VR technology is advancing rapidly and that future development might lead to more life-like virtual experiences of nature. It is however likely that, matter how much the technology will improve, virtual nature will never be able to fully replicate the holistic, multi-sensory and potentially elating experience of the real outdoors. The voice of one of the participants in our VR trials is telling in this regard: 'Nature will always win for me. It is less stressful, you know where you are, you can stop and look, for example, at birds anytime' (Female, 22 years old).

Challenges associated with IVN technology

Immersion and presence

The concepts of immersion and presence are key aspects of virtual environments. Immersion is defined as the extent to which a computer-generated environment is 'capable of delivering an inclusive, extensive, surrounding, and vivid illusion of reality to the senses of a human participant' (Slater & Wilbur, 1997). The level of immersion depends solely on the technological aspects of the virtual environment, such as field of view, display resolution and frame rate (Bowman & McMahan, 2007). In other words, the level of immersion is directly linked to the system being used for the virtual representation, and one can objectively evaluate the systems level of immersion. Two people that use the same technology to display a virtual environment will be provided with the same level of immersion. Presence, on the other hand, describes the subjective feeling of 'being in the virtual environment' (Slater & Wilbur, 1997). This concept describes the psychological feeling of no longer being present in the physical location and rather being fully present in the virtual location. Thus, two different people can use a system with the same level of immersion, but experience different levels of presence.

Immersion and presence are closely related and it is believed that a highly immersive system increases the likelihood of inducing high levels of presence. Consider a comparison of a painting and a head-mounted display, and let us assume that both of them portray a visual representation of nature. The painting is obviously a low-tech representation of nature and is considered the least immersive of the two, but it may still induce the feeling of being present in the painting (i.e. presence). The head-mounted display, on the other hand, is a highly immersive system, which increases the likelihood of inducing a feeling of being present in the virtual environment. However, it is far from guaranteed and depends on several other factors, such as personality traits and most notably cyber sickness.

The virtual environment's ability to deliver a sense of presence is pivotal to its effectiveness, and relates to the ability of the virtual environment to fulfil the purposes set by the virtual environment (Botella, Fernandez-Alvarez, Guillen, Garcia-Palacios, & Banos, 2017; Steuer, 1992; Triberti, Repetto, & Riva, 2014). This relation between presence and effectiveness of a virtual environment, suggest that presence in IVN is key to induce psychophysiological benefits comparable to actual nature.

Cyber sickness

Virtual environments do not come without complications. Cyber sickness is a well-known malaise and can occur in most virtual environments presented through a visual medium, including cell phones, computer screens and head-mounted displays. Cyber sickness mimics the symptoms of motion sickness, inducing feelings of dizziness, nausea and general discomfort (Smith, 2015), and is considered a specific type of visually induced motion sickness (Kennedy, Drexler, & Kennedy, 2010). Cyber sickness is reported to occur in as many as 100% of viewers depending on the technology used, the duration of immersion and the content of the virtual environment (Allen, Hanley, Rokers, & Green, 2016; Merhi, Faugloire, Flanagan, & Stoffregen, 2007; Murata, 2004).

This modern day malaise is not only unpleasant, but also lowers the sense of presence in virtual environments (Weech, Kenny, & Barnett-Cowan, 2019). This is unfortunate, as the combination of cyber sickness and reduced sense of presence will logically take away from the desired psychophysiological benefits of IVN. Furthermore, visual displays that are considered more advanced and immersive, such as head-mounted displays, generally induce higher levels of cyber sickness (Sharples, Cobb, Moody, & Wilson, 2008). However, this may not relate directly to the type of display. The most advanced types of displays are also the newest, which limits the time manufacturers have had to optimize the associated hardware and software. This creates a paradox: the most advanced displays may provide higher degrees of presence, but these displays may at the same time be more prone to induce cyber sickness.

Researchers and manufacturers are scrambling to find strategies to make highly immersive systems that induce high levels of presence, while trying to reduce the impact of cyber sickness. Luckily, this work seems to be moving in the right direction. Manufacturers continuously improve their technology and researchers have identified several factors that contribute to or limit the susceptibility to cyber sickness, such as habituation, exposure time, scene oscillation, movement lag and type of display (Calogiuri et al., 2018; Duzmanska, Strojny, & Strojny, 2018; Gavgani,

Nesbitt, Blackmore, & Nalivaiko, 2017; Lo & So, 2001; Sharples et al., 2008). This combined effort holds promise for the future of IVN and the day virtual environments can reliably create life-like experiences may be here sooner rather than later.

Technological nature, better than no nature? Some examples

IVN as a palliative treatment in clinical care or home settings

The field of clinical care is probably where IVN has proliferated the most. The interest in the use of VR technology as part of the prevention and treatment of both mental and physiological health problems initiated as far back as the 1990s, and has continued to increase since (Chirico et al., 2016; White et al., 2018). Although researchers have warned about the need for well-designed studies to show its cost-effectiveness, there is consistent evidence demonstrating that the use of VR technology in clinical settings is both feasible and safe, and often results in high patient satisfaction (Dascal et al., 2017). In a recent review of literature, White et al. conclude that IVN is a useful tool to integrate traditional treatments and promote greater health outcomes in contexts in which contact with real nature is not possible or not recommended, for example when dealing with individuals at high-risk of injury or when meteorological conditions might cause harm to patients (White et al., 2018). More specifically, in their review, White et al. summarize the literature on effective application of IVN in the following fields:

pain management,
neurological disorders and stroke rehabilitation,
distraction and relaxation tool in cancer treatment,
mental health and well-being, including eating disorders, obesity, phobias, anxiety, agitation and depression,
cognitive rehabilitation.

Furthermore, they discuss the extent to which IVN relates to the mediating mechanisms linking natural environments and health, as proposed by the World Health Organization (see Box 15.1), concluding that IVN can play a role in relation to each of them.

BOX 15.1 WORLD HEALTH ORGANIZATION'S PROPOSED PATHWAYS LINKING THE OBSERVED HEALTH OUTCOMES AND URBAN GREEN AND BLUE INFRASTRUCTURE (WHO, 2016):

- Relaxation and restoration
- Improved social capital
- Improved functioning of the immune system
- Enhanced physical activity, improved fitness and reduced obesity

- Anthropogenic noise buffering and production of natural sounds
- Reduced exposure to air pollution
- Reduction of the urban heat island effect
- Enhanced pro-environmental behaviour
- Optimized exposure to sunlight and improved sleep

IVN in the workplace as a strategy to reduce and prevent work-related stress

Work-related stress is considered one of the most challenging issues in occupational safety and employees' health (European Agency for Safety and Health at Work, 2018). European studies show that work-related stress is an extremely extended phenomenon. The fourth European Working Conditions Survey found that a large number of employees believed their health was at risk due to stress at work, with the highest prevalence observed in Greece (55%), Slovenia (38%) and Sweden (38%). The reported health impact of work-related stress tended to be higher among the new member states (30% in average) than in the EU-15 (Parent-Thirion, 2007). Such a widespread phenomenon has significant and real costs for society: it has been estimated that about half of the missed working days were somewhat associated with work-related stress, costing the EU-15 approximately €20,000 million annually (Hassard, 2011).

The cost of work-related stress is often linked with the emergence of mental health disorders. A meta-analysis found a moderate level of evidence from multiple prospective studies for high job demands, low job control, high effort-reward imbalance, low relational justice, low procedural justice, role stress, bullying and low social support in the workplace leading to greater risk of developing work-related stress and mental health problems such as depression and anxiety (Harvey et al., 2017). It is estimated that about 83 million European citizens have experienced at least one mental disorder (including psychoses, depression, anxiety, eating disorders, and problems arising from substance use) in the past year. In spite of such a great burden, mental health problems are often under-treated; for example it is estimated that three out of four people suffering from major depression *do not* receive adequate treatment (WHO Europe, 2018).

The term *nature-based interventions*, as discussed in Chapter 2, refers to interventions that aim to enhance and promote health by developing strategies to expose people to nature by facilitating recovery from or even preventing the occurrence of stress. This concept is often translated by inserting elements of nature into work environments or by facilitating access to a natural environment during worktime. Based on the growing evidence of the health-enhancing effects of nature-based solutions in urban settings (van den Bosch & Sang, 2017), as well as a large body of literature showing the health benefits of interacting with nature in reducing stress (Hartig, Mitchell, De Vries, & Frumkin, 2014), nature-based interventions have been proposed as a cost-effective strategy to promote health and well-being in the workplace.

A scoping review from 2014 also supported the health-promoting effects of so-called *indoor nature exposure* (indoor environments that contain real or representations of nature-based stimuli that engage a variety of senses), emphasizing that the health benefits of indoor nature exposure often occur by facilitating reduction of and recovery from stress (Mcsweeney, Rainham, Johnson, Sherry, & Singleton, 2014). A simple (and common) way to expose employees to nature is by making use of nature elements within the indoor spaces (e.g. potted plants and images portraying natural landscapes). A whole field of *biofilic* indoor architecture has been developed as a form of indoor nature exposure. Some studies have also investigated the effectiveness of implementing nature-based solutions that aim to facilitate employees spending time in natural environments, such as walks in nature during lunch-time (Brown, Barton, Pretty, & Gladwell, 2014) and green exercise group sessions for employees (Calogiuri et al., 2016a). However, experiences of this type are often subject to a number of barriers, such as weather conditions and accessibility to quality outdoor natural environments. Moreover, in some circumstances, outdoor natural settings pose many threats to health and well-being, especially when engaged in exercise in conditions of high levels of air pollution (Sinharay et al., 2018).

The advent of VR technology might represent a further advancement in this field by allowing more immersive and life-like experience of nature in indoor settings, possibly leading to a new field of *IVN-based interventions.* Digital images of nature have been used in studies of micro-breaks (short informal work-day based respite activities designed to restore psychological resources, Sonnentag & Fritz, 2007) in prior research (Lee, Williams, Sargent, Farrell, & Williams, 2014). In an experiment, the researchers compared two groups after viewing images of a roof scene. One group viewed a "green roof" while the other group viewed a concrete roof, during a 40-second work break during a sustained attention task. The findings showed, as predicted, a positive impact on cognitive performance among the nature scene group with a decrease in performance among the comparison condition. Developing higher fidelity IVN-based interventions could amplify these effects and are worthy of exploration. Although there is a lack of scientific literature investigating the effectiveness of implementing IVN-based solutions in the workplace, evidence exists supporting the effectiveness of IVN to elicit stress reduction in experimental trials on healthy adults (Plante et al., 2003; Valtchanov, Barton, & Ellard, 2010; Yu et al., 2018). Exposure to IVN was found to provide greater reductions of anxiety and improvements in affect as compared to simply watching images of nature from a screen in situations of acute emotional strain (Liszio & Masuch, 2018). This suggests that IVN might have a greater potential to promote health and well-being among employees when compared with other forms of indoor nature exposure.

IVN in school settings as a supplement to psycho-cognitive development

In his book *Last Child in the Woods: Saving Our Children from Nature Deficit Disorder*, Richard Louv (2008) brings attention to the societal cost of the diminished time that today's children spend in contact with nature. 'Nature-deficit disorder' is not a recognized medical diagnosis, but a generic term referring to a series of health challenges linked to a reduced time spent outdoors in contact with nature, such as attention difficulties, increased risk for physical and mental problems, vision deficits, obesity and Vitamin D deficiency. In addition, the progressive disconnection from nature can result in less concerns for environmental issues, which can lead to a collective disengagement, with environmentally sustainable behaviours that harm the planet as well as its inhabitants. According to Louv, therefore, direct exposure to nature is essential for healthy childhood development and for the physical and emotional health of future adults. A large body of literature does support such a position. A large portion of the population do not engage with nature on a regular basis: recent estimates show that in the United Kingdom, for instance, almost 60% of the adult population does not spend time out in nature during a typical week (White et al., 2016). Although in Norway a larger portion of people (up to 60%) engages nature on a weekly base, a recent study shows that younger people are significantly less engaged in nature than older adults are (Calogiuri, Patil, & Aamodt, 2016).

Exposure to nature is an effective supplement in tackling health challenges of central relevance for children and young people's development. For instance, Mennis, Mason, and Ambrus (2018) found that the presence of greenspaces within adolescents' living environments was associated with a reduction in levels of psychological stress. Participation in green exercise and outdoor recreation activities can lead to higher levels of self-esteem, well-being, and a more positive perceived body image in adolescents (Barton, Bragg, Pretty, Roberts, & Wood, 2016; Swami, Barron, & Furnham, 2018; Wood, Sandercock, & Barton, 2014). Exposure to nature during childhood can also lead to greater engagement with nature-based physical activity in adulthood (Calogiuri, 2016; Thompson, Aspinall, & Montarzino, 2008), thus promoting life-long physical and mental health.

The topic of environmental sustainability has been emerging as a major social issue in the present century, not only in environmental sciences but also in public health. The WHO warns about the risks posed by environmental issues, such as air, water and soil pollution, chemical exposures, climate change and ultraviolet radiation. Such challenges are a particular threat to future generations, and even more so for the most disadvantaged groups in the population. 'Protecting the planet' is one of the main objectives of the Sustainable Development Goals outlined by the United Nations, with five of the 17 goals being closely linked with environmental sustainability issues. Because issues of environmental sustainability are in large part about human choices and actions, psychologists have been interested in understanding what makes people embrace more sustainable ways of living. In particular, the concept of nature connectedness, i.e. an individual's feeling of being emotionally connected to the natural world, has emerged as a key psychological component fostering sustainable behaviour (Geng, Xu, Ye, Zhou, & Zhou, 2015). Not only is nature connectedness an important component fostering sustainable behaviour, it has also been associated with positive health outcomes. For instance, a meta-analysis by Capaldi et al. showed that individuals who are more connected to nature tend to experience more positive affect, vitality, and life satisfaction compared to those less connected to nature (Capaldi, Dopko, & Zelenski, 2014). Individuals with stronger emotional attachment to nature were also found to be more likely to meet the minimum recommended levels for physical activity (Calogiuri, 2016).

Alongside the increasing commercialization and popularity of VR technology, there has been a growing interest in using VR as a possible supplement in school-based teaching and learning (Parsons et al., 2017). Similarly, for schools with poor access to quality spaces where the pupils can engage with nature, IVN can represent a useful tool to supplement interaction with real nature. Although there is a lack of studies specifically investigating children's psychophysiological responses to IVN, evidence exists of VR's capacity to reduce children's experience of aversive stimuli and reduce anxiety levels (Parsons et al., 2017). Additionally, as VR is seen as a tool that provides safe environments for pupils and students to gain skills, IVN might be used to facilitate initial mastery experiences that might help in reducing children's fears or insecurities when exploring outdoors (see also Chapter 9). The research literature provides useful information for designing advertisements to promote green exercise participation in different target groups (Gavarkovs, 2016), which can be used to develop tailored IVN encouraging children to visit real natural environments.

IVN, a useful tool in environmental research?

In disciplines such as (but not limited to) environmental psychology, public health and sport sciences, a number of researchers are interested in understanding how different environments influence people's emotions, behaviours and health. Such knowledge can assist, for instance, architects designing outdoor or indoor environments that help people recovering from stress, policy makers taking informed decisions about regulations relative to public spaces, or coaches to understand how to gain best benefits from sport practice and exercise. Comparing how people respond to different environments, however, is not an easy task. Conducting rigorous research studies, in fact, requires that researchers eliminate possible confounders that might lead to false results (see Chapter 2). This requires, for example, standardizing environmental conditions and blinding the participants as well as the examiners to the conditions each individual is exposed to.

To comply, as far as possible, to such requirements, researchers have often used pictures or videos of various environments as a mean of exposure. The advantage of this approach is that, in so doing, the researcher can conduct the study in a laboratory, thus maintaining a greater control on the environmental conditions. The disadvantage, of course, is that viewing a picture or a video of an environment makes the assumption that people might respond in the exact same way as they would if they were actually in the real environment. In this sense, it seems obvious how the use of VR technology could, by providing more immersive experiences and excluding any visual contact with the laboratory setting, help in conducting studies that are more valid. Earlier we presented the study by Yu et al. (2018) in which a classical paradigm used in environmental psychology research is replicated. The findings of this study indicated that using VR technology as a means of exposure was effective in eliciting psychological emotional responses similar to those previously found in studies *in vivo*, but not similar physiological responses. At the same time, a study by Liszio and Masuch (2018) showed that exposure to a IVN had a more powerful impact on psychological recovery after pre-induced stress as compared with viewing the same natural environment on a screen.

The aforementioned studies suggest that, although IVN might still be far from providing the whole range of psychophysiological responses that people experience in real environments, this technology might still represent a better compromise when trying to balance methodological rigour and life-like experiences. Although IVN may not allow a full blinding of the participants to which experimental condition they are allocated, it may at least avoid disclosing the condition allocation until the very beginning of the exposure, reducing possible expectation bias. Using head-mounted devices as the means of exposure also means that the condition allocation is not disclosed to the examiner.

More challenging, however, appears the application of IVN technology in green exercise research. Green exercise research is characterized by the necessity of combining physical activity with exposure to nature. Many studies have been conducted *in vivo*, often comparing exercising in natural settings with indoor settings. This can lead to possible confounders as different physical environments are likely to differ in terms of, for example, terrain/pendency, environmental temperature, noises, lighting, etc. To overcome this challenge, some green exercise studies have been conducted in laboratory settings in which the participants viewed images or videos of different environments (e.g. a natural environment v. a urban setting) projected onto a screen whilst exercising on a treadmill or an indoor bike (see for example Akers et al., 2012; Plante, Cage, Clements, & Stover, 2006; Pretty, Peacock, Sellens, & Griffin, 2005; White, Pahl, Ashbullby, Burton, & Depledge, 2015; Yeh, Stone, Churchill, Brymer, & Davids, 2017). Criticism of such an approach has also risen, especially in relation to its ability to provide realistic experiences of exercising in different settings. Considering the methodological challenges described above, the introduction of VR and, especially, IVN in green exercise research might thus represent an advantage. However, combining IVN and physical activity conveys some challenges, mainly associated with the issue of sensory conflict leading to cyber sickness.

VR systems exist that allow synchronization of head-mounted devices with sensors that register the participants' movements and translate them into movement of the virtual avatars. These systems, however, allow a relatively small range of motion (e.g. within a $5m^2$ area) and thus do not allow physical activities such as walking or running for longer distances. The gaming industry has been working on the development of special treadmills and stationary bikes that allow performance of endurance exercise while the participant is being exposed to IVN. Cyber sickness remains however a challenge for many users. In one of our studies, in fact, we not only found a significant difference between participants' psychological responses to a bout of green exercise *in vivo* as compared with *in virtuo* (IVN), but also that cyber sickness had a dramatic impact on people's emotional responses. A number of participants also complained of difficulties in balancing and frustration in feeling that their own movements did not fully match the movements of their virtual self (Calogiuri et al., 2018). VR technology is advancing rapidly, so some of the challenges discussed above might (hopefully) be addressed in a relatively near future. Until then, however, we urge caution in the use of IVN for exercise for research purposes, and we call for more research into how to make IVN technology more effective while avoiding possible side-effects for the participants (see Box 15.2 for a list of recommended areas of research).

BOX 15.2 RECOMMENDATIONS FOR FUTURE RESEARCH

- Investigate the extent to which IVN, can compare to experiences in real nature;
- Investigate the extent to which IVN can effectively enhance feelings of connectedness with nature and persuade people to visit real nature (possibly with follow-up studies);
- Identify strategies to effectively and realistically combine IVN exposure with endurance physical activities (e.g. walking, running, biking);
- Identify strategies to improve immersion and increase presence in IVN (e.g. multi-sensory aspects such as soundscape);
- Investigate possible long-term side-effects of exposure to IVN (e.g. long-term ailment, disturbance of the vestibular system, reduction in sight, etc.);
- Measure individual differences in nature connectedness, preferences for different types of landscapes and gender differences;
- Employ experimental designs that enable appropriate controls and comparisons (e.g. VR of urban green vs VR of urban built environments);

- Develop a better understanding of the individual characteristics that are associated with higher predisposition to cyber sickness, and identify strategies to reduce it (without sacrificing immersion);
- Develop a better understanding of how long-term exposure to IVN (intended as both prolonged duration of the exposure and repeated exposures) leads to habituation in terms of presence, cyber sickness, and the participants' psychophysiological responses.

Can IVN help reconnecting people with real nature?

In 2014, 54% of the world's population resided in cities, and the UN estimates that by 2050 this proportion will reach 66%. Cities are also expanding, possibly resulting in many people becoming distanced from natural environments and, for example, children not knowing what natural features like grass or earth feel like. The WHO acknowledges the importance of urban settlements integrating elements of nature as part of ensuring a healthy environment for people to live (WHO, 2016). Alongside rational urban planning that leaves space for nature in cities, it is however important to find strategies to strengthen people's bonds with nature and natural places. In an urbanized society, many individuals do not engage with nature on a regular basis. For instance, in the UK less than 40% of people visit and spend time in natural environments during a typical week (White et al., 2016). Even in Norway, where there is a strong tradition for outdoor recreations and more than 90% of the population live in proximity to some natural environment, about 40% of adults do not visit natural environments during a regular week (Calogiuri et al., 2016b). At the same time, people living in urban settlements are more likely to spend time in indoor settings, for example by exercising in gyms (Calogiuri et al., 2016b).

IVN has been proposed as part of the solution in augmenting people's interaction with nature (Smith, 2015); concerns have been raised, however, about the risks that increasing use of IVN might lead to people replacing real nature with virtual nature, thus accelerating the progressive disconnection of humans from the natural world. IVN might, on the other hand, not only be used to 'supplement' people's lack of interaction with real nature, but as an instrument to reconnect people to nature and persuade them to visit real natural environments. A simple way in which IVN can persuade people to visit natural environments is by providing information about places to explore and the type of facilities and features the environment offers. Furthermore, pleasant experiences associated with viewing IVN might also serve as a form of positive reinforcement that can enhance people's attitudes towards nature-based recreations, which can be further strengthened by modelling messages eliciting vicarious experiences of mastery (Calogiuri & Chroni, 2014; Calogiuri, Nordtug, & Weydahl, 2015).

Another way can be explained under the prism of Rachel and Stephen Kaplan's Attention Restoration Theory (ART). ART postulates that restoration from cognitive stress (which is caused by prolonged focus on tasks that are not perceived as interesting) can be elicited by triggering a form of attention that is spontaneous and 'effortless', in the theory referred to as *fascination*. Because of some characteristic features such as the clouds moving in the sky and leaves waving in the breeze, natural environments are considered as having high fascinating qualities: such environments have the ability to trigger people's attention in a spontaneous and effortless fashion, leading to positive emotional responses while at the same time avoiding excessive psychological arousal ('soft' fascination). Alongside fascination, three other environmental characteristics can elicit attention-restoration processes: compatibility (a match between the environment's characteristics and a person's inclinations at a given moment), extent (the degree to which an environment is perceived as being coherently ordered), and being away (the extent to which the environment provides the opportunity to break with daily routines). These environmental qualities not only have contributed to explaining the positive affective responses associated with nature, but could also contribute to explaining motivational process that drive people to visit natural environments. Recommendations for advertising of natural environments have indeed stressed the importance of present views of natural environments with highly restorative value in line with ART (Gavarkovs, 2016).

Characteristics of the IVN technology, as well as the extent to which this provides an immersive and pleasant experiencc, might influence its effectiveness in persuading people to visit natural environments. As discussed above, it is plausible to expect that the greater the experience of presence, the greater the IVN's effectiveness. Another common challenge associated with VR technology is the tendency for some users to exhibit of cyber sickness. Cyber sickness was in fact found to dramatically impact participants' experience of and affective responses to an IVN (Calogiuri et al., 2018). On the other hand, preliminary findings from our studies suggest that the ratings of perceived environmental restorativeness that participants assign to an IVN strongly correlate with their reported willingness to visit the natural environment in reality as well as with changes in the extent to which they intend to engage in green exercise in the future.

The aforementioned preliminary findings aside, to the best of our knowledge to date there is no scientific evidence supporting the effectiveness of viewing IVN in persuading people to visit real natural environments. There seems however to be some interest in such a strategy from private and public agencies. For example, the travel agency Visit Norway has developed a webpage[1] where users can view breathtaking IVN using a personal head-mounted device, alongside practical information about the location and how to travel to it. Our experiences in developing interventions for cities, for example, have also highlighted the potential for IVN as an engagement tool in the co-creation of nature-based solutions. Previous engagement tools to display in an authentic way differences in air pollution across cities (e.g. London, Mumbai, etc.)

used Pollution Pods (see www.michaelpinsky.com). IVN can potentially increase the acceptability of current or planned green infrastructure, for example. One novel approach would be to investigate the application of IVN to provide a well-being and stress-reduction intervention for those in space-flight, which is becoming an increasing possibility over recent years. Researchers have described space as an extreme environment for the human body as micro-gravity leads to muscular atrophy among other challenges (Demontis et al., 2017). This is a burgeoning line of research enquiry with recent studies attempting to explore the role of psychological interventions to assist in adaptation and recovery from exposure to micro-gravity (Guillot & Debarnot, 2019).

Conclusions

A promising future exists for technological nature but the extent to which we engage, for example, with IVN-based interventions is likely to be influenced by a shift in the paradigm. We cannot simply view these possible experiences as, without nature, they are potentially more than a proxy too. They have indeed a huge potential in augmenting the limited nature contact we may have in future cities and workplaces. As consumers we also need to be mindful of the unintended consequences of digital nature. For example, does a workplace-based intervention simply add to the media immersion common in our agile workplace, and rather than acting as a recovery strategy, it may instead simply be an additional stressor.

Note

1 www.visitnorway.com/media/news-from-norway/experience-norways-spectacular-landscapes-through-a-vr-headset/

References

Akers, A., Barton, J., Cossey, R., Gainsford, P., Griffin, M., & Micklewright, D. (2012). Visual color perception in green exercise: Positive effects on mood and perceived exertion. *Environmental Science & Technology*, *46*(16), 8661–8666. doi:10.1021/es301685g

Allen, B., Hanley, T., Rokers, B., & Green, C. S. (2016). Visual 3D motion acuity predicts discomfort in 3D stereoscopic environments. *Entertainment Computing*, *13*, 1–9. doi:10.1016/j.entcom.2016.01.001

Barton, J., Bragg, R., Pretty, J., Roberts, J., & Wood, C. (2016). The wilderness expedition: An effective life course intervention to improve young people's well-being and connectedness to nature. *Journal of Experiential Education*, *39*(1), 59–72. doi:10.1177/1053825915626933

Botella, C., Fernandez-Alvarez, J., Guillen, V., Garcia-Palacios, A., & Banos, R. (2017). Recent progress in virtual reality exposure therapy for phobias: A systematic review.

Current Psychiatry Reports, *19*(7), 42. Retrieved from www.ncbi.nlm.nih.gov/pubmed/28540594

Bowler, D. E., Buyung-Ali, L. M., Knight, T. M., & Pullin, A. S. (2010). A systematic review of evidence for the added benefits to health of exposure to natural environments. *BMC Public Health*, *10*, 456. doi:10.1186/1471-2458-10-456

Bowman, D. A., & McMahan, R. P. (2007). Virtual reality: How much immersion is enough? *Computer*, *40*(7), 36. doi:10.1109/Mc.2007.257

Brown, D. K., Barton, J. L., Pretty, J., & Gladwell, V. F. (2014). Walks4Work: Assessing the role of the natural environment in a workplace physical activity intervention. *Scandinavian Journal of Work and Environment Health*, *40*(4), 390–399. doi:10.5271/sjweh.3421

Calogiuri, G. (2016). Natural environments and childhood experiences promoting physical activity, examining the mediational effects of feelings about nature and social networks. *International Journal of Environmental Research and Public Health*, *13*(4), 439. doi:10.3390/ijerph13040439

Calogiuri, G., & Chroni, S. (2014). The impact of the natural environment on the promotion of active living: An integrative systematic review. *BMC Public Health*, *14*, 873. doi:10.1186/1471-2458-14-873

Calogiuri, G., Evensen, K., Weydahl, A., Andersson, K., Patil, G., Ihlebaek, C., & Raanaas, R. K. (2016a). Green exercise as a workplace intervention to reduce job stress. Results from a pilot study. *Work*, *53*(1), 99–111. doi:10.3233/wor-152219

Calogiuri, G., Litleskare, S., Fagerheim, K. A., Rydgren, T. L., Brambilla, E., & Thurston, M. (2018). Experiencing nature through immersive virtual environments: Environmental perceptions, physical engagement, and affective responses during a simulated nature walk. *Frontiers in Psychology*, *8*(2321). doi:10.3389/fpsyg.2017.02321

Calogiuri, G., Nordtug, H., & Weydahl, A. (2015). The potential of using exercise in nature as an intervention to enhance exercise behavior: Results from a pilot study. *Perceptual and Motor Skills*, *121*(2), 350–370. doi:10.2466/06.PMS.121c17x0

Calogiuri, G., Patil, G. G., & Aamodt, G. (2016b). Is green exercise for all? A descriptive study of green exercise habits and promoting factors in adult norwegians. *International Journal of Environmental Research and Public Health*, *13*(11), 1165. doi:10.3390/ijerph13111165

Capaldi, C. A., Dopko, R. L., & Zelenski, J. M. (2014). The relationship between nature connectedness and happiness: A meta-analysis. *Frontiers in Psychology*, *5*, 976. doi:10.3389/fpsyg.2014.00976

Chirico, A., & Gaggioli, A. (2019). When virtual feels real: Comparing emotional responses and presence in virtual and natural environments. *Cyberpsychology, Behavior, and Social Networking*, *22*(3), 220–226. doi:10.1089/cyber.2018.0393

Chirico, A., Lucidi, F., De Laurentiis, M., Milanese, C., Napoli, A., & Giordano, A. (2016). Virtual reality in health system: Beyond entertainment: A mini-review on the efficacy of VR during cancer treatment. *Journal of Cell Physiology*, *231*(2), 275–287. doi:10.1002/jcp.25117

Dascal, J., Reid, M., IsHak, W. W., Spiegel, B., Recacho, J., Rosen, B., & Danovitch, I. (2017). Virtual reality and medical inpatients: A systematic review of randomized, controlled trials. *Innovations in Clinical Neuroscience*, *14*(1–2), 14.

Demontis, G.C., Germani, M.M., Caiani, E.G., Barravecchia, I., Passino, C. & Angeloni, D. (2017). Human pathophysiological adaptations to the space environment. *Frontiers in Physiology*, *8*, 547. doi:10.3389/fphys.2017.00547

Duzmanska, N., Strojny, P., & Strojny, A. (2018). Can simulator sickness be avoided? A review on temporal aspects of simulator sickness. *Frontiers in Psychology, 9*, 2132. doi:10.3389/fpsyg.2018.02132

European Agency for Safety and Health at Work. (2018). *Psychosocial risks and stress at work*. Retrieved from https://osha.europa.eu/en/themes/psychosocial-risks-and-stress

Gavarkovs, A. G. (2016). Nature-based physical activity advertising: Recommendations based on attention restoration theory and psychoevolutionary theory. *WURJ: Health and Natural Sciences, 6*(1), 4. doi:10.5206/wurjhns.2015-16.4

Gavgani, A. M., Nesbitt, K. V., Blackmore, K. L., & Nalivaiko, E. (2017). Profiling subjective symptoms and autonomic changes associated with cybersickness. *Autonomic Neuroscience, 203*, 41–50. doi:10.1016/j.autneu.2016.12.004

Geng, L., Xu, J., Ye, L., Zhou, W., & Zhou, K. (2015). Connections with nature and environmental behaviors. *PloS One, 10*(5), e0127247. doi:10.1371/journal.pone.0127247

Guillot, A. & Debarnot, U. (2019). Benefits of motor imagery for human space flight: A brief review of current knowledge and future applications. *Frontiers in Physiology, 10*, 396. doi:10.3389/fphys.2019.00396

Hartig, T., Mitchell, R., De Vries, S., & Frumkin, H. (2014). Nature and health. *Annual Review of Public Health, 35*, 207–228. doi:10.1146/annurev-publhealth-032013-182443

Harvey, S. B., Modini, M., Joyce, S., Milligan-Saville, J. S., Tan, L., Mykletun, A., … Mitchell, P. B. (2017). Can work make you mentally ill? A systematic meta-review of work-related risk factors for common mental health problems. *Occupational & Environmental Medicine, 74*. doi:10.1136/oemed-2016-104015

Hassard, J., & Cox, T. (2011). Work-related stress: Nature and management. *OSHwiki*. Retrieved from https://oshwiki.eu/wiki/Work-related_stress:_Nature_and_management#Work-related_stress:_reported_prevalence_and_costs

Kahn, P. H. (2018). Technological nature. In M. van Den Boch & W. Bird (Eds.), *Oxford Textbook of Nature and Public Health: The Role of Nature in Improving the Health of a Population* (pp. 160–164). Oxford: Oxford University Press.

Kahn, P. H., Severson, R. L. & Ruckert, J. H. (2009). The human relation with nature and technological nature. *Current Directions in Psychological Science, 18*(1), 37–42.

Kennedy, R. S., Drexler, J., & Kennedy, R. C. (2010). Research in visually induced motion sickness. *Applied Ergonomics, 41*(4), 494–503. doi:10.1016/j.apergo.2009.11.006

Lahart, I., Darcy, P., Gidlow, C. & Calogiuri, G. (2019). The effects of green exercise on physical and mental wellbeing: A systematic review. *International Journal of Environmental Research and Public Health, 16*(8), 1352.

Lee, K. E, Williams, K. J.H, Sargent, L. D, Farrell, C., & Williams, N. S. (2014). Living roof preference is influenced by plant characteristics and diversity. *Landscape and Urban Planning, 122*, 152–159. doi:10.1016/j.landurbplan.2013.09.011

Liszio, S., & Masuch, M. (2018). *The relaxing effect of virtual nature: Immersive technology provides relief in acute stress situations*. Paper presented at the 23rd Annual CyberPsychology, CyberTherapy & Social Networking Conference.

Lo, W. T., & So, R. H. Y. (2001). Cybersickness in the presence of scene rotational movements along different axes. *Applied Ergonomics, 32*(1), 1–14. doi:10.1016/S0003-6870(00)00059-4

Loomis, J. M., Blascovich, J. J., & Beall, A. C. (1999). Immersive virtual environment technology as a basic research tool in psychology. *Behavior Research Methods, Instruments, & Computers, 31*(4), 557–564. doi:10.3758/BF03200735

Louv, R. (2008). *Last Child in the Woods: Saving Our Children from Nature-Deficit Disorder*. Carolina: Algonquin.

Mcsweeney, J., Rainham, D., Johnson, S. A., Sherry, S. B., & Singleton, J. (2014). Indoor nature exposure (INE): A health-promotion framework. *Health Promotion International, 30*(1), 126–139. doi:10.1093/heapro/dau081

Mennis, J., Mason, M., & Ambrus, A. (2018). Urban greenspace is associated with reduced psychological stress among adolescents: A Geographic Ecological Momentary Assessment (GEMA) analysis of activity space. *Landscape and Urban Planning, 174*, 1–9. doi:10.1016/j.landurbplan.2018.02.008

Merhi, O., Faugloire, E., Flanagan, M., & Stoffregen, T. A. (2007). Motion sickness, console video games, and head-mounted displays. *Human Factors, 49*(5), 920–934. doi:10.1518/001872007X230262

Murata, A. (2004). Effects of duration of immersion in a virtual reality environment on postural stability. *International Journal of Human-Computer Interaction, 17*(4), 463–477. doi:10.1207/s15327590ijhc1704_2

Parent-Thirion, A. (2007). *Fourth European Working Conditions Survey*. Luxembourg: Office for official Publ. of the European Communities. https://www.eurofound.europa.eu/publications/report/2007/working-conditions/fourth-european-working-conditions-survey

Parsons, T. D., Riva, G., Parsons, S., Mantovani, F., Newbutt, N., Lin, L., … Hall, T. (2017). Virtual reality in pediatric psychology. *Pediatrics, 140*(Suppl. 2), S86–S91. doi:10.1542/peds.2016-1758I

Passmore, H-A. & Holder, M. D. (2017). Noticing nature: Individual and social benefits of a two-week intervention. *The Journal of Positive Psychology, 12*(6), 537–546. doi:10.1080/17439760.2016.1221126

Plante, T. G., Aldridge, A., Su, D., Bogdan, R., Belo, M., & Kahn, K. (2003). Does virtual reality enhance the management of stress when paired with exercise? An exploratory study. *International Journal of Stress Management, 10*(3), 203. doi:10.1037/1072-5245.10.3.203

Plante, T. G., Cage, C., Clements, S., & Stover, A. (2006). Psychological benefits of exercise paired with virtual reality: Outdoor exercise energizes whereas indoor virtual exercise relaxes. *International Journal of Stress Management, 13*(1), 108. doi:10.1037/1072-5245.13.1.108

Pretty, J., Peacock, J., Sellens, M., & Griffin, M. (2005). The mental and physical health outcomes of green exercise. *International Journal of Environmental Health Research, 15*(5), 319–337. doi:10.1080/09603120500155963

Sharples, S., Cobb, S., Moody, A., & Wilson, J. R. (2008). Virtual Reality Induced Symptoms and Effects (VRISE): Comparison of Head Mounted Display (HMD), desktop and projection display systems. *Displays, 29*(2), 58–69. doi:10.1016/j.displa.2007.09.005

Sinharay, R., Gong, J., Barratt, B., Ohman-Strickland, P., Ernst, S., Kelly, F. J., … Chung, K. F. (2017). Respiratory and cardiovascular responses to walking down a traffic-polluted road compared with walking in a traffic-free area in participants aged 60 years and older with chronic lung or heart disease and age-matched healthy controls: A randomised, crossover study. *The Lancet, 391*(10118), 339–349. doi:10.1016/S0140-6736(17)32643-0

Slater, M., & Wilbur, S. (1997). A framework for immersive virtual environments (FIVE): Speculations on the role of presence in virtual environments. *Presence-Teleoperators and Virtual Environments, 6*(6), 603–616. doi:10.1162/pres.1997.6.6.603

Smith, J. W. (2015). Immersive virtual environment technology to supplement environmental perception, preference and behavior research: A review with applications.

International Journal of Environmental Research in Public Health, 12(9), 11486–11505. doi:10.3390/ijerph120911486

Sonnentag, S., & Fritz, C. (2007). The Recovery Experience Questionnaire: Development and validation of a measure for assessing recuperation and unwinding from work. *Journal of Occupational Health Psychology, 12*(3), 204. doi:10.1037/1076-8998.12.3.204

Steuer, J. (1992). Defining virtual reality - dimensions determining telepresence. *Journal of Communication, 42*(4), 73–93. doi:10.1111/j.1460-2466.1992.tb00812.x

Swami, V., Barron, D., & Furnham, A. (2018). Exposure to natural environments, and photographs of natural environments, promotes more positive body image. *Body Image, 24*, 82–94.

Thompson, C. W., Aspinall, P., & Montarzino, A. (2008). The childhood factor: Adult visits to green places and the significance of childhood experience. *Environment and Behavior, 40*(1), 111–143.

Triberti, S., Repetto, C., & Riva, G. (2014). Psychological factors influencing the effectiveness of virtual reality-based analgesia: A systematic review. *Cyberpsychology, Behavior, and Social Networking, 17*(6), 335–345. doi:10.1089/cyber.2014.0054

Valtchanov, D., Barton, K. R., & Ellard, C. (2010). Restorative effects of virtual nature settings. *Cyberpsychology, Behavior, and Social Networking, 13*(5), 503–512.

van den Bosch, M., & Sang, Å. O. (2017). Urban natural environments as nature-based solutions for improved public health–A systematic review of reviews. *Environmental Research, 158*, 373–384.

Weech, S., Kenny, S., & Barnett-Cowan, M. (2019). Presence and cybersickness in virtual reality are negatively related: A review. *Frontiers in Psychology, 10*, 158. doi: ARTN15810.3389/fpsyg.2019.00158

White, M., Elliott, L., Taylor, T., Wheeler, B., Spencer, A., Bone, A., … Fleming, L. (2016). Recreational physical activity in natural environments and implications for health: A population based cross-sectional study in England. *Preventive Medicine, 91*, 383–388.

White, M. P., Pahl, S., Ashbullby, K. J., Burton, F., & Depledge, M. H. (2015). The effects of exercising in different natural environments on psycho-physiological outcomes in post-menopausal women: A simulation study. *International Journal of Environmental Research and Public Health, 12*(9), 11929–11953.

White, M. P., Yeo, N. L., Vassiljev, P., Lundstedt, R., Wallergård, M., Albin, M., & Lõhmus, M. (2018). A prescription for "nature"–The potential of using virtual nature in therapeutics. *Neuropsychiatric Disease and Treatment, 14*, 3001.

WHO Europe. (2018). *Prevalence of mental disorders*. Retrieved from www.euro.who.int/en/health-topics/noncommunicable-diseases/mental-health/data-and-resources

Wood, C., Sandercock, G., & Barton, J. (2014). Interactions between physical activity and the environment to improve adolescent self-esteem: A randomised controlled trial. *International Journal of Environament and Health*, 7. doi:10.1504/IJENVH.2014.067359

World Health Organization. (2016). *Urban Green Spaces and Health. A Review of Evidence*. Copenhagen: WHO Regional office for Europe. Retrieved from www.euro.who.int/__data/assets/pdf_file/0005/321971/Urban-green-spaces-and-health-review-evidence.pdf?ua=1%20WorldHealth%20Organization%202016

Yeh, H.-P., Stone, J. A., Churchill, S. M., Brymer, E., & Davids, K. (2017). Physical and emotional benefits of different exercise environments designed for treadmill running. *International Journal of Environonmental Research and Public Health, 14*(7), 752.

Yu, C.-P., Lee, H.-Y., & Luo, X.-Y. (2018). The effect of virtual reality forest and urban environments on physiological and psychological responses. *Urban Forestry & Urban Greening, 35*, 106–114.

16

DREADMILLS

Is there such a thing as sustainable exercise?

Aoife A. Donnelly, Marlena Tomkalska and Tadhg E. MacIntyre

1. Introduction

There is a complex set of factors that influences physical activity levels on an individual basis, many of which are still poorly understood without solid quantification (Trost, Owen, Bauman, Sallis, & Brown, 2002). Convenience and cost would suggest that going for a run straight out the door would be an attractive option for many people. However, convenience does not always lead to action and some studies have even shown that participants in unsupervised activity who live closer to the exercise setting are in fact more likely to drop out (Marlatt & Gordon, 1980). Weather has a direct effect on participation in a variety of physical activities. In some climates exercising outdoors might be impossible in certain seasons and indeed climate has been shown to influence choices with regards to such activities (Dishman, Sallis, & Orenstein, 1985).

To overcome many of these perceived barriers, some people may use gyms, community centres or boot camp type classes, many of which offer structured activities and an opportunity to work in a community environment. Studies show that an opportunity to socialise in exercise clubs and group fitness classes increases the commitment to regular gym visits (IHRSA, 2014). A need to be a part of a sport community has strongly influenced the development of the fitness market. Today, the industry witnesses a rapid growth of fitness facilities that create a cult and tribe-like experience, for instance boxing clubs or CrossFit studios. Booth, Owen, Bauman, Clavisi, and Leslie (2000) found that regular physical activity is impacted by the friend effect, while many studies postulate that access to good recreational facilities impacts levels of physical activity (MacDougall, Cooke, Owen, Willson, & Bauman, 1997; Mitchell & Olds, 1999). Gyms and indoor fitness facilities are popular choices in urban settings where access to outdoor recreational infrastructure might be limited or in cities struggling with ambient air pollution or extreme hot/cold weather periods. Many gyms and fitness centres also offer additional facilities like swimming pools, sauna and wellness treatments attracting more customers.

As a result the fitness industry is booming (see Box 16.1). An unprecedented growth and development within the health and fitness sector generates an estimated $85.2 billion in industry revenue worldwide (IHRSA, 2017). Combined with expenditures on gym gear, fitness gadgets, supplements and personal meal plans the global wellness market is worth over $3.4 trillion (even greater than the pharmaceutical industry) (Global Wellness Institute, 2016).

BOX 16.1 HEALTH AND FITNESS STATISTICS

In Ireland, a total of 0.5 million people are members of 710 health and fitness clubs and 53% of the population declare themselves to be physically active (Deloitte, 2018). Irish Sport Monitor indicates that gym-type activities are the most popular type of sport amongst the Irish population (Sports Ireland, 2017). Likewise, fitness is also the biggest sport on a global scale with 27% of adult populations attending fitness facilities of some description (Les-Mills Global Consumer Fitness Survey, 2013).

A Healthy Ireland Survey in 2016 showed that over a half of responders are aware of the recommended minimum of 150 minutes of physical activity while almost 91% are willing to pursue an active lifestyle (Healthy Ireland, 2016).

The growth of gym culture is driven by many factors, not least of which is a substantial improvement in health literacy. Modern society is exposed to health-related information through many channels (mass media, the education system and public health interventions). Decreasing prevalence of tobacco and alcohol consumption reflects an overall positive attitude towards low-risk lifestyle behaviours. Undoubtedly, an increase in general health awareness and understanding of physical and mental wellbeing benefits arising from participation in sport constitutes a significant positive social change.

A growing number of gyms and fitness centres are heavily influenced by the demand of the millennial generation, the largest proportion of gym users. This cohort are often considered to be adventurous, goal-oriented and technology-savvy people. To meet the demand, industry has responded with new high-end facilities and speciality studios offering trending community-based fitness programme and flexible membership options (Shea, 2016).

Social media plays an important role in shaping gym culture. Visually-oriented platforms are flooded with messages depicting ideal body image. An interesting shift has been observed from the traditionally promoted standards of thin women to a new *fit ideal* – a strong and toned female physique, characterised as “healthy and achievable” (Alleva, 2018). Furthermore, there is a new online movement of *fitspo* – fit inspirational quotes attached to pictures glamorising fit bodies. The result is the creation of social pressures to engage in fitness and chase the desired body outline and is a key catalyst behind the gym culture phenomenon.

2. Indoor air pollution in exercise facilities

It is generally accepted that exercising in industrialised and high-emission zones reduces the benefit of physical activity and possibly compromises athletes' health and performance. A common misconception is that indoor air is cleaner and healthier than outdoor air. In fact, indoor air pollution is considered to be one of the top five environmental hazards to human health with some contaminates existing in concentrations two to five times higher than in surrounding ambient air (Environmental Protection Agency, EPA, 2017b). About 70,000 synthetic chemicals have been identified in residential and public indoor spaces and the human toxicity for many of them remains unknown (Alberta Environmental Health, 2012). A systematic review found that 9 out of 12 studies reviewed (on indoor air quality of environments used for physical exercise) concluded that there was higher indoor-to-outdoor ratio of air pollution (Andrade & Dominski, 2018).

Poor indoor air quality can be defined by the excessive presence of gases and particles, produced internally or infiltrated from external sources, that affect the health and comfort of occupants. Energy efficient constructions often rely on mechanical ventilation to improve the quality of indoor air. Even though the primary function of artificial ventilation systems is to dilute and remove any impurities, they often become a source of contamination themselves. Improperly designed, positioned and maintained Heating Ventilation Air-Conditioning Systems (HVAC) support harbourage and dispersion of microorganisms. Insufficient ventilation rates increase the relative humidity leading to formation of mould and bio-aerosols. Various bacteria, viruses and sensitising agents are engulfed by water droplets and become airborne. Inadequate supply of fresh air increases the concentration of pollutants given off by construction materials, furnishings, equipment, cleaning detergents and pest control chemicals. On the other hand, open windows or cracks and crevices in old structures are pathways by which external combustion-related pollutants such as carbon monoxide, nitrogen dioxide and its oxides, polycyclic aromatic hydrocarbons and particulate matter can ingress into buildings. Furthermore, the prevalence of synthetic materials in interior finishes can contribute to the accumulation of toxic substances.

Multiuser exercise facilities often have a variety of characteristics that can promote poor air quality (location, ventilation type, furnishings and building materials and type of activity that is taking place inside). Higher concentrations of pollutants related to vehicular exhaust emissions are detected in the premises adjacent to heavy traffic roads (Ramos, Wolterbeek, & Almeida, 2014). Humans are considered as important sources of pollution. Gatherings of people in enclosed spaces results in a reduction in oxygen levels and an increase in carbon dixoxide (CO_2), temperature, humidity, bioaerosols and odours (NPTEL.ac.ie, 2014). "Metabolic processes can generate about 500 chemical compounds discharged through sweat glands and respiration track" (Wang, 2010) such as pathogenic bacteria, ammonia and dead skin fall-off. Interestingly, dead skin cells make up 90% of the dust composition (Wang, 2010). Furthermore, sweating and breathing creates water vapour, supporting aerosol formation and resuspension of particulates. Intensity of physical activity also appears to be crucial as movement can cause resuspension of particles and higher levels of CO_2. Ramos et al. (2014) found that the concentration of this human respiration by-product has been detected as substantially greater during high intensity classes. A yoga class with 24 participants was found to have an average CO_2 concentration of 959mg/m^3 while a body attack class with 20 participants had a concentration of 1774mg/m^3 (Ramos et al., 2014).

Although, CO_2 is more commonly considered as a comfort parameter rather than directly as a pollutant, its elevated levels indicate insufficient ventilation rates and possible build-up of harmful contaminants and particulate matter (Zitnik et al., 2016). It is well established that exposure to particulate matter can reduce life expectancy, and an increase by 10μg/m^3 in concentration of coarse and fine particulates is associated with up to 1% higher rates of daily cardio-respiratory morbidity (Newell, Kartsonaki, Lam, & Kurmi, 2017). While the detrimental effects on physical health are well established, some recent studies linked an exposure to $PM_{2.5}$ with greater psychological distress and impaired cognitive functions (Sassa et al., 2017). The presence of inhalable fractions of particulate matter in indoor exercise facilities is directly attributable to occupancy, intensity of activities, outdoor-indoor transfer and the use of "gym-chalk" – powdered products.

Volatile Organic Hydrocarbons (VOCs) are substances that are found in the vapour state at room temperature. Over 300 VOCs can be found in gymnasiums including benzene, formaldehyde, dichloromethane, tetrachloromethane, non-methane products, halocarbons and oxygenates (Carlisle & Sharp, 2001). Exposures are associated with various neurological and respiratory ailments, from irritation of eye and respiratory mucus membranes to responses like dizziness, vomiting, dyspnea and loss of memory (Hajian & Mohaghegh, 2015). Ramos et al. (2014) found exceedances of VOCs in 82% of monitored fitness centres and the elevated levels could have originated from alcohol-based hand disinfectants, new furnishings or synthetic flooring materials and exercise mats. Composite wood, laminate and rubber-derived floorings commonly used in sport facilities are important sources of formaldehyde. Its evaporation increases substantially with a rise in temperature and humidity levels (Parthasarathy et al., 2011). Usually, high concentrations of VOCs and formaldehyde are associated with newly opened premises.

Indoor air pollution – a silent killer

Episodes of nausea, headaches and eye-nose-throat irritations are the most widely reported acute symptoms arising from an exposure to unsatisfactory indoor climate. Poor indoor air quality appears to be the key driving factor for Sick Building Syndrome (nonspecific feelings of illness and comfort decrease linked to a time spent in a particular building). Since the popularisation of airtight constructions in mid-1980s, the rates of complaints about indoor discomfort have increased significantly (US EPA, 1991). Even though ill-effects are short-lasting and may simply disappear after leaving a building, they may indicate a presence of internal pollutants and more severe adverse health impacts in the long run. Inhalation of polluted air takes a heavy toll on cardiovascular and respiratory systems leading to premature deaths from strokes, pneumonia, ischaemic heart diseases, chronic obstructive pulmonary diseases and lung cancers (World Health Organization, WHO, 2014). According to WHO (2014) statistics, indoor air pollution accounts for 3.8 million deaths per year globally. Whether it is from a modern tightly insulated building or a simple household with open stoves (utilising fossil fuels for cooking and heating purposes?), prolonged exposures to indoor airborne contaminants have a detrimental impact on the health of buildings' occupants. Considering the fact that "people spend about 90 to 95% of their time indoors", the quality of indoor air is of paramount importance to the public health (EPA, 2017a).

Physical activity is known to have tremendous benefits for humans' overall health and wellbeing. Conclusive evidence exists that regular and sufficient doses of daily sports practice helps protect against many chronic conditions, including the leading mortality causes – the cardiovascular and pulmonary diseases. The inconvenient question arises about a counterbalancing effect of exercising in polluted indoor spaces. Unlike the outdoor environments where natural atmospheric forces can reduce the concentration of pollutants through the dispersion process, enclosed fitness facilities present a greater risk for the accumulation of harmful substances.

A large body of scientific research shows an increased susceptibility to poor quality air during exercising. Three essential factors necessary to establish risk from air pollution include a concentration of pollutant, exposure time and volume of air breathed (Watson, Bates, & Kennedy, 1988; Scientific Committee on Health and Environmental Risk, 2007). The volume of inhaled air is the most significant factor for health vulnerability of professional and recreational athletes. During an exercise session, an individual may go through several physiological changes which include increase in minute ventilation, air flow velocity, pulmonary diffusion capacity and air inhalation through the mouth (Hajian & Mohaghegh, 2015). Hence, the mechanism of adverse health impacts is trifold. The increasing ventilation rates during exercise amplify the amount of pollutants inhaled during exercise, and inhalation through the mouth causes large particles and soluble vapours to enter the body as the normal filtration through the nostrils is bypassed when inhaled through the mouth. Increased airflow velocity during exercise allows large particles to enter deeper into the respiratory tract and the increased pulmonary diffusion capacity boosts the diffusion of pollutant gas within the body (Alves et al. 2013). A higher cardiac pulse rate accelerates blood circulation distributing toxins more rapidly (Flynn, Matz, Woolf, & Wright, 2000). As a result, a 90-minute workout indoors predisposes a sport practitioner to six times greater doses of coarse particles compared to the same dose outdoors without exercising (Zitnik et al., 2016).

BOX 16.2 EXPOSURE TO INDOOR AIR POLLUTION IN GYMS – A CASE STUDY (TOMKALSKA, 2018)

Context: People go to gyms to improve health, fitness level and appearance. However, poor indoor air quality may jeopardise their effort to stay healthy. A monitoring programme carried out in 2017 across various types of exercise facilities in Dublin evaluated the overall air quality as unsatisfactory.

Methods: 12 gyms and 14 fitness centres were randomly chosen for the study, including recreational facilities such as indoor trampoline parks and kids' play centres. Measurements of selected airborne contaminates, PM_{10} and $PM_{2.5}$ as well as comfort parameters, namely temperature, carbon dioxide and relative humidity, were conducted in both, cardio and weight-lifting zones. Proposed division is based on variation in heart rate and respiration between those activities. Each gym was assessed during the peak and off-peak times to observe the exercise induced changes in the gym's atmosphere. The results were compered against limit values adopted from the Portuguese indoor air quality legislation Portaria n.º 353-A/2013.

Results: This research found that mean concentrations of coarse particulate matter and comfort parameters in all facilities breached the recommended thresholds. The main sources that compromise the air quality identified in the survey of the Dublin gym-goers (n=120) include overcrowded spaces (63.3%), poor ventilation (56.7%), poor housekeeping (45%), cleaning detergents (35.8%) and mould (33.3%). The indoor air quality in the fitness classes were identified to be significantly worse than in the gymnasiums. Also, the cardio zones were found to be more polluted than free-weights areas.

Implications: Increased minute ventilation during intensive fitness classes escalates the susceptibility to air pollutants. According to the findings of Ramos, Reis, Almeida, Wolterbeek, and Almeida (2015), the inhaled dose of pollutants during aerobic classes can double the dose in slow pace exercises. Therefore, Dublin indoor workout enthusiasts practising cardio workout or attending high intensity classes are at risk of greater exposure to air pollutants.

Indoor air quality in exercise facilities – an unregulated public health issue

In spite of a significant effort that has been made to control sources of emissions and the quality of ambient air, the quality of indoor air remains mostly unaddressed. More worryingly, some contaminants are reported to be found at considerably higher concentrations inside buildings compared to environmental levels. While even low level exposure to air pollution has negative health impacts, scientific evidence exists to suggest that increased minute ventilation during physical activity renders the sport practitioners more vulnerable to poor indoor air quality. Studies on air pollution in sport and leisure facilities demonstrate the presence of harmful pollutants at concerning levels. Considering the overall time spent indoors and greater pollutants uptake when performing physical activity, the quality of air in gyms and fitness studios is an emerging, yet neglected, environmental health risk to public health. Aside from in Portugal, there is no specific regulation governing indoor air quality in public spaces, including indoor sports environments. In 2010, the WHO produced guidelines on selected indoor air pollutants that can serve as basis for formulation of national legislations. Portuguese authorities transformed the guidelines into legally enforceable standard, Portaria n.°353A/2013. The legislation comprises the indoor air limit values for the pollutants $PM_{2.5}$, CO_2, PM_{10}, VOC and CH_2O and O_3. It is worth noting that exposure thresholds were adopted only for selected contaminates, ignoring factors such as changes in respiratory parameters during exercising and the total amount of time in indoor spaces.

To potentiate the benefits of physical activities in indoor spaces, it is crucial to regulate the aspect of indoor air quality in exercise facilities. There is an urgent need for a specific legislation that would prescribe evidence-based health protecting limits for common gym pollutants, specify air-exchange rates and identify safe building/interior materials. It is important to monitor the air quality to maintain healthy indoor environments for sports practice.

BOX 16.3 PERCEPTION OF INDOOR AIR QUALITY BY GYM USERS – A CASE STUDY (TOMKALSKA, 2018)

Description: A medium-sized fitness studio is exclusively used for yoga practice. The room comprises of a laminate flooring but each attendee brings their own rubber exercise mat. For the purpose of hot-yoga classes, the air-conditioning unit is turned off and additional portable heaters are used to increase the room temperature above 25°C. There are no means of natural ventilation or other air-cleaning measures.

Air quality: During an hour-long hot-yoga session air quality was monitored for concentrations of PM_{10} and $PM_{2.5}$ and following comfort parameters: CO_2, temperature and relative humidity. Air samples were been found of a terribly poor quality. The concentration of the fine particulates was six times greater and the coarse particulates five times greater than recommended limits. The temperature was 22°C above the recommended 18°C, whereas humidity was found to be exceeding the optimal 60% by 26%. Also, the CO_2 was exceptionally high, breaching the limit of 1250ppm by 6800ppm.

Perception: Attendees (n=20) were asked in an anonymous survey if they ever experienced any negative health symptoms after a class in that facility. Most predominately reported ill-effects were headaches, fatigue and eye-nose-throat irritations. Responders were able to indicate potential sources of air pollution, namely crowding, poor air circulation, poor temperature management or unpleasant chemical odour. However, the majority ranked the air quality as good (60%) and excellent (20%). Moreover, 90% admitted that they never been concerned about the air quality having any negative health impacts.

Awareness: The hot-yoga case study provides evidence of the poor awareness of the air quality amongst indoor sport practitioners. Positive opinions on the air quality go against complaints about health issues and physical conditions like crowding and stale air. This suggests a casual attitude and significant knowledge gap about the importance of good indoor air quality in exercise facilities.

Conclusion: A high-temperature and humid indoor climate is desired for the hot-yoga class in order to promote better flexibility and toxin release. At the same time, these conditions promote poor air quality: higher temperature and moisture content support evaporation of formaldehyde and other VOCs from synthetic flooring, yoga mats and other resin-based finishes; changing yoga poses boosts suspension of particles while the humid air acts as a dispersion vector.

Potential solutions: Good air quality is a prerequisite to a healthy indoor environment.

In order to potentiate benefits from indoor physical activity it is necessary to optimise the ventilation systems and address sources of pollution. A purpose-built yoga studio should utilise low-VOC materials such as solid hardwood, bamboo, natural cork or polished concrete. During the class, a combination of increased air-exchange rates and use of air-filtration technology should be employed to allow for a constant supply of clean air. The room should be ventilated and wet-cleaned in between classes. Finally, class bookings should always be below the maximum occupancy permitted.

3. Increased food consumption due to exercise

In an era where food sustainability is a topic of concern, should we really be encouraging people to expend more energy, only to consume more food as a result? Does increased exercise actually intensify the ever growing burden on global food resources? In fact, many people allude to a suppression of hunger which occurs in the hours proceeding intensive exercise. However, this short lived effect does not appear to have an overall impact on energy intake. Is there a lagged effect, whereby energy consumption in increased in the days following exercise? Somewhat counterintuitively conclusive evidence that increased physical activity results in increased energy intake has been slow to emerge (King, Tremblay, & Blundell, 1997). Martins, Morgan, Bloom, and Robertson (2007) found a decrease in hunger scores (during the exercise period) but an increase in absolute energy intake for the active cohort in their study which compared a group of cycling subjects with a group who rested. Accounting for the energy expended during the exercise itself produced a significant decrease in relative energy intake, a similar finding to that of Holliday and Blannin, 2017. How this would translate to the longer term is unclear. Some studies have suggested that some people compensate for increased energy expenditure by increasing food intake, while others do not (Blundell, Stubbs, Hughes, Whybrow, & King, 2003). Other confounding factors relate to the type of exercise carried out, with some studies suggesting that high intensity intermittent exercise training (HIIT) might result in decreased energy intake when compared with moderate intensity continuous exercise training (MICT) (Sim, Wallman, Fairchild, & Guelfi, 2015).

Exercise may also have an effect on our food choices. For example do we consume more protein (which may have been more energy intensive to produce in the first instance) following exercise, or do we increase our overall carbohydrate intake in the longer term? The energy requirements of exercise will no doubt influence our food choices, but what we choose is highly individualised and will be influenced by our nutritional education, the purpose of the exercise (weight loss or elite athlete training) and a plethora of other factors.

It is no doubt possible to make ethical food choices that are good for our health and environmentally sustainable no matter what level of physical activity we are involved in. The non-vegetarian diet places a far greater burden on the environment than the vegetarian diet, using more primary energy, more fertiliser, more water and more pesticides (Marlow et al., 2009). The dietary trend towards increased meat consumption and processed foods can also be linked to many chronic non-communicable diseases that reduce life expectancy (Tilman & Clark, 2014). One only has to look at the ever expanding list of professional vegan or vegetarian athletes to see that meat is not the only solution to a demanding exercise regime.

The overall effect therefore of a more active population on food demand is a complex subject and there is no straightforward answer as to whether it increases global demand for food. What is clear however, is that a more active population is a healthier population with a reduced burden on healthcare systems. Deaths from chronic diseases (many of which have modifiable health-risk factors such as physical inactivity) are projected to continue to rise (Oldridge, 2008) as will the future healthcare costs of a sedentary population. An educated population can make informed and ethical choices with regards to the food they eat and thus be kinder not only to their own bodies but also to the environment.

4. Active travel versus car, bus and train

Active travel is increasingly seen as a way to improve personal health through exercise while simultaneously reducing one's carbon footprint, lessening congestion and helping to lower roadside pollution (de Nazelle et al., 2011; Gotschi et al., 2015; Grange, Dirks, Costello, & Salmond, 2014). Despite strategies to improve efficiency and reduce the number of private vehicles in cities, pollution remains a problem. While recent research has indicated that active commuting provides benefits to health (Royal College of Physicians, 2016), the fact remains that active commuters may be exposed to higher levels of roadside pollutants than those who choose to travel by car, bus or train (Farrell et al., 2016; Peters et al., 2014).

So how then can active travel be promoted and developed without exposing commuters to an unreasonable level of pollution? A simple solution to reduce population exposure is to segregate the pollutant source (vehicle) and receptor (population). There is little doubt that given the choice, most of us would prefer to walk on a footpath which was segregated (preferably by greenery) and somewhat distant from the road and, indeed, studies have shown how increasing the distance between the pedestrian and congested roads reduces personal exposure to traffic pollution (de Hartog, Boogaard, Nijland, & Hoek, 2010; Garcia, Cerdeira, Coelho, Kumar, & Carvalho, 2014; Jarjour et al., 2013).

As increasing numbers of people live in cities internationally, it is important to augment the use of green space for people to exercise in the city areas as well. The provision of such green spaces in city centres has the potential to increase active commuting uptake and in turn make it healthier than the status quo. There are many other factors that influence whether an individual will partake in active travel, and these factors vary on a day to day basis as well as in the longer term. Broach, Dill, and Gliebe (2012) in their study in Portland, Oregan, USA found that that cyclists are sensitive to the effects of distance, turn frequency, slope, intersection control (e.g. presence or absence of traffic signals), and traffic volumes. Bike lanes more or less exactly offset the negative effects of adjacent traffic.

5. Concluding remarks

The interdisciplinary research agenda must consider the interactions which exist between human health, ecosystem health and the built environment (Tzoulas et al., 2007). If we want to develop a more environmentally conscious population that is also healthier, we need to design multilevel interventions that do not simply target the individual but look more broadly at the physical environment in which we live (Sallis et al., 2006). Where we live, where we work, where we spend our recreational time, and how we move between these areas all impact our health. Collaborative research can inform policy so that communities can be designed not only to be healthier but also to be more sustainable in the long term (see Figure 16.1). Sprawling cities do not favour the healthy active lifestyle, as people are forced to use cars to get around. Many cities are no longer walkable and there is frequently a lack of safe footpaths or bike lanes. All of this is leading to an increase in obesity rates and an increase in pollution as people drive more. If we designed our urban areas so that workplaces, amenities and homes were close to each other there is little doubt that people would make active travel choices and use public transport more (Frumkin, Frank, & Jackson, 2004).

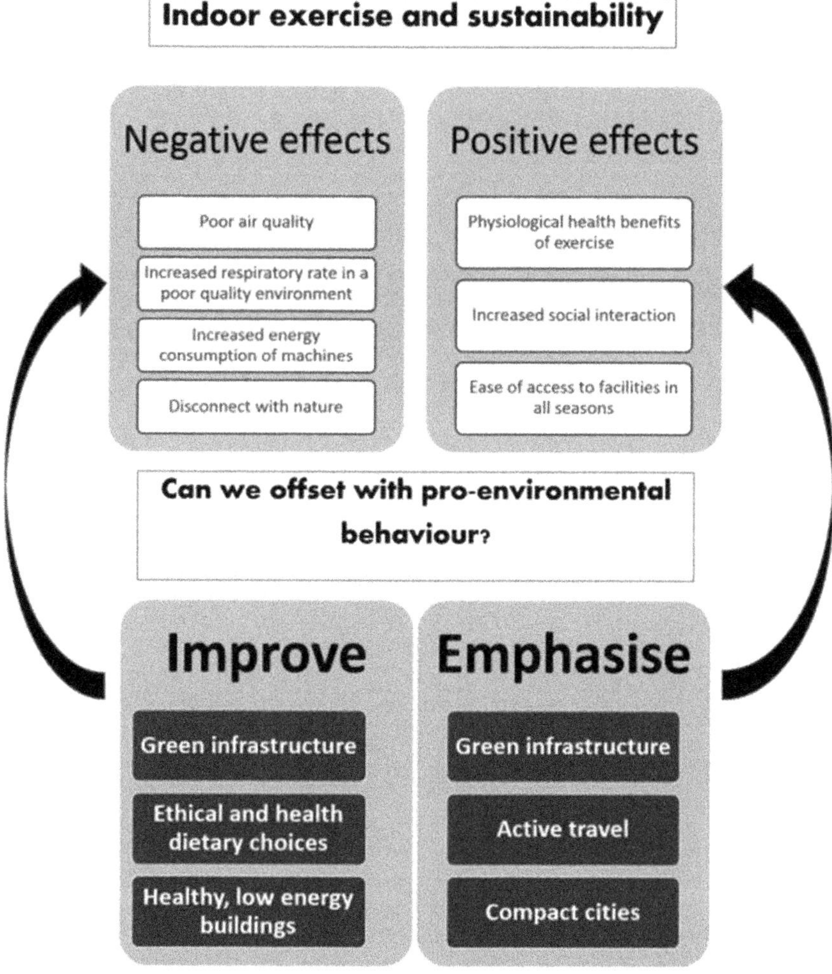

FIGURE 16.1 Indoor exercise and sustainability

References

Alberta Environmental Health (2012). *Environmental public health indoor air quality manual.* [online] Available at: https://open.alberta.ca/dataset/bea93036-a8f4-4a16-bcca-d7e83c0157e0/resource/f7e4ae01-4cda-4229-b581-924cf30a8d45/download/indoor-air-quality-manual-2012.pdf

Alleva, J. (2018). *"Strong is the new skinny": Do women like their bodies more?* [online] Available at: www.psychologytoday.com/intl/blog/mind-your-body/201802/strong-is-the-new-skinny-do-women-their-bodies-more

Alves, C.A., Calvo, A.I., Castro, A., Fraile, R., Evtyugina, M., Bate-Epey, E.F. (2013). Indoor air quality in two university sports facilities. *Aerosol and Air Quality Research, 13,* 1723-1730.

Andrade, A., & Dominski, F.H. (2018). Indoor air quality of environments used for physical exercise and sports practice. *Journal of Environmental Management, 206,* 577–586.

Blundell, J. E., Stubbs, R. J., Hughes, D. A., Whybrow, S., & King, N. A. (2003). Cross talk between physical activity and appetite control: Does physical activity stimulate appetite? *Proceedings of the Nutrition Society, 62*(3), 651–661.

Booth, M. L., Owen, N., Bauman, A., Clavisi, O., & Leslie, E. (2000). Social–Cognitive and perceived environment influences associated with physical activity in older Australians. *Preventive Medicine, 31*(1), 15–22.

Broach, J., Dill, J., & Gliebe, J. (2012). Where do cyclists ride? A route choice model developed with revealed preference GPS data. *Transportation Research Part A: Policy and Practice, 46*(10), 1730–1740.

Carlisle, A. & Sharp, N. (2001). Exercise and outdoor ambient air pollution. *British Journal of Sports Medicine, 1*(35), 214–222. Available at: www.researchgate.net/publication/11865829

de Hartog, J. J., Boogaard, H., Nijland, H., & Hoek, G. (2010). Do the health benefits of cycling outweigh the risks? *Environmental Health Perspectives, 118*(8), 1109–1116. doi:10.1289/ehp.0901747

Deloitte. (2018). *European health and fitness market report 2018.* [online] Available at: www.irelandactive.ie/contentfiles/EuropeActive_Deloitte_EHFMR_2018_IE.PDF

de Nazelle, A., Nieuwenhuijsen, M. J., Antó, J. M., Brauer, M., Briggs, D., Braun-Fahrlander, C., … Lebret, E. (2011). Improving health through policies that promote active travel: A review of evidence to support integrated health impact assessment. *Environment International, 37*(4), 766–777. doi:10.1016/j.envint.2011.02.003

Dishman, R. K., Sallis, J. F., & Orenstein, D. R. (1985). The determinants of physical activity and exercise. *Public Health Reports, 100*(2), 158.

Environmental Protection Agency (EPA). (2017a). *Indoor air quality.* [online] Available at: www.epa.gov/indoor-air-quality-iaq/volatile-organic-compounds-impact-indoor-air-quality

Environmental Protection Agency (EPA). (2017b). *What are the trends in indoor air quality and their effects on human health?* [online] Available at: https://cfpub.epa.gov/roe/chapter/air/indoorair.cfm

Farrell, W., Weichenthal, S., Goldberg, M., Valois, M.-F., Shekarrizfard, M., & Hatzopoulou, M. (2016). Near roadway air pollution across a spatially extensive road and cycling network. *Environmental Pollution, 212,* 498–507. doi:10.1016/j.envpol.2016.02.041

Flynn, E., Matz, P., Woolf, A., & Wright, R. (2000). *Indoor air pollutants affecting child health.* [pdf]: p. 1. Available at: www.allergycosmos.co.uk/wp-content/uploads/2010/02/IndoorAirPolution.pdf

Frumkin, H., Frank, L., & Jackson, R. J. (2004). *Urban Sprawl and Public Health: Designing, Planning, and Building for Healthy Communities*. Washington DC: Island Press.

Garcia, J., Cerdeira, R., Coelho, L., Kumar, P., & Carvalho, M. d. G. (2014). Influence of pedestrian trajectories on school children exposure to PM_{10}. *Journal of Nanomaterials, 2014*, 9. doi:10.1155/2014/505649

Global Wellness Institute. (2016). *Global wellness institute study*. [online] Available at: www.globalwellnessinstitute.org/global-wellness-institute-study-34-trillion-global-wellness-market-is-now-three-times-larger-than-worldwide-pharmaceutical-industry/

Gotschi, T., Tainio, M., Maizlish, N., Schwanen, T., Goodman, A., & Woodcock, J. (2015). Contrasts in active transport behaviour across four countries: How do they translate into public health benefits? *Preventive Medicine, 74*, 42–48. doi:10.1016/j.ypmed.2015.02.009

Grange, S. K., Dirks, K. N., Costello, S. B., & Salmond, J. A. (2014). Cycleways and footpaths: What separation is needed for equivalent air pollution dose between travel modes? *Transportation Research Part D: Transport and Environment, 32*, 111–119. doi:10.1016/j.trd.2014.07.014

Hajian, M. & Mohaghegh, S. (2015). Indoor air pollution in exercise centers. *International Journal of Medical Toxicology and Forensic Medicine, 5*(1), 22–31. Available at: http://journals.sbmu.ac.ir/ijmtfm/article/viewFile/IJMTFM-6442/pdf_41

Healthy Ireland. (2016). *Healthy Ireland survey 2016: Summary of findings*. Dublin: Government Publications.

Holliday, A., & Blannin, A. (2017). Appetite, food intake and gut hormone responses to intense aerobic exercise of different duration. *Journal of Endocrinology, 235*(3), 193–205.

International Health, Racquet and Sports-club Association (IHRSA). (2014). Focus on member loyalty. [online] Available at: http://hub.ihrsa.org/member-retention-report

International Health, Racquet and Sports-club Association (IHRSA). (2017). *Global report-state of the health club industry*. [online] Available at: www.ihrsa.org/publications/the-2017-ihrsa-global-report

Jarjour, S., Jerrett, M., Westerdahl, D., de Nazelle, A., Hanning, C., Daly, L., … Balmes, J. (2013). Cyclist route choice, traffic-related air pollution, and lung function: A scripted exposure study. *Environmental Health, 12*(1), 1–12. doi:10.1186/1476-069x-12-14

King, N. A., Tremblay, A., & Blundell, J. E. (1997). Effects of exercise on appetite control: Implications for energy balance. *Medicine & Science in Sports & Exercise, 29*(8), 1076–1089.

LesMills. (2013) *Global consumer fitness survey*. [online] Available at: https://w2.lesmills.com/files/GlobalCentral/Fitness%20is%20the%20worlds%20biggest%20sport.pdf

MacDougall, C., Cooke, R., Owen, N., Willson, K., & Bauman, A. (1997). Relating physical activity to health status, social connections and community facilities. *Australian and New Zealand Journal of Public Health, 21*(6), 631–637.

Marlatt, G. A., & Gordon, J. R. (1980). Determinants of Relapse: Implications for the Maintenance of Behavior Change. In P. O. Davidson & S. M. Davidson (Eds.), *Behavior medicine: Changing health lifestyles* (pp. 410–452). New York: Brunner/Mazel.

Marlow, H. J., Hayes, W. K., Soret, S., Carter, R. L., Schwab, E. R., & Sabate, J. (2009). Diet and the environment: Does what you eat matter? *The American Journal of Clinical Nutrition, 89*(5), 1699S–1703S.

Martins, C., Morgan, L. M., Bloom, S. R., & Robertson, M. D. (2007). Effects of exercise on gut peptides, energy intake and appetite. *Journal of Endocrinology, 193*(2), 251–258.

Mitchell, S., & Olds, R. (1999). Psychological and perceived situational predictors of physical activity: A cross-sectional analysis. *Health Education Research, 14*(3), 305–313.

Newell, K., Kartsonaki, C., Lam, H., & Kurmi, O. (2017). Cardiorespiratory health effects of particulate ambient air pollution exposure in low-income and middle-income countries: A systematic review and meta-analysis. *Lancet Planetary Health, 1*(9), 355–356. Available at: www.sciencedirect.com/science/article/pii/S2542519617301663?via%3Dihub

NPTEL.ac.ie. (2014). *Indoor air pollution.* [online] Available at: http://nptel.ac.in/courses/105102089/air%20pollution%20(Civil)/Module-6/1.htm

Oldridge, N. B. (2008). Economic burden of physical inactivity: Healthcare costs associated with cardiovascular disease. *European Journal of Cardiovascular Prevention & Rehabilitation, 15*(2), 130–139.

Parthasarathy, S., Randy, M.L., Russell, M. L., & Apte, M. G. (2011). Effect of temperature and humidity on formaldehyde emissions in temporary housing units. *Journal of the Air & Waste Management Association, 61*(6), 689–694. Available at: www.tandfonline.com/doi/pdf/10.3155/1047-3289.61.6.689

Peters, J., Van Den Bossche, J., Reggente, M., Van Poppel, M., De Baets, B., & Theunis, J. (2014). Cyclist exposure to UFP and BC on urban routes in Antwerp, Belgium. *Atmospheric Environment, 92*, 31–43. doi:10.1016/j.atmosenv.2014.03.039

Ramos, C.A., Reis, J.F., Almeida, T., Wolterbeek, H.T., & Almeida, S.M. (2015). Estimating the inhaled dose of pollutants during indoor physical activity. *Science of the Total Environment, 527–528*, 111–118. Available at: www.sciencedirect.com.ditlib.dit.ie/science/article/pii/S0048969715300541

Ramos, C.A., Wolterbeek, H.T., & Almeida, S.M. (2014). Exposure to indoor air pollutants during physical activity in fitness centres. *Building and Environment, 82*, 349–360. Available at: www.sciencedirect.com/science/article/pii/S0360132314002856

Royal College of Physicians. (2016). *Every Breath We Take: The Lifelong Impact of Air Pollution Report of a Working Party.* London: RCP.

Sassa, V., Kravitz-Wirtzb, N., Karceskia, S.M., Hajatc, A., Crowdera, K., & Takeuchid, D. (2017). The effects of air pollution on individual psychological distress. *Health and Place, 47*, 72–79. Available at: www.sciencedirect.com/science/article/pii/S1353829217303088#!

Sallis, J. F., Cervero, R. B., Ascher, W., Henderson, K. A., Kraft, M. K., & Kerr, J. (2006). An ecological approach to creating active living communities. *Annual Review of Public Health, 27*, 297–322.

Scientific Committee on Health and Environment Risk. (2007). *Opinion on risk assessment on indoor air quality.* [pdf]: pp. 3–32. Available at: http://ec.europa.eu/health/ph_risk/committees/04_scher/docs/scher_o_055.pdf

Shea, M. (2016). *Millennials are killing gyms, too.* [online] Available at: https://nypost.com/2016/10/17/millennials-are-killing-gyms-too/

Sim, A. Y., Wallman, K. E., Fairchild, T. J., & Guelfi, K. J. (2015). Effects of high-intensity intermittent exercise training on appetite regulation. *Medicine & Science in Sports & Exercise, 47*(11), 2441–2449.

Sports Ireland. (2017). Irish sport monitor annual report 2017. [online] Available at: www.sportireland.ie/Research/Irish%20Sports%20Monitor%202017%20-%20Half%20Year%20Report/Irish%20Sports%20Monitor%202017.pdf

Tilman, D., & Clark, M. (2014). Global diets link environmental sustainability and human health. *Nature, 515*(7528), 518.

Tomkalska, M. (2018). An investigation into indoor air quality in exercise facilities. Unpublished Masters dissertation, TU Dublin.

Trost, S. G., Owen, N., Bauman, A. E., Sallis, J. F., & Brown, W. (2002). Correlates of adults' participation in physical activity: Review and update. *Medicine & Science in Sports & Exercise, 34*(12), 1996–2001.

Tzoulas, K., Korpela, K., Venn, S., Yli-Pelkonen, V., Ka⊠mierczak, A., Niemela, J., & James, P. (2007). Promoting ecosystem and human health in urban areas using Green Infrastructure: A literature review. *Landscape and Urban Planning, 81*(3), 167–178.

US EPA. (1991). *Building Air Quality: A guide for building owners and facility managers.* DC: US GOV.

Wang, X. (2010). *Indoor air quality analysis.* Degree programme in Chemistry and Technology. Available at: www.theseus.fi/handle/10024/16515.

World Health Organization (WHO). (2014). *Indoor air pollution.* [online] Available at: www.who.int/news-room/fact-sheets/detail/household-air-pollution-and-health

Žitnik, M., Bu⊠ar, K., Hiti, B., Barba, Ž., Rupnik, Z., Založnik, A., ... & Žibert, J. (2016). Exercise-induced effects on a gym atmosphere. *Indoor air, 26*(3), 468-477.

17

MINDFULNESS AND GREEN EXERCISE

Enhancing our relationship with physical activity and the natural world

Kat Longshore, Michelle M. McAlarnen, Ryan Sappington and Dominic Harmon

Introduction

Let's get some green exercise by taking a walk on a nature trail. As we walk, we notice what the earth feels like under our feet – soft but firm, with the occasional crunch of leaves or pebbles. We feel the gentle breeze on our skin as it blows our hair off our forehead, we smell the pine needles and it sparks a memory of the winter holidays, we hear the chirp of a bird off in the distance and then a bark of a dog somewhere down the trail and feel a connection to nature, our body feels alive and alert. After a mile or so, we begin to climb a hill and as our legs tire we think, "How much longer?" The dog barks again and we wonder why the owner cannot keep it quiet. Now the air is stiffer and hot and we wish that breeze would return …

"Ugh is it over yet?"

"Still two miles to go … maybe we should have just gone to the gym. At least there we could watch a tv show while we walked …."

This green exercise example illustrates the three central themes of this chapter.

Theme 1: mindfulness as a way of enhancing and broadening the green exercise experience

What happened on our nature trail? For starters, there was much of which to be aware! Including our sensory experience, smell, touch, sight, sound, our emotions (i.e. from joy to annoyance), and our thoughts, wanted and unwanted. Experience ebbed and flowed, from pleasant to unpleasant to neutral, and back again. What we resisted, physical sensations, sounds, thoughts, all persisted. At times we wanted it just to be over, but the more we tried to distract ourselves, the longer it felt. We sometimes found it hard to have compassion for ourselves and others. In these ways, we begin to see how we can utilize mindfulness to leverage the benefits of green exercise.

One of the primary reasons we have for engaging in green exercise is, presumably, to enjoy and be with nature – that we believe there is some benefit to that experience. Otherwise, we would workout at home, in a gym, or in another built environment. Many times, we bring the same mindless behaviours to "get through" the green exercise. Unfortunately, this behaviour defeats the purpose and could negate the benefits we hope to have from green exercise. Mindfulness can help bring us back to our present experience, embrace nature, allow the green environment to be a part of our experience, and thus, leverage those perceived and real benefits.

Theme 2: mindfulness during green exercise as a tool for attention restoration

Our nature walk above also illustrates how our attention during physical activity can become disjointed and fragmented. We become overstimulated and overwhelmed by unpleasant sensations (e.g., soreness, fatigue, pain, loud noises, hot temperatures), and quickly distanced from the pleasant ones. We can become cognitively and emotionally consumed with escaping the discomfort and *just getting through* the activity. In time, our attention to our inner and outer experience – and by extension, our relationship with exercise and nature – can become tainted. Our discussion of mindfulness in this chapter will also focus on the restorative effects mindfulness practice can have on our attention.

Theme 3: mindfulness as a tool for cultivating compassion for self and others

If we reflect some more on our walk on the nature trail, we might also see that the experience lacked some compassion. We were not very kind to ourselves as we experienced leg fatigue, the hot stiff air, and our desire to escape that which was uncomfortable. Rather than seeing it as a part of the experience, we just wanted it to go away. What was also perhaps lacking was an overall appreciation of what our body is doing for us at this moment: walking – a wonderfully complex process involving electrical and chemical signals speeding throughout our central and peripheral nervous system, combining the input and processing of sensory experience, proprioception, movement, and coordination! It was also very convenient for us to go to the nature trail, but once there we lost the wonder for that opportunity. We ruminated on the accessibility of the gym. Instead, we could have brought some compassion or awareness that not everyone has this sort of access to green spaces, and maybe that is reason enough alone to absorb and appreciate the whole experience fully. Access to green exercise and its benefits intersects with social justice issues and perspectives. We can use mindfulness to extend compassion to others and cultivate greater awareness of social justice issues in the green movement.

Mindfulness basics

What is mindfulness?

Mindfulness has been defined in a number of ways and by many people. One of the most cited definitions is Kabat-Zinn (1994) who defined mindfulness as, "paying attention in a particular way: on purpose, in the present moment, and nonjudgmentally" (p. 4). Bishop and colleagues (2004), defined mindfulness as having two components, "self-regulation of attention … maintained on immediate experience, thereby allowing for increased recognition of mental events in the present moment and adopting a particular orientation toward one's experiences in the present moment, … characterized by curiosity, openness, and acceptance" (p. 232).

These classic definitions allude to the core principles of mindfulness: being in the moment, noticing what's happening right now, being open to all experience, having kindness for self and others, and recognizing that being mindful is an ongoing process. Another way to think about being mindful is to imagine its opposite, mindlessness. Mindlessness can be described as not paying attention to the task at hand, operating on autopilot, fantasizing, rushing, unaware, careless, spaced-out (Siegel, 2012).

It is worth noting that these definitions and much of the current understanding and teaching of mindfulness in Western (i.e. the United States & Europe) culture are a secularized version, detaching mindfulness from its Buddhist roots (Baer, 2003; Kabat-Zinn, 2003). Mindfulness has been around for thousands of years, a testament to its power and appeal. Though the core concepts have been retained, they are often presented differently and with different "goals" for the practice (Shonin & Van Gordon, 2015).

What does the research say about mindfulness?

Ample research in psychology and psychotherapy is available showing positive benefits of mindfulness and meditation practice. A few of these benefits include (a) stress reduction (Chiesa & Serretti, 2009; Khoury, Sharma, Rush, & Fournier, 2015; Victorson et al., 2015), (b) increased attention and concentration (Jha et al., 2015; Rooks, Morrison, Goolsarran, Rogers, & Jha, 2017) through reduced mind-wandering (Mrazek, Franklin, Phillips, Baird, & Schooler, 2013), and (c) increased emotional regulation through increased cognitive and somatic awareness (Baer, 2003; Holzel et al., 2011). For a review of the state of the evidence for mindfulness across domains and primary outcomes, particularly in the management of stress and anxiety and mood disorders (i.e. depression), see McAlarnen and Longshore (2017). More recently, researchers have compared across mindfulness-based interventions (MBI; Goyal et al., 2014) possible mechanisms by which mindfulness enables change (Gu, Strauss, Bond, & Cavanagh, 2015; van der Velden et al., 2015), and reviewed different delivery methods of MBIs (Spijkerman, Pots, & Bohlmeijer, 2016; Visted, Vøllestad, Nielsen, & Nielsen, 2014). Mindfulness research has gained momentum in other domains and subspecialties of psychology, such as healthcare (Gotink et al., 2015) and sport and exercise psychology (Sappington & Longshore, 2015).

One outcome and area of research particularly relevant to mindfulness and green exercise is the experience of flow which is defined as, "being so involved in an activity that nothing else seems to matter" (Csikszentmihalyi, 1990, p. 3). Flow is often regarded as an optimal performance state, a pleasurable experience, and something to be achieved. Csikszentmihalyi's research indicated that individuals are most likely to experience flow at the intersection of "difficulty" and "ability." In other words, when the challenge of an activity is in balance with an individual's skill level, they are more likely to achieve a flow state. Similarly, when exercising, it is essential to find a space in which one's skills are appropriately aligned with the challenge. Mindful engagement during green exercise may enhance flow. Dispositional mindfulness is linked to dispositional flow and mindfulness training has been found to increase flow (Kaufman et al., 2009).

Applying the tenets of mindfulness to bodily movement is not an entirely new concept. Established forms of mindful movement include practices such as Yoga, Tai Chi, and Qi Qong. All forms of mindful movement emphasize (a) alignment of the breath and the movement of the body, (b) becoming intimately aware of the sensations of the body during movement, (c) focusing on the present moment (e.g., the movement performing right now), and (d) letting go of judgment of the experience (e.g., I am not flexible enough, I cannot do what that other person is doing). These movement practices have demonstrated initial support for reductions in stress, anxiety, and depression (Büssing, Michalsen, Khalsa, Telles, & Sherman, 2012; Wang, Bannuru, Ramel, Kupelnick, Scott, & Schmid, 2010; Zeng, Luo, Xie, Huang, & Cheng, 2014).

What does it mean to be mindful?

A central concept in mindfulness is impermanence or the notion that everything is ever changing and thus nothing stays the same. When we relate this to our experience, we see that things never stay positive or negative. Instead, our experience is always changing. We wake up on the wrong side of the bed, the day feels miserable, and maybe it stays that way for a couple of hours. Then a few things go our way, we start to feel better, and by the end of the day we reflect on the great day we had. An adage in the mindfulness community is, "The only constant is change." In any moment, we can feel or think differently than the last moment. These ebbs and flows offer us flexibility, knowing that whatever is happening right now will not be happening forever, whether we want it to or not. This flexibility teaches us to be with the experience; if it is pleasant, we can savour the positive emotions, and if it is unpleasant, we can rest in it and build our tolerance for it, trusting in the knowledge that neither will last forever.

Another component of mindfulness is acceptance, which rests in the concept of nonjudgment of experience. This is done by bringing an attitude of curiosity and openness to whatever is happening now. Most of our time during the day is spent judging our experience – this is good, that is bad, I like that, I do not like this. This tendency creates discomfort, suffering, and our desire to want to hang on to the "good" and avoid the "bad." Mindfulness encourages us, instead, to describe the experience as an observer. For example, you are outside running, the sun is warm, you feel relaxed, and you think, "This run is great. I want all my runs to be this great." The next thing you know, it starts to rain. You come around a corner and discover that your favourite running path is blocked off due to construction. Turning around to head the other direction, you step into a deep muddy puddle, ruining your brand new running shoes. Nothing has changed in your experience of *running*, except for the surrounding conditions, over which you have no control. However, you now decide that this is an unpleasant run. Your judgment of the weather, the construction workers, and muddy puddles dictated your impression of the run. Could these instances instead be another part of the experience?

An essential part of mindfulness is increasing awareness of one's whole experience, all-encompassing, not just of our internal environment (e.g. thoughts and feelings), but also of physical sensations and our external environment taken in through our senses. What does the grass smell like? What does the wind or sun feel like? How many branches are on that tree and what do the leaves look like? Is that a bird chirping, how does it hit my ear? Is that tightness in my calf? Rather than trying to ignore any of these sensations, go to it and investigate the sensation. What does it feel like? Is it tightness, soreness, or pain? Have I felt it before? Is it hindering or just unpleasant? Is the sun on my face hot, unpleasant, or warming? Perhaps allow the sensations some time to pass on their own without even needing to do anything to get rid of them or change them.

Another element of mindfulness is changing one's relationship to experience, thoughts, and feelings. Mindfulness does not change the situation, it doesn't "get rid of" the stress, but instead changes our relationship to the stress. We all have certain situations, people, or circumstances that lead to stress – are "stressors" in our life. For example, we get an email about an unexpected meeting, our significant other says we need to talk, and traffic leads to arriving late. No matter how hard we try to avoid them, potential stressors will occur and by building our tolerance for stress and stress-inducing situations, we can change our relationship to the experience. While we can do nothing to turn back the time and have our alarm go off, we can accept that it happened, allow some frustration to be present, and by not holding on to wanting it to be different, let it pass.

Exercise is a perfect example of this process of building tolerance to a situation, emotion, thought, or physical sensation (i.e., cross-stressor adaptation hypothesis, see Sothmann, Buckworth, Clayton, Cox, White-Welkley, & Dishman, 1996). When we begin to move our bodies, it can be hard, it may hurt, and we find we may be sore or tired afterward. Over time, that same physical activity becomes easier, our bodies have built a tolerance, and increased exercise would be needed for the same level of original difficulty. Remember the hill from the earlier nature trail example? Suppose you want to be able to climb to the top of that hill and in the beginning you can only get half-way before turning back. Over time, you find you can get further and further up the hill, until one day you are standing at the top. Your body has adapted to the movement; much like with mindfulness, our minds adapt to life events.

Finally, mindfulness is not complete without kindness and compassion, for self and others. Through the practice of mindfulness, we realize our role in causing our suffering through judgment, resistance to experience and change, lack of awareness, distraction, detachment from our bodies, and need to control that which cannot be controlled. A necessary understanding in the practice of mindfulness is that life is inherently full of both pleasure and pain, happiness, and suffering. When we see the truth of our suffering, this experience opens us up to be able to appreciate the suffering of others. We can say, "It is not just me who does this, it is the human condition, so if I feel this suffering, then I can see the suffering you feel as well." In this way, we can begin to build compassion for others, knowing they are doing their best. In turn, this helps us have more compassion for ourselves, "I'm not the only one." What if we could be kind to ourselves? The cultivation of compassion, through practicing nonjudgment, increasing awareness of experience, and building tolerance and less resistance, can then be applied to many aspects of our lives and indeed, green exercise.

Restorative attention

Before turning our discussion to the intersection of mindfulness and green exercise, we want first to note a common aspect of exercise in the modern age: the use of technology (e.g., music, television) as a means of distracting or dividing our attention during physical activity. Of course, there are times when the use of technology serves to bring one more authentically into the exercise experience, perhaps even helping us coordinate our bodily movement with a rhythm. In this case, the use of music is *a deliberate choice* made for the purpose of enhancing our workout, rather than giving us something to distract ourselves from the discomfort. Similarly, consider athletes who use music during a pre-competition routine to prepare their mind and body (Weinberg & Gould, 2018. In this case, as well as cases in which music is used to facilitate exercise, the intention is to achieve physiological or psychological arousal. In other words, we make music *part* of our experience, rather than depending on it to *get through* the experience.

One way to think about attention during exercise is to consider the extent to which we are actively exerting control over it. William James (1892) identified two types of attention, distinguished by the amount of effort involved in their use.

Involuntary attention refers to attention that requires no effort. You might think about a time when you were "zoning out," perhaps as a passenger in the car or on public transportation, and suddenly your attention is yanked in a certain direction when something exciting or interesting happens. James (1892) described stimuli that bring forth involuntary attention as having a "direct exciting quality." In contrast, turning one's attention deliberately toward a stimulus or forcing oneself to pay attention to something that is not particularly interesting requires a good deal of effort. James referred to this as voluntary attention; clinical neurologists now refer to it as directed attention (Morecraft, Geula, & Mesulam, 1993). This effortful, directed attention is not unlimited and can be depleted, as you have likely experienced towards the end of a full day of meetings! When directed attention fatigue occurs in response to intense and sustained mental effort, mental fatigue results (Kaplan & Berman, 2010).

When it comes to directed attention, we often use two different techniques: dissociation or association. Dissociation is actively distracting oneself from experience and association is actively paying attention to the experience in which we are taking part. During exercise, the experience might include bodily sensations, respiration, muscle pain, exertion level, emotions, and thoughts (Lind, Welch, & Ekkekakis, 2009). For many, exercise only feels possible when it is accompanied by our favourite playlist or a television in front of our treadmill – both examples of dissociation. On the other hand, running without music and intentionally being aware of your breathing rate, how much effort you are giving, or the feel of the ground under your feet are examples of association. In their review, Lind and colleagues (2009) found that while exercisers and athletes typically use a combination of dissociation and association techniques, association techniques have consistently been found to be the most beneficial strategy for performance. Again, the use of technology during exercise is not always a bad thing, but the question is whether it is used to enhance the experience or to "get away from" it.

Now that we have identified two types of attention (involuntary and directed), as well as two techniques for "controlling" attention (dissociation and association), there seems to be an emerging paradox, or at the very least, a challenge. Ideally, we want to avoid "dissociating" from our exercise experience, as it means we are less authentically engaged in that experience, and perhaps getting less out of it. However, "associating" (i.e., directing our attention) *too strongly* into the experience may result in the depletion of cognitive resources, increased mental fatigue, and a shortened workout because we allow the physical discomfort to overwhelm us. Somehow, we need to strike a balance, whereby we become *deliberate observers* of our physical experience, while we avoid the cognitive depletion that can come from sustained, rigid association in the activity.

Mindfulness can be conceptualized as a form of attention training (Kabat-Zinn, 1990) that allows us to sustain a healthy awareness of our experience, without becoming overwhelmed or cognitively drained by it. Similarly, attention restoration theory has been proposed as a potential approach to facilitating mental recovery (Kaplan & Berman, 2010) and suggests that directed attention might be more likely to recover if it is allowed to rest.

Attention restoration theory is closely tied to the green exercise movement, given the cognitive benefits that can come from engaging with nature. Research indicates that merely viewing natural scenery (i.e., images of nature in paintings, photographs, slides, videos, computer displays) fosters attention restoration (Laumann, Garling, & Morten Stormark, 2003; Tennessen & Cimprich, 1995). Tennessen and Cimprich (1995) found that college students who had views of only natural elements through their dormitory windows performed better on tests of directed attention than students who had views that were partly natural or entirely built. Berto (2005) tested attentional capacity in college students before and after they viewed photographs previously judged to be restorative (nature scenes) or nonrestorative (non-nature scenes). Improvement was only found in students who viewed nature scenes, suggesting that ten minutes of viewing nature scenes improves directed attention. Studies that expose participants to sounds of nature demonstrate similar effects. Abbott, Taff, Newman, Benfield, and Mowen (2016) found that during recovery from a mentally fatiguing task, participants who listened to natural sound out-performed the others, indicating that natural sounds can facilitate attention restoration.

It is no surprise, then, that exercise in nature also fosters attention restoration. This benefit occurs in studies where exercise is controlled (Rogerson & Barton, 2015) and uncontrolled. In healthy populations, several studies using objective measures of attention have found restorative attention benefits (Berman, Jonides, & Kaplan, 2008; Duvall, 2011; Rogerson & Barton, 2015). For example, Duvall (2011) suggested that promoting cognitive engagement with the environment may make it easier for individuals to achieve the psychological benefits typically associated with outdoor physical activity (30-minute rural walk), even in settings that are less than ideal.

Bringing mindfulness to green exercise

Our discussion of the idiosyncratic benefits of both mindfulness and green exercise – with regard to our awareness, the nonjudgmental acceptance of our inner and outer experience, our tolerance for discomfort, our compassion for ourselves and others, and the restoration of our attention – brings us to the intersection of the two. The following sections will explore how this intersection can guide us in building a healthier relationship with our bodies, the experience of physical activity in and out of traditionally "green" spaces, and the natural world.

Mindfulness, green exercise, and our bodies

The intersection of green exercise and mindfulness can offer a wonderful space for mending and enhancing the relationship between mind and body. As human beings, we can have complicated relationships with our physical sense of self. We are constantly flooded with a stream of messaging from fitness magazines, television advertisements, and clothing stores that suggest to us that we should be skinnier, taller, more muscular, more tanned, and fitter. These messages can, over time, condition us to believe that we are neither attractive nor athletic enough to be accepted and that we must always be striving to reach the outrageous standards of beauty that society has constructed. We can develop feelings of frustration, shame, embarrassment, resentment, and jealousy when it comes to thinking about our bodies, and these feelings can, in turn, develop into mental health issues (e.g., anxiety, depression, eating disorders).

In response, many of us turn to our neighbourhood gyms and fitness centres. We hire trainers, we read fitness and health magazines, and we subscribe to motivational YouTube channels that help us stay on track when it comes to our new fitness regimen. Though these steps might move us in the direction of building healthier, more physically active lives, *they hardly liberate us from societal standards of beauty or physical "normalcy,"* nor do they mend the complicated relationships we have with our bodies. In fact, in many ways, when we engage in modern versions of exercise in community workout spaces, we can be inundated with these societal pressures to an even greater degree.

Consider, for example, the experience of working out in a public gym or fitness/recreation centre. These can be useful community spaces for physical activity, social engagement, and healthy living; however, there is a dark side to these environments. These settings can be breeding grounds for judgment, social comparison, body shaming, insecurity, segregation, and exclusion, based merely on the physical layout and the patterns of behaviour that emerge. Large, open workout rooms with clear glass and mirrors can make these spaces feel uncomfortable and unwelcoming for many in the population who may not fit into the narrow definition of "athletic" or "attractive." In turn, these spaces start to become divided.

For individuals who are differently abled, the pressures of socialized ideals of beauty and attraction, as well as the unwelcoming environment of exercise settings can be compounded by the daily task of living in a world (and accessing a gym) that is often not built for them. Add in the ways in which gyms can feel performative, and these spaces can foster feelings of discomfort for many. How the world perceives or treats us can mould our relationship with our body. It influences how we feel when we step into these public realms and how we are told, implicitly or explicitly, on a regular basis that we should look different.

Green exercise, on the other hand, can offer a starkly different experience. Jogging or walking in natural environments can provide the welcome relief that comes from being largely free from feeling judged or unwelcome. Bringing exercise and physical activity into green spaces can serve to, in some ways, free us from the pressures of socialized norms around fitness, movement, and attractiveness. Adding mindfulness to exercising in green spaces shifts one's attention from other people and judgment to the environment and acceptance of one's experience. To be mindful in a green space is to be aware of the open and expansive environment, the change that is ever present and welcomed in nature, and the stimulation of all of one's senses (the colours, textures, aromas, sounds, temperatures). In these ways, mindfulness works to foster the environment-mind-body connection, helping us make intimate contact with our thoughts and emotions, and observe how they manifest in our physical sensations. Over time, mindful green exercise can help us better understand our relationship with our body, observe how this relationship has become abusive or unhealthy, and seek to mend it.

Using mindfulness to work through (resting in) discomfort

As discussed in the previous section, the practice of mindfulness can be thought of as finding and resting in, the "space between stimulus and response" (Frankl, 1985). Consider the experience of being run off the trail by a bike, or arriving at the gym to see no open treadmills. In these moments, one may feel suddenly overwhelmed by feelings of anger or annoyance. In response, many of us might react impulsively, perhaps by screaming at the cyclist, or by expressing our frustration when we approach the gym counter about how long we were waiting. Though it may feel good now to act on our displeasure, the catharsis rarely lasts long. Instead, in some cases, the problem is exacerbated (e.g., the person behind the counter snaps back at us) and we are left with residual feelings of regret or shame over having acted out.

There is an alternative to this process, however. By bringing mindfulness to a particular moment, one seeks to exist, even momentarily, in the space between the stimulus (i.e., what angers us) and the way we react to it. One can readily apply this approach to the act of exercising. Though it might be rare to experience such strong emotions as anger while working out, it is true that physical activity can create feelings of minor to extreme discomfort. It can be tempting to dissociate from these experiences – to avoid or reduce the physical distress by multitasking (e.g., watching television on the treadmill, listening to music out on the trail). In some cases, we might stop the activity entirely at the first hint of pain. Though these strategies may offer us a reprieve from the discomfort of our workout, over time, we can become conditioned, in some ways, to feel as though *we cannot exercise without these strategies*. Concurrently, we might come to resent, dread, or fear exercise, because it is an experience that, in our mind, "requires" dissociation.

What if, instead of choosing to dissociate in these moments (because it is a choice!), one chooses to exist entirely in the discomfort, even for a brief moment? Mindfulness encourages us to pause before instinctively pushing this pain away or trying to banish it. It encourages us to welcome it into our experience. Of course, this process is easier said than done. In many cases, it might mean changing our entire relationship with exercise. It requires practice, and it is entirely reasonable to start small. For example, if you start to feel a burning sensation in your legs while walking or running, rather than slowing down or stopping entirely, consider posing this question to yourself inwardly, "Am I able to welcome this discomfort at this moment?" We could even bring some compassion to this experience of discomfort. "It is okay for this to feel hard. I have not done this before." Take our earlier hill example; you started only able to walk half-way up the hill and after moving through some discomfort over time were able to get all the way to the top. We may even recognize that we are not alone, "I am not the only one who has felt discomfort making a change, and others have gone through this too." Of course, this does not mean that one should not pause or stop physical activity in moments of more intense discomfort or pain, as doing so can prevent injury.

What if there is no green?

Thus far, we have discussed green exercise mainly in a manner that implies that green spaces are readily accessible to everyone. However, we know this is not the case, and many readers may be balking, because, "Green exercise is great in theory, but I do not live in an area with access to parks, scenic trails, and the trees. I am in a small apartment in the middle of a city." With urban areas growing in geographical size and population, large segments of the population do not live within walking distance of greenery.

At face value, urban spaces offer a stark contrast from what we might picture when we think of "green exercise." The noise, speed, and sharpness of urban living can make a run along city sidewalks feel dramatically unlike what we might feel when we jog through the wooded path, or along farmlands, mountains, and rivers. The unforgiving nature of asphalt or concrete, the sharp corners and edges of buildings and skyscrapers, the sounds and smells rising up through the subway vents, the honking of car horns, perhaps even the cold glares of pedestrians who are pushing past each other – it all seems so abrasive and distant from the peace and serenity that nature offers. How can one possibly hope to engage in "green exercise" in these spaces?

First – and this is easier said than done – ask yourself, "How can mindfulness help me notice the green that *remains* in these environments?" Shift your awareness away from the busy streets and car horns to the plants outside windows or office buildings, small squared off sections of grass between streets and dried out leaves littering the sidewalk. Notice how the trees along roadways stand in sharp defiance against their human-made surroundings, as their roots break apart and push up entire sections of concrete. Bring your attention to large rocks, pebbles, or dirt crunching beneath your feet. When we mindfully immerse ourselves into the present moment in a city, we can find vestiges of greenery almost everywhere.

This approach, of course, is no easy task. Cities can feel over-stimulating, and the sights, sounds, and smells can very quickly drown out any small moment of intimacy we might feel when we see a solitary tree along a busy urban street. *However, what is mindfulness if it is not a continuous cycle of returning to those moments of intimacy, even when they are regularly interrupted?* Cities, in a way, offer us the ultimate challenge when it comes to mindfully engaging in green exercise, and as such, they can help us become more compassionate and patient in our meditative practice.

Second – and perhaps, a more significant challenge – mindfulness offers a means by which we can cultivate a softer relationship with our outer world, even if it completely lacks greenery. Recall our earlier discussion about how mindfulness is not about "getting rid" of discomfort but changing our relationship to it. We are socialized to dichotomously categorize the external world into urban and rural, natural and not when all humans and materials derive from nature (see Van Gordon, Shonin, & Richardson, 2018). However, even the unnaturally gray and black façade of buildings, which seem like the epitome of "anti-green," can trace their materials back to nature. Granted, it requires mental agility to experience a skyscraper as a part of the green exercise experience, and in no way are we suggesting that they are not an affront to the notion of environmental protection and the conservation of natural resources. However, when it comes to exercising in ways that get us more in touch and in tune with our surroundings, it is important to explore and be curious about what is already there (see Box 17.1). In this sense, we can use mindfulness to expand our definition of "green" and become more intimately aware of how built structures came to be.

BOX 17.1 PRACTICAL SUGGESTIONS FOR BEING MINDFUL DURING GREEN EXERCISE

Pay attention to your sensory experience.

- Allow the sensation to arise and to pass, without too much analysis.
- Notice how the air feels as it makes contact with your skin, is it cool, warm, sticky, wet, scratchy, soft?
- Notice what you see, pay attention to the detail, the color, texture, size. Look to the left and right, up and down.
- Notice what aromas or smells are present, perhaps freshly cut grass, moisture in the air, tree sap or leaves, or open water.
- Notice what sounds are a part of your experience, sounds from animals, the wind moving through the trees, or your feet as they hit the ground or crunch the earth.Pay attention to your body.
- What does it feel like to move?
- What parts of your body call out for your attention? What sensation is then present there?
- When you notice some discomfort, can you give it some attention and allow it some space to work itself out?

- Notice how the signals from your body change throughout your exercise.Pay attention to your internal experience of thoughts and emotions.
- What sorts of thoughts are you having? What sorts of emotions are you having?
- How much are your thoughts or emotions connected to the experience or your interpretation or judgment of the experience?
- Notice how your thoughts and emotions change throughout your exercise.

Use the breath.

- Keep an eye on your breath throughout the green exercise. Notice how it shifts, and changes becomes shallower or deeper depending on the exertion.
- The breath happens in real-time. Anytime you feel distracted or not present with your green environment, pay attention to the breath, it will bring you back to the moment.

Take a pause.

- Every so often, take a pause and experience the green around you. When you come to the top of a hill or the edge of a clearing, take a moment to appreciate the green space.
- Take a pause every so often to appreciate yourself, your body, and the effort you are putting into exercise.

Bring the Compassion.

- Can you notice when you are unkind to yourself, for example, when it gets hard, or your body will not move the way you want it?
- Can you instead say, "I am doing my best," "this is a moment of suffering but everyone suffers sometimes," or "may I love and accept myself at this moment."

Mindfulness and environmental (in)justice in green environments

We want to pause and reflect on some larger implications of the green exercise movement. This section presents questions that emerged from our reflections on nature and built environments as we reviewed literature in public health, urban planning, green exercise, mindfulness, social and environmental justice, and sport and fitness culture.

This section is not comprehensive, and we encourage readers to pursue the references and additional research. Despite its brevity, we believe its inclusion helps to illustrate our complex relationship with green exercise and the related movements in urban design and fitness. This section exemplifies how a mindful approach to green exercise can cultivate compassion for humans and non-humans and connect to social justice concerns. We hope to deepen the conversation around green exercise by articulating our questions and critiques of an activity we purport.

Who has access to green exercise?

We discussed how to find green wherever we are, but we also recognize that there are socio-spatial and socio-cultural discrepancies to access (see Wolch, Byrne, & Newell, 2014). Because green spaces are restorative environments that offer psychological and physiological benefits (King, Stokols, Talen, Brassington, & Killingsworth, 2002; Thompson et al., 2012), it is an environmental justice issue when access differs by social class, racial-ethnic communities, place of living, ableness, and other vital demographic groupings (Wolch et al., 2014).

The location and number of public parks are often used to assess different communities' access to green spaces (though parks vary in their amount of "green"). Research on the relationship between demographic, cultural, local histories (i.e., socio-cultural) and physical (i.e., socio-spatial) factors and access to parks is inconsistent and complex (Wen, Zhang, Harris, Holt, & Croft, 2013). White and more affluent communities tend to have more access to urban green spaces (Wolch et al., 2014) and parks (Wen et al., 2013), though the opposite has also been found (e.g., less affluent have more access to public parks, Barbosa et al., 2007). There is also evidence of no disparity between racial-ethnic and socio-economic groups and park access (Wen et al., 2013). An important factor that might underscore these results is the difference between social access and physical access (Wen et al., 2013). Social access encompasses "socio-demographic features, such as safety, traffic, and walkability that might directly affect park utilization" (Wen et al., 2013, p. 6; see also Byrne, 2012; Wolch et al., 2014), whereas physical access refers to the existence of a park and its spatial distance to the surrounding neighbourhood, especially concerning walkability and public transport.

Communities may have varying degrees of social and physical access that may support or hinder park use. In urban areas, disruptive environmental conditions that induce neighbourhood disorder and environmental stress (see King et al., 2002) may exist and inhibit park use, even if it is spatially close. In rural areas, the distance from the park can inhibit use (Wen et al., 2013). Wen and colleagues (2013) encouraged increasing social access for urban parks and physical access to parks in rural communities.

Last, even if parks and similar green spaces (e.g., benches by creeks, trails, gardens) are socio-spatially and socio-culturally accessible, for whom are they designed?

Are considerations made for differently abled populations so that they can access and participate in the park, trail, nature-based/green tourism, or other green space? Though limitations might exist for some natural formations, all can benefit and use public parks and many trails through inclusive play design (e.g., Jeanes & Magee, 2012; Playworld Systems Inc., 2015) and accessible tourism strategies (see Buhalis & Darcy, 2011).

How is green space integrated into built environments and what are its implications?

As built environments incorporate green, there are potential harmful social and environmental consequences. Urban areas and the inner ring of suburban areas are traditionally inhabited by lower socio-economic populations and racial-ethnic minorities (Wolch et al., 2014). It is these communities who can most benefit from active and passive green space as one way to confront public health challenges (Wolch et al., 2014), but because urban parks serve a dense population with limited public space, parks and related green space can be overcrowded. These green spaces may provide fewer psychological and physical benefits to users because of location, accessibility, and equipment. Locations near automobile traffic might mean poor air health quality and loud noises, which diminish its restorative environment and benefits. It might even produce health problems. Automobile-centric infrastructure might limit walkability, even to nearby parks, if the quality of pedestrian infrastructure is low. Parks may not have active spaces with updated play equipment or may require personal equipment. Depending on the income level of individuals and access to community recreation and resources, such supplemental play equipment may not be available (Wolch et al., 2014).

Social and physical access challenges can incentivize a community to revitalize or add new green spaces. Green space development, meant to improve a community's health and aesthetics, can increase property values, cost of living, and desirability. Therein, lies the "urban green space paradox" (Kruger & Gibbs, 2007). These changes push out the community it is intended to serve, including businesses linked to that population (Zukin et al., 2009) and also persons experiencing homelessness (Dooling, 2009). Renovations attract new residents (usually of higher socio-economic status) who can afford the new cost of living (Wolch et al., 2014). The increased land value forces inhabitants to leave for poorer neighborhoods beset by high pollutants and poor environmental conditions. These conditions are exactly what the green space development aimed to diminish. Further, the displacement of longtime inhabitants disrupts the history, culture, community, and sense of place for neighbourhoods and forces these families and individuals into new communities. The green space intervention had a paradoxical effect and reinforced class structure, land use, and public health disparities. This situation is why Wolch and colleagues argue for "just green enough" interventions in which the dosage and spread of green added to impoverished, racial-ethnic minority communities is de-centralized, targeted, and small scale. This purposeful greening provides public health benefits but does not prompt gentrified development (Curran & Hamilton, 2012; Wolch et al., 2014). This approach is particularly relevant when green space development derives from the local community and government with a public health focus.

This section discussed bringing green into residential and commercial spaces and this phenomenon sparked some questions for us. As we try to balance our relationship with nature by bringing more of it into built environments, do we move farther from nature? In other words, do we move farther from nature as we move it closer to us? For example, new children's play centres boast replica rocks to climb, streams, and nature-related activities (e.g., examining butterflies; see Zimmermann, 2017 for examples of indoor nature recreation centre). On the one hand, these complexes offer a place for children to engage in free play, participate in educational activities, be in and connect to nature or nature-like settings without the impact of weather conditions, and play in a safe, potentially convenient environment compared to the distance to local, regional, and national parks. On the other hand, high entry fees and varied access via public transportation can limit accessibility and reinforce class structure. To participate, families need enough disposable income, flexible work hours or a schedule that aligns with the play center's open hours, and reliable transportation. Additionally, children and adults are not engaging directly with nature, but with a crafted version. What are the implications of these encounters for children and adults psychologically, physiologically, socially, and their development of nature-based skills? If we believe we can "create" nature when we need it, do we lose our awe of it and our responsibility to care for it?

How does green exercise affect non-human beings?

Mansfield (2009) recounted a disconcerting experience during a "boot camp" fitness session at a park. As the sessions grew in attendance, runners overflowed the trail and trampled the adjacent areas. The size and noise of the group kept animals away. The instructor's bellowed orders drowned the chirping of birds and rustling of leaves. Though in green space, this experience hardly seemed restorative for the participants or respectful to the non-humans who inhabited the park. There was a disconnect between the space, what it could offer humans and non-humans, and how it was used and experienced.

This observation by Mansfield (2009) encourages us to reflect on incongruencies within the sport and fitness cultures, especially the environmental impact of sport and fitness products. Does cutting trees to build football pitches count as green? What about pouring tons (literally) of mud in a field or trail for Tough-Mudder-like events? Who and what is harmed in the name of sport, exercise, and fitness, even when green space is created? Mega-events, such as the Olympics, World Cup, and Super Bowl are the epitome of sport and require extensive built and green space. Research on environmental and social impacts of mega-events is nuanced and complicated. There are some expected, short-term benefits to hosting mega-events, but also there are detriments to the cities, people, and environments as stadiums are built and communities displaced (Chappelet, 2008; Essex & Chalkley, 1998; Kim, Gursoy, & Lee, 2006; Malfas, Theodoraki, & Houlihan, 2004). In the realm of adventure, ecotourism, and traditional travel, there can be an ecological cost to the pristine, sensitive terrain (Wong, 2004). This realization prompted research, activism, and interventions toward sustainable tourism (McCool & Moisey, 2001) to protect plant-life, animal-life, and the land, which have worth as separate entities and a right to habitat, safety, and survival. These life forms are integral to sustained human life and well-being. We are left to wonder about the degree to which the spaces surrounding sport, fitness, and exercise activities disregard the non-human for the human and its short and long-term implications.

As the mainstream fitness and sport culture incorporates green exercise, there is an increased tendency to see green exercise as a commodity and something to sell and market. Green capitalism means that consumption is prioritized (Mansfield, 2009) even if it is consumption of sustainable, environment-friendly materials and activities. As a commodity, its definition of success is growth and production of equipment, material, space. Thus, more materials are produced, more outdoor sport and fitness events are held, more tours to witness natural beauty are taken and more paved (and unpaved) trails created. These activities can support physical activity, mental and physical health, and appreciation for nature. They also require energy to make, transport, sell, and dispose of even when produced from sustainable or recycled materials and made in environmentally conscious ways.

Bringing mindfulness to green exercise also implores us to consider how we may contribute to green capitalism through our purchases and green space use. It is easy and understandable to get swept into green capitalism, especially when it does seem to align with our intentions and belief systems. But, our mindfulness practice and connection with nature can help us pause to expand our compassion as we realize that we are in nature and nature in us (see Van Gordon et al., 2018). Kaza (2008) in *Mindfully Green: A personal and spiritual guide to whole earth thinking* details how to bring a mindful green practice to reduce harm to nature and notice the suffering of animals, water, and food sources (and ultimately humans and the world through these acts). This examination of the ecosystem and how we support or diminish its health through our daily acts is a great resource and meditation as we seek to practice green, mindfully.

Living the questions

We consider these questions crucial to a more nuanced examination of the green exercise movement and imperative as practitioners and researchers who espouse mindfulness in our professional and personal lives. We must give ourselves permission to ask the uncomfortable questions and see the complex interaction between green exercise and land and residential policy, social and economic stratification, marginalized and oppressed populations, and non-human populations and their habitats. As the momentum continues to green the built environment, unexpected implications for humans, non-humans, and space may arise. We encourage professionals and students to examine *how* and *for whom* green exercise is developed and commodified.

Summary

The intersection of mindfulness and green exercise can have restorative benefits for our attention, better our relationship with our body, and create space between stimuli and our learned response. Some initial ways to integrate mindfulness to exercise were offered, which might help us find beauty and nature even in the most urban environments – or reconnect with the everyday green in our lives that we overlook. Finally, a mindful practice can extend our compassion to humans and non-humans, and allow us to consider the environmental and social justice issues embedded in access to green exercise.

References

Abbott, L. C., Taff, D., Newman, P., Benfield, J. A., & Mowen, A. J. (2016). The influence of natural sounds on attention restoration. *Journal of Park and Recreation Administration, 34*, 5–15.

Baer, R. A. (2003). Mindfulness training as a clinical intervention: A conceptual and empirical review. *Clinical Psychology: Science and Practice, 10*, 125–143.

Barbosa, O., Tratalos, J. A., Armswoth, P. R. Davies, R. G., Fuller, R. A, Johnson, P., & Gaston, K. J. (2007). Who benefits form access to green space? A case study from Sheffield, UK. *Landscape and Urban Planning, 83*, 187–195.

Berto, R. (2005). Exposure to restorative environments helps restore attentional capacity. *Journal of Environmental Psychology, 25*, 249–259.

Berman, M. G., Jonides, J., & Kaplan, S. (2008). The cognitive benefits of interacting with nature. *Psychological Science, 19*, 1207–1212.

Bishop, S. R., Lau, M., Shapiro, S., Carlson, L., Anderson, N. D., Carmody, J., … & Devins, G. (2004). Mindfulness: A proposed operational definition. *Clinical Psychology: Science and Practice, 11*(3), 230–241.

Buhalis, D., & Darcy, S. (Eds.). (2011). *Accessible Tourism: Concepts and Issues*. Buffalo, NY: Channel View Publications.

Büssing, A., Michalsen, A., Khalsa, S., Telles, S., & Sherman, K. J. (2012). Effects of yoga on mental and physical health: A short summary of reviews. *Evidence-Based Complementary and Alternative Medicine*, 1–7. doi:10.1155/2012/165410

Byrne, J. (2012). When green is White: The cultural politics of race, nature, and social exclusion in a Los Angeles urban national park. *Geoforum, 43*(3), 595–611.

Chappelet, J. L. (2008). Olympic environmental concerns as a legacy of the winter games. *The International Journal of the History of Sport, 25*(14), 1884–1902.

Chiesa, A., & Serretti, A. (2009). Mindfulness-based stress reduction for stress management in healthy people: A review and meta-analysis. *The Journal of Alternative and Complementary Medicine, 15*, 593–600.

Curran, W., & Hamilton, T. (2012). Just green enough: Contesting environmental gentrification in Greenpoint, Brooklyn. *Local Environment, 17*, 1027–1042.

Csikszentmihalyi, M. (1990). *Flow: The Psychology of Optimal Performance*. New York, NY: Harper & Row.

Dooling, S. (2009). Ecological gentrification: A research agenda exploring justice in the city. *International Journal of Urban and Regional Research, 33*, 621–639.

Duvall, J. (2011). Enhancing the benefits of outdoor walking with cognitive engagement strategies. *Journal of Environmental Psychology, 31*, 27–35.

Essex, S., & Chalkley, B. (1998). Olympic games: Catalyst of urban change. *Leisure Studies, 17*(3), 187–206.

Frankl, V. E. (1985). *Man's Search for Meaning*. New York, NY: Simon and Schuster.

Gotink, R. A., Chu, P., Busschbach, J. J., Benson, H., Fricchione, G. L., & Hunink, M. M. (2015). Standardised mindfulness-based interventions in healthcare: An overview of systematic reviews and meta-analyses of RCTs. *PloS One, 10*(4), e0124344.

Goyal, M., Singh, S., Sibinga, E. M., Gould, N. F., Rowland-Seymour, A., Sharma, R., … Ranasinghe, P. D. (2014). Meditation programs for psychological stress and well-being: A systematic review and meta-analysis. *JAMA Internal Medicine, 174*, 357–368.

Gu, J., Strauss, C., Bond, R., & Cavanagh, K. (2015). How do mindfulness-based cognitive therapy and mindfulness-based stress reduction improve mental health and wellbeing? A systematic review and meta-analysis of mediation studies. *Clinical Psychology Review, 37*, 1–12.

Holzel, B. K., Carmody, J., Vangel, M., Yerramsetti, S. M., Gard, T., & Lazar, S. W. (2011). Mindfulness practice leads to increases in regional brain gray matter density. *Psychiatry Research: Neuroimaging, 19*(1), 36–43.

James, W. (1892). *Psychology: The Briefer Course*. New York, NY: Holt.

Jeanes, R. & Magee, J. (2012). 'Can we play on the swings and the roundabouts?': Creating inclusive play spaces for disabled young people and their families. *Leisure Studies, 31*(2), 193–210.

Jha, A. P., Morrison, A. B., Dainer-Best, J., Parker, S., Rostrup, N., & Stanley, E. A. (2015). Minds "at attention": Mindfulness training curbs attentional lapses in military cohorts. *PloS One, 10*(2), e0116889.

Kabat-Zinn, J. (1990). *Full Catastrophe Living: How to Cope with Stress, Pain and Illness Using Mindfulness Meditation*. New York, NY: Random House.

Kabat-Zinn, J. (1994). *Wherever You Go, There You Are: Mindfulness Meditation in Everyday Life*. New York, NY: Hyperion.

Kabat-Zinn, J. (2003). Mindfulness-based interventions in context: Past, present, and future. *Clinical Psychology: Science and Practice, 10*, 144–156.

Kaplan, S., Berman, M. G. (2010). Directed attention as a common resource for executive functioning and self-regulation. *Perspectives on Psychological Science, 5*(1), 43–57.

Kaza, S. (2008). *Mindfully Green: A Personal and Spiritual Guide to Whole Earth Thinking*. Boston, MA: Shambhala Publications.

Khoury, B., Sharma, M., Rush, S. E., & Fournier, C. (2015). Mindfulness-based stress reduction for healthy individuals: A meta-analysis. *Journal of Psychosomatic Research, 78*, 519–528.

Kim, H. J., Gursoy, D., Lee, S.-B. (2006). The impact of the 2002 World Cup on South Korea: Comparisons of pre- and post-games. *Tourism Management, 27*, 86–96.

King, A. C., Stokols, D., Talen, E., Brassington, G. S., & Killingsworth, R. (2002). Theoretical approaches to the promotion of physical activity. *American Journal of Preventative Medicine, 23*(2), 12–25.

Kruger, R., & Gibbs, D. (Eds.). (2007). *The Sustainable Development Paradox*. New York, NY: Guilford.

Laumann, K., Garling, T., Morten Stormark, K. (2003). Selective attention and heart rate responses to natural and urban environments. *Journal of Environmental Psychology, 23*, 125–134.

Lind, E., Welch, A. S., & Ekkekakis, P. (2009). Do 'mind over muscle' strategies work? *Sports Medicine, 39*(9), 743–764.

Malfas, M., Theodoraki, E., & Houlihan, B. (2004). Impacts of the Olympic Games as mega-events. *Municipal Engineers, 157*(ME3), 209–220.

Mansfield, L. (2009). Fitness cultures and environmental (in)justice? *International Review for the Sociology of Sport, 44*(4), 345–362.

McAlarnen, M. M., & Longshore, K. (2017). Evidence-based mindfulness: Proceed with caution. In S. J. Zizzi & M. B. Anderson (Eds.), *Being Mindful in Sport and Exercise Psychology: Pathways for Practitioners and Students* (pp. 31–62). Morgantown, WV: Fitness Information Technology.

McCool, S. F., & Moisey, R. N. (Eds.). (2001). *Tourism, Recreation, and Sustainability: Linking Culture and the Environment* (2nd ed.). Cambridge, MA: CABI International.

Morecraft, R. J., Geula, C., Mesulam, M. M. (1993). Architecture of connectivity within a cingulo-fronto-parietal neurocognitive network for directed attention. *Archives of Neurology, 50*, 279–284.

Mrazek, M. D., Franklin, M. S., Phillips, D. T., Baird, B., & Schooler, J. W. (2013). Mindfulness training improves working memory capacity and GRE performance while reducing mind wandering. *Psychological Science, 24*(5), 776–781.

Playworld Systems, Inc. (2015). *Inclusive play design guide*. Retrieved from www.accessibleplayground.net/wp-content/uploads/2016/05/Inclusive-Play-Design-Guide-LowRes-2.pdf

Rogerson, M., & Barton, J. (2015). Effects of the visual exercise environments on cognitive directed attention, energy expenditure and perceived exertion. *International Journal of Environmental Research and Public Health, 12*, 7321–7336.

Rooks, J. D., Morrison, A. B., Goolsarran, M., Rogers, S. L., & Jha, A. P. (2017). "We are talking about practice": The influence of mindfulness vs. relaxation training on athletes' attention and well-being over high-demand intervals. *Journal of Cognitive Enhancement, 1*(2), 141–153.

Sappington, R. & Longshore, K. (2015). Systematically reviewing the efficacy of mindfulness- based interventions for enhanced athletic performance. *Journal of Clinical Sport Psychology, 9*, 232–262.

Shonin, E., & Van Gordon, W. (2015). The lineage of mindfulness. *Mindfulness, 6*, 141–145.

Siegel, R. (2012). *Mindfulness in psychotherapy*. Continuing Education Seminar presented at J&K Seminars, Lancaster, PA.

Sothmann, M. S., Buckworth, J., Clayton, R. P., Cox, R. H., White-Welkley, J., & Dishman, R. (1996). Exercise training and the cross-stressor adaptation hypothesis. *Exercise and Sport Science Reviews, 24*(1), 267–288.

Spijkerman, M. P. J., Pots, W. T. M., & Bohlmeijer, E. T. (2016). Effectiveness of online mindfulness-based interventions in improving mental health: A review and meta-analysis of randomised controlled trials. *Clinical Psychology Review, 45*, 102–114.

Tennessen, C. M., Cimprich, B. (1995). Views to nature; effects on attention. *Journal of Environmental Psychology, 16*, 77–85.

Thompson, C. W., Roe, J., Aspinall, P., Mitchell, R., Clow, A., Miller, D. (2012). More green space is linked to less stress in deprived communities: Evidence from salivary cortisol patterns. *Landscape and Urban Planning, 105*, 221–229.

Van Gordon, W., Shonin, E., & Richardson, M. (2018). Mindfulness and nature. *Mindfulness*. doi:10.1007/s12671-018-0883-6

van der Velden, A. M., Kuyken, W., Wattar, U., Crane, C., Pallesen, K. J., Dahlgaard, J., … & Piet, J. (2015). A systematic review of mechanisms of change in mindfulness-based cognitive therapy in the treatment of recurrent major depressive disorder. *Clinical Psychology Review, 37*, 26–39.

Victorson, D., Kentor, M., Maletich, C., Lawton, R. C., Kaufman, V. H., Borrero, M., & Berkowitz, C. (2015). Mindfulness meditation to promote wellness and manage chronic disease: A systematic review and meta-analysis of mindfulness-based randomized control trials relevant to lifestyle medicine. *American Journal of Lifestyle Medicine, 9*, 185–211.

Visted, E., Vøllestad, K., Nielsen, B., & Nielsen, G. H. (2014, June). The impact of group-based mindfulness training on self-reported mindfulness: A systematic review and meta- analysis. *Mindfulness, 6*(3), 1–23.

Wang, C., Bannuru, R., Ramel, J., Kupelnick, B., Scott, T., & Schmid, C. H. (2010). Tai chi on psychological well-being: Systematic review and meta-analysis. *BMC Complementary and Alternative Medicine, 10*(23). Retrieved from www.biomedcentral.com/1472-6882/10/23

Wen, M., Zhang, X., Harris, C. D., Holt, J. B., & Croft, J. B. (2013). Spatial disparities in the distribution of parks and green spaces in the USA. *Annuals of Behavioral Medicine, 45*(1), 18–27.

Wolch, J. R., Byrne, J., Newell, J. P. (2014). Urban green space, public health, and environmental justice: The challenge of making cities 'just green enough'. *Landscape and Urban Planning, 125*, 234–244.

Wong, P. P. (2004). Environmental impacts of tourism. In A. A. Lew, C. M. Hall, & A. M. Williams (Eds.), *A Companion to Tourism* (pp. 450–461). Maiden, MA: Blackwell Publishing Ltd.

Zeng, Y., Luo, T., Xie, H., Huang, M., & Cheng, A. (2014). Health benefits of qigong or tai chi for cancer patients: A systematic review and meta-analyses. *Complementary Therapies in Medicine, 22*(1), 173–186. doi:10.1016/j.ctim.2013.11.010

Zimmermann, J. (2017, June). Insider badlands. *Bethesda Beat*. Retrieved from www.bethesdamagazine.com/Bethesda-Beat/2017/Inside-Badlands-Play-Space-Rockville/

Zukin, S., Trujillo, V., Frase, P., Jackson, D., Recuber, T., & Walker, A. (2009). New retail capital and neighborhood change: Boutiques and gentrification in New York City? *City and Community, 8*(1), 47–64.

18

NATURE-BASED SOLUTIONS AND INTERVENTIONS IN CITIES

A look ahead

Tadhg E. MacIntyre, Christopher Gidlow, Méliné Baronian, Mark Nieuwenhuijsen, Marcus Collier, Susan Gritzka and Giles Warrington

Introduction

Cities are growing and densifying, as discussed in Chapter 2, and have ageing populations. Urbanisation and climate change present a unique set of consequences for environmental and human health (van den Bosch & Depledge, 2015). We know that current urbanisation processes have led to widespread sprawl, and that this has had an extremely detrimental effect on the biodiversity and ecosystem services in peri-urban and rural hinterlands. We also know that the optimal way to address this, within the cities of the future, is to infill 'empty' spaces, brownfield sites, and other areas that are classified as 'unused' (Song et al., 2019). So what little biodiversity can be found in the cities of today is now even more threatened. Wildlife aside for a moment, densification also poses many other potentially new and conflicting challenges, the principal of which is how do we provide multi-functional, open, healthy spaces when we are also densifying? With cities getting bigger and fuller, but not necessarily richer, many citizens, especially those in lower economic brackets, will be unable to regularly access rural hinterlands or wilderness areas for recreation and relaxation. The de-naturisation of our cities can lead to nature deficit disorder (Louv, 2008) and impact across generations (see Chapter 9) and is one of the many impacts of urbanisation.

This challenge of urbanisation is among the five societal challenges highlighted in Chapter 2. The others, mental health, physical inactivity, climate change and air pollution, are part of a nexus of problems that together represent wicked problems. The complexity of the problems obscures our capacity to develop solutions in a definitive manner. In our efforts to meet the UN Sustainable Development Goals (SDGs) our city-makers will increasingly encounter inadvertent conflicts on how to simultaneously meet these goals while fulfilling demands to also create and maintain healthy, liveable cities. The UN SDG11 to 'Make cities and human settlements inclusive, safe, resilient and sustainable' is interlinked with Climate Action (SGG 13), with Reduced Inequalities (SDG 10) and Responsible Consumption and Production (SDG 12). The specific objective 'increasing access to urban green spaces' (11.7) is mirrored by the New Urban Agenda adopted at Habitat III and supported by the recommendation of the European Commission working group and the WHO Regional Office for Europe (2016) on universal access to a green space (defined as living within a 300m linear distance of a green space ≥ 0.5 ha). One initiative to achieve these goals and tackle wicked problems is nature-based solutions (Nesshöver et al., 2017).

Nature-based solutions – what are they?

Nature-based solutions (NBS) is a relatively new term within natural environment management discourse that has been considered in great detail elsewhere (e.g. Kabisch, Horst, Stadler, & Bonn, 2017; Nesshöver et al., 2017; Raymond et al., 2017). NBS have been defined as 'solutions to societal challenges that are inspired and supported by nature, which are cost-effective, provide simultaneous environmental, social and economic benefits, and help build resilience' (European Commission, 2016, p. 1). Nesshöver et al. (2017) noted how NBS are the latest in a line of ideas related to concepts such as 'sustainable development', 'natural capital' and 'ecosystem services'; terms that have been described as 'clunky' and 'chewy' ways to describe efforts to preserve and protect the natural world (Editorial, 2017).

Where NBS might stand apart from these earlier ecosystem-based concepts is, first, in the positive framing. The aim to 'explicitly link positive outcomes for society ("solutions") with a notion of "nature" as something helpful for these aims' (Nesshöver et al., 2017, p. 1216) speaks to more than merely reducing the risk of environmental hazards. Second, NBS give genuine prominence to the co-benefits for human health and well-being of actions (or solutions) that use nature to mitigate against wider societal challenges, such as climate change, food security or water resource management (Kabisch et al., 2017). Indeed, the importance of health-related outcomes is reflected in the call to include physical health, mental health and well-being indicators (alongside others) to assess the effectiveness of NBS (Kabisch et al., 2016).

Yet, this shift in focus to recognise the positive outcomes that are characteristic of the NBS concept (rather than risk mitigation) has yet to be fully reflected in the research funding landscape. While Horizon 2020 funding is estimated to have committed over €185m to NBS since 2014, only in 2019 did a call prioritise health and well-being consequences. This call, referred to as SC5-5-14-2019, is termed 'Visionary and integrated solutions to improve well-being and health in cities' and marked a watershed in funding under the EU environment call. For the first time in NBS research and innovation actions, the 'co-benefits' to health and well-being were prioritised over the 'benefits' to the environment. Thus, arguably NBS have overlooked a deep understanding of human-nature interaction as a key determinant of the state of the environment, acceptability of NBS and citizen's health, mental health and well-being.

In the context of NBS, seen by many as 'the next big thing' for simultaneously tackling urban climate issues, behavioural change and social cohesion, and augmenting health and well-being in cities, this chapter aims to articulate a multi-dimensional focus on green exercise, health, mental health and well-being, which builds upon the reciprocal benefits gained from human-nature interactions. NBS are reviewed in terms of how green exercise can be considered as a possible intervention with a focus on health and well-being. The remainder of the chapter considers: urban greening as an example of a nature-based solution that is directly relevant to green exercise; implications and unintended consequences of NBS for different socio-demographic groups; the role of stakeholder engagement and co-creation in NBS; the synergies of NBS with developments in the mental health, well-being and psychology fields; and the role of digital innovation.

Urban greening

Perhaps the most directly relevant example of NBS in relation to green exercise is urban greening (Bowler, Buyung-Ali, Knight, & Pullin, 2010). This can be achieved through: provision of urban green space, including greenways or green corridors, either retrospectively or through design of new neighbourhoods; general greening of the urban infrastructure, through introducing street trees and other vegetation; and architectural approaches, such as introducing green roofs and green walls to buildings (see the EU Turas FP7 project and Oppla). All have the potential to mitigate the environmental risks of rising temperatures, and noise and air pollution (Kabisch et al., 2016; Xing, Jones, & Donnison, 2017). Tree canopy, for example, mitigates against air pollution and notably tree coverage has been demonstrated to vary widely across cities (Pauleit, Ennos, & Golding, 2005).

Urban green spaces and green corridors are associated with a wide range of health indicators that may be explained by a combination of (a) mitigation (e.g. of co-hazards of noise and air pollution), (b) psychological benefits, (c) enriched biodiversity enhancing immune function (Aerts, Honnay, & Van Nieuwenhuyse, 2018), (d) safety and social cohesion, and (e) increased physical activity (Triguero-Mas et al., 2015).

In the context of green exercise, we can consider increasing the provision of urban green spaces and green corridors. Green spaces are defined as the land that is partly or completely covered with grass, trees, shrubs or other vegetation, and can include parks, community gardens and cemeteries (US EPA, 2017). The availability of green space is necessary for, but not does not guarantee, green exercise. Both surrounding greenness and physical access to green space have been used to assess contact to green space (see Dadvand & Nieuwenhuijsen, 2018). As discussed in other chapters of this book (Chapters 2 and 4), there is mixed evidence to support the assumption that if people have better access to green space, they will become more active by using it as a place to exercise (Kaczynski et al., 2014; Kaczynski & Henderson, 2007; Lachowycz & Jones, 2011). Therefore, to realise co-benefits related to green exercise as a result of NBS might require additional 'nature-based interventions'; for example, to incorporate features that have been linked with higher levels of park-based physical activity (Kaczynski, Potwarka, & Saelens, 2008).

Moreover, the physical infrastructure of NBS could be complemented through other interventions and programmes to engage local residents with those spaces. The World Health Organization (WHO) review concluded that urban green space interventions were most beneficial for health when adopting a dual approach: combining physical improvements with a social engagement/participation element that promotes the green space and reaches out to new target groups (WHO, 2017). A similar conclusion was drawn from a systematic review of urban green space interventions to improve physical activity (Hunter et al., 2015). While highlighting the many limitations of the evidence-base, the review authors reported that physical activity increases were most likely when physical changes were combined with physical activity programmes that encouraged their use.

'Greenways' or 'green corridors' have been described as linear green spaces that typically follow natural or manmade features such as rivers or railways (Lynch, 2018). They have the potential to increase levels of active travel (Dallat et al., 2013; Goodman, Sahlqvist, & Ogilvie, 2014) and, thereby reduce emission from motorised transport, in addition to the primary benefit of reduced emissions from lower car use. Citizens spending time in green spaces has been linked with lower rates of depression, lower blood pressure and greater social cohesion within the community (Shanahan et al., 2016). Improving neighbourhood walkability and active transport infrastructure enhances physical activity in children and adults (Smith et al., 2017). Active commuting reduces risk of cardiovascular disease, cancer and mortality (Celis-Morales et al., 2017). Walking in busy urban streets dampens the benefits of physical activity, and has negative health consequences in older adults compared to walking in green areas (Sinahray et al., 2017) so there is an imperative to ensure that active travel and social connectivity across urban communities is feasible by green routes as part of an overall urban greening approach. Building cities inspired by nature through urban greening, and relying on the collective skills and know-how of the citizens, inhabitants and municipal organisations to provide the public services of tomorrow, would give nature in the city a completely different and more prominent place.

Examples of the NBS functions, supporting strategies, and impact in terms of opportunities for green exercise are illustrated in Figure 18.1.

Implications of NBS for different socio-demographic groups

The WHO Europe review of urban green space and health concluded that 'urban green space has health benefits, particularly for economically deprived communities, children, pregnant women and senior citizens' (WHO, 2016, p. 40). This is also reflected in the UN SDG Target 11.7 'to provide universal access to […] green and public spaces, particularly for women and children, older persons and persons with disabilities'.

Indeed, protecting equitable accessibility, equal distribution and supply of high-quality green areas and public spaces for all communities is of tremendous importance to avoid inadvertently accelerating gentrification, segregation and socio-spatial inequalities. Kabisch et al. (2016) note the potential adverse consequences of introducing new or restoring existing green spaces, effects variously referred to as the 'green paradox', 'eco- or ecological gentrification' or 'environmental gentrification.' That is, by making areas more attractive,

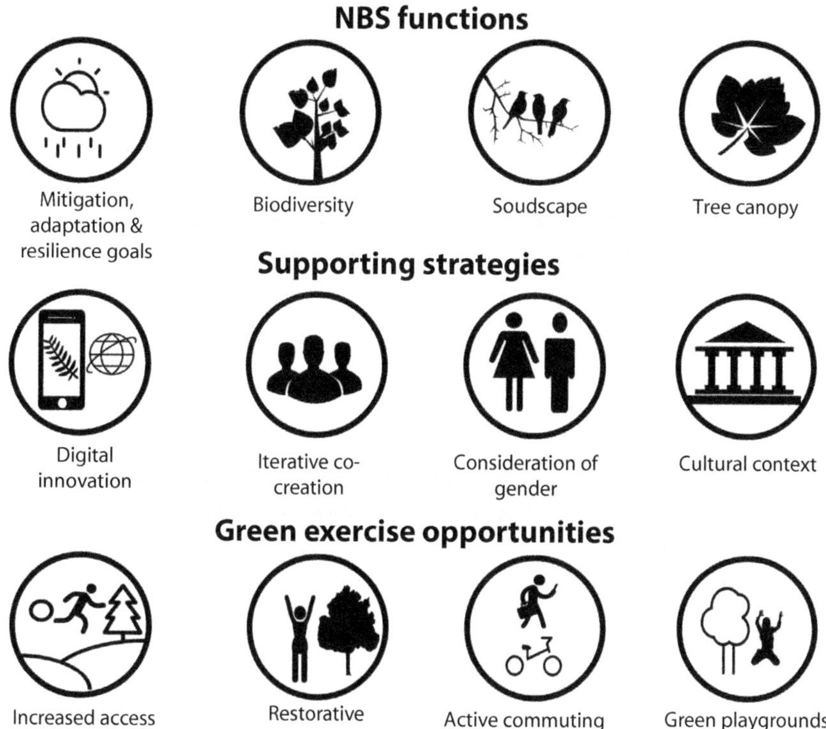

FIGURE 18.1 Potential implementation strategy for green corridors

urban greening could lead to increased property prices, attract an influx of affluent residents, in turn, displacing the most socially disadvantaged. New York City's High Line Park has been used as an example of 'green' gentrification (Maantay & Maroko, 2018).

Disadvantaged population groups often live in neighbourhoods with reduced availability and/or quality of green space, compared with more affluent areas (CABE, 2010; Gidlow et al., 2018; Vaughan et al., 2013). And yet, epidemiological studies often find that the apparent protective health effects of living in greener areas are strongest in more socioeconomically disadvantaged individuals (WHO, 2016). Therefore, NBS offer a means of reducing socioeconomic disparities in the availability of urban green space, contributing to efforts to reduce inequalities in health.

Given the noted benefits of urban green space for older and younger groups, multi-generational consequences must also be considered. For example, there is some evidence that children benefit the most from access to green space. Dadvand et al. (2017), in a longitudinal study of 500 children, reported that children with higher greenness around their homes (e.g. residential surrounding greenness at 100, 300 and 500 metres distance), had better scores in attention tests. In terms of promoting green exercise in children through encouraging use of urban green space, the aforementioned dual approach of physical infrastructure and engagement activities is recommended (WHO, 2017). For children, this could include single basketball hoops (pop-up recreational areas), quiet restorative spaces for rest, and green playgrounds (see Chapter 9). But the consequences for other potential user groups must be considered. The diverse make-up of the local population (e.g. gender, age, ethnicity, physical ability) and their different requirements in urban green spaces should be considered to avoid exclusive usage of implemented areas only by certain populations, and the lack of usage by others (e.g. Gidlow & Ellis, 2011). This imperative leads on to another fundamental feature of NBS, stakeholder involvement.

Co-creation and co-implementation

According to Raymond et al. (2017) NBS were 'founded on the concept of participatory process involving the various stakeholders but also includes the idea of alternative routes and/or possible feedbacks between one stage and the previous' (p. 18). Thus a key feature of NBS is the need to involve key stakeholders as part of multi-disciplinary teams for their design, implementation and evaluation. Within this, of critical importance are the target user groups. It is widely recognised in community development and, more recently in neighbourhood design and planning, that for communities to embrace changes or programmes, they should be involved in their design (Kabisch et al., 2017). In the context of trying to increase green exercise as a co-benefit of urban greening (as part of a wider NBS approach), local residents need to be part of a co-design and co-implementation process.

One potential reason for the need for participatory approaches is to ensure the local preferences for green infrastructure are considered and positive attitudes are cultivated towards the current NBS and possible future iterations. Managing negative perceptions of stakeholders has been noted in models of NBS implementation (Raymond et al., 2017). However, this is a narrow set of criteria relative to the potential attitudinal factors that may influence acceptability of an intervention. To explain, Eurobarometer surveys are regularly conducted to assess attitudes towards physical activity and sport, the environment and more precisely, NBS (e.g. Eurobarometer 444, 2015). On a national level, attitudinal variation has been assessed with largely representative sampling across EU27. For example, 83% of respondents across the EU were in favour of the promotion of NBS, but only 30% of Estonians surveyed would like more natural features compared to 46% in France. In contrast to the positive regard for NBS, over one quarter of Europeans (28%) fear that these new natural areas would not be properly maintained. City, district and community level attitudes towards the environment, NBS and specific interventions should be assessed in advance of implementation. Potentially applying this assessment well in advance of initiation could help predict which areas would benefit most from NBS.

Methods such as public participation Geographical Information Systems (PPGIS, sometimes referred to as Volunteered GIS, or VGIS) offer a means of gathering community perspectives. There is variation in the specific name and definition for these approaches whereby the public uses various forms of geospatial technologies to participate in public processes, such as mapping and decision making (Tulloch, 2008). They tend to involve participants identifying spatial locations on a map, either hardcopy or digital, using stickers, markers, or digital annotations. Over the past two decades, PPGIS approaches have been used in general community and neighbourhood planning (e.g. Sieber, 2006).

With respect to urban parks, PPGIS has been used variously to understand the perspectives of the local population, such as: identifying green spaces and or greenways of particular importance; identifying values that people attach to urban parks; measuring self-reported park-based physical activity (in different areas of green spaces) and perceived benefits of urban parks; and forest design (Brown, 2009; Brown, Schebella, & Weber, 2014; Brown & Weber, 2011). The flexibility of such approaches means that they can be applied to a variety of contexts where understanding public perceptions of the local natural environment is the main objective.

This need to consider local, cultural context in the design and planning of NBS also links to the need to consider the potential to ameliorate or exacerbate inequalities in access, use and the associated health benefits of urban green space. Additional considerations are all the public services that a city can provide to its inhabitants. Public transport, roads, public buildings, lighting, rainwater management and waste treatment would become the driving force for improving the well-being and health of the inhabitants. Nature becomes a vector of well-being through the public services offered by the city, and is central to a city's function rather than being an add-on.

A shift towards benefits to mental health and psychological well-being

A key barrier in NBS implementation identified at the 2017 EU NBS workshop is the lack of standardisation in NBS evaluation procedures, including human health and well-being metrics (European Commission, 2017). This problem has created a knowledge gap in the research, as noted previously in Chapter 2. The inability to use sophisticated tools, inventories and assessment techniques to measure mental health and well-being, in particular, has limited the potential of NBS in terms of co-benefits and potentially overlooked a major factor supporting their efficacy. Evidence linking a reduced risk of mental health problems and better mental health outcomes to the greenness of the living environment is relatively strong (Gascon et al., 2015; Shanahan et al., 2016). As noted earlier, a distinct feature of NBS is the positive framing, giving prominence to the health benefits of nature-based environmental intervention. This aligns well with the paradigm shift within psychology to focus on 'positive' mental health and psychological well-being (Seligman & Csikszentmihalyi, 2000). Mental illness and mental health are not viewed as being at either end of a continuum, but present two distinct axes (Keyes, 2007). Mental health ranges from flourishing (i.e. positive mental health) to languishing; mental illness and the absence of mental illness represent a distinct axis. Mental health is unobservable and identified only by subjective well-being measures (e.g. self-reported mood, quality of life satisfaction and psychological resilience). Resilience or the 'capacity to maintain regular functioning through diverse challenges or to rebound through the use of facilitative resources' (Bryan, O'Shea, & MacIntyre, 2017, p. 8) can be successfully developed using online training, overcoming adversity (e.g. challenges in a green playground; see also Chapter 9) and by increasing social connections to increase psychological resources (e.g. prosocial behaviour).

Arguably, previous theories of human-nature interactions have had limited explanatory value and focused on a narrow set of outcomes (e.g. Stress Reduction Theory, Ulrich et al., 1991; Attention Restoration Theory, Kaplan, 1989). There are other theoretical approaches that could be applied to advance our exploration of the potential benefits of NBS for mental health and well-being including (a) Psychological Recovery Theory (Sonnentag, Venz, & Casper, 2017); (b) Generalised Unsafety Theory of Stress (GUTS; Brosschot, Verkuil, & Thayer, 2018) and (c) Habit Formation. Firstly, nature contact increases positive emotions which can be used subsequently to promote well-being during a period of stress – nature has both restorative and proactive coping functions (Sonnentag et al., 2017). Positive emotions may lead to prosocial behaviour and connecting with others which is vital to combat the isolation symptomatic of urban living. And according to GUTS, stress in urban areas is not only linked to stressful events but is ubiquitous. Consequently, instead of developing interventions to help cope with daily stressors, life events or trauma, it is necessary to engage with preventative approaches with regular nature contact integral to protecting well-being over the long-term. Accumulating evidence supports this approach as urban settings are linked to negative mental health outcomes, higher levels of stress and reduced social cohesion. Habit formation (i.e., when a plan to start an activity is accessed without conscious effort) when supported by technology can lead to long-term adherence to sustainable behaviours (Stawarz, Cox, & Blandford, 2015).

Digital innovation

Digital natives, those born after the widespread adoption of digital technology (e.g. age 10–39 years) are central to our future and of key interest as they are easily accessible through, and receptive to, digital innovations. The adoption of healthy lifestyle habits by this generation will foresee a range of what are termed therapeutic lifestyle changes which will buffer future stressors, have co-benefits for health and well-being and create more sustainable lifestyles (Walsh, 2011). This will help to protect against health risks (e.g. non-communicable diseases) and ensure positive attitudes towards urban change. This in turn increases the likelihood that future projects and innovations are well-received.

Cutting-edge transversal digital innovations that could be part of the overall NBS approach include *soundscape, digital placemaking, emotional mapping, technological nature* and *immersive Virtual Reality (VR) experience*. The latter two components have been discussed in detail in Chapter 15, so we will not delve too deeply on these topics.

As outlined in Chapter 2, *soundscape* concerns the sounds perceived and understood by the individual citizen or community and is influenced by the structure of the urban environment. A key issue is to understand how soundscape affects a citizen's psychological and physiological health. Restorative spaces established along green routes can be enhanced by focusing on the detailed acoustic design, which extends far beyond limiting the sound level. Consideration of the acoustic environment aligned with the intended use of the space is proposed, encompassing optimal acoustic environments for various areas, from lively to peaceful, from natural to more urban settings.

A digital placemaking toolkit can be integrated into NBS interventions to employ crowdsourcing, geo-tagged pictures and associated meta-data to build an alternative cartography of a city weighted for positive emotions (e.g. emotional mapping), air quality and multi-sensual mapping. *Digital placemaking* uses location-specific digital technology to support and facilitate public life, community interaction, place attachment and place efficiencies, to foster deeper relationships between citizens and public spaces. *Emotional mapping* (Redi, Aiello, Schifanella, & Quercia, 2018) can further leverage online feeds and the associated meta-data to build an alternative cartography weighted for positive emotions, adding a layer where citizens' opinions and emotions are modelled in time and space at scale. This can enable the implementation of new forms of services, e.g. an emotions-driven routing engine that is able to suggest a happy and pleasant path over the shortest distance, and urban design policies that favour the human factor over a city built around efficiency, predictability and security alone.

Technological nature (i.e. technologies that mediate, stimulate, promote, and/or augment human-nature contact, Kahn, 2018) can plausibly be applied as a strategy to familiarise, bond and attach with green infrastructure innovations. And as discussed in Chapter 15, VR offers a potential engagement tool for citizen involvement which has shown to be key to understanding of urban issues (e.g. 2015 ArtCOP festival).

Conclusion

The concept of NBS has gained prominence in the last few years and begun to permeate discourse in related practice, policy and research. The grander aim of addressing climate change and related environmental risks notwithstanding, there is undoubtedly more space within NBS for health (and, therefore, green exercise), compared with other ecosystem-based approaches. The literature identifies many challenges in developing an evidence-base and the need to draw on good-practice examples to guide action in its absence (Kabisch et al., 2017). However, as van den Bosch and Nieuwenhuijsen (2017) state, we have a sufficient understanding of the potential benefits of greening our cities (and the high likelihood that these benefits outweigh any potential risks) to warrant action now. Based on the information in this book and the ever-growing literature, and considering green exercise in the context of NBS, urban greening efforts might not increase overall physical activity in the local population, unless combined with programmes to engage people with the green spaces and be active, but should increase green exercise, particularly for parks that support physical activity and traffic-free greenways that support active travel. This, in turn, might promote additional psychological and health benefits for people exercising in the green spaces (although robust research is required to demonstrate this; see Chapter 4). It is imperative that socio-demographic characteristics of the local population and implications for equitable access are considered, and that the NBS approach is co-created alongside these key target groups to ensure equitable access and interventions that support a diverse range of users. The city of tomorrow may be greener, more liveable and perhaps less dense because its natural spaces will no longer be spaces for leisure and sporting activities activity, but spaces capable of guaranteeing the city's public services in a sustainable way. The innovative and positive focus of NBS opens the door to embrace other psychological theories to understand the potential impact, and the range of digital innovations that can be used to augment/facilitate environmental and engagement interventions. And finally, given the severe health-warnings that come with some of the evidence to support the added health benefits of green exercise (see Chapter 4), it is imperative that innovation in measurement and assessment, and robust research design is used to determine the impact of NBS in future urban contexts.

References

Aerts, R., Honnay, O., & Van Nieuwenhuyse, A. (2018). Biodiversity and human health: Mechanisms and evidence of the positive health effects of diversity in nature and green spaces. *British Medical Bulletin, 127*(1), 5–22. doi:10.1093/bmb/ldy021

Art Cop Festival. www.artcop21.com

Bowler, D. E., Buyung-Ali, L. M., Knight, T. M., & Pullin, A. S. (2010). Urban greening to cool towns and cities: A systematic review of the empirical evidence. *Landscape and Urban Planning, 97*(3), 147–155. doi:10.1016/j.landurbplan.2010.05.006

Brosschot, J., Verkuil, B., & Thayer, J. (2018). Generalized unsafety theory of stress: Unsafe environments and conditions, and the default stress response. *International Journal of Environmental Research and Public Health, 15*(3), 464. doi:10.3390/ijerph15030464

Brown, G. (2009). Public participation GIS : A new method for use in national forest planning. *Forest Science, 55*(2), 166–182. doi:10.1093/forestscience/55.2.166

Brown, G., Schebella, M. F., & Weber, D. (2014). Using participatory GIS to measure physical activity and urban park benefits. *Landscape and Urban Planning, 121*, 34–44. doi:10.1016/j.landurbplan.2013.09.006

Brown, G., & Weber, D. (2011). Public participation GIS: A new method for national park planning. *Landscape and Urban Planning, 102*(1), 1–15. doi:10.1016/j.landurbplan.2011.03.003

Bryan, C., O'Shea, D., & MacIntyre, T. (2017). Stressing the relevance of resilience: A systematic review of resilience across the domains of sport and work. *International Review of Sport and Exercise Psychology*, 1–41. doi:10.1080/17500984X.2017.1381140

CABE. (2010). *Urban Green Nation: Building the Evidence Base*. London: Author.

Celis-Morales, C. A., Lyall, D. M, Welsh, P., Anderson, J., Steell, L., Yibing, G., et al. (2017). Association between active commuting and incident cardiovascular disease, cancer, and mortality: Prospective cohort stud. *BMJ, 357*, j1456. doi:10.1136/bmj.j1456

Dadvand, P. & Nieuwenhuijsen, M. (2018). Green space and health. In M. Nieuwenhuijsen & H. Khreis (Eds.), *Integrating Human Health into Urban and Transport Planning: A Framework* (pp. 409–423). New York: Springer.

Dadvand, P., Tischer, C., Estarlich, M., Llop, S., Dalmau-Bueno, A., López-Vicente, M., … Rodriguez-Dehli, C. (2017). Lifelong residential exposure to green space and attention: A population-based prospective study. *Environmental Health Perspectives, 125*(9), 097016. doi:10.1289/EHP694

Dallat, M. A. T., Soerjomataram, I., Hunter, R. F., Tully, M. A., Cairns, K. J., & Kee, F. (2013). Urban greenways have the potential to increase physical activity levels cost-effectively. *The European Journal of Public Health*. doi:10.1093/eurpub/ckt035

Editorial. (2017). 'Nature-based solutions' is the latest green jargon that means more than you might think. *Nature, 541*, 133–134. doi:10.1038/541133b

EPA (2017). What is open space/green space? www3.epa.gov/region1/eco/uep/openspace.html

Turas FP7 Project (2019). www.turas-cities.com

Eurobarometer (2015). Special Eurobarometer 444: Citizens' view on nature-based solutions. https://data.europa.eu/euodp/data/dataset/S2081_84_4_444_ENG

European Commission. (2016). *Topics: Nature-based solutions*. https://ec.europa.eu/research/environment/index.cfm?pg=nbs

European Commission (2017). Workshop with horizon 2020 SC5 programme committee representatives and experts from Member States and Associated Countries (MS/AC). June 2017.

Gascon, M., Triguero-Mas, M., Martínez, D., Dadvand, P., Forns, J., Plasència, A., & Nieuwenhuijsen, M. J. (2015). Mental health benefits of long-term exposure to residential green and blue spaces: A systematic review. *International Journal of Environmental Research and Public Health, 12*(4), 4354–4379. doi:10.3390/ijerph120404354

Gidlow, C. J., & Ellis, N. J. (2011). Neighbourhood green space in deprived urban communities: Issues and barriers to use. *Local Environment, 16*, 989–1002. doi:10.1080/13549839.2011.582861

Gidlow, C. J., van Kempen, E., Smith, G. R., Triguero-Mas, M., Kruize, H., Gražulevičienė, R., … Nieuwenhuijsen, M. J. (2018). Development of the Natural Environment Scoring Tool (NEST). *Urban Forestry & Urban Greening, 29*, 322–333. doi:10.1016/j.ufug.2017.12.007

Goodman, A., Sahlqvist, S., & Ogilvie, D. (2014). New walking and cycling routes and increased physical activity: One- and 2-year findings from the UK iConnect study. *American Journal of Public Health, 104*(9), e38–e46. doi:10.2105/AJPH.2014.302059

Hunter, R. F., Christian, H., Veitch, J., Astell-Burt, T., Hipp, J. A., & Schipperijn, J. (2015). The impact of interventions to promote physical activity in urban green space: A systematic review and recommendations for future research. *Social Science & Medicine, 124*, 246–256. doi:10.1016/j.socscimed.2014.11.051

Kabisch, N., Frantzeskaki, N., Pauleit, S., Naumann, S., Davis, M., Artmann, M., … Bonn, A. (2016). Nature-based solutions to climate change mitigation and adaptation in urban areas: Perspectives on indicators, knowledge gaps, barriers, and opportunities for action. *Ecology and Society, 21*(2), 39. doi:10.5751/ES-08373-210239

Kabisch, N., Horst, K., Stadler, J., & Bonn, A. (2017). *Nature Based Solutions to Climate Change Adaptation in Urban Areas: Linkages between Science, Policy and Practice*. New York: Springer Open.

Kaczynski, A., Besenyi, G., Stanis, S., Koohsari, M., Oestman, K., Bergstrom, R., … Reis, R. (2014). Are park proximity and park features related to park use and park-based physical activity among adults? Variations by multiple socio-demographic characteristics. *International Journal of Behavioral Nutrition and Physical Activity, 11*(1), 146. doi:10.1186/s12966-014-0146-4

Kaczynski, A. T., & Henderson, K. A. (2007). Environmental correlates of physical activity: A review of evidence about parks and recreation. *Leisure Sciences, 29*, 315–354. doi:10.1080/01490400701394865

Kaczynski, A. T., Potwarka, L. R., & Saelens, B. E. (2008). Association of park size, distance, and features with physical activity in neighborhood parks. *American Journal of Public Health, 98*(8), 1451–1456. doi:10.2105/AJPH.2007.129064

Kahn, P. H. (2018). Technological nature. In M. van Den Bosch & W. Bird (Eds.), *Oxford Textbook of Nature and Public Health: The Role of Nature in Improving the Health of a Population* (pp. 160–164). Oxford: Oxford University Press.

Kaplan, R. (1989). *The Experience of Nature: A Psychological Perspective*. Cambridge: Cambridge University Press.

Keyes, C. (2007). Towards a mentally flourishing society: Mental health promotion, not cure. *Journal of Public Mental Health, 6*(2), 4–7. doi:10.1108/17465729200700009

Lachowycz, K., & Jones, A. P. (2011). Greenspace and obesity: A systematic review of the evidence. *Obesity Reviews, 12*(5), e183–e189. doi:10.1111/j.1467-789X.2010.00827.x

Louv, R. (2008). *Last Child in the Woods: Saving Our Children from Nature-Deficit Disorder.* Carolina: Algonquin.

Lynch, A. J. (2018). Creating effective urban greenways and stepping-stones: Four critical gaps in habitat connectivity planning research. *Journal of Planning Literature.* doi:10.1177/0885412218798334

Maantay, J. A., & Maroko, A. R. (2018). Brownfields to greenfields: Environmental justice versus environmental gentrification. *International Journal of Environmental Research and Public Health, 15*(10), 2233. doi:10.3390/ijerph15102233

Nesshöver, C., Assmuth, T., Irvine, K. N., Rusch, G. M., Waylen, K. A., Delbaere, B., ... Wittmer, H. (2017). The science, policy and practice of nature-based solutions: An interdisciplinary perspective. *Science of the Total Environment, 579*, 1215–1227. doi:10.1016/j.scitotenv.2016.11.106

Oppla. (2019). https://oppla.eu

Pauleit, S., Ennos, R., & Golding, Y. (2005). Modeling the environmental impacts of urban land use and land cover change – A study in Merseyside, UK. *Landscape and Urban Planning, 71*(2–4), 295–310. doi:10.1016/j.landurbplan.2004.03.009

Raymond, C. M., Frantzeskaki, N., Kabisch, N., Berry, P., Breil, M., Nita, M. R., ... Calfapietra, C. (2017). A framework for assessing and implementing the co-benefits of nature-based solutions in urban areas. *Environmental Science and Policy, 77*, 15–24. doi:10.1016/j.envsci.2017.07.008

Redi, M., Aiello, L. M., Schifanclla, R., & Quercia, D. (2018). The spirit of the city: Using social media to capture neighborhood ambiance. *Proceedings of the ACM on Human-Computer Interaction, 2 (CSCW)* (p. 144). doi:10.1145/3274413

Seligman, M. E. P., & Csikszentmihalyi, M. (Eds.). (2000). Positive psychology—An introduction. *American Psychologist, 55*, 5–14. doi:10.1007/978-94-017

Shanahan, D. F., Bush, R., Gaston, K. J., Lin, B. B., Dean, J., Barber, E., Fuller, R. (2016). Health benefits from nature experiences depend on dose. *Scientific Reports, 6*, 28551. doi:10.1038/srep11610

Sieber, R. (2006). Public participation geographic information systems: A literature review and framework. *Annals of the Association of American Geographers, 96*(3), 491–507. doi:10.1111/j.1467-8306.2006.00702.x

Sinahray, R., Gong, J., Barratt, B., Ohman-Strickland, P., Ernst, S., Kelly, F. J., ... Chung, K. F. (2017). Respiratory and cardiovascular responses to walking down a traffic-polluted road compared with walking in a traffic-free area in participants aged 60 years and older with chronic lung or heart disease and age-matched healthy controls: A randomised, crossover study. *The Lancet, 391*(10118), 339–349. doi:10.1016/S0140-6736(17)32643-0

Smith, M., Hosking, J., Woodward, A., Witten, K., MacMillan, A., Field, A., ... Mackie, H. (2017). Systematic literature review of built environment effects on physical activity and active transport–An update and new findings on health equity. *International Journal of Behavioral Nutrition and Physical Activity, 14*(1), 158. doi:10.1186/s12966-017-0613-9

Song, Y., Kirkwood, N., Maksimović, Č., Zhen, X., O'Connor, D., Jin, Y., & Hou, D. (2019). Nature based solutions for contaminated land remediation and brownfield redevelopment in cities: A review. *Science of the Total Environment, 663*, 568–579. doi:10.1016/j.scitotenv.2019.01.347

Sonnentag, S., Venz, L., & Casper, A. (2017). Advances in recovery research: What have we learned? What should be done next? *Journal of Occupational Health Psychology, 22*(3), 365–380. doi:10.1037/ocp0000079

Stawarz, K., Cox, A. L., & Blandford, A. (2015). Beyond self-tracking and reminders: Designing smartphone apps that support habit formation. In *Proceedings of the 33rd Annual ACM Conference on Human Factors in Computing Systems* (pp. 2653–2662). New York: ACM.

Triguero-Mas, M., Dadvand, P., Cirach, M., Martínez, D., Medina, A., Mompart, A., ... Nieuwenhuijsen, M. J. (2015). Natural outdoor environments and mental and physical health: Relationships and mechanisms. *Environment International*, 77, 35–41. doi:10.1016/j.envint.2015.01.012

Tulloch, D. (2008). Public participation GIS (PPGIS). In K. Kemp (Ed.), *Encyclopedia of Geographic Information Science* (pp. 352–355). Thousand Oaks, CA: SAGE Publications, Inc. doi:10.4135/9781412953962

Turas FP7 Project. (2019). www.turas-cities.com

Ulrich, R. S., Simons, R. F., Losito, B. D., Fiorito, E., Miles, M. A., & Zelson, M. (1991). Stress recovery during exposure to natural and urban environments. *Journal of Environmental Psychology, 11*(3), 201–230. doi:10.1016/S0272-4944(05)80184-7

van den Bosch, M. & Depledge, M. (2015). Healthy people with nature in mind. *BMC Public Health, 15*, 1232. doi:10.1186/s12889-015-2574-8

van den Bosch, M., & Nieuwenhuijsen, M. (2017). No time to lose – Green the cities now. *Environment International, 99*, 343–350. doi:10.1016/j.envint.2016.11.025

Vaughan, K. B., Kaczynski, A. T., Stanis, S. A. W., Besenyi, G. M., Bergstrom, R., & Heinrich, K. M. (2013). Exploring the distribution of park availability, features, and quality across Kansas City, Missouri by income and race/ethnicity: An environmental justice investigation. *Annals of Behavioral Medicine, 45*(Suppl. 1). doi:10.1007/s12160-012-9425-y

Walsh, R. (2011). Lifestyle and mental health. *American Psychologist, 66*(7), 579–592. doi:10.1037/a0021769

World Health Organization. (2016). *Urban Green Spaces and Health*. Copenhagen: WHO Regional Office for Europe.

World Health Organization. (2017). *Urban Green Space Interventions and Health: A Review of Impacts and Effectiveness*. Copenhagen: W. R. O. for Europe.

Xing, Y., Jones, P., & Donnison, I. (2017). Characterisation of nature-based solutions for the built environment. *Sustainability, 9*(1), 149. doi:10.3390/su9010149

INDEX